First published in Great Britain 2023 by Farshore
An imprint of HarperCollins*Publishers*
1 London Bridge Street, London, SE1 9GF
www.farshore.co.uk

HarperCollins*Publishers*
Macken House, 39/40 Mayor Street Upper,
Dublin 1, D01 C9W8, Ireland

Written by Mara Alperin

BEANO.COM

ISBN 978 0 0085 3696 1
Printed in Great Britain
002

Stay safe online. Any website addresses listed in this book are correct at the time of going to print. However, Farshore is not responsible for content hosted by third parties. Please be aware that online content can be subject to change and websites can contain content that is unsuitable for children. We advise that all children are supervised when using the internet.

MIX
Paper | Supporting responsible forestry
FSC™ C007454

This book is produced from independently certified FSC™ paper to ensure responsible forest management.

For more information visit: www.harpercollins.co.uk/green

BEANO®

WOULD YOU RATHER?

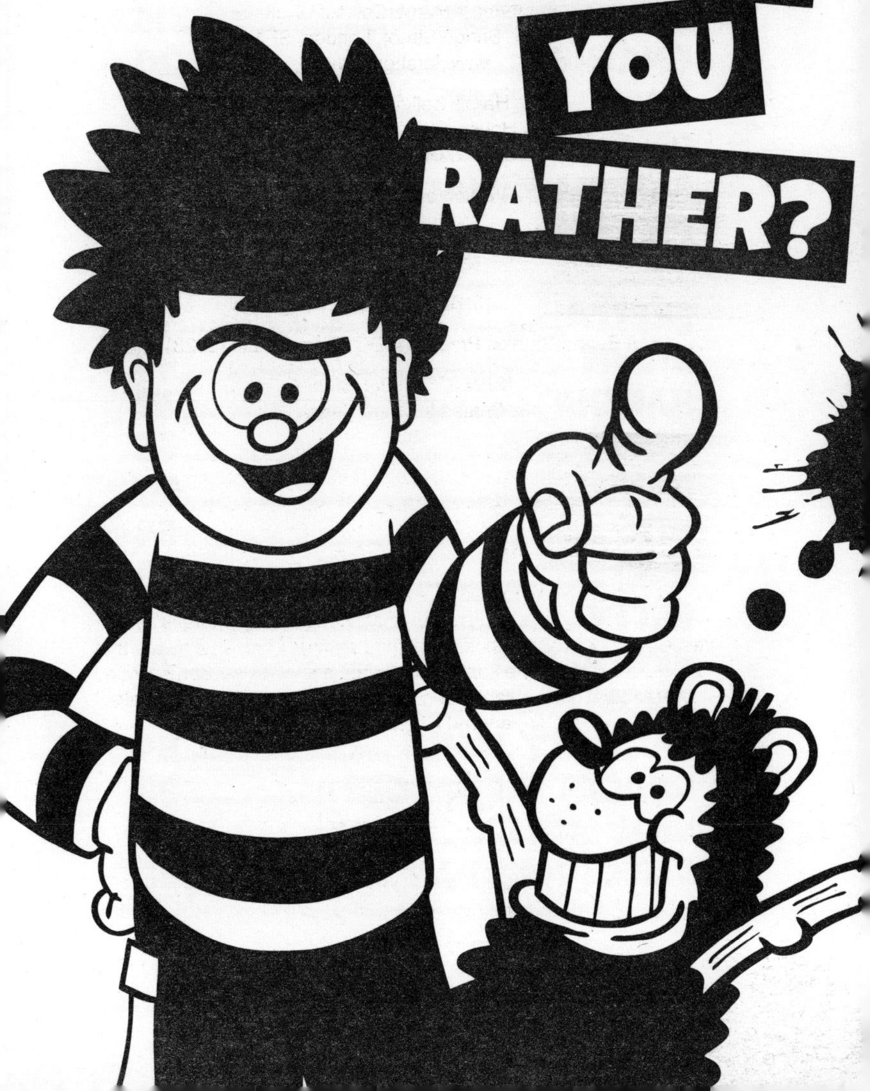

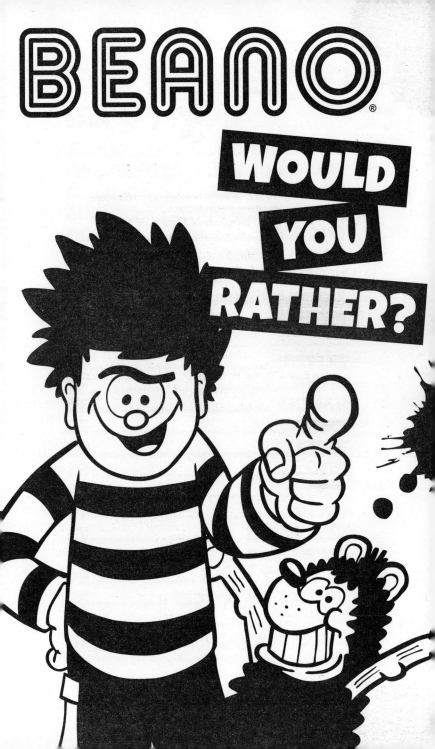

CONTENTS

INTRODUCTION

'Hurry up, Dennis, we're going to be late!' called Rubi as she raced down Bash Street School's corridor with their invention balanced precariously on her lap. 'The Science Fair has already started!'

'I'm coming, I'm coming!' Dennis's muffled voice came from behind the large piece of cardboard he was carrying.

In truth, most of the words on their presentation board bamboozled him. He was the ideas guy in this duo, though Rubi had firmly shot down some of his best ones: electronic slingshot, fart gun, sausage simulator. Instead, they (namely Rubi) had invented a MIND* reader, which allowed them to hear everyone's numskulls – the beings that live inside your head. But it was Dennis who'd had the

*Marvellous Imagination Neurotransmission Device

blamazing idea of just how to use it.

'Keep up, Gnasher! It's your fault we're late. Did you really need the third sausage stop?'

'**Gnash!**' barked Gnasher, which Dennis understood to mean *Of course!*

The three of them burst into the school hall, which was already buzzing with noise and activity.

'Ahh, there you are!' Miss Mistry shouted over the crowd. 'Your table is over there by the stage.'

'Thanks, Miss!' Rubi said and zoomed off again, quicker than Dennis could keep up.

Dennis heaved their presentation board onto the table and rubbed at the sausage-grease marks.

'Are you ready?' he asked Rubi . . .

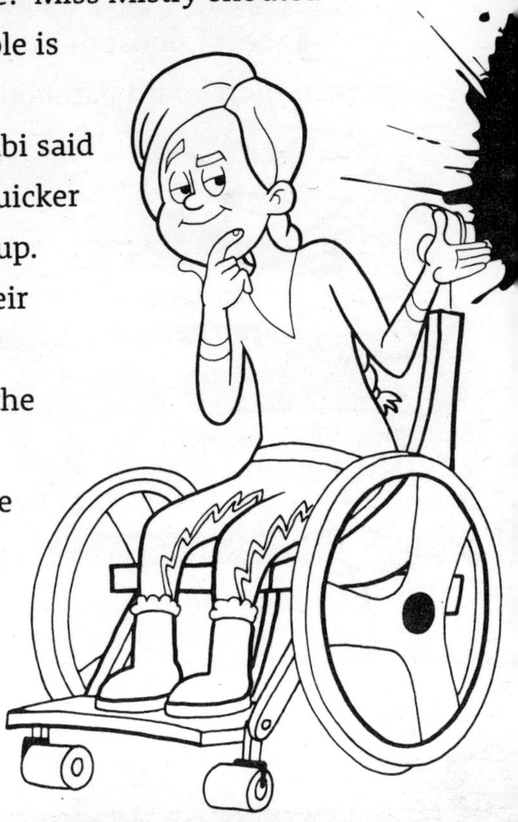

PROFESSOR VON SCREWTOP

'Nearly ready!' Rubi cheered. 'Oh, Dad, can I test my latest invention on you? Make sure you mind the curly thingy-ma-wires.'

'Well, I suppose I wouldn't mind helping out,' Professor Von Screwtop replied with a grin.

'Great! Let's see what your numskulls make of this!'

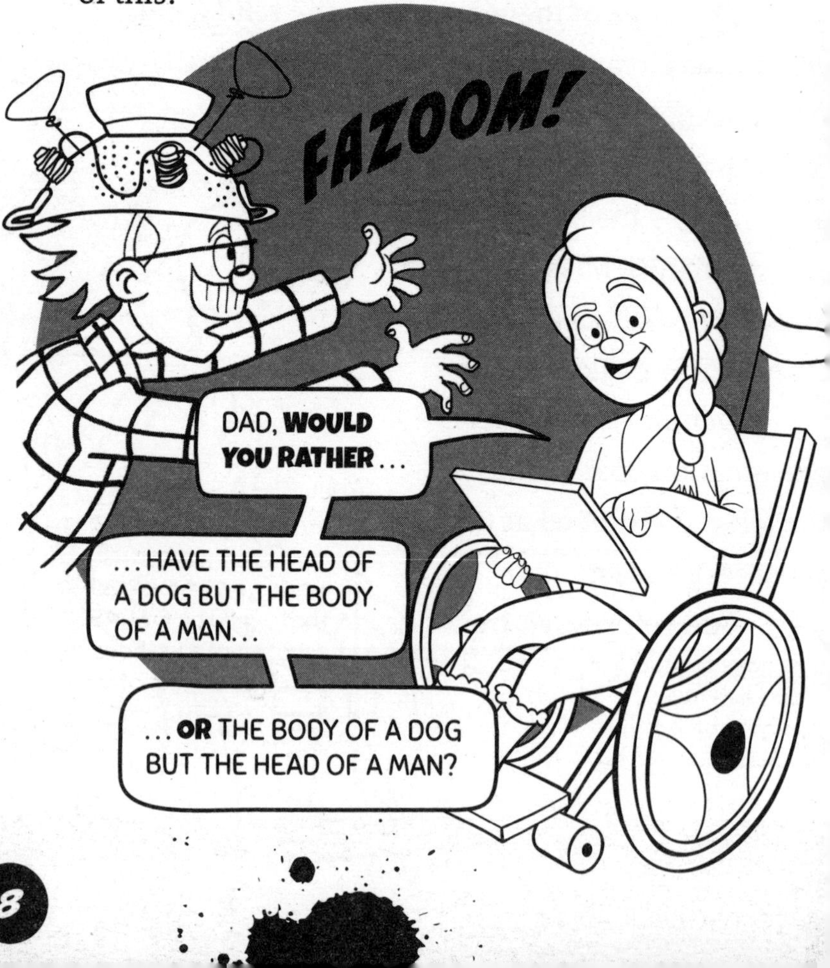
FAZOOM!
DAD, **WOULD YOU RATHER**...
...HAVE THE HEAD OF A DOG BUT THE BODY OF A MAN...
...**OR** THE BODY OF A DOG BUT THE HEAD OF A MAN?

WHAT DO PROFESSOR VON SCREWTOP'S NUMSKULLS THINK?

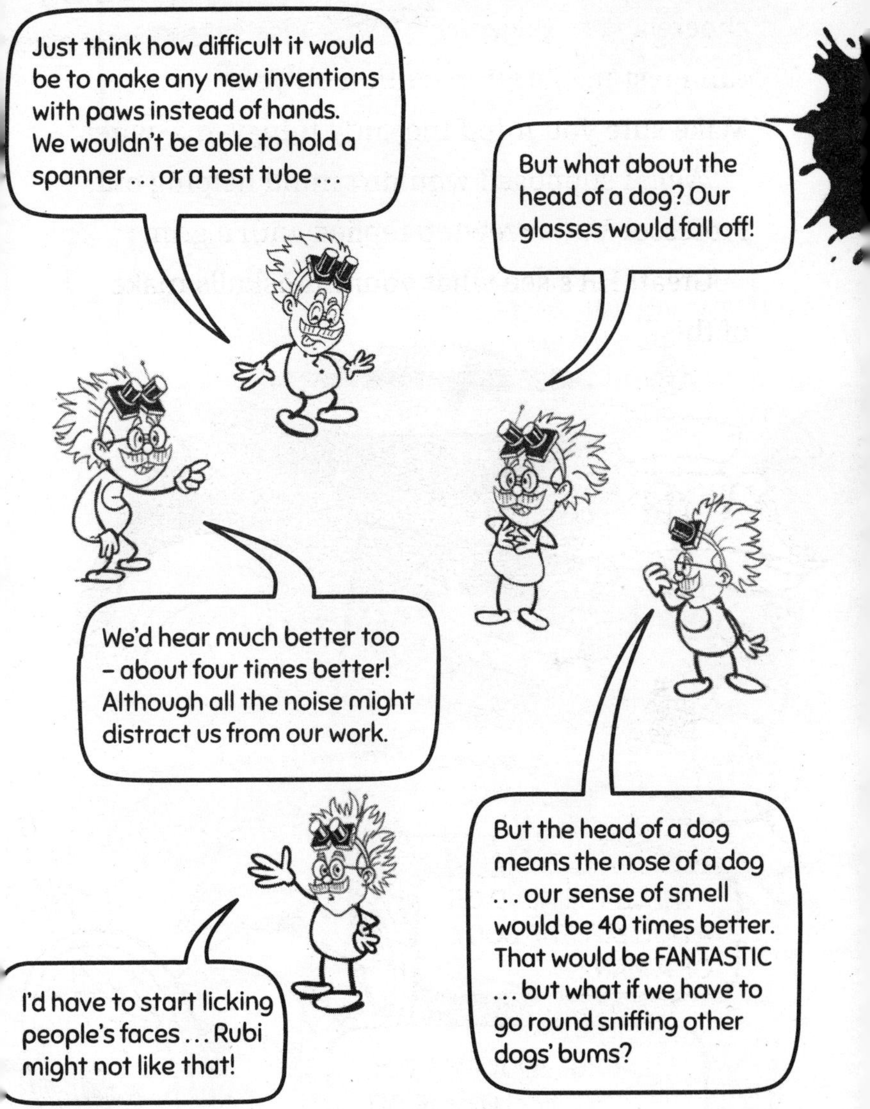
Just think how difficult it would be to make any new inventions with paws instead of hands. We wouldn't be able to hold a spanner . . . or a test tube . . .
But what about the head of a dog? Our glasses would fall off!
We'd hear much better too – about four times better! Although all the noise might distract us from our work.
But the head of a dog means the nose of a dog . . . our sense of smell would be 40 times better. That would be FANTASTIC . . . but what if we have to go round sniffing other dogs' bums?
I'd have to start licking people's faces . . . Rubi might not like that!

WHAT WOULD YOU DO?

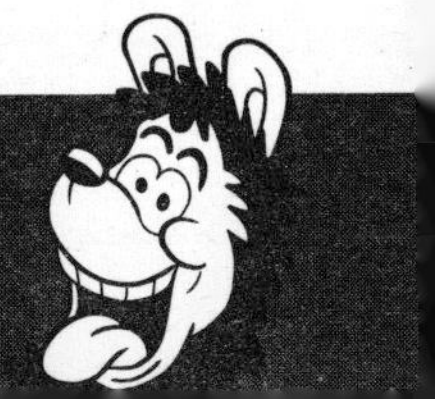

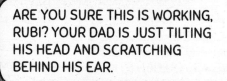

ARE YOU SURE THIS IS WORKING, RUBI? YOUR DAD IS JUST TILTING HIS HEAD AND SCRATCHING BEHIND HIS EAR.

WOOPS, FORGOT TO TURN UP THE VOLUME. THERE'S MORE, **DAD** – WOULD YOU CHANGE YOUR MIND WITH THESE **VARIATIONS**?

- YOUR HUMAN BODY CAN'T STOP WAGGING ITS BUM
- YOU TALK LIKE A HUMAN, BUT BARK EVERY TIME YOU SEE A SQUIRREL

- YOUR BODY MAY BE HUMAN, BUT YOUR FARTS SMELL LIKE A DOG'S
- YOU EAT HUMAN FOOD, BUT ALWAYS HAVE DOG BREATH

- YOUR DOG HEAD TALKS LIKE THE KING
- YOUR DOG BODY LOOKS LIKE ONE OF THE ROYAL CORGIS

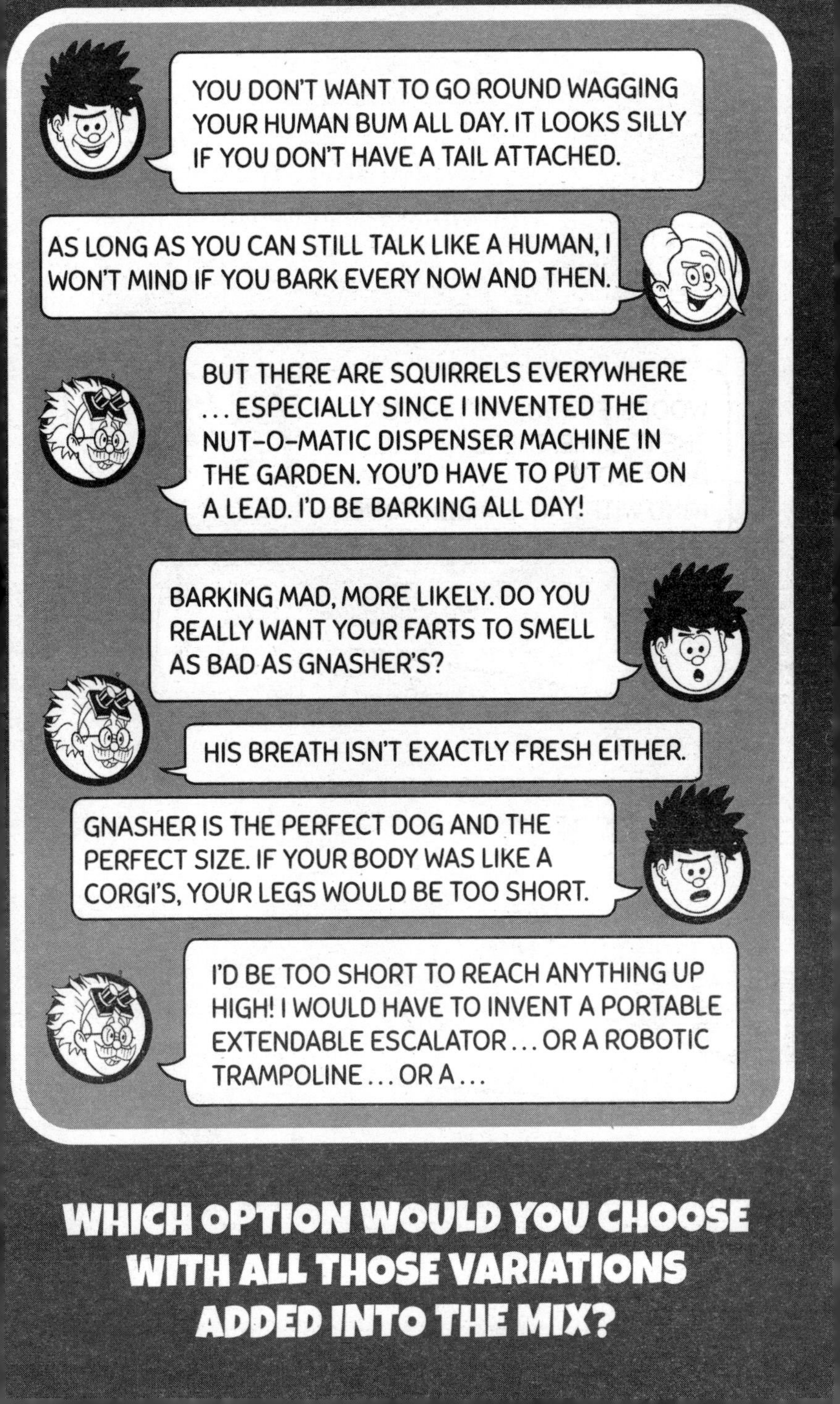
YOU DON'T WANT TO GO ROUND WAGGING YOUR HUMAN BUM ALL DAY. IT LOOKS SILLY IF YOU DON'T HAVE A TAIL ATTACHED.
AS LONG AS YOU CAN STILL TALK LIKE A HUMAN, I WON'T MIND IF YOU BARK EVERY NOW AND THEN.
BUT THERE ARE SQUIRRELS EVERYWHERE ... ESPECIALLY SINCE I INVENTED THE NUT-O-MATIC DISPENSER MACHINE IN THE GARDEN. YOU'D HAVE TO PUT ME ON A LEAD. I'D BE BARKING ALL DAY!
BARKING MAD, MORE LIKELY. DO YOU REALLY WANT YOUR FARTS TO SMELL AS BAD AS GNASHER'S?
HIS BREATH ISN'T EXACTLY FRESH EITHER.
GNASHER IS THE PERFECT DOG AND THE PERFECT SIZE. IF YOUR BODY WAS LIKE A CORGI'S, YOUR LEGS WOULD BE TOO SHORT.
I'D BE TOO SHORT TO REACH ANYTHING UP HIGH! I WOULD HAVE TO INVENT A PORTABLE EXTENDABLE ESCALATOR ... OR A ROBOTIC TRAMPOLINE ... OR A ...

WHICH OPTION WOULD YOU CHOOSE WITH ALL THOSE VARIATIONS ADDED INTO THE MIX?

DENNIS MENACE

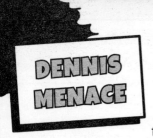

'Gather round, gather round!' shouted Rubi. 'You are about to witness science and comedy history being made! This here is a MIND* reader. Watch as I demonstrate it on my partner, Dennis.'

*Marvellous Imagination Neurotransmission Device

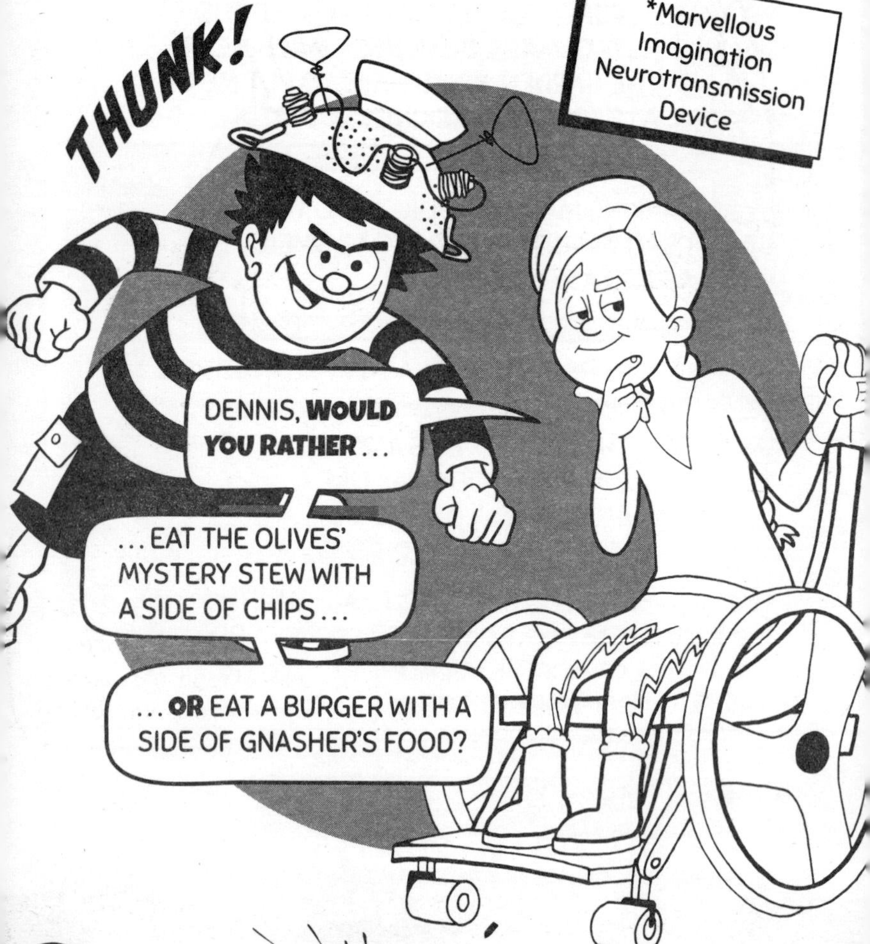
THUNK!
DENNIS, **WOULD YOU RATHER** . . .
. . . EAT THE OLIVES' MYSTERY STEW WITH A SIDE OF CHIPS . . .
. . . **OR** EAT A BURGER WITH A SIDE OF GNASHER'S FOOD?

WHAT DO DENNIS'S NUMSKULLS THINK?

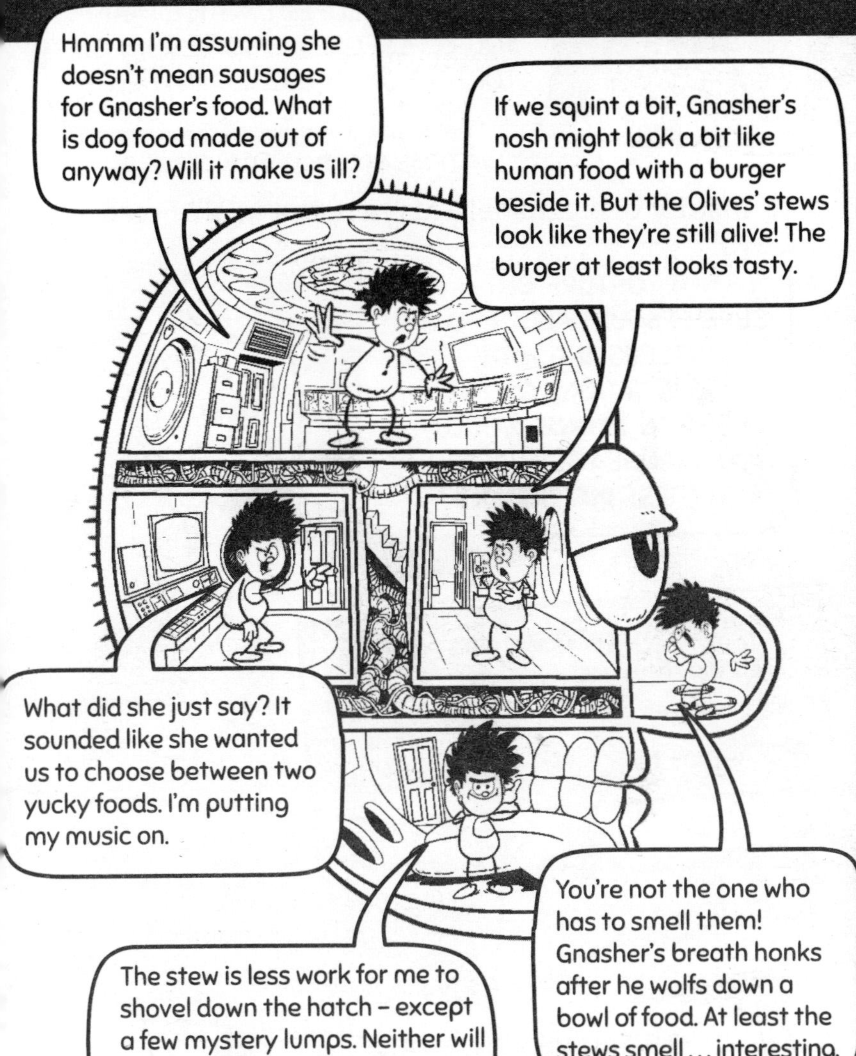
Hmmm I'm assuming she doesn't mean sausages for Gnasher's food. What is dog food made out of anyway? Will it make us ill?
If we squint a bit, Gnasher's nosh might look a bit like human food with a burger beside it. But the Olives' stews look like they're still alive! The burger at least looks tasty.
What did she just say? It sounded like she wanted us to choose between two yucky foods. I'm putting my music on.
You're not the one who has to smell them! Gnasher's breath honks after he wolfs down a bowl of food. At least the stews smell . . . interesting.
The stew is less work for me to shovel down the hatch – except a few mystery lumps. Neither will make the Tumskulls happy . . . but the chips and burger might make it easier for them.

WHAT WOULD YOU DO?

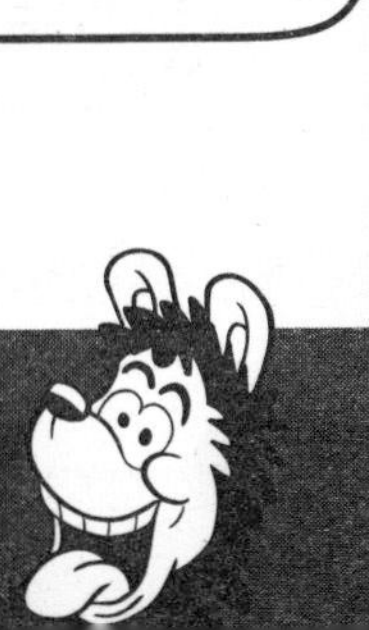

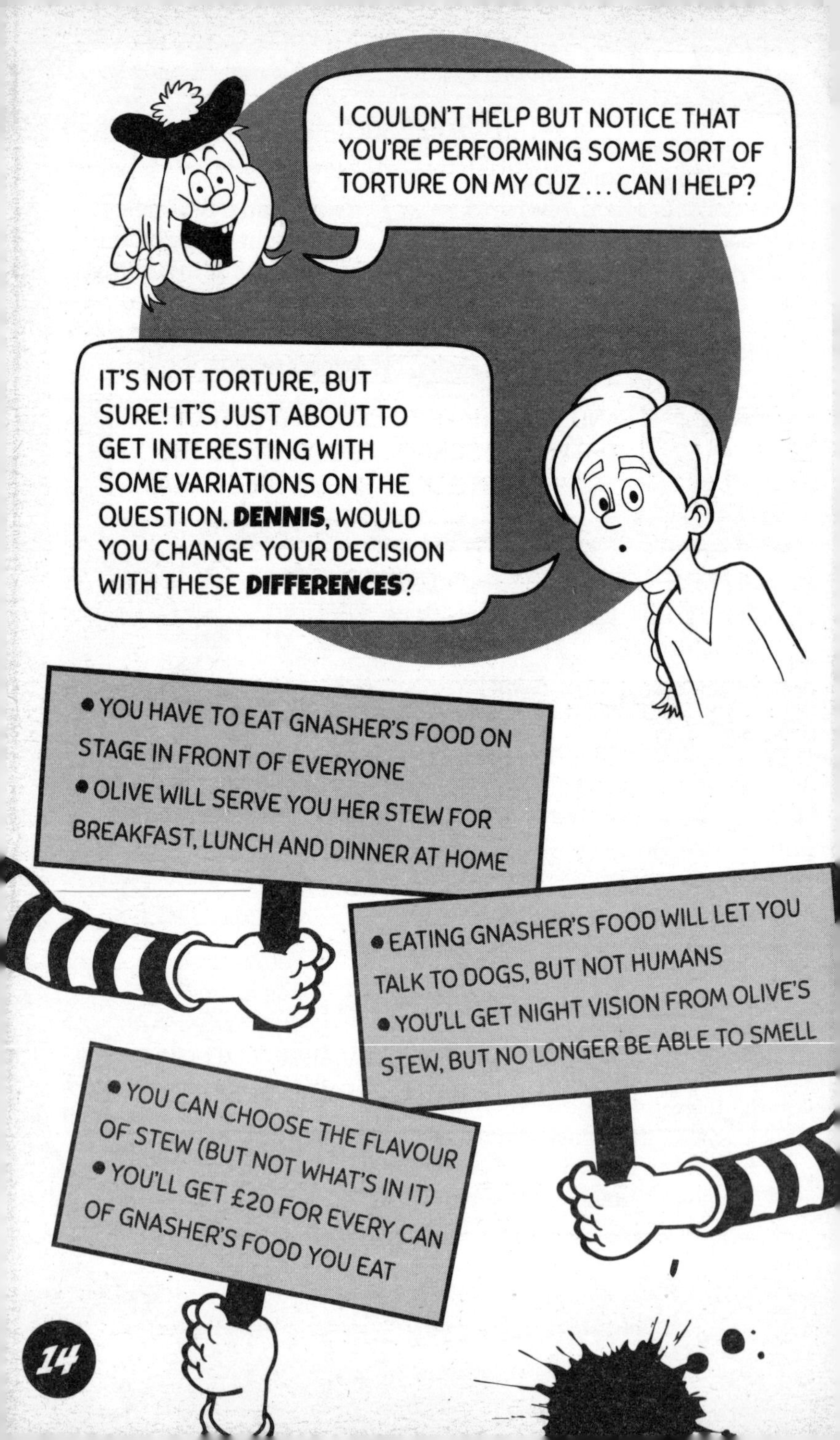
I COULDN'T HELP BUT NOTICE THAT YOU'RE PERFORMING SOME SORT OF TORTURE ON MY CUZ . . . CAN I HELP?
IT'S NOT TORTURE, BUT SURE! IT'S JUST ABOUT TO GET INTERESTING WITH SOME VARIATIONS ON THE QUESTION. **DENNIS**, WOULD YOU CHANGE YOUR DECISION WITH THESE **DIFFERENCES**?
• YOU HAVE TO EAT GNASHER'S FOOD ON STAGE IN FRONT OF EVERYONE
• OLIVE WILL SERVE YOU HER STEW FOR BREAKFAST, LUNCH AND DINNER AT HOME
• EATING GNASHER'S FOOD WILL LET YOU TALK TO DOGS, BUT NOT HUMANS
• YOU'LL GET NIGHT VISION FROM OLIVE'S STEW, BUT NO LONGER BE ABLE TO SMELL
• YOU CAN CHOOSE THE FLAVOUR OF STEW (BUT NOT WHAT'S IN IT)
• YOU'LL GET £20 FOR EVERY CAN OF GNASHER'S FOOD YOU EAT

BLIMEY, CUZ. YOU COULD BE RICH IF YOU EAT GNASHER'S FOOD FOR A WEEK!

URGH, NO WAY. EVEN IF I CAN DISGUISE IT WITH THE BURGERS, IT'D STILL BE A MEATY JELLY!

AND YOU'D HAVE TO DO IT IN FRONT OF THE WHOLE SCHOOL TOO! YOU'D BE THE LAUGHING STOCK OF BASH STREET. AGAIN.

HEY! I'VE NEVER BEEN A LAUGHING STOCK. AND I'D RATHER THAT THAN OLIVE FEEDING ME AT HOME!

YEAH, ONCE A DAY AT SCHOOL IS BAD ENOUGH. AND IF THEY DID LAUGH AT YOU, YOU COULD TALK TO YOUR NEW DOG PALS AND GET 'EM!

BUT I ALREADY UNDERSTAND GNASHER, AND HE'S THE ONLY DOG I NEED TO TALK TO!

AND IF YOU HAVE NIGHT VISION, YOU COULD BE MY, I MEAN, BATMIN'S FAITHFUL SIDEKICK!

WHICH OPTION WOULD YOU CHOOSE WITH ALL THOSE VARIATIONS ADDED INTO THE MIX?

Minnie looked amazed.

'Can I try it out? If Dennis can do it, I can definitely handle it.'

'Sure,' Rubi replied. 'Just put the MIND reader on your head like this.'

'I know what to do,' Minnie declared, and thrust the device upon her head.

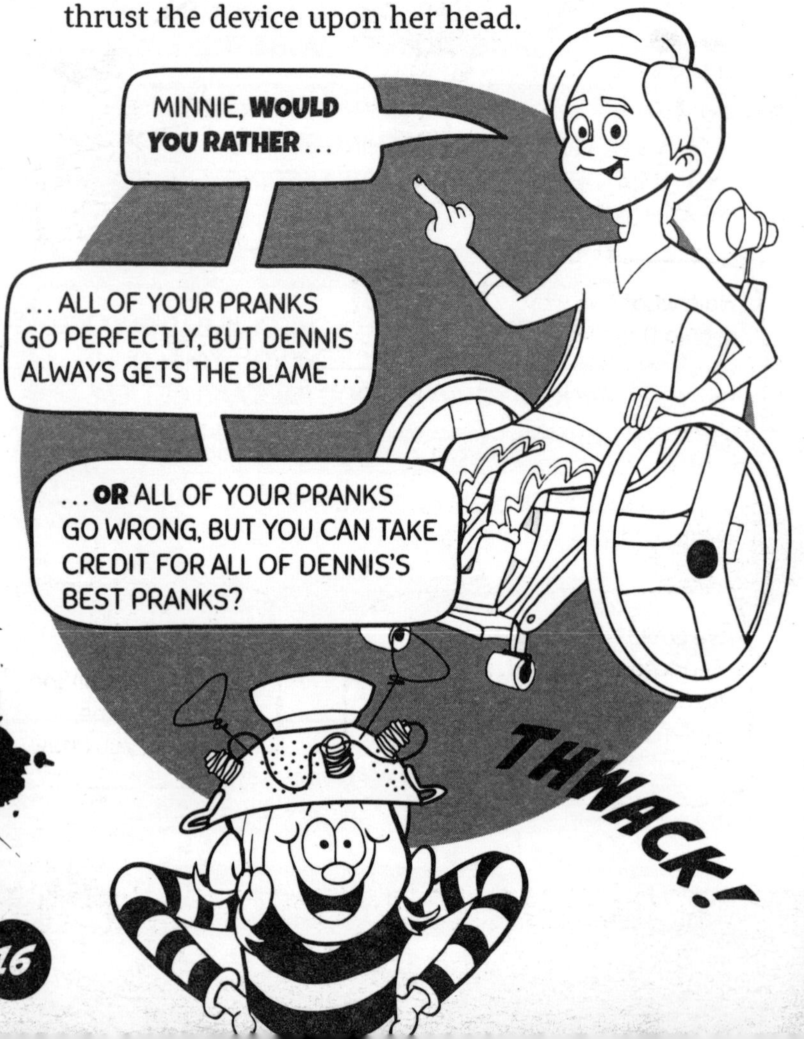
MINNIE, **WOULD YOU RATHER** ...
...ALL OF YOUR PRANKS GO PERFECTLY, BUT DENNIS ALWAYS GETS THE BLAME...
...**OR** ALL OF YOUR PRANKS GO WRONG, BUT YOU CAN TAKE CREDIT FOR ALL OF DENNIS'S BEST PRANKS?
THWACK!

WHAT DO MINNIE'S NUMSKULLS THINK?

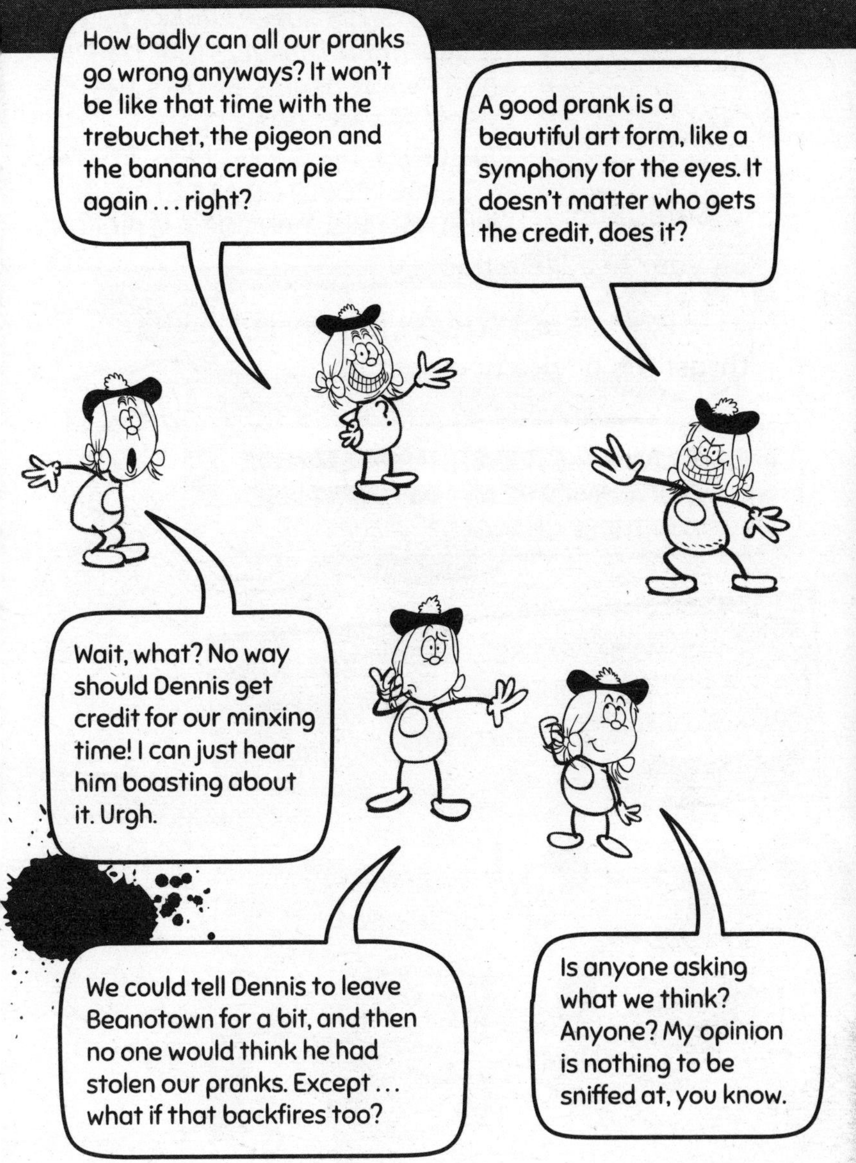
How badly can all our pranks go wrong anyways? It won't be like that time with the trebuchet, the pigeon and the banana cream pie again . . . right?
A good prank is a beautiful art form, like a symphony for the eyes. It doesn't matter who gets the credit, does it?
Wait, what? No way should Dennis get credit for our minxing time! I can just hear him boasting about it. Urgh.
We could tell Dennis to leave Beanotown for a bit, and then no one would think he had stolen our pranks. Except . . . what if that backfires too?
Is anyone asking what we think? Anyone? My opinion is nothing to be sniffed at, you know.

WHAT WOULD YOU DO?

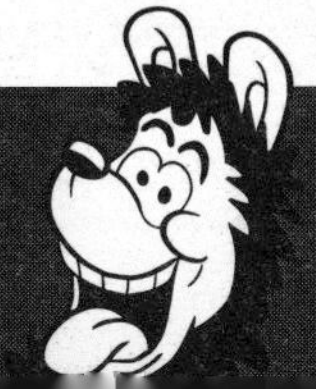

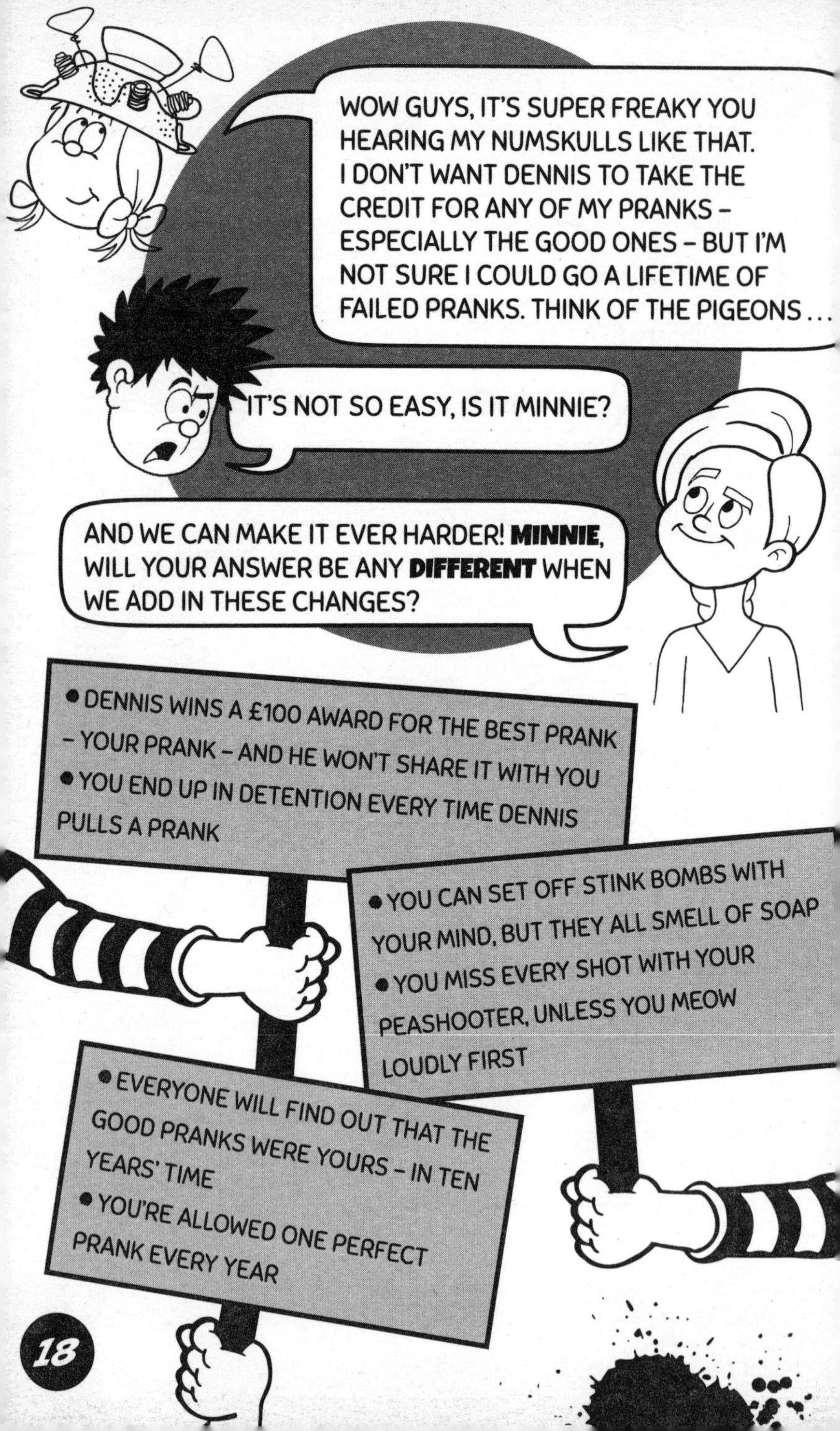
WOW GUYS, IT'S SUPER FREAKY YOU HEARING MY NUMSKULLS LIKE THAT. I DON'T WANT DENNIS TO TAKE THE CREDIT FOR ANY OF MY PRANKS – ESPECIALLY THE GOOD ONES – BUT I'M NOT SURE I COULD GO A LIFETIME OF FAILED PRANKS. THINK OF THE PIGEONS . . .
IT'S NOT SO EASY, IS IT MINNIE?
AND WE CAN MAKE IT EVER HARDER! **MINNIE**, WILL YOUR ANSWER BE ANY **DIFFERENT** WHEN WE ADD IN THESE CHANGES?
• DENNIS WINS A £100 AWARD FOR THE BEST PRANK – YOUR PRANK – AND HE WON'T SHARE IT WITH YOU
• YOU END UP IN DETENTION EVERY TIME DENNIS PULLS A PRANK
• YOU CAN SET OFF STINK BOMBS WITH YOUR MIND, BUT THEY ALL SMELL OF SOAP
• YOU MISS EVERY SHOT WITH YOUR PEASHOOTER, UNLESS YOU MEOW LOUDLY FIRST
• EVERYONE WILL FIND OUT THAT THE GOOD PRANKS WERE YOURS – IN TEN YEARS' TIME
• YOU'RE ALLOWED ONE PERFECT PRANK EVERY YEAR

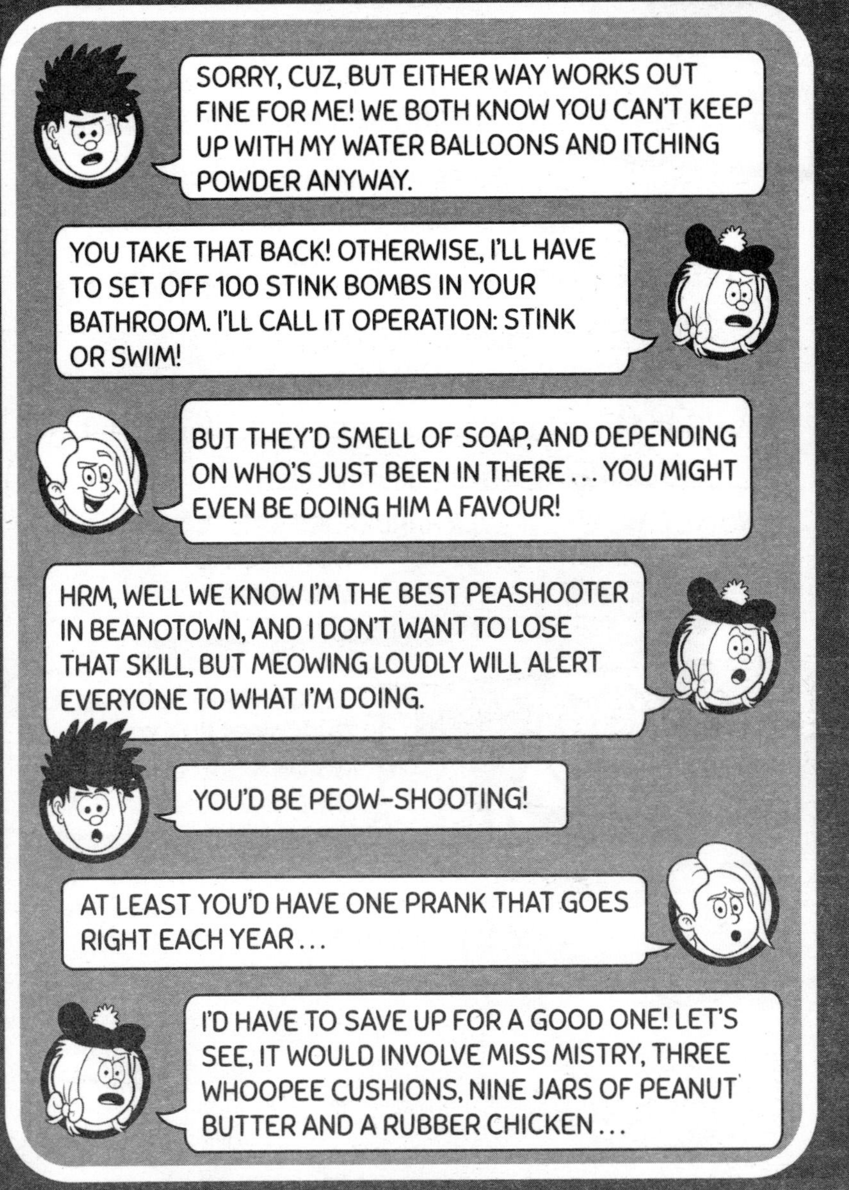
SORRY, CUZ, BUT EITHER WAY WORKS OUT FINE FOR ME! WE BOTH KNOW YOU CAN'T KEEP UP WITH MY WATER BALLOONS AND ITCHING POWDER ANYWAY.
YOU TAKE THAT BACK! OTHERWISE, I'LL HAVE TO SET OFF 100 STINK BOMBS IN YOUR BATHROOM. I'LL CALL IT OPERATION: STINK OR SWIM!
BUT THEY'D SMELL OF SOAP, AND DEPENDING ON WHO'S JUST BEEN IN THERE... YOU MIGHT EVEN BE DOING HIM A FAVOUR!
HRM, WELL WE KNOW I'M THE BEST PEASHOOTER IN BEANOTOWN, AND I DON'T WANT TO LOSE THAT SKILL, BUT MEOWING LOUDLY WILL ALERT EVERYONE TO WHAT I'M DOING.
YOU'D BE PEOW-SHOOTING!
AT LEAST YOU'D HAVE ONE PRANK THAT GOES RIGHT EACH YEAR...
I'D HAVE TO SAVE UP FOR A GOOD ONE! LET'S SEE, IT WOULD INVOLVE MISS MISTRY, THREE WHOOPEE CUSHIONS, NINE JARS OF PEANUT BUTTER AND A RUBBER CHICKEN...

WHICH OPTION WOULD YOU CHOOSE WITH ALL THOSE VARIATIONS ADDED INTO THE MIX?

GNASHER

'So who else can your machine work on?' Minnie asked. 'Teachers? Parents? Pets?'

'I know just who to try next,' Dennis replied. 'Oh Gnasher . . .'

'Gnash!' *Right gnow? Do I have to?*

'Good boy, Gnasher!' Dennis said, plonking the MIND reader upon Gnasher's head.

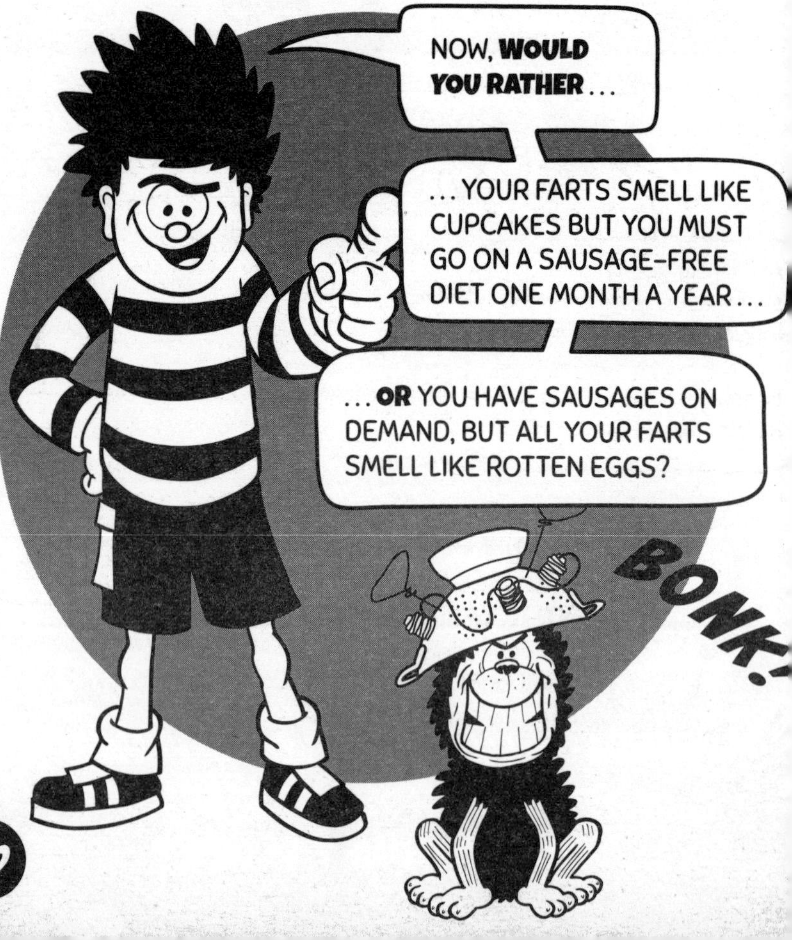
NOW, WOULD YOU RATHER . . .
. . . YOUR FARTS SMELL LIKE CUPCAKES BUT YOU MUST GO ON A SAUSAGE-FREE DIET ONE MONTH A YEAR . . .
. . . OR YOU HAVE SAUSAGES ON DEMAND, BUT ALL YOUR FARTS SMELL LIKE ROTTEN EGGS?
BONK!

WHAT DO GNASHER'S NUMSKULLS THINK?

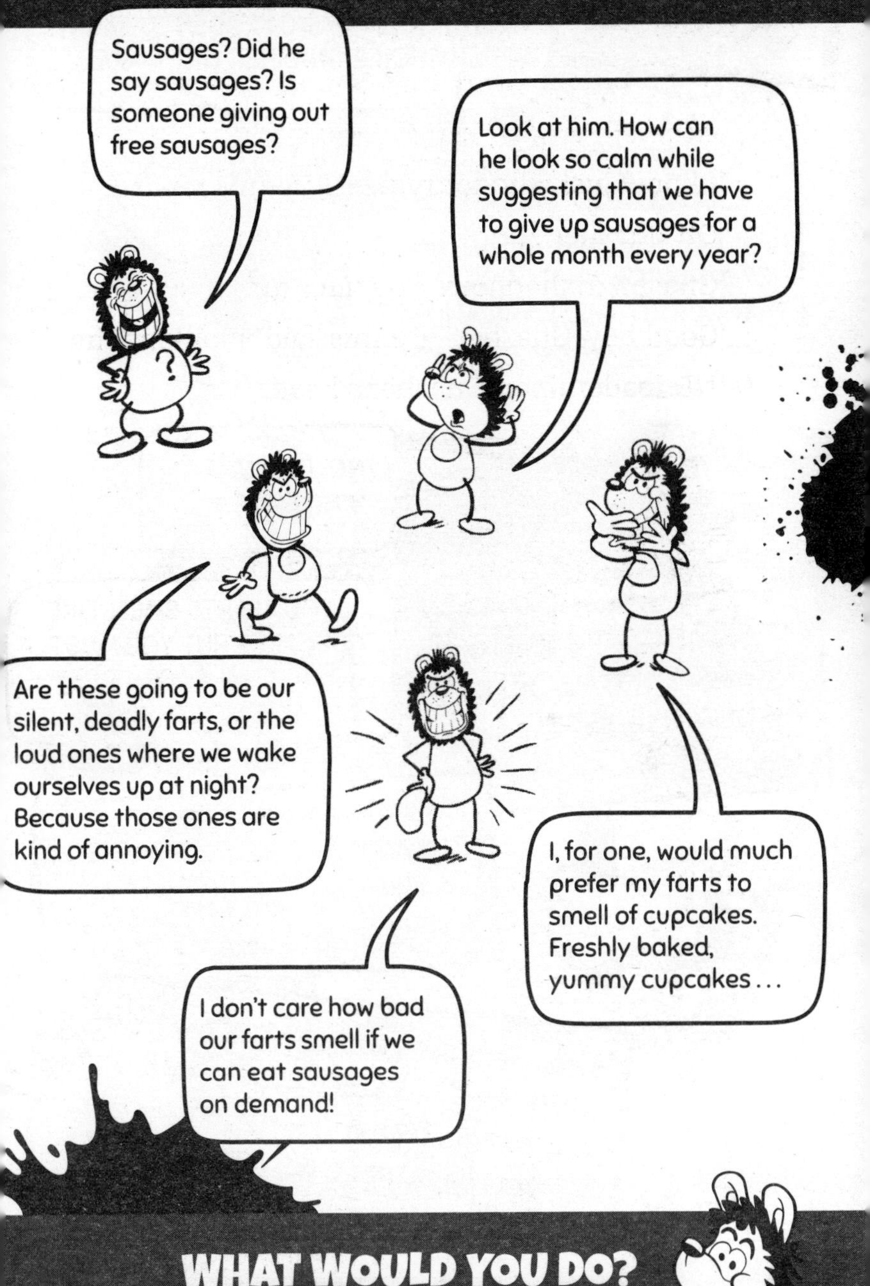

Sausages? Did he say sausages? Is someone giving out free sausages?
Look at him. How can he look so calm while suggesting that we have to give up sausages for a whole month every year?
Are these going to be our silent, deadly farts, or the loud ones where we wake ourselves up at night? Because those ones are kind of annoying.
I, for one, would much prefer my farts to smell of cupcakes. Freshly baked, yummy cupcakes . . .
I don't care how bad our farts smell if we can eat sausages on demand!

WHAT WOULD YOU DO?

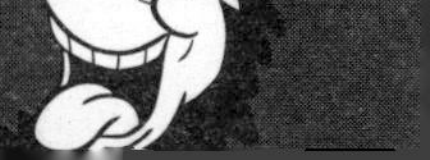

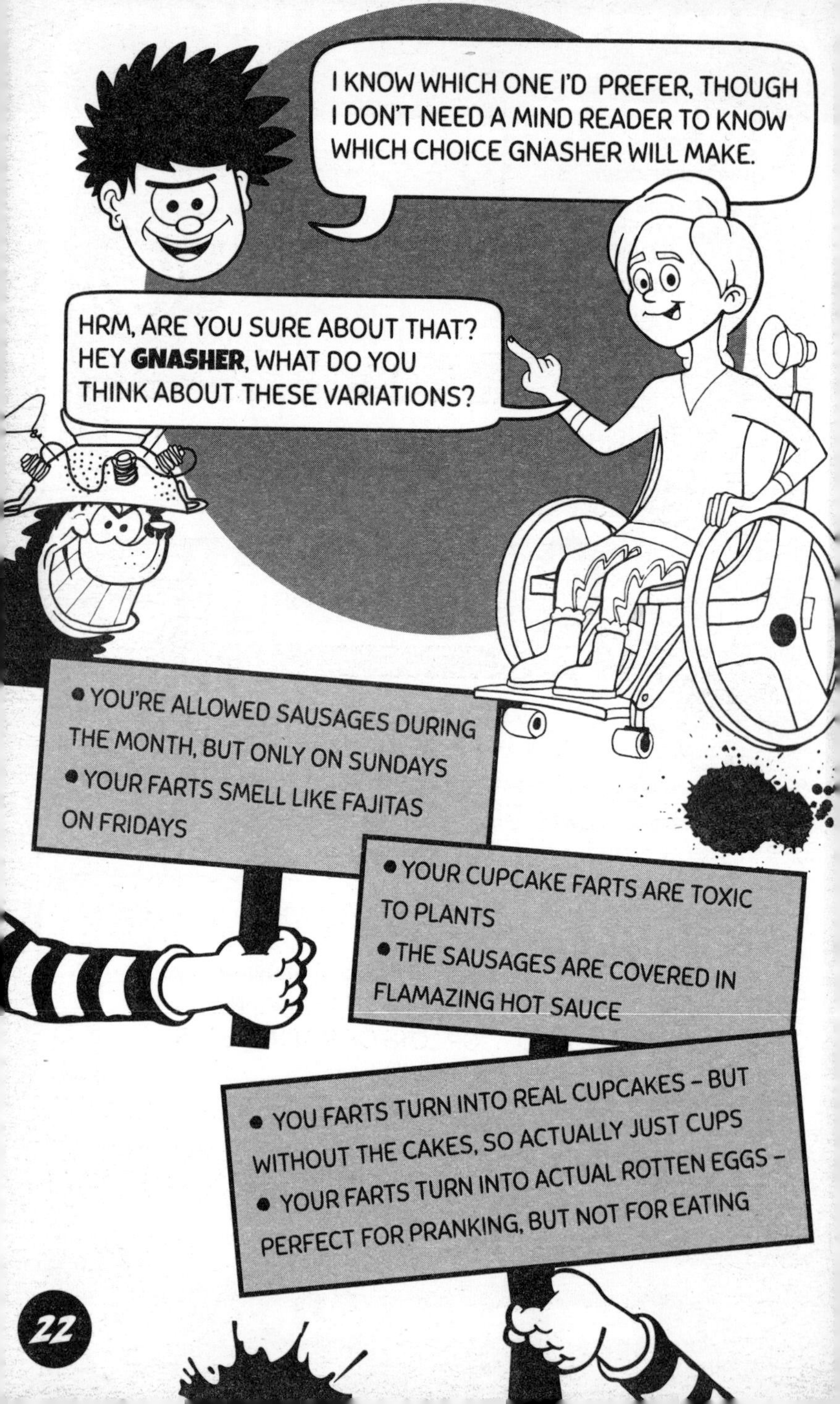
I KNOW WHICH ONE I'D PREFER, THOUGH I DON'T NEED A MIND READER TO KNOW WHICH CHOICE GNASHER WILL MAKE.
HRM, ARE YOU SURE ABOUT THAT? HEY **GNASHER**, WHAT DO YOU THINK ABOUT THESE VARIATIONS?
• YOU'RE ALLOWED SAUSAGES DURING THE MONTH, BUT ONLY ON SUNDAYS
• YOUR FARTS SMELL LIKE FAJITAS ON FRIDAYS
• YOUR CUPCAKE FARTS ARE TOXIC TO PLANTS
• THE SAUSAGES ARE COVERED IN FLAMAZING HOT SAUCE
• YOU FARTS TURN INTO REAL CUPCAKES – BUT WITHOUT THE CAKES, SO ACTUALLY JUST CUPS
• YOUR FARTS TURN INTO ACTUAL ROTTEN EGGS – PERFECT FOR PRANKING, BUT NOT FOR EATING

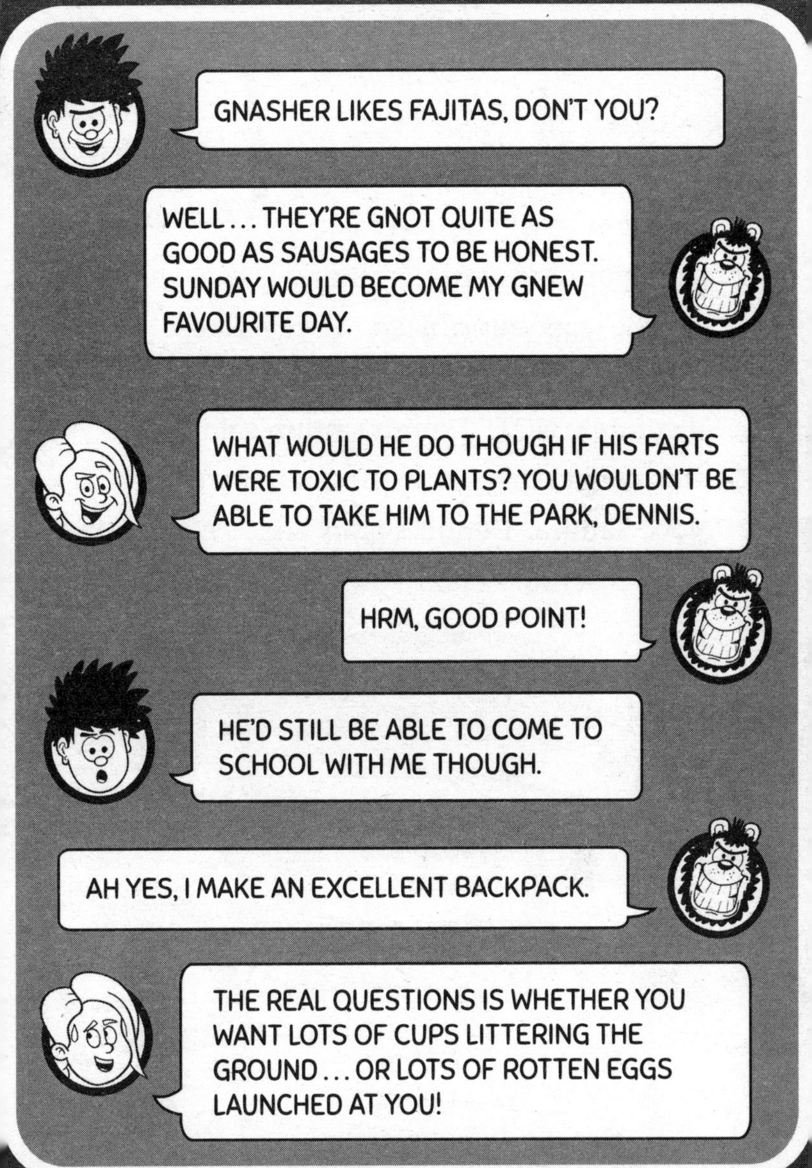
GNASHER LIKES FAJITAS, DON'T YOU?
WELL... THEY'RE GNOT QUITE AS GOOD AS SAUSAGES TO BE HONEST. SUNDAY WOULD BECOME MY GNEW FAVOURITE DAY.
WHAT WOULD HE DO THOUGH IF HIS FARTS WERE TOXIC TO PLANTS? YOU WOULDN'T BE ABLE TO TAKE HIM TO THE PARK, DENNIS.
HRM, GOOD POINT!
HE'D STILL BE ABLE TO COME TO SCHOOL WITH ME THOUGH.
AH YES, I MAKE AN EXCELLENT BACKPACK.
THE REAL QUESTIONS IS WHETHER YOU WANT LOTS OF CUPS LITTERING THE GROUND... OR LOTS OF ROTTEN EGGS LAUNCHED AT YOU!

WHICH OPTION WOULD YOU CHOOSE WITH ALL THOSE VARIATIONS ADDED INTO THE MIX?

Meanwhile, the rest of Dennis's family had wandered over.

'Den-den bowl on head!' Bea giggled, pointing at her brother.

'Does it work on babies?' Minnie asked. 'You could try it on Bea!'

'Absolutely NOT!' Dennis's mum said before Dennis could reply. 'It might not be safe.'

'Now, Sandra,' Dennis's gran said. 'Why don't I try it for Dennis? Make sure it's safe first.'

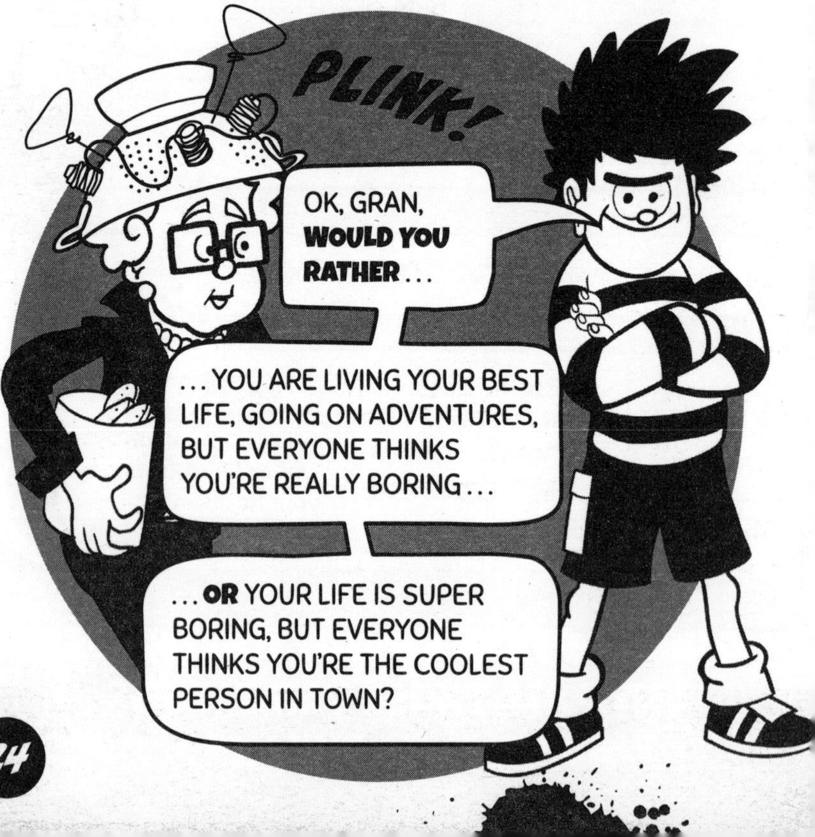
PLINK!
OK, GRAN, **WOULD YOU RATHER** . . .
. . . YOU ARE LIVING YOUR BEST LIFE, GOING ON ADVENTURES, BUT EVERYONE THINKS YOU'RE REALLY BORING . . .
. . . **OR** YOUR LIFE IS SUPER BORING, BUT EVERYONE THINKS YOU'RE THE COOLEST PERSON IN TOWN?

WHAT DO GRAN MENACE'S NUMSKULLS THINK?

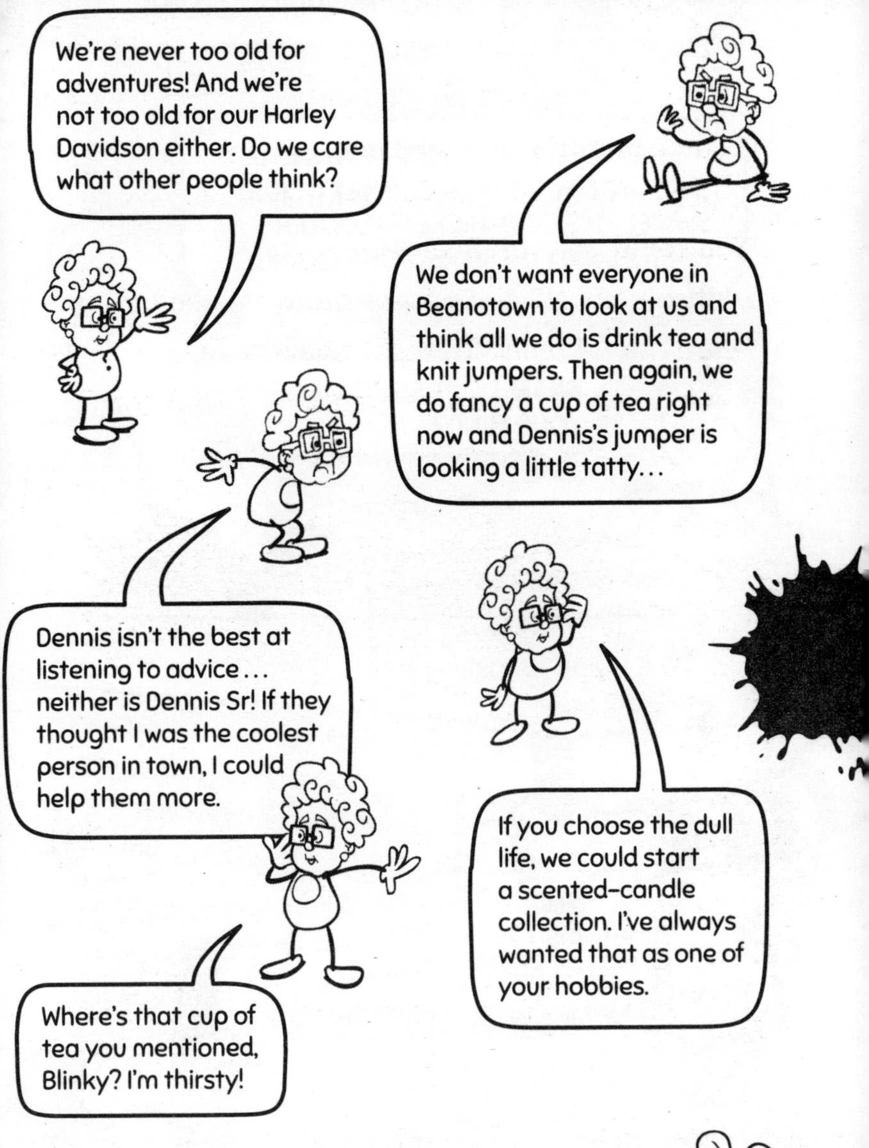
We're never too old for adventures! And we're not too old for our Harley Davidson either. Do we care what other people think?
We don't want everyone in Beanotown to look at us and think all we do is drink tea and knit jumpers. Then again, we do fancy a cup of tea right now and Dennis's jumper is looking a little tatty...
Dennis isn't the best at listening to advice... neither is Dennis Sr! If they thought I was the coolest person in town, I could help them more.
If you choose the dull life, we could start a scented-candle collection. I've always wanted that as one of your hobbies.
Where's that cup of tea you mentioned, Blinky? I'm thirsty!

WHAT WOULD YOU DO?

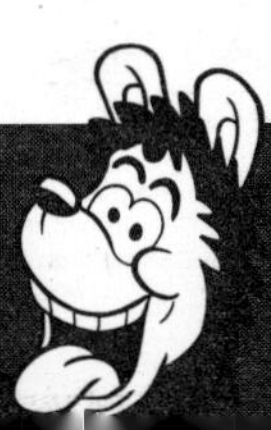

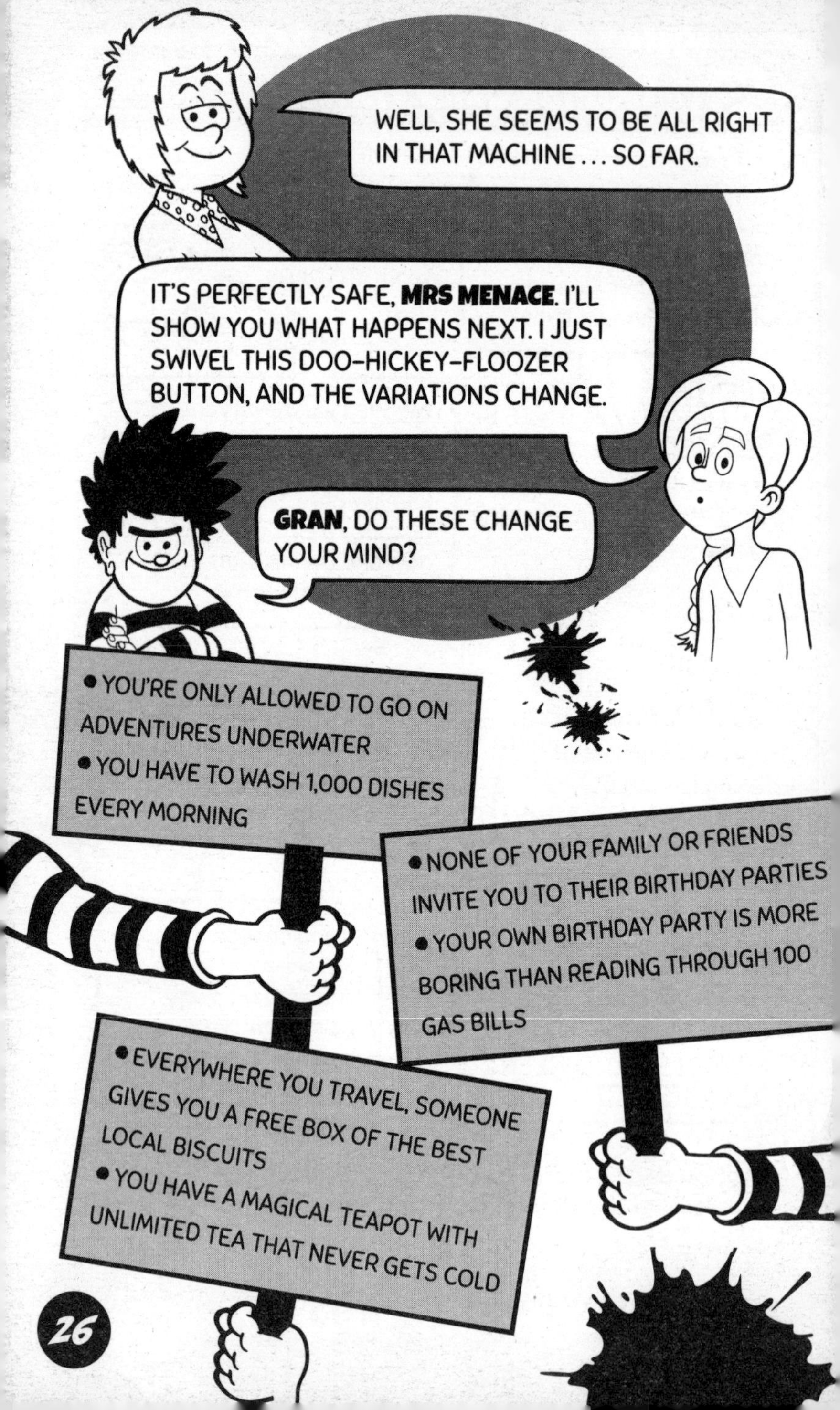

WELL, SHE SEEMS TO BE ALL RIGHT IN THAT MACHINE . . . SO FAR.
IT'S PERFECTLY SAFE, **MRS MENACE**. I'LL SHOW YOU WHAT HAPPENS NEXT. I JUST SWIVEL THIS DOO–HICKEY–FLOOZER BUTTON, AND THE VARIATIONS CHANGE.
GRAN, DO THESE CHANGE YOUR MIND?
• YOU'RE ONLY ALLOWED TO GO ON ADVENTURES UNDERWATER
• YOU HAVE TO WASH 1,000 DISHES EVERY MORNING
• NONE OF YOUR FAMILY OR FRIENDS INVITE YOU TO THEIR BIRTHDAY PARTIES
• YOUR OWN BIRTHDAY PARTY IS MORE BORING THAN READING THROUGH 100 GAS BILLS
• EVERYWHERE YOU TRAVEL, SOMEONE GIVES YOU A FREE BOX OF THE BEST LOCAL BISCUITS
• YOU HAVE A MAGICAL TEAPOT WITH UNLIMITED TEA THAT NEVER GETS COLD

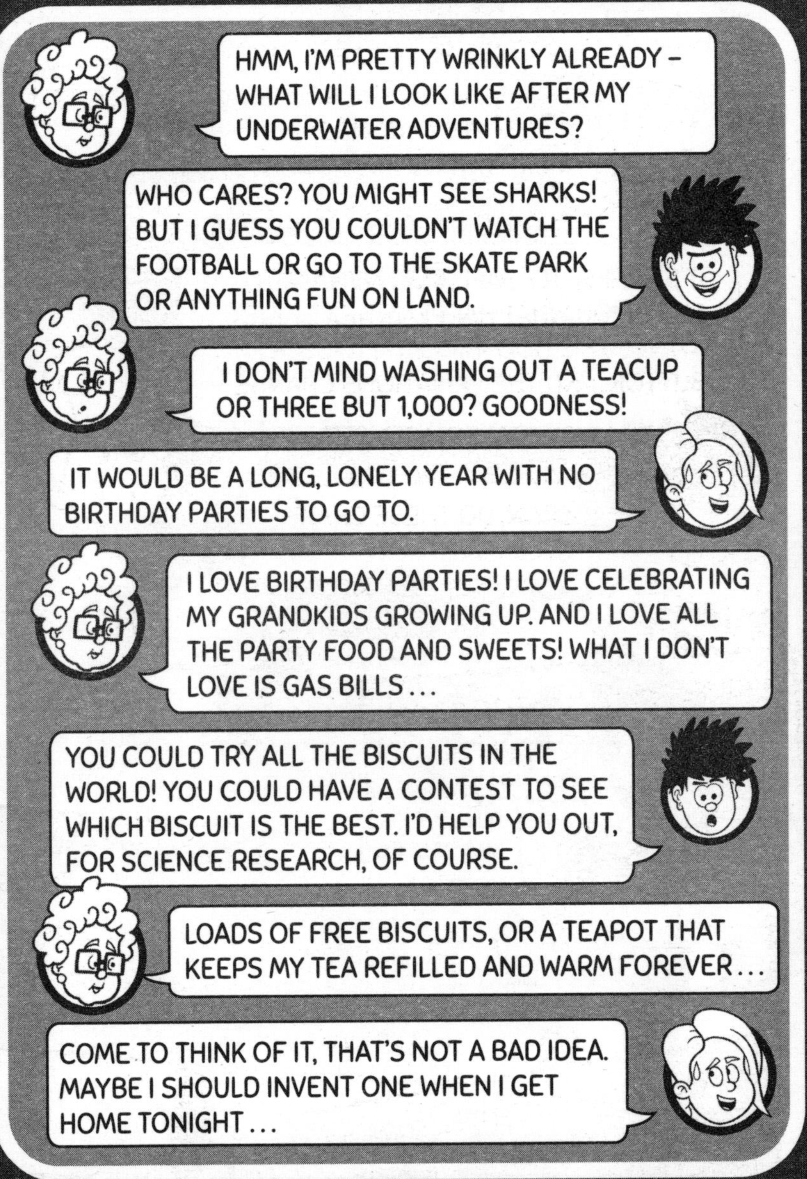
HMM, I'M PRETTY WRINKLY ALREADY – WHAT WILL I LOOK LIKE AFTER MY UNDERWATER ADVENTURES?
WHO CARES? YOU MIGHT SEE SHARKS! BUT I GUESS YOU COULDN'T WATCH THE FOOTBALL OR GO TO THE SKATE PARK OR ANYTHING FUN ON LAND.
I DON'T MIND WASHING OUT A TEACUP OR THREE BUT 1,000? GOODNESS!
IT WOULD BE A LONG, LONELY YEAR WITH NO BIRTHDAY PARTIES TO GO TO.
I LOVE BIRTHDAY PARTIES! I LOVE CELEBRATING MY GRANDKIDS GROWING UP. AND I LOVE ALL THE PARTY FOOD AND SWEETS! WHAT I DON'T LOVE IS GAS BILLS . . .
YOU COULD TRY ALL THE BISCUITS IN THE WORLD! YOU COULD HAVE A CONTEST TO SEE WHICH BISCUIT IS THE BEST. I'D HELP YOU OUT, FOR SCIENCE RESEARCH, OF COURSE.
LOADS OF FREE BISCUITS, OR A TEAPOT THAT KEEPS MY TEA REFILLED AND WARM FOREVER . . .
COME TO THINK OF IT, THAT'S NOT A BAD IDEA. MAYBE I SHOULD INVENT ONE WHEN I GET HOME TONIGHT . . .

WHICH OPTION WOULD YOU CHOOSE WITH ALL THOSE VARIATIONS ADDED INTO THE MIX?

DENNIS MENACE SR

'This is such a cool invention, Rubi! You should be very proud,' said Dennis Sr.

'Dennis came up with the plan for how to use the MIND reader,' Rubi added loyally.

'I knew my son was a genius,' Dennis Sr said proudly, ruffling Dennis's hair. 'I don't suppose I could try it out?'

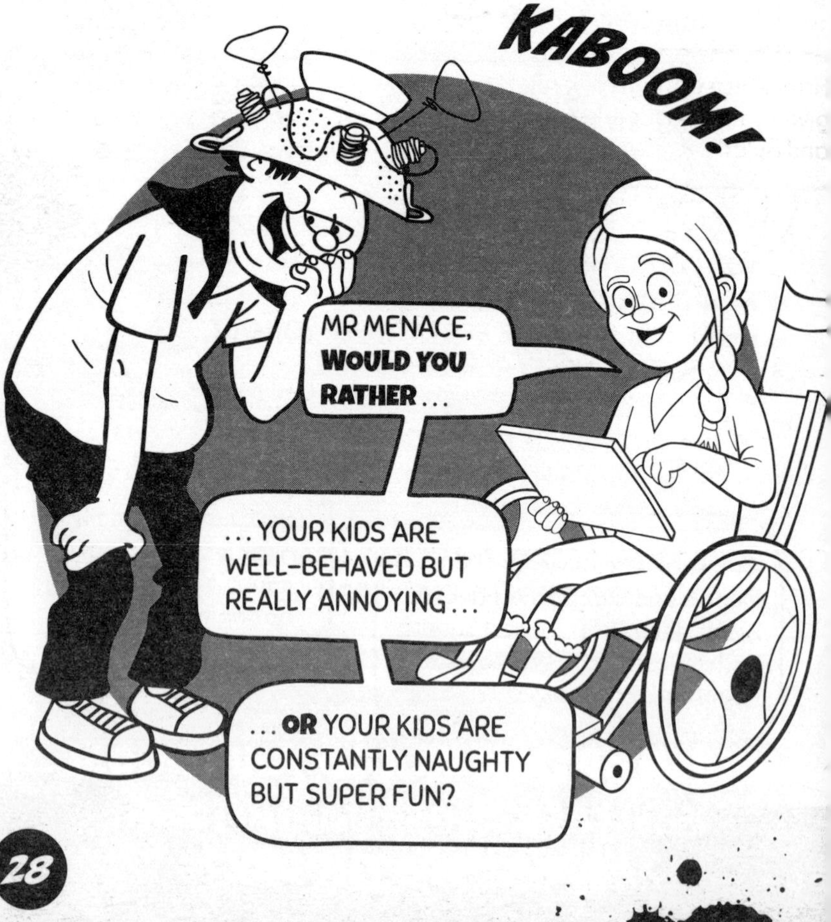
KABOOM!
MR MENACE, **WOULD YOU RATHER** . . .
. . . YOUR KIDS ARE WELL-BEHAVED BUT REALLY ANNOYING . . .
. . . **OR** YOUR KIDS ARE CONSTANTLY NAUGHTY BUT SUPER FUN?

WHAT DO DENNIS SR'S NUMSKULLS THINK?

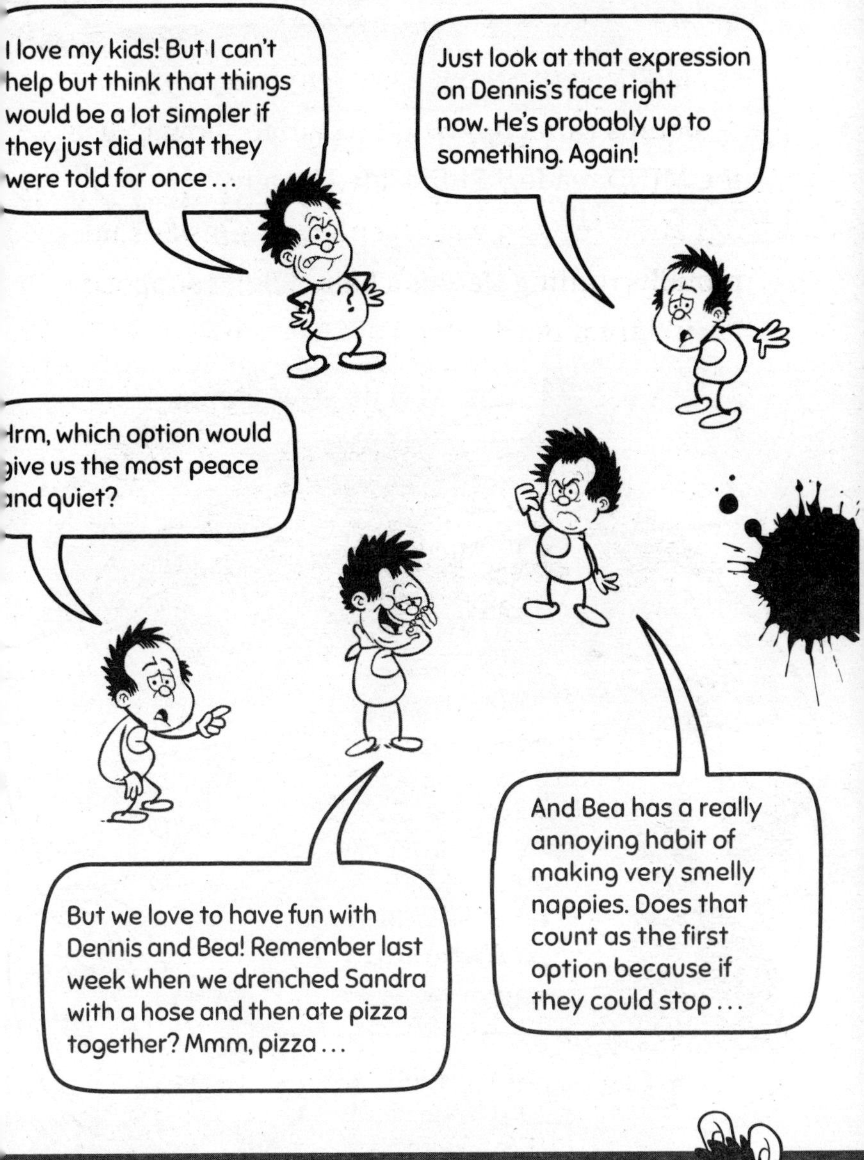

WHAT WOULD YOU DO?

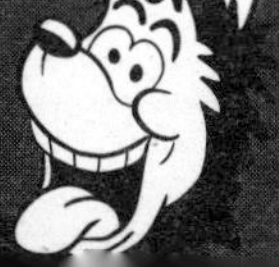

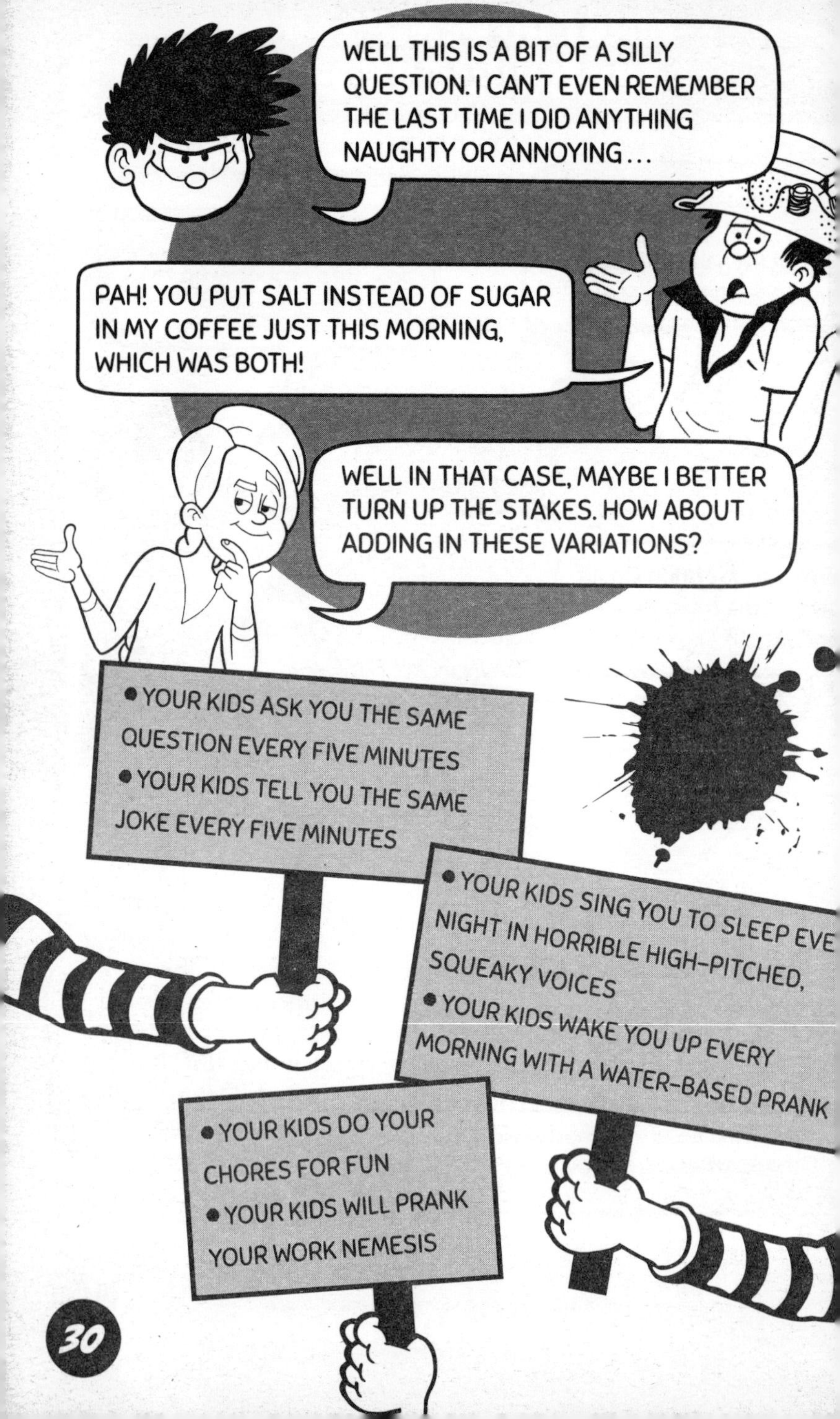

WELL THIS IS A BIT OF A SILLY QUESTION. I CAN'T EVEN REMEMBER THE LAST TIME I DID ANYTHING NAUGHTY OR ANNOYING...
PAH! YOU PUT SALT INSTEAD OF SUGAR IN MY COFFEE JUST THIS MORNING, WHICH WAS BOTH!
WELL IN THAT CASE, MAYBE I BETTER TURN UP THE STAKES. HOW ABOUT ADDING IN THESE VARIATIONS?
• YOUR KIDS ASK YOU THE SAME QUESTION EVERY FIVE MINUTES
• YOUR KIDS TELL YOU THE SAME JOKE EVERY FIVE MINUTES
• YOUR KIDS SING YOU TO SLEEP EVE NIGHT IN HORRIBLE HIGH-PITCHED, SQUEAKY VOICES
• YOUR KIDS WAKE YOU UP EVERY MORNING WITH A WATER-BASED PRANK
• YOUR KIDS DO YOUR CHORES FOR FUN
• YOUR KIDS WILL PRANK YOUR WORK NEMESIS

I STILL THINK SOMETHING'S WRONG WITH THE QUESTION! IT SHOULD BE ASKING YOU WHETHER YOU THINK I'M AWESOMELY EPIC, OR EPICALLY AWESOME. RIGHT? AM I? AM I?

YOU'RE ALREADY ASKING THE SAME QUESTION OVER AND OVER AGAIN!

AT LEAST DENNIS'S JOKES ARE FUNNY ... THE FIRST TIME ROUND.

HEY!

IT'S SO HARD TO GET A GOOD NIGHT'S SLEEP ALREADY! WHAT IF I CAN'T SLEEP THROUGH HIGH-PITCHED, SQUEAKY VOICES OR WATER THROWN IN MY FACE?

CAN YOU IMAGINE IF DENNIS AND BEA STARTED DOING YOUR CHORES ... FOR FUN?

IF ONLY! THEN I'D HAVE SO MUCH MORE TIME TO RELAX IN MY SHED ... OR IN MY FAVOURITE OLD COMFY CHAIR ...

OH, BUT I COULD PULL SUCH A BLAMAZING PRANK ON YOUR WORK NEMESIS! I'D PUT INVISIBLE GLUE ALL OVER THEIR PAPERCLIPS, SO THEY WOULD BE STUCK AT WORK!

WHICH OPTION WOULD YOU CHOOSE WITH ALL THOSE VARIATIONS ADDED INTO THE MIX?

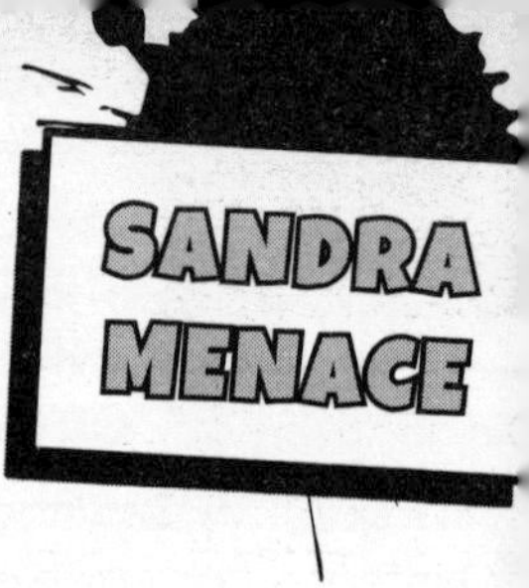
SANDRA
MENACE

'What do you think, Mum?' Dennis tried. 'Will you have a turn now?'

'It's for science,' Rubi added sweetly.

'Well . . .'

'GO ON!' shouted Dennis, Rubi, Dennis Senior and Gran together.

'Oh all right!'

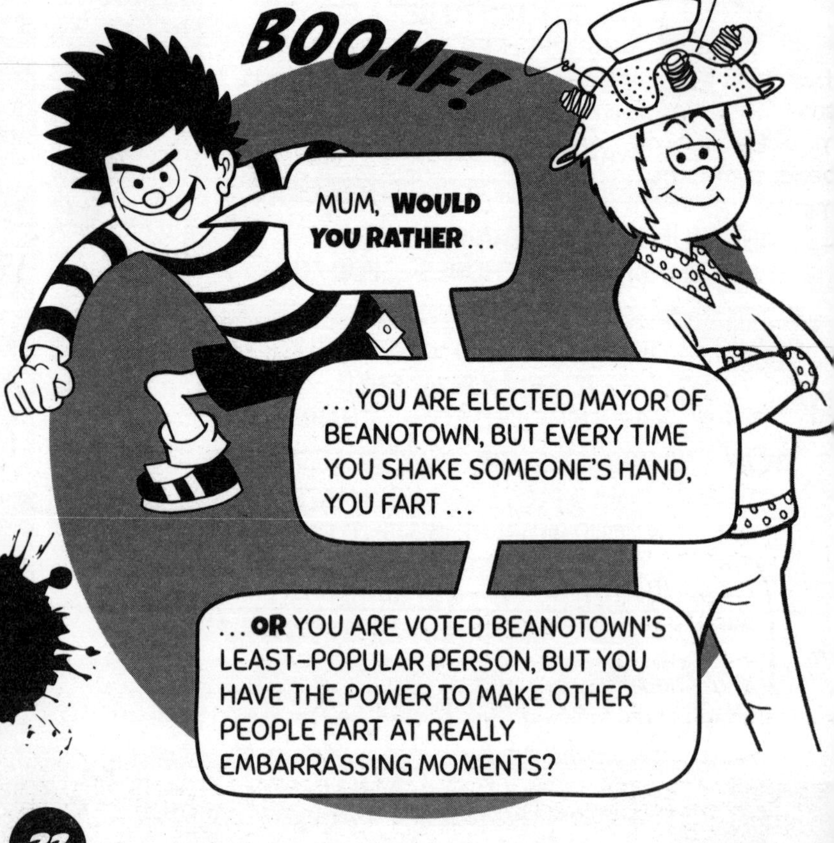
BOOMF!
MUM, **WOULD YOU RATHER**...
...YOU ARE ELECTED MAYOR OF BEANOTOWN, BUT EVERY TIME YOU SHAKE SOMEONE'S HAND, YOU FART...
...**OR** YOU ARE VOTED BEANOTOWN'S LEAST-POPULAR PERSON, BUT YOU HAVE THE POWER TO MAKE OTHER PEOPLE FART AT REALLY EMBARRASSING MOMENTS?

WHAT DO SANDRA MENACE'S NUMSKULLS THINK?

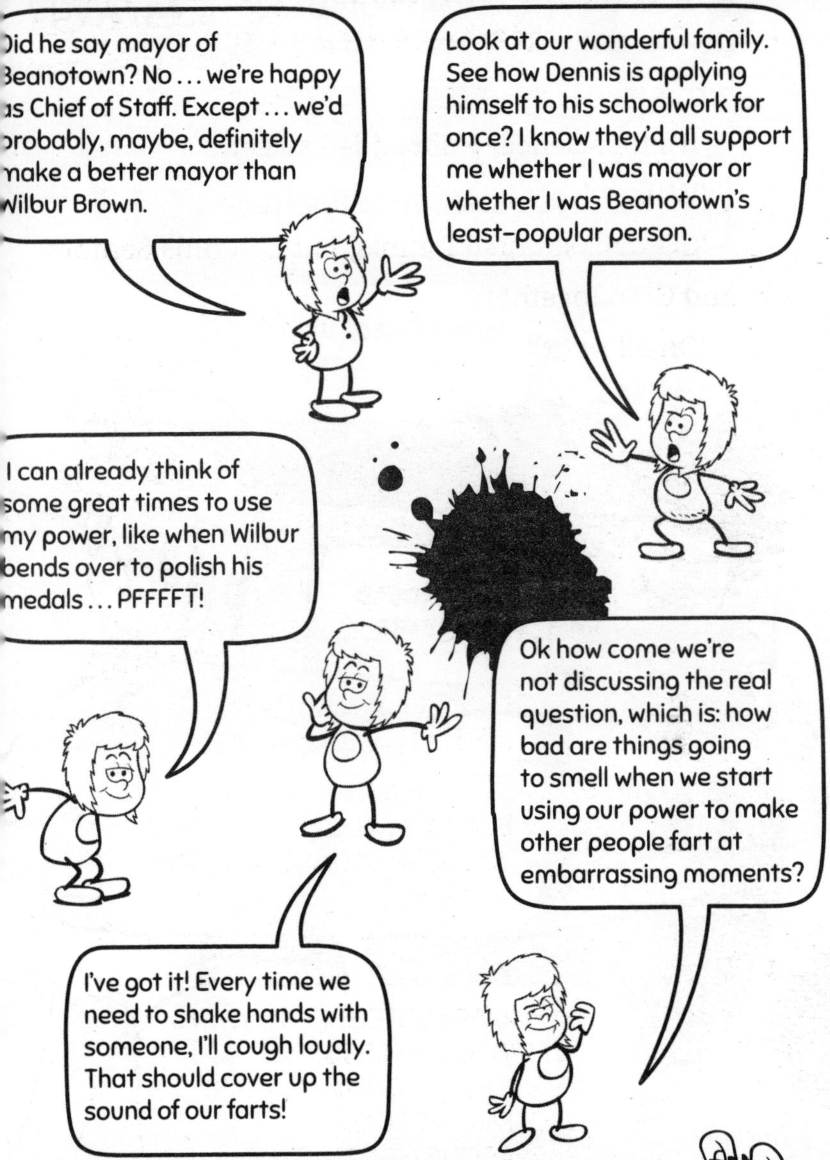

WHAT WOULD YOU DO?

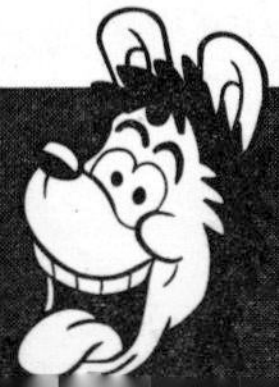

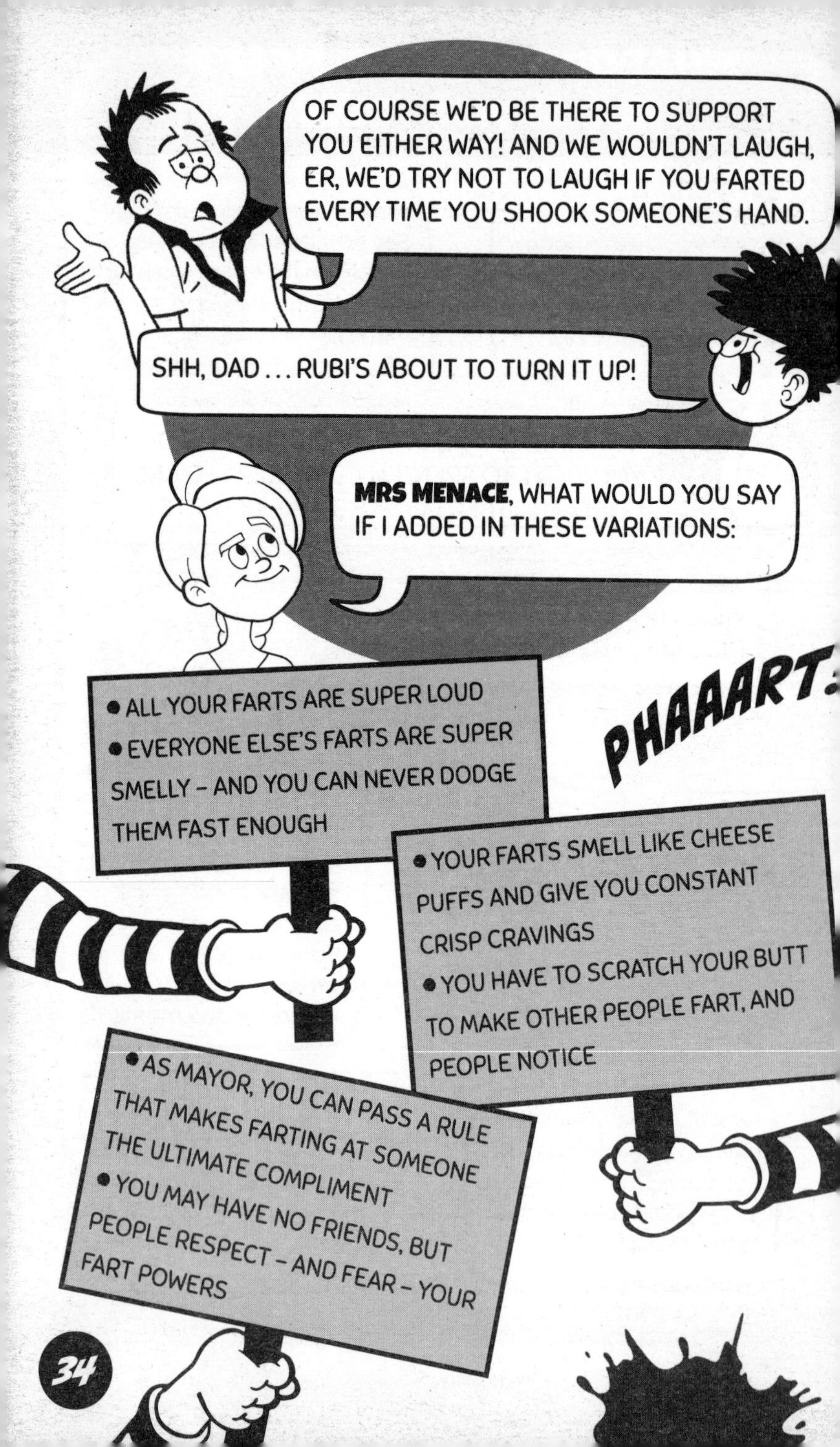

OF COURSE WE'D BE THERE TO SUPPORT YOU EITHER WAY! AND WE WOULDN'T LAUGH, ER, WE'D TRY NOT TO LAUGH IF YOU FARTED EVERY TIME YOU SHOOK SOMEONE'S HAND.
SHH, DAD . . . RUBI'S ABOUT TO TURN IT UP!
MRS MENACE, WHAT WOULD YOU SAY IF I ADDED IN THESE VARIATIONS:
• ALL YOUR FARTS ARE SUPER LOUD • EVERYONE ELSE'S FARTS ARE SUPER SMELLY – AND YOU CAN NEVER DODGE THEM FAST ENOUGH
PHAAART!
• YOUR FARTS SMELL LIKE CHEESE PUFFS AND GIVE YOU CONSTANT CRISP CRAVINGS • YOU HAVE TO SCRATCH YOUR BUTT TO MAKE OTHER PEOPLE FART, AND PEOPLE NOTICE
• AS MAYOR, YOU CAN PASS A RULE THAT MAKES FARTING AT SOMEONE THE ULTIMATE COMPLIMENT • YOU MAY HAVE NO FRIENDS, BUT PEOPLE RESPECT – AND FEAR – YOUR FART POWERS

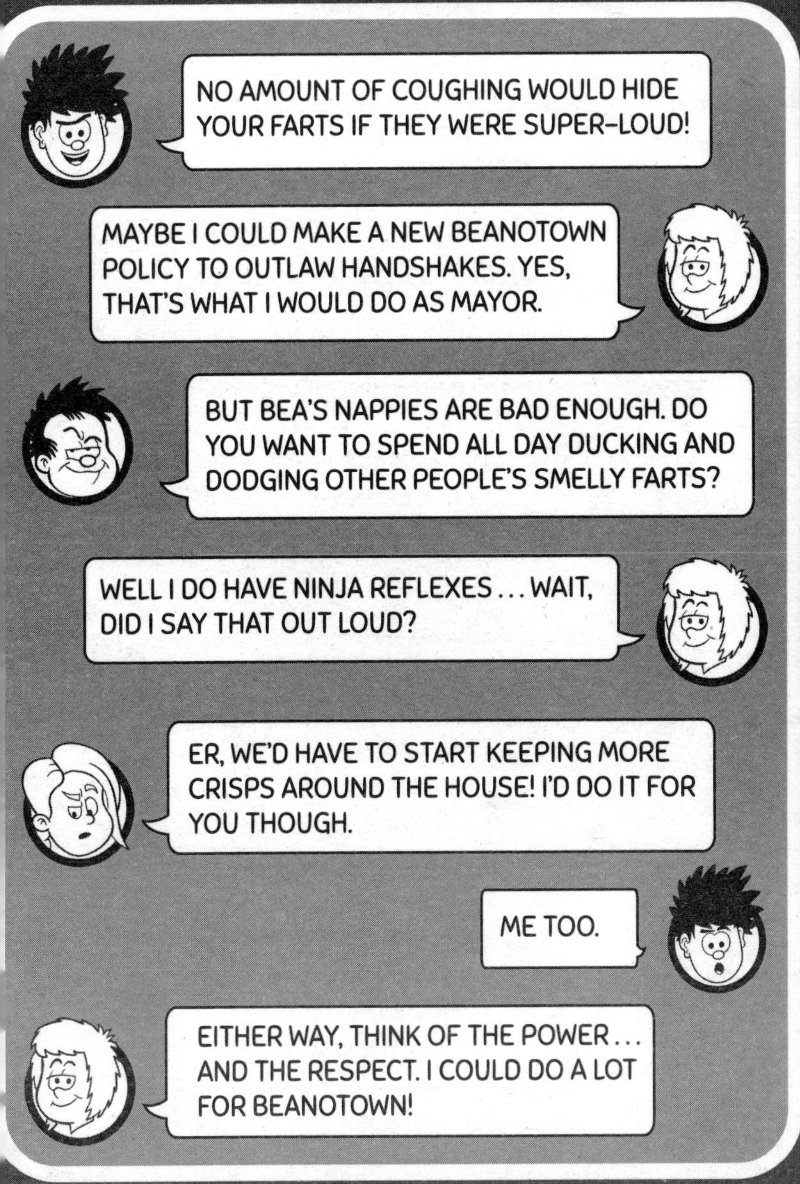
NO AMOUNT OF COUGHING WOULD HIDE YOUR FARTS IF THEY WERE SUPER-LOUD!
MAYBE I COULD MAKE A NEW BEANOTOWN POLICY TO OUTLAW HANDSHAKES. YES, THAT'S WHAT I WOULD DO AS MAYOR.
BUT BEA'S NAPPIES ARE BAD ENOUGH. DO YOU WANT TO SPEND ALL DAY DUCKING AND DODGING OTHER PEOPLE'S SMELLY FARTS?
WELL I DO HAVE NINJA REFLEXES . . . WAIT, DID I SAY THAT OUT LOUD?
ER, WE'D HAVE TO START KEEPING MORE CRISPS AROUND THE HOUSE! I'D DO IT FOR YOU THOUGH.
ME TOO.
EITHER WAY, THINK OF THE POWER . . . AND THE RESPECT. I COULD DO A LOT FOR BEANOTOWN!

WHICH OPTION WOULD YOU CHOOSE WITH ALL THOSE VARIATIONS ADDED INTO THE MIX?

PIE FACE

'Hey, Pie Face! Want to take part in an experiment?' Dennis called.

'I don't know guys . . . that looks dangerous.'

'It involves pies,' Rubi promised.

'I'm in!'

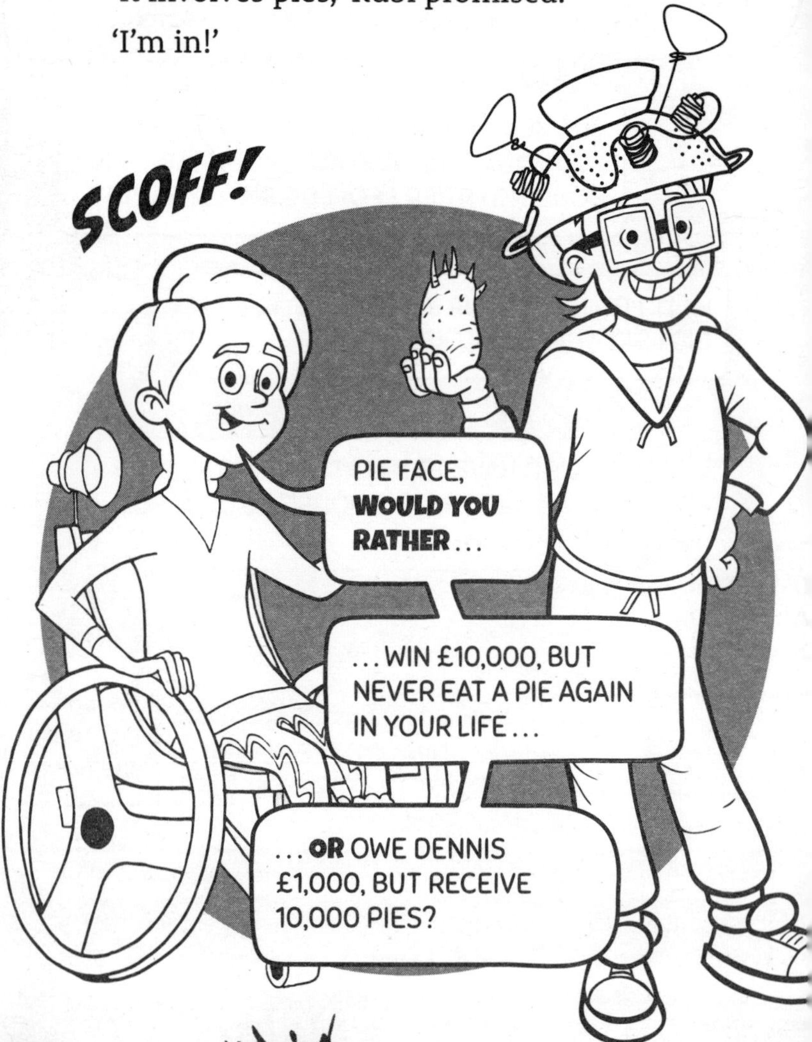

SCOFF!
PIE FACE, **WOULD YOU RATHER** . . .
. . . WIN £10,000, BUT NEVER EAT A PIE AGAIN IN YOUR LIFE . . .
. . . **OR** OWE DENNIS £1,000, BUT RECEIVE 10,000 PIES?

WHAT DO PIE FACE'S NUMSKULLS THINK?

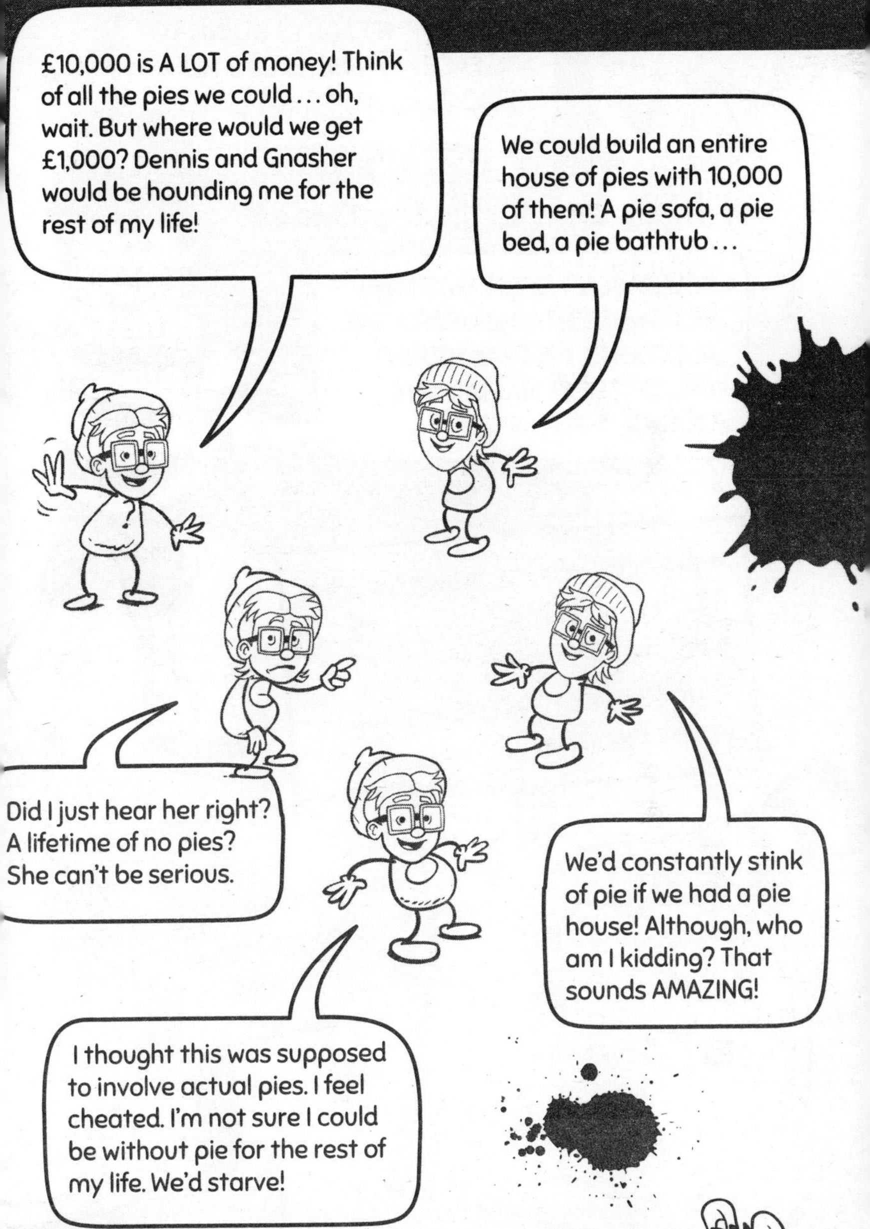
£10,000 is A LOT of money! Think of all the pies we could . . . oh, wait. But where would we get £1,000? Dennis and Gnasher would be hounding me for the rest of my life!
We could build an entire house of pies with 10,000 of them! A pie sofa, a pie bed, a pie bathtub . . .
Did I just hear her right? A lifetime of no pies? She can't be serious.
We'd constantly stink of pie if we had a pie house! Although, who am I kidding? That sounds AMAZING!
I thought this was supposed to involve actual pies. I feel cheated. I'm not sure I could be without pie for the rest of my life. We'd starve!

WHAT WOULD YOU DO?

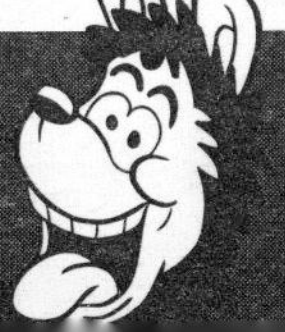

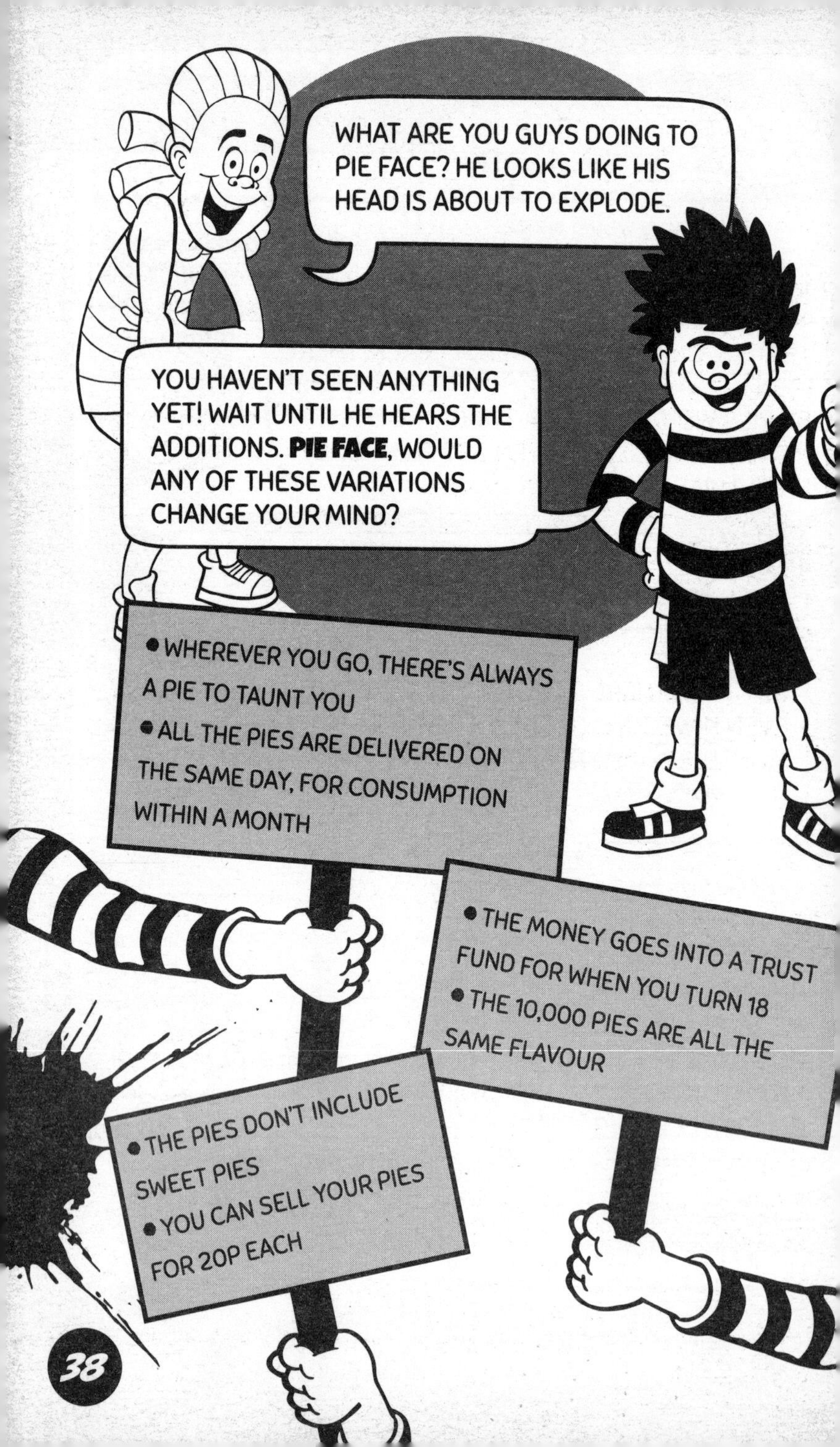
WHAT ARE YOU GUYS DOING TO PIE FACE? HE LOOKS LIKE HIS HEAD IS ABOUT TO EXPLODE.
YOU HAVEN'T SEEN ANYTHING YET! WAIT UNTIL HE HEARS THE ADDITIONS. PIE FACE, WOULD ANY OF THESE VARIATIONS CHANGE YOUR MIND?
• WHEREVER YOU GO, THERE'S ALWAYS A PIE TO TAUNT YOU
• ALL THE PIES ARE DELIVERED ON THE SAME DAY, FOR CONSUMPTION WITHIN A MONTH
• THE MONEY GOES INTO A TRUST FUND FOR WHEN YOU TURN 18
• THE 10,000 PIES ARE ALL THE SAME FLAVOUR
• THE PIES DON'T INCLUDE SWEET PIES
• YOU CAN SELL YOUR PIES FOR 20P EACH

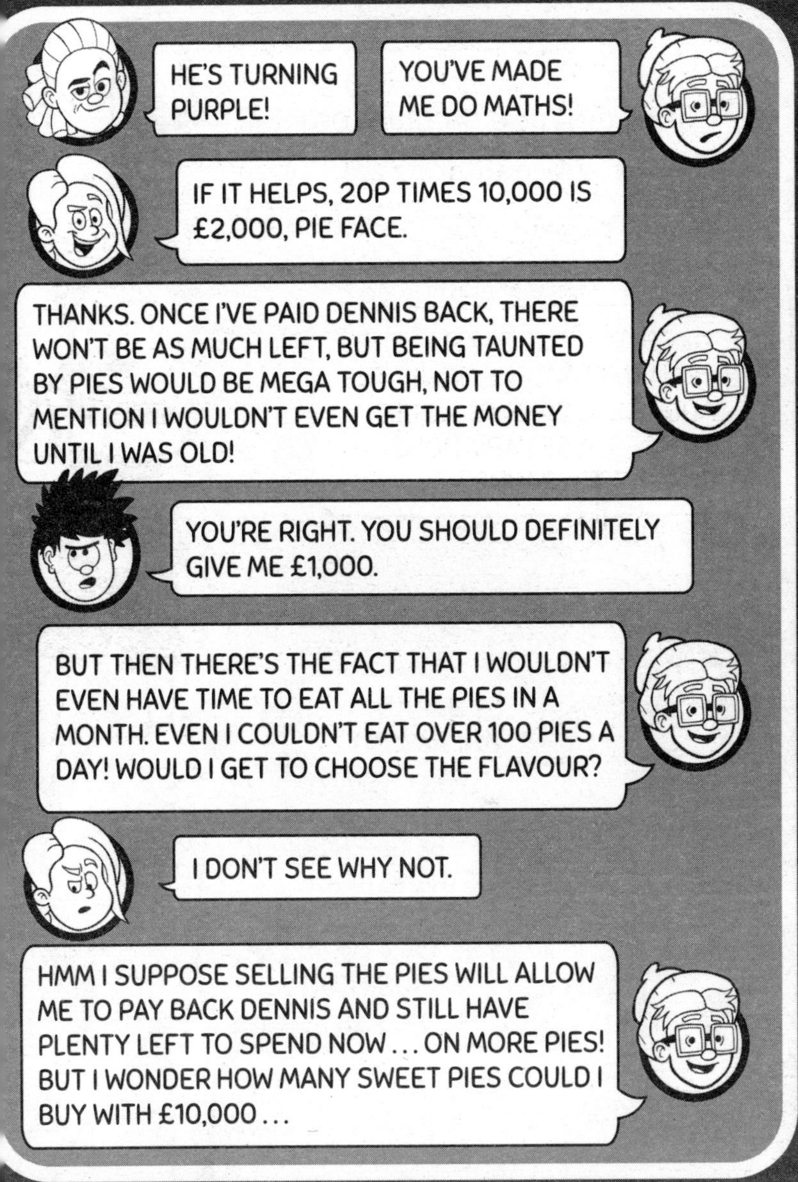
HE'S TURNING PURPLE!
YOU'VE MADE ME DO MATHS!
IF IT HELPS, 20P TIMES 10,000 IS £2,000, PIE FACE.
THANKS. ONCE I'VE PAID DENNIS BACK, THERE WON'T BE AS MUCH LEFT, BUT BEING TAUNTED BY PIES WOULD BE MEGA TOUGH, NOT TO MENTION I WOULDN'T EVEN GET THE MONEY UNTIL I WAS OLD!
YOU'RE RIGHT. YOU SHOULD DEFINITELY GIVE ME £1,000.
BUT THEN THERE'S THE FACT THAT I WOULDN'T EVEN HAVE TIME TO EAT ALL THE PIES IN A MONTH. EVEN I COULDN'T EAT OVER 100 PIES A DAY! WOULD I GET TO CHOOSE THE FLAVOUR?
I DON'T SEE WHY NOT.
HMM I SUPPOSE SELLING THE PIES WILL ALLOW ME TO PAY BACK DENNIS AND STILL HAVE PLENTY LEFT TO SPEND NOW . . . ON MORE PIES! BUT I WONDER HOW MANY SWEET PIES COULD I BUY WITH £10,000 . . .

WHICH OPTION WOULD YOU CHOOSE WITH ALL THOSE VARIATIONS ADDED INTO THE MIX?

JJ

'Want a turn next, JJ?' Rubi asked. 'The current conditions are conducive for optimum performance of voluntary experimentees.'

'You mean you want me to try it out,' JJ translated.

'That's just what I said!'

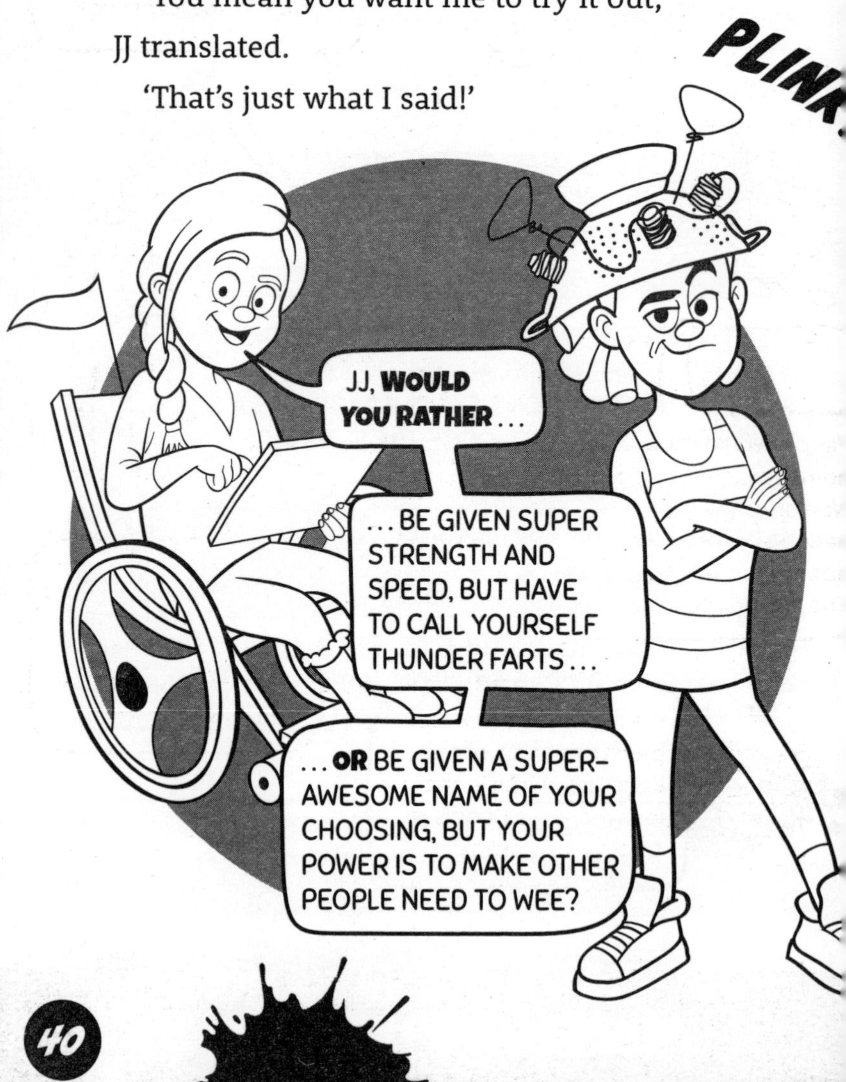
PLINK
JJ, **WOULD YOU RATHER** . . .
. . . BE GIVEN SUPER STRENGTH AND SPEED, BUT HAVE TO CALL YOURSELF THUNDER FARTS . . .
. . . **OR** BE GIVEN A SUPER-AWESOME NAME OF YOUR CHOOSING, BUT YOUR POWER IS TO MAKE OTHER PEOPLE NEED TO WEE?

WHAT DO JJ'S NUMSKULLS THINK?

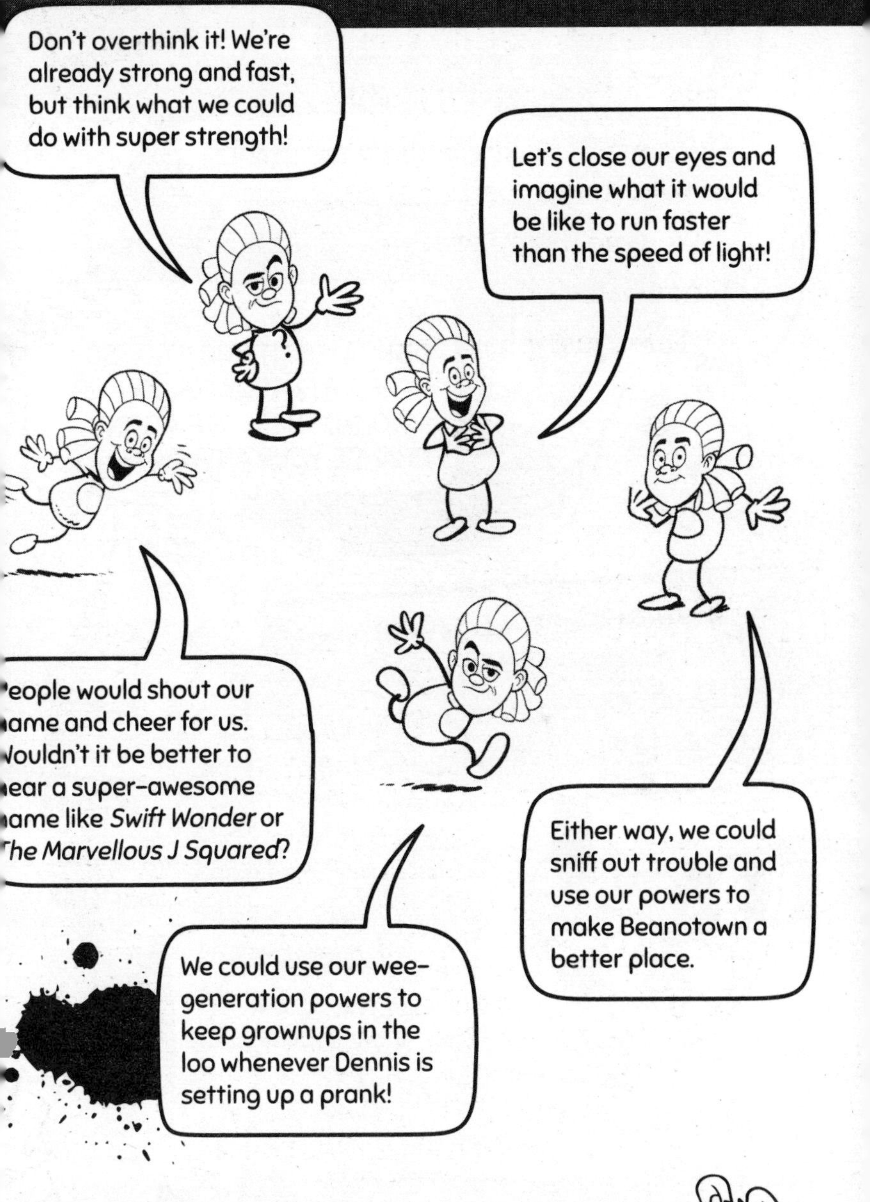

WHAT WOULD YOU DO?

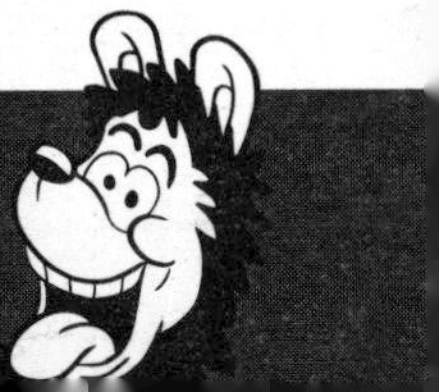

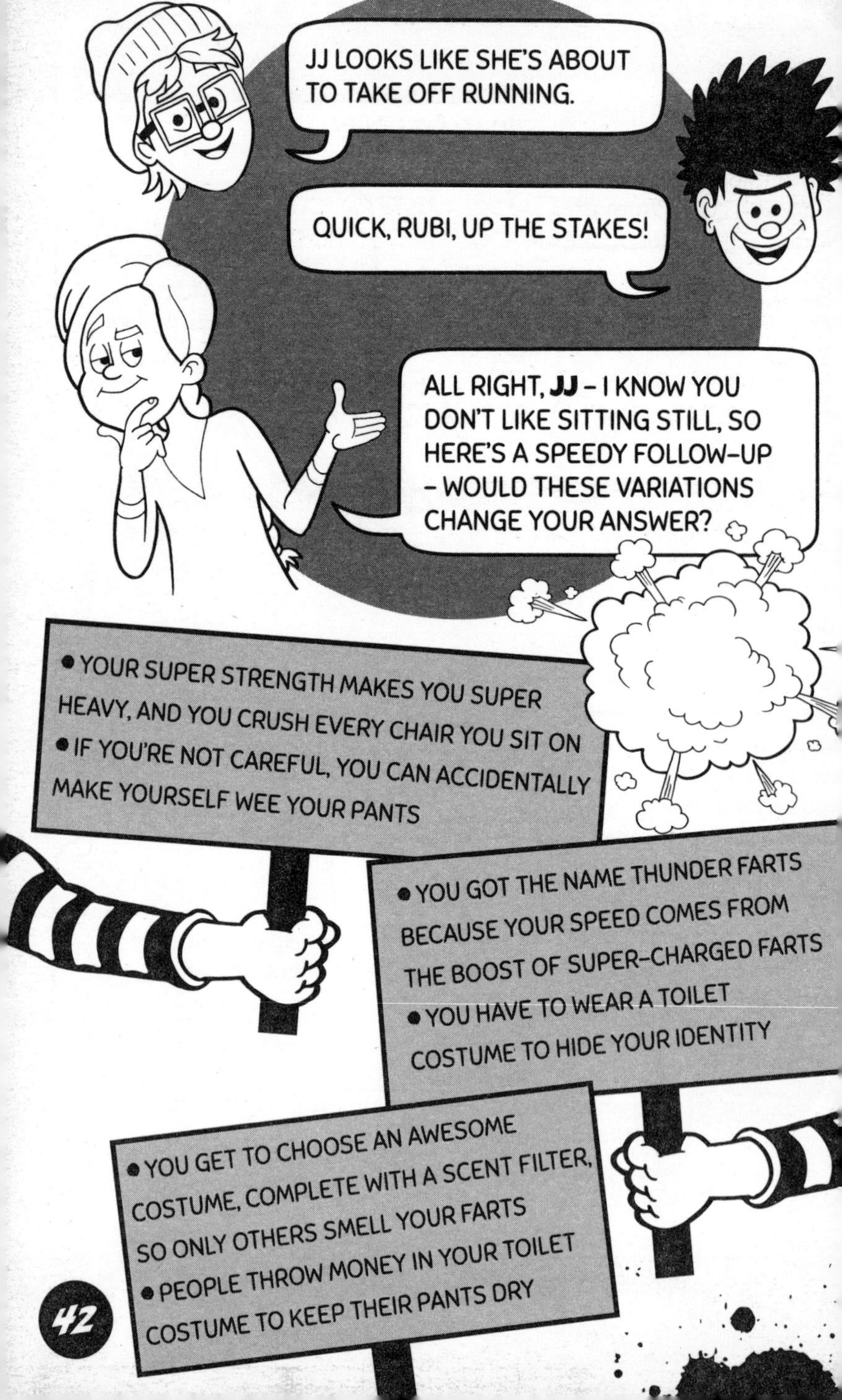
JJ LOOKS LIKE SHE'S ABOUT TO TAKE OFF RUNNING.
QUICK, RUBI, UP THE STAKES!
ALL RIGHT, **JJ** – I KNOW YOU DON'T LIKE SITTING STILL, SO HERE'S A SPEEDY FOLLOW-UP – WOULD THESE VARIATIONS CHANGE YOUR ANSWER?
• YOUR SUPER STRENGTH MAKES YOU SUPER HEAVY, AND YOU CRUSH EVERY CHAIR YOU SIT ON
• IF YOU'RE NOT CAREFUL, YOU CAN ACCIDENTALLY MAKE YOURSELF WEE YOUR PANTS
• YOU GOT THE NAME THUNDER FARTS BECAUSE YOUR SPEED COMES FROM THE BOOST OF SUPER-CHARGED FARTS
• YOU HAVE TO WEAR A TOILET COSTUME TO HIDE YOUR IDENTITY
• YOU GET TO CHOOSE AN AWESOME COSTUME, COMPLETE WITH A SCENT FILTER, SO ONLY OTHERS SMELL YOUR FARTS
• PEOPLE THROW MONEY IN YOUR TOILET COSTUME TO KEEP THEIR PANTS DRY

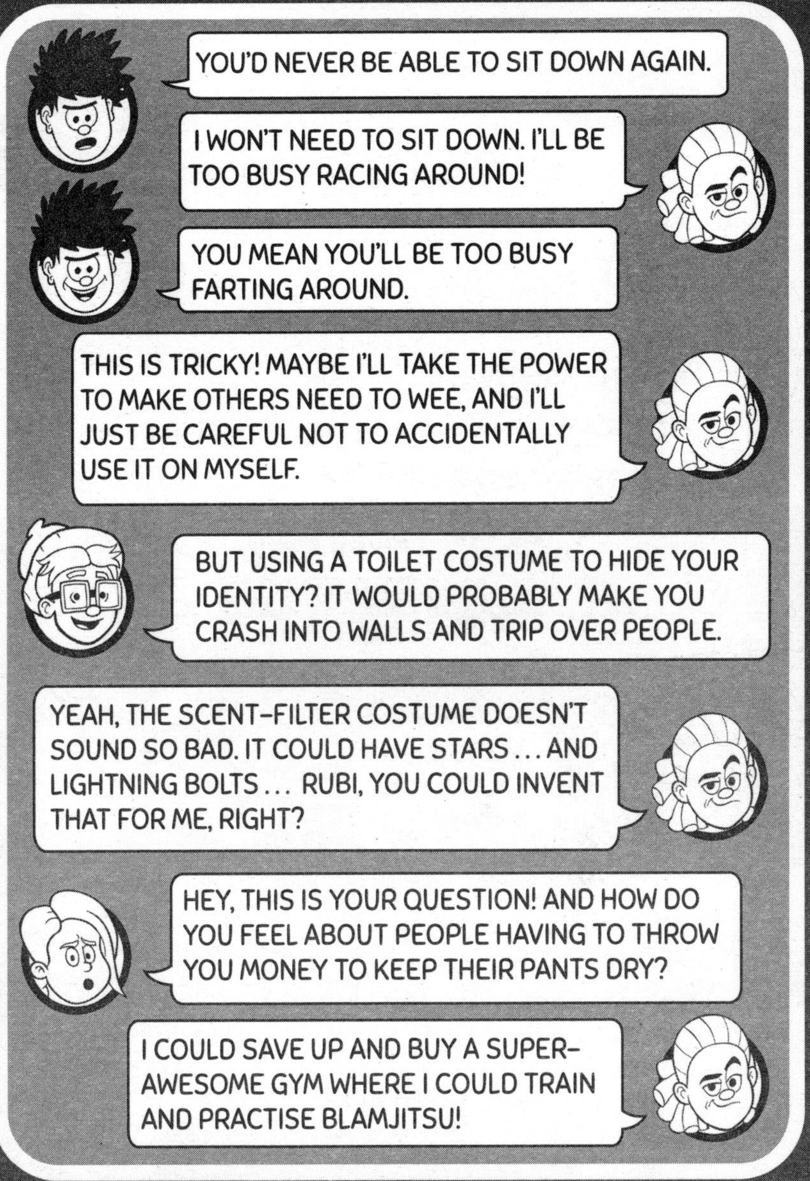
YOU'D NEVER BE ABLE TO SIT DOWN AGAIN.
I WON'T NEED TO SIT DOWN. I'LL BE TOO BUSY RACING AROUND!
YOU MEAN YOU'LL BE TOO BUSY FARTING AROUND.
THIS IS TRICKY! MAYBE I'LL TAKE THE POWER TO MAKE OTHERS NEED TO WEE, AND I'LL JUST BE CAREFUL NOT TO ACCIDENTALLY USE IT ON MYSELF.
BUT USING A TOILET COSTUME TO HIDE YOUR IDENTITY? IT WOULD PROBABLY MAKE YOU CRASH INTO WALLS AND TRIP OVER PEOPLE.
YEAH, THE SCENT–FILTER COSTUME DOESN'T SOUND SO BAD. IT COULD HAVE STARS . . . AND LIGHTNING BOLTS . . . RUBI, YOU COULD INVENT THAT FOR ME, RIGHT?
HEY, THIS IS YOUR QUESTION! AND HOW DO YOU FEEL ABOUT PEOPLE HAVING TO THROW YOU MONEY TO KEEP THEIR PANTS DRY?
I COULD SAVE UP AND BUY A SUPER–AWESOME GYM WHERE I COULD TRAIN AND PRACTISE BLAMJITSU!

WHICH OPTION WOULD YOU CHOOSE WITH ALL THOSE VARIATIONS ADDED INTO THE MIX?

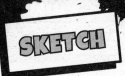

SKETCH

Sketch had been watching the experiments from nearby and drawing them on her tablet.

'Hey Sketch! Come and try it out,' Rubi said. 'It's awesome!'

'Yeah, it's pretty wild,' JJ said.

'I'll draw my own conclusions!' Sketch said and set aside her tablet.

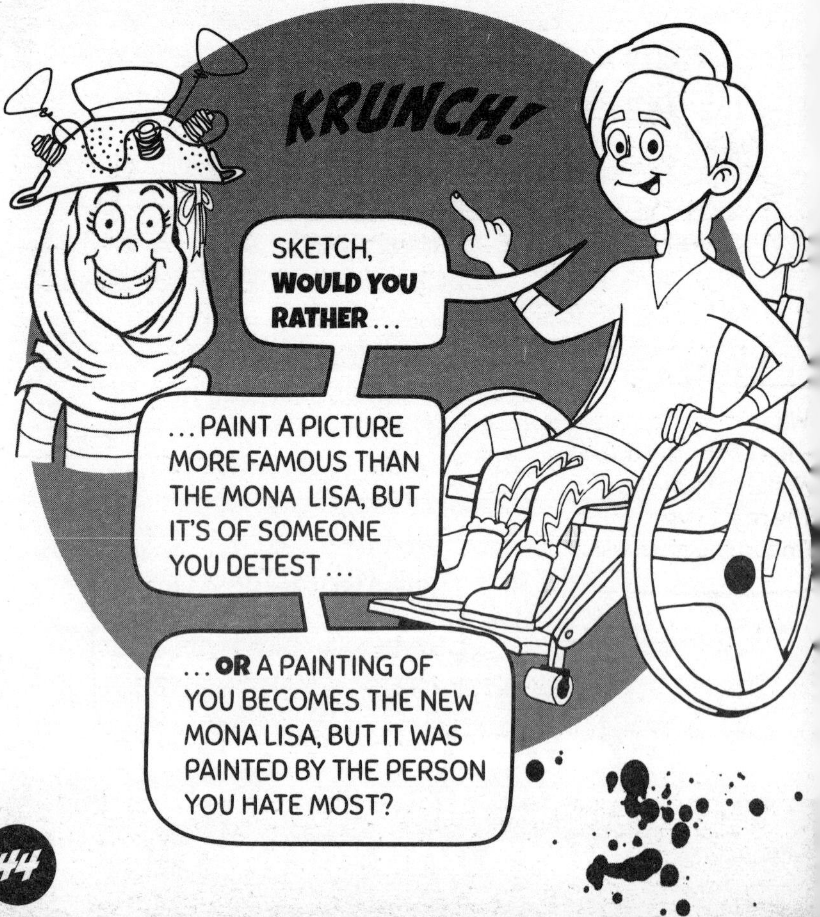
KRUNCH!
SKETCH, **WOULD YOU RATHER** . . .
. . . PAINT A PICTURE MORE FAMOUS THAN THE MONA LISA, BUT IT'S OF SOMEONE YOU DETEST . . .
. . . **OR** A PAINTING OF YOU BECOMES THE NEW MONA LISA, BUT IT WAS PAINTED BY THE PERSON YOU HATE MOST?

WHAT DO SKETCH'S NUMSKULLS THINK?

Did she say the Mona Lisa? That painting is a masterpiece! If we painted something even more famous, we'd probably go down in history as the world's greatest artist! Who cares if it's of someone we don't like?

The Mona Lisa's eyes follow you around! Does that mean our nemesis's eyes would follow us around? Because that would be too creepy!

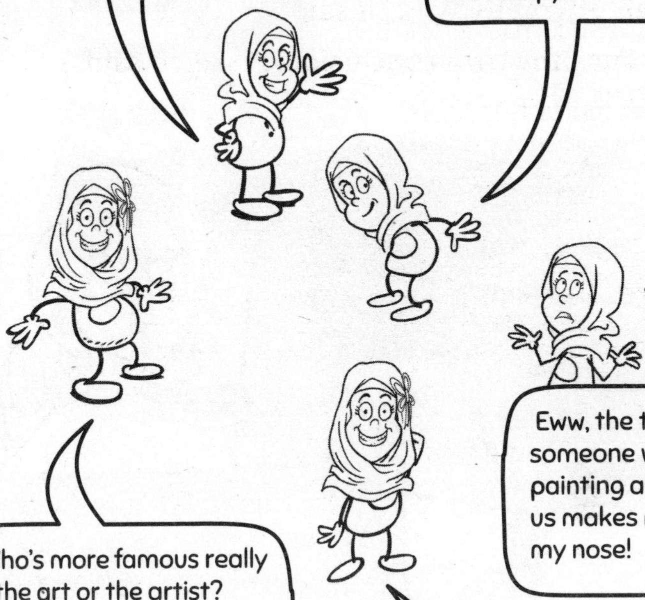

Eww, the thought of someone we hate painting a portrait of us makes me wrinkle my nose!

Who's more famous really – the art or the artist? Wait, that's pretty deep. The rest of you can decide. I'm turning my music up!

Doesn't it take a long time to pose for a portrait? Would we be able to take a break for snacks? I'm asking for a friend, of course . . .

WHAT WOULD YOU DO?

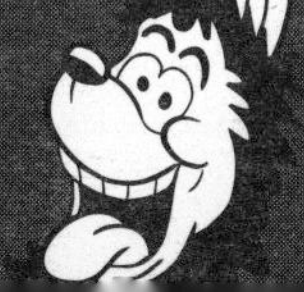

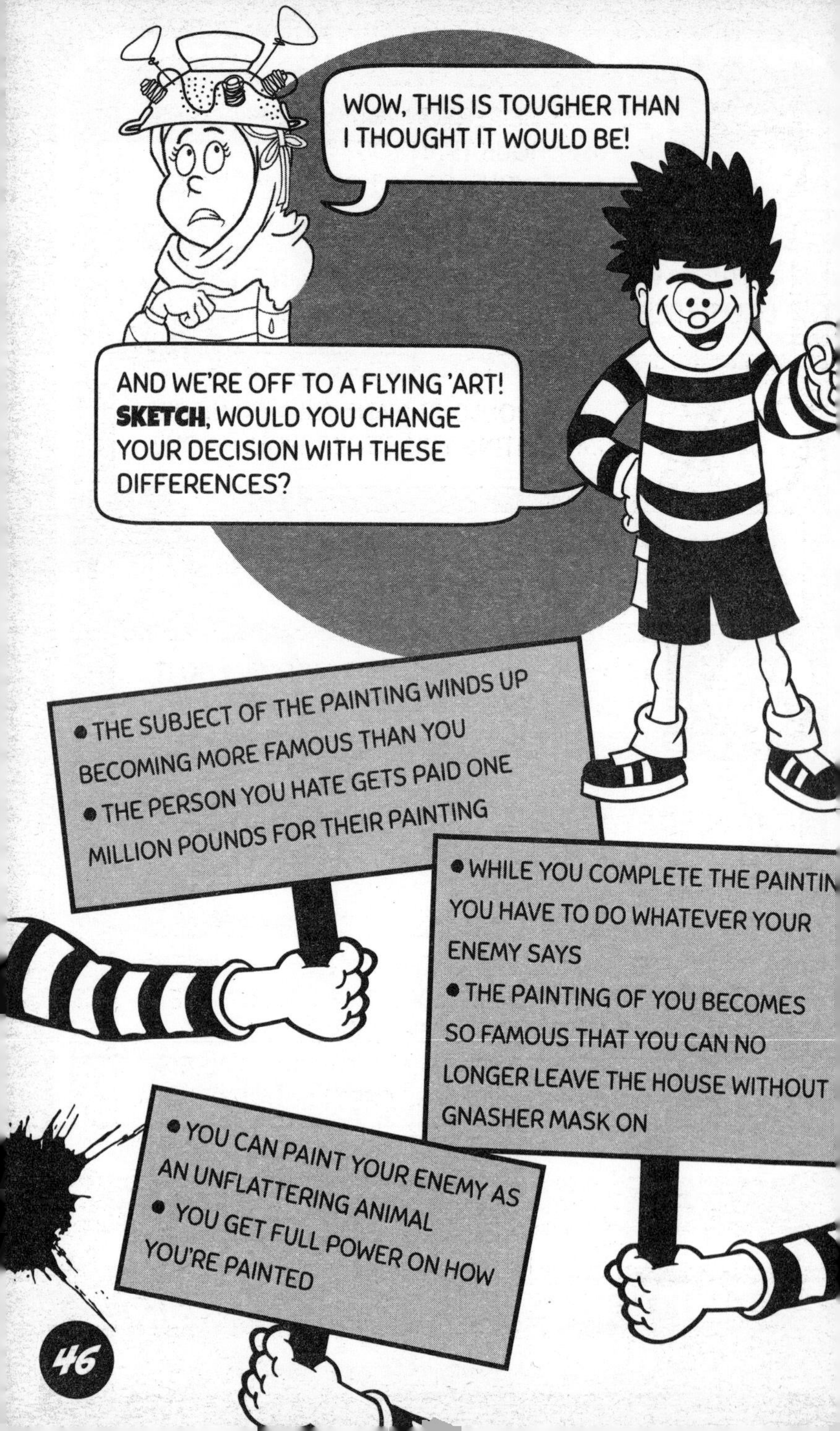
WOW, THIS IS TOUGHER THAN I THOUGHT IT WOULD BE!
AND WE'RE OFF TO A FLYING 'ART! **SKETCH**, WOULD YOU CHANGE YOUR DECISION WITH THESE DIFFERENCES?
• THE SUBJECT OF THE PAINTING WINDS UP BECOMING MORE FAMOUS THAN YOU
• THE PERSON YOU HATE GETS PAID ONE MILLION POUNDS FOR THEIR PAINTING
• WHILE YOU COMPLETE THE PAINTIN YOU HAVE TO DO WHATEVER YOUR ENEMY SAYS
• THE PAINTING OF YOU BECOMES SO FAMOUS THAT YOU CAN NO LONGER LEAVE THE HOUSE WITHOUT GNASHER MASK ON
• YOU CAN PAINT YOUR ENEMY AS AN UNFLATTERING ANIMAL
• YOU GET FULL POWER ON HOW YOU'RE PAINTED

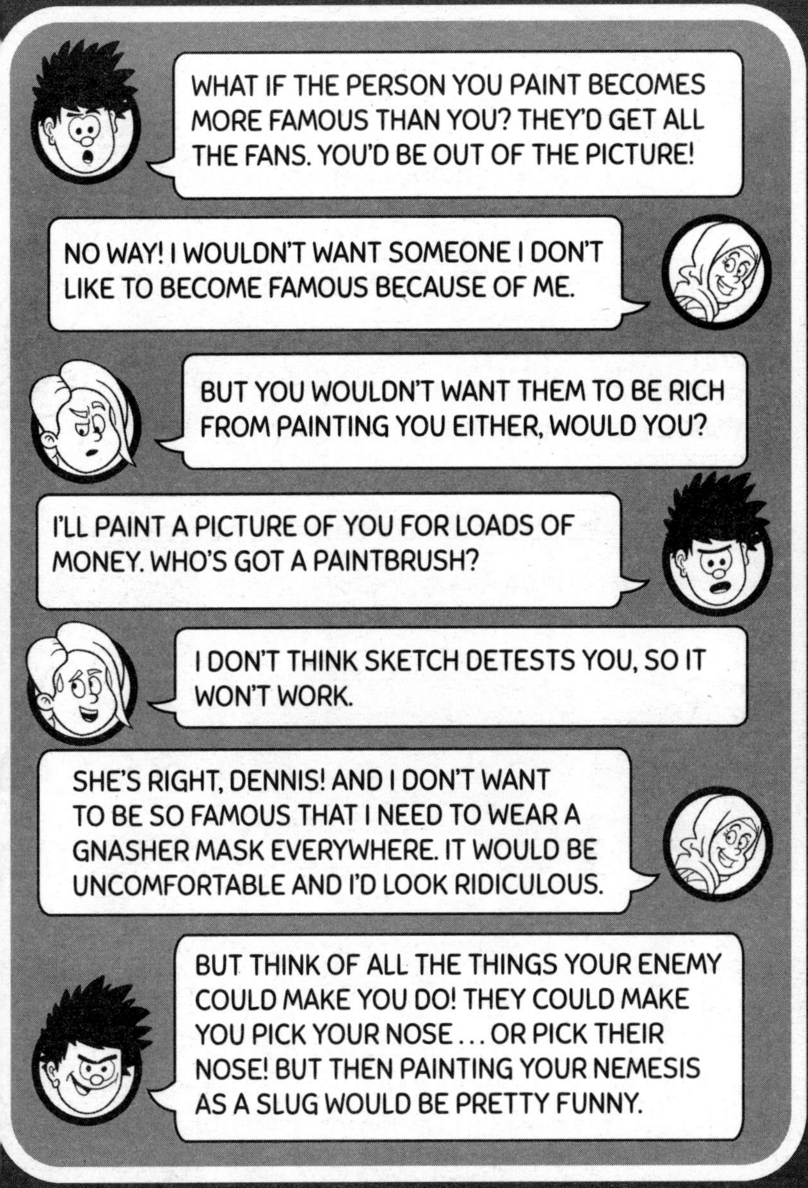
WHAT IF THE PERSON YOU PAINT BECOMES MORE FAMOUS THAN YOU? THEY'D GET ALL THE FANS. YOU'D BE OUT OF THE PICTURE!
NO WAY! I WOULDN'T WANT SOMEONE I DON'T LIKE TO BECOME FAMOUS BECAUSE OF ME.
BUT YOU WOULDN'T WANT THEM TO BE RICH FROM PAINTING YOU EITHER, WOULD YOU?
I'LL PAINT A PICTURE OF YOU FOR LOADS OF MONEY. WHO'S GOT A PAINTBRUSH?
I DON'T THINK SKETCH DETESTS YOU, SO IT WON'T WORK.
SHE'S RIGHT, DENNIS! AND I DON'T WANT TO BE SO FAMOUS THAT I NEED TO WEAR A GNASHER MASK EVERYWHERE. IT WOULD BE UNCOMFORTABLE AND I'D LOOK RIDICULOUS.
BUT THINK OF ALL THE THINGS YOUR ENEMY COULD MAKE YOU DO! THEY COULD MAKE YOU PICK YOUR NOSE . . . OR PICK THEIR NOSE! BUT THEN PAINTING YOUR NEMESIS AS A SLUG WOULD BE PRETTY FUNNY.

WHICH OPTION WOULD YOU CHOOSE WITH ALL THOSE VARIATIONS ADDED INTO THE MIX?

STEVIE

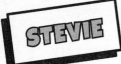

Stevie Star walked past. As usual, he held his phone up, smiling into the camera.

'Stevie, want to try out my latest invention?' Rubi asked.

'Sure,' he said. 'My viewers are gonna love this . . .' He turned back to his camera. 'Hey everyone, we're live at the Beanotown Science Fair, and I'm about to take part in a never-before-seen experiment. Crazy, right?

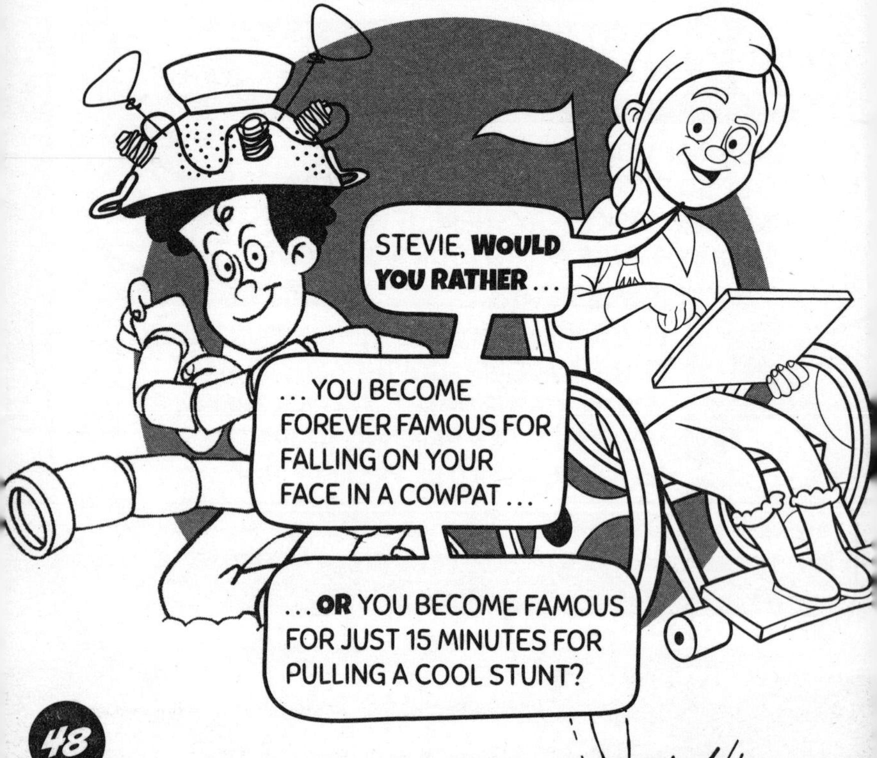

STEVIE, **WOULD YOU RATHER** . . .
. . . YOU BECOME FOREVER FAMOUS FOR FALLING ON YOUR FACE IN A COWPAT . . .
. . . **OR** YOU BECOME FAMOUS FOR JUST 15 MINUTES FOR PULLING A COOL STUNT?

WHAT DO STEVIE'S NUMSKULLS THINK?

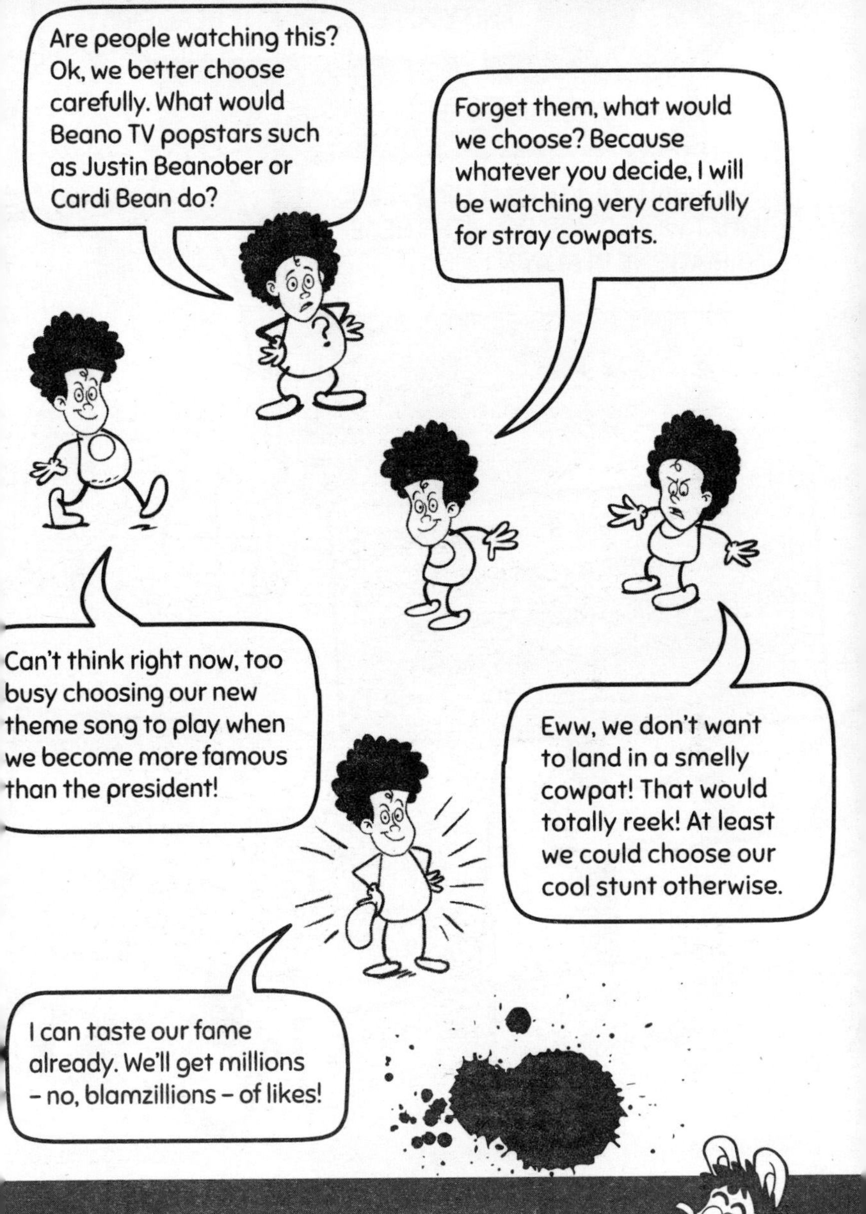
Are people watching this? Ok, we better choose carefully. What would Beano TV popstars such as Justin Beanober or Cardi Bean do?
Forget them, what would we choose? Because whatever you decide, I will be watching very carefully for stray cowpats.
Can't think right now, too busy choosing our new theme song to play when we become more famous than the president!
Eww, we don't want to land in a smelly cowpat! That would totally reek! At least we could choose our cool stunt otherwise.
I can taste our fame already. We'll get millions – no, blamzillions – of likes!

WHAT WOULD YOU DO?

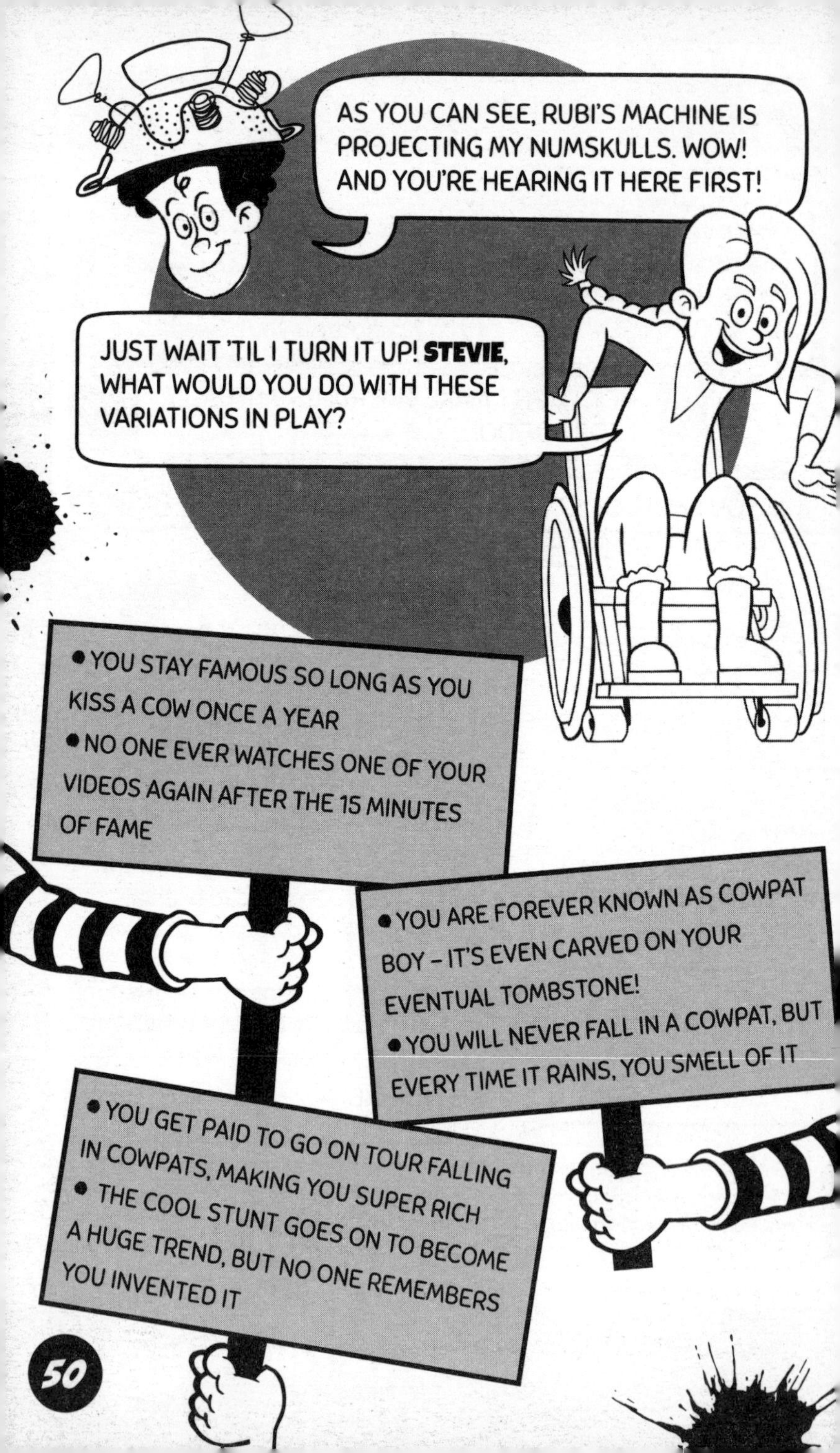
AS YOU CAN SEE, RUBI'S MACHINE IS PROJECTING MY NUMSKULLS. WOW! AND YOU'RE HEARING IT HERE FIRST!
JUST WAIT 'TIL I TURN IT UP! STEVIE, WHAT WOULD YOU DO WITH THESE VARIATIONS IN PLAY?
• YOU STAY FAMOUS SO LONG AS YOU KISS A COW ONCE A YEAR
• NO ONE EVER WATCHES ONE OF YOUR VIDEOS AGAIN AFTER THE 15 MINUTES OF FAME
• YOU ARE FOREVER KNOWN AS COWPAT BOY – IT'S EVEN CARVED ON YOUR EVENTUAL TOMBSTONE!
• YOU WILL NEVER FALL IN A COWPAT, BUT EVERY TIME IT RAINS, YOU SMELL OF IT
• YOU GET PAID TO GO ON TOUR FALLING IN COWPATS, MAKING YOU SUPER RICH
• THE COOL STUNT GOES ON TO BECOME A HUGE TREND, BUT NO ONE REMEMBERS YOU INVENTED IT

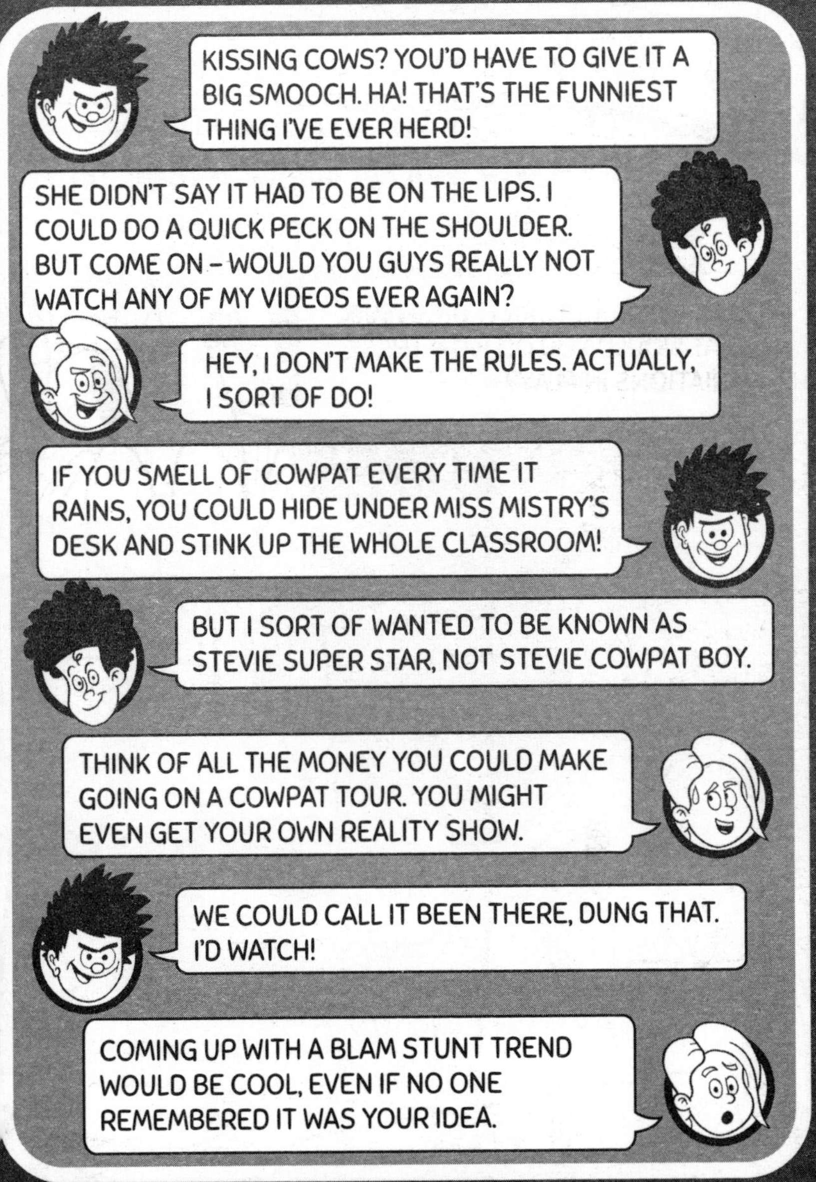
KISSING COWS? YOU'D HAVE TO GIVE IT A BIG SMOOCH. HA! THAT'S THE FUNNIEST THING I'VE EVER HERD!
SHE DIDN'T SAY IT HAD TO BE ON THE LIPS. I COULD DO A QUICK PECK ON THE SHOULDER. BUT COME ON – WOULD YOU GUYS REALLY NOT WATCH ANY OF MY VIDEOS EVER AGAIN?
HEY, I DON'T MAKE THE RULES. ACTUALLY, I SORT OF DO!
IF YOU SMELL OF COWPAT EVERY TIME IT RAINS, YOU COULD HIDE UNDER MISS MISTRY'S DESK AND STINK UP THE WHOLE CLASSROOM!
BUT I SORT OF WANTED TO BE KNOWN AS STEVIE SUPER STAR, NOT STEVIE COWPAT BOY.
THINK OF ALL THE MONEY YOU COULD MAKE GOING ON A COWPAT TOUR. YOU MIGHT EVEN GET YOUR OWN REALITY SHOW.
WE COULD CALL IT BEEN THERE, DUNG THAT. I'D WATCH!
COMING UP WITH A BLAM STUNT TREND WOULD BE COOL, EVEN IF NO ONE REMEMBERED IT WAS YOUR IDEA.

WHICH OPTION WOULD YOU CHOOSE WITH ALL THOSE VARIATIONS ADDED INTO THE MIX?

HARSHA

'I heard laughing,' said Harsha, coming over with her family. 'Is there fun going on here? If so, I want to be involved.'

'Sure, you can go next!' Rubi replied. 'Are you ready for your question?'

'Yup . . . and make it a good one!'

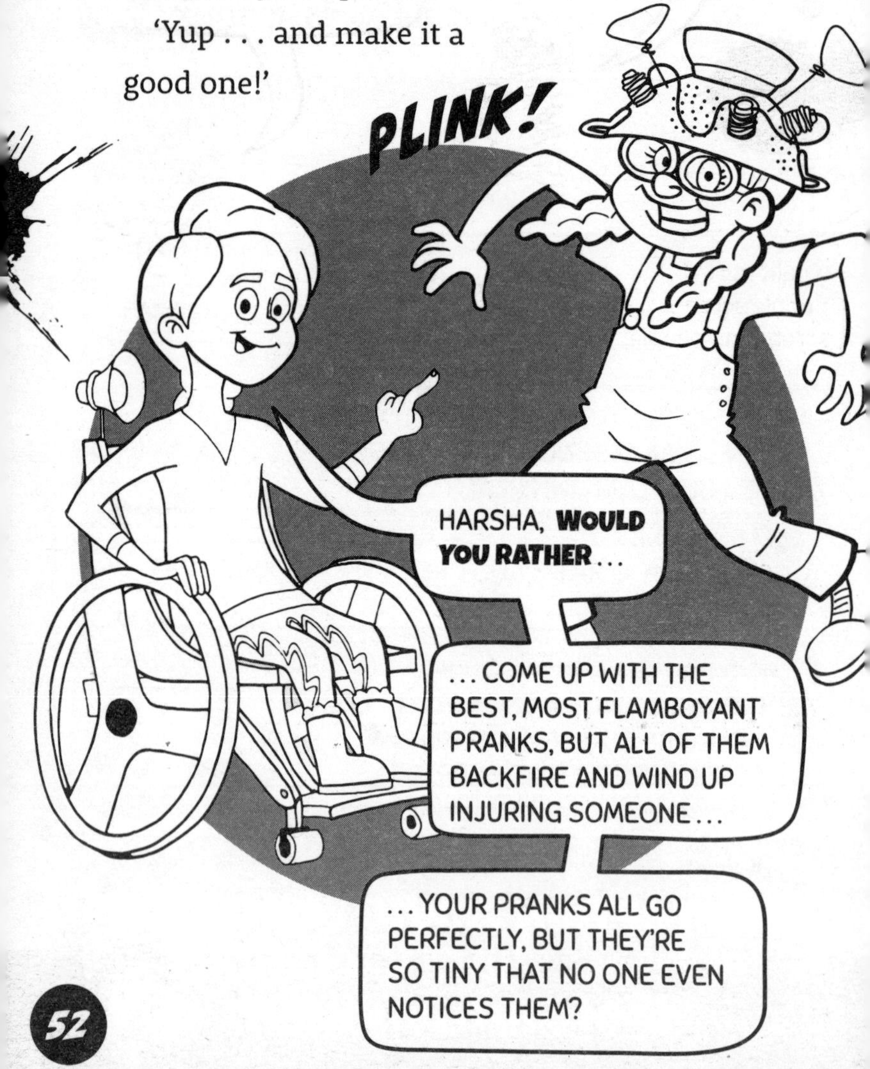

PLINK!
HARSHA, **WOULD YOU RATHER**...
... COME UP WITH THE BEST, MOST FLAMBOYANT PRANKS, BUT ALL OF THEM BACKFIRE AND WIND UP INJURING SOMEONE...
... YOUR PRANKS ALL GO PERFECTLY, BUT THEY'RE SO TINY THAT NO ONE EVEN NOTICES THEM?

WHAT DO HARSHA'S NUMSKULLS THINK?

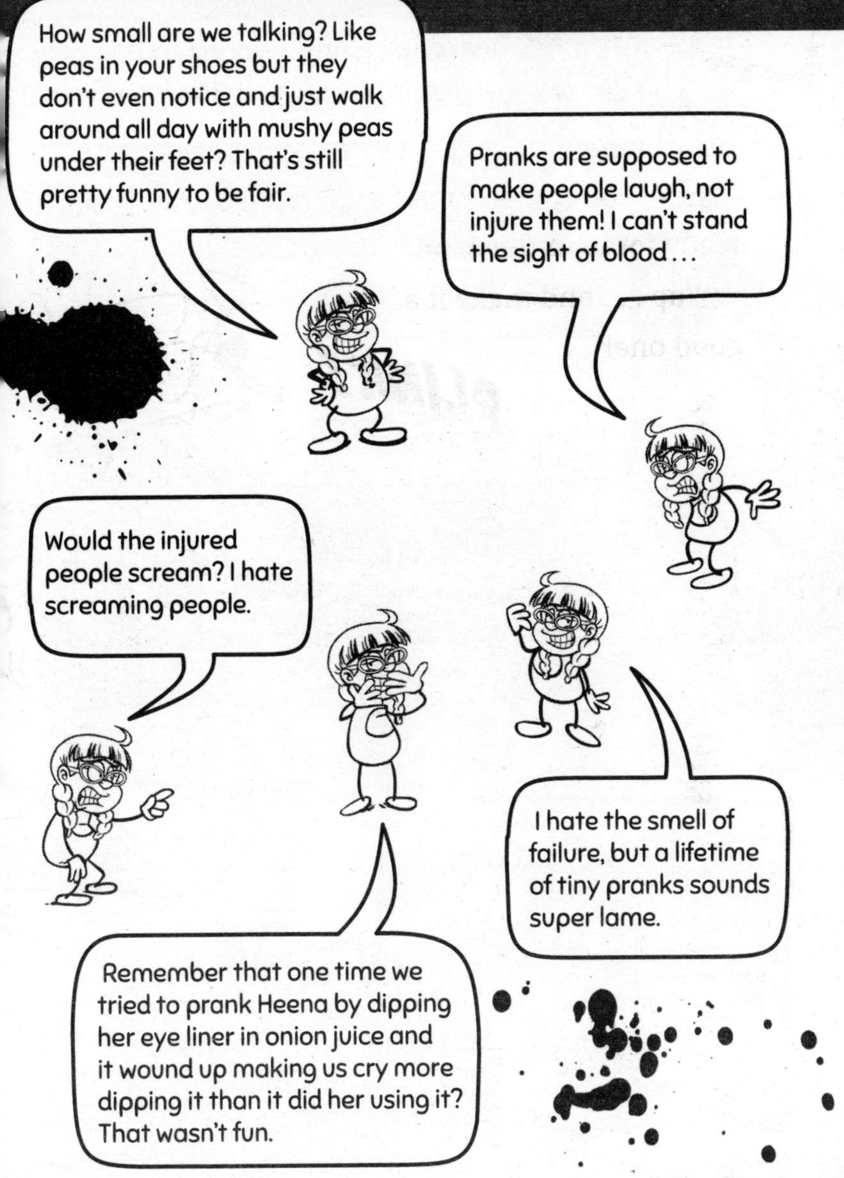
How small are we talking? Like peas in your shoes but they don't even notice and just walk around all day with mushy peas under their feet? That's still pretty funny to be fair.
Pranks are supposed to make people laugh, not injure them! I can't stand the sight of blood . . .
Would the injured people scream? I hate screaming people.
I hate the smell of failure, but a lifetime of tiny pranks sounds super lame.
Remember that one time we tried to prank Heena by dipping her eye liner in onion juice and it wound up making us cry more dipping it than it did her using it? That wasn't fun.

WHAT WOULD YOU DO?

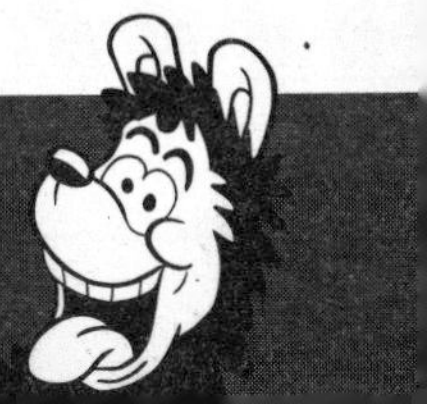

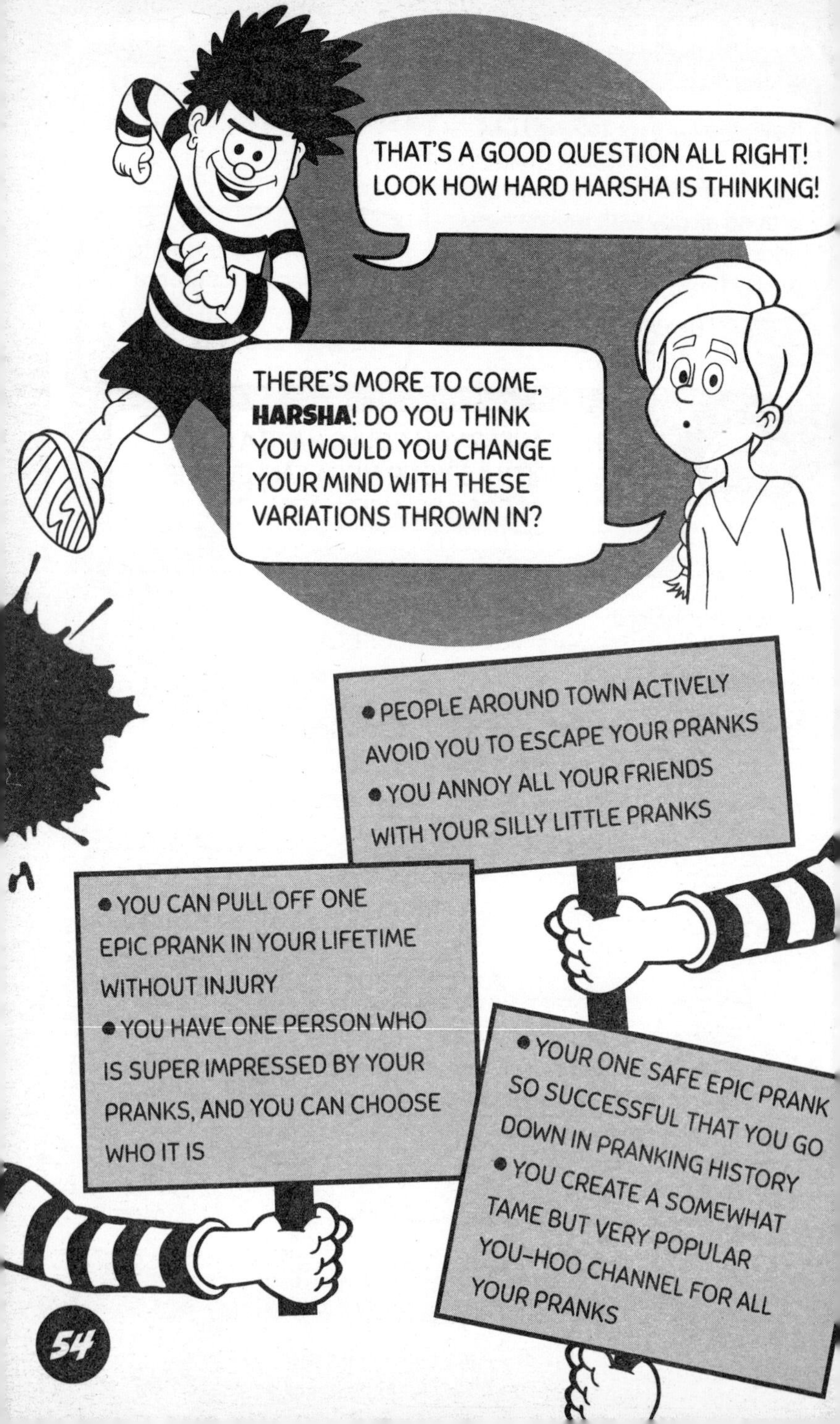

THAT'S A GOOD QUESTION ALL RIGHT! LOOK HOW HARD HARSHA IS THINKING!
THERE'S MORE TO COME, **HARSHA**! DO YOU THINK YOU WOULD YOU CHANGE YOUR MIND WITH THESE VARIATIONS THROWN IN?
• PEOPLE AROUND TOWN ACTIVELY AVOID YOU TO ESCAPE YOUR PRANKS
• YOU ANNOY ALL YOUR FRIENDS WITH YOUR SILLY LITTLE PRANKS
• YOU CAN PULL OFF ONE EPIC PRANK IN YOUR LIFETIME WITHOUT INJURY
• YOU HAVE ONE PERSON WHO IS SUPER IMPRESSED BY YOUR PRANKS, AND YOU CAN CHOOSE WHO IT IS
• YOUR ONE SAFE EPIC PRANK SO SUCCESSFUL THAT YOU GO DOWN IN PRANKING HISTORY
• YOU CREATE A SOMEWHAT TAME BUT VERY POPULAR YOU-HOO CHANNEL FOR ALL YOUR PRANKS

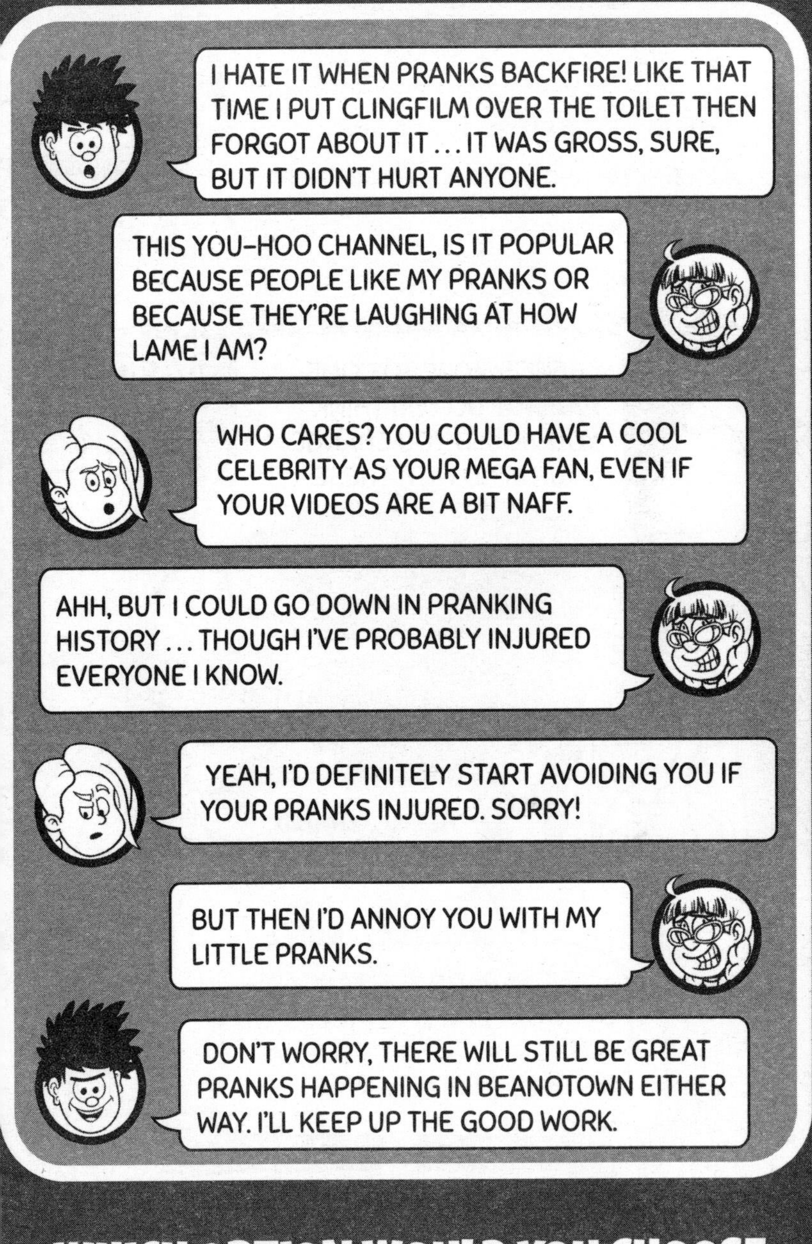
I HATE IT WHEN PRANKS BACKFIRE! LIKE THAT TIME I PUT CLINGFILM OVER THE TOILET THEN FORGOT ABOUT IT . . . IT WAS GROSS, SURE, BUT IT DIDN'T HURT ANYONE.
THIS YOU-HOO CHANNEL, IS IT POPULAR BECAUSE PEOPLE LIKE MY PRANKS OR BECAUSE THEY'RE LAUGHING AT HOW LAME I AM?
WHO CARES? YOU COULD HAVE A COOL CELEBRITY AS YOUR MEGA FAN, EVEN IF YOUR VIDEOS ARE A BIT NAFF.
AHH, BUT I COULD GO DOWN IN PRANKING HISTORY . . . THOUGH I'VE PROBABLY INJURED EVERYONE I KNOW.
YEAH, I'D DEFINITELY START AVOIDING YOU IF YOUR PRANKS INJURED. SORRY!
BUT THEN I'D ANNOY YOU WITH MY LITTLE PRANKS.
DON'T WORRY, THERE WILL STILL BE GREAT PRANKS HAPPENING IN BEANOTOWN EITHER WAY. I'LL KEEP UP THE GOOD WORK.

WHICH OPTION WOULD YOU CHOOSE WITH ALL THOSE VARIATIONS ADDED INTO THE MIX?

Harsha waved over her older sister. 'Come on, Heena, you have to try this.'

'No way.'

'Come on. Come onnnnn! I'll keep asking until you do it . . .'

Heena rolled her eyes. 'Fine, go on then.'

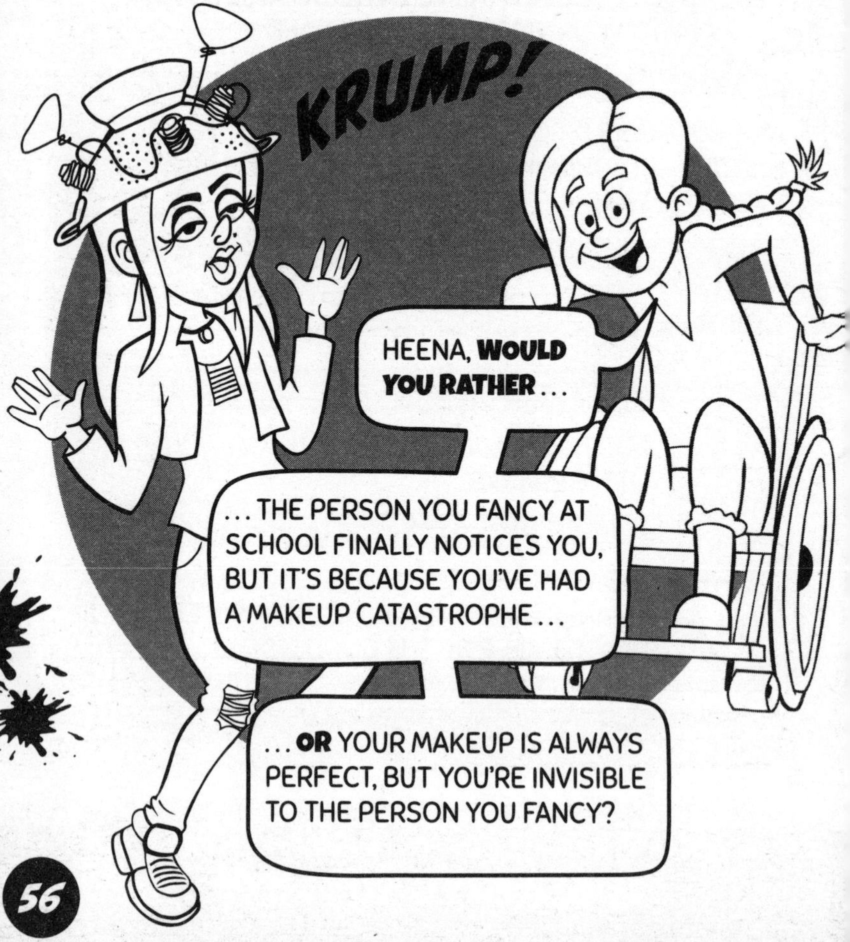
KRUMP!
HEENA, **WOULD YOU RATHER** . . .
. . . THE PERSON YOU FANCY AT SCHOOL FINALLY NOTICES YOU, BUT IT'S BECAUSE YOU'VE HAD A MAKEUP CATASTROPHE . . .
. . . **OR** YOUR MAKEUP IS ALWAYS PERFECT, BUT YOU'RE INVISIBLE TO THE PERSON YOU FANCY?

WHAT DO HEENA'S NUMSKULLS THINK?

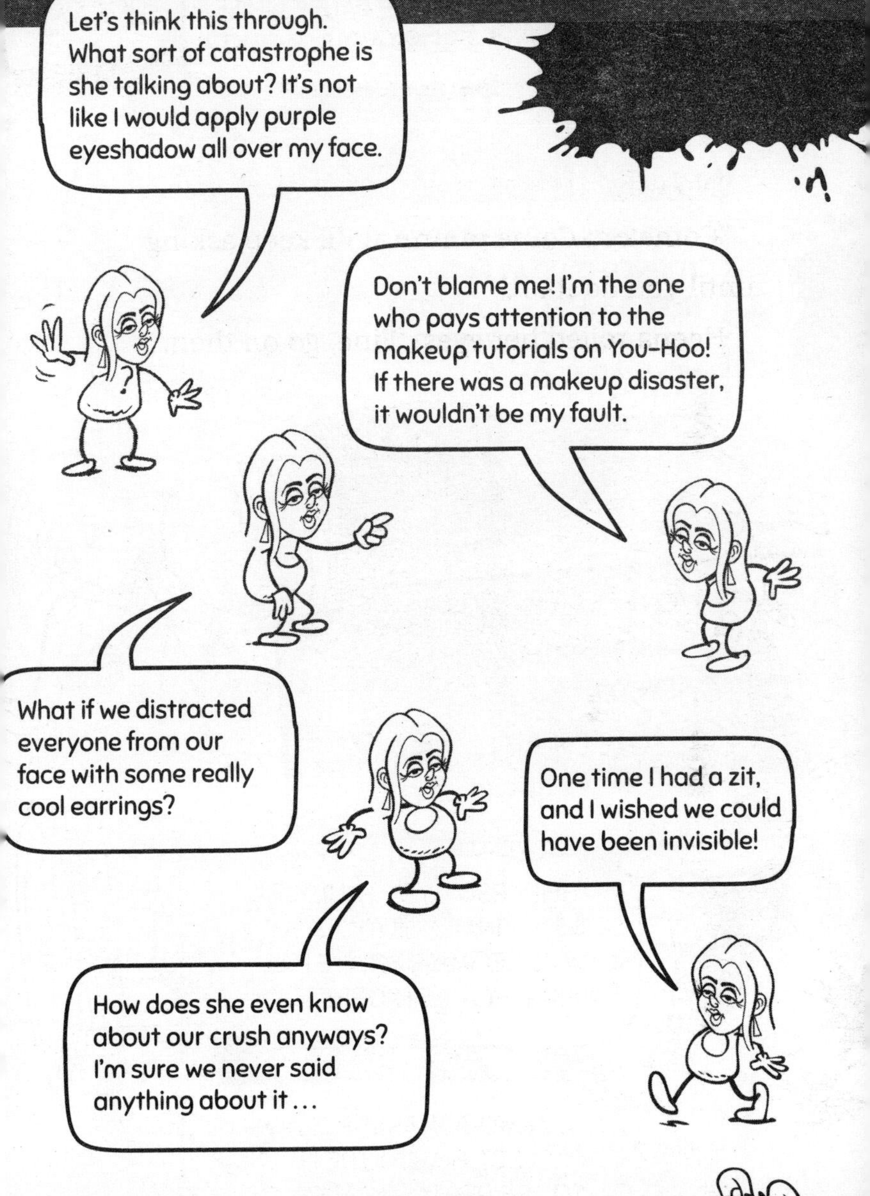

Let's think this through. What sort of catastrophe is she talking about? It's not like I would apply purple eyeshadow all over my face.
Don't blame me! I'm the one who pays attention to the makeup tutorials on You-Hoo! If there was a makeup disaster, it wouldn't be my fault.
What if we distracted everyone from our face with some really cool earrings?
One time I had a zit, and I wished we could have been invisible!
How does she even know about our crush anyways? I'm sure we never said anything about it . . .

WHAT WOULD YOU DO?

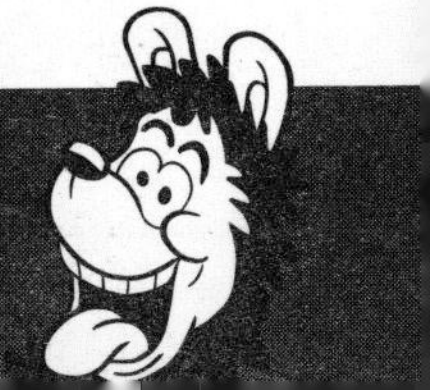

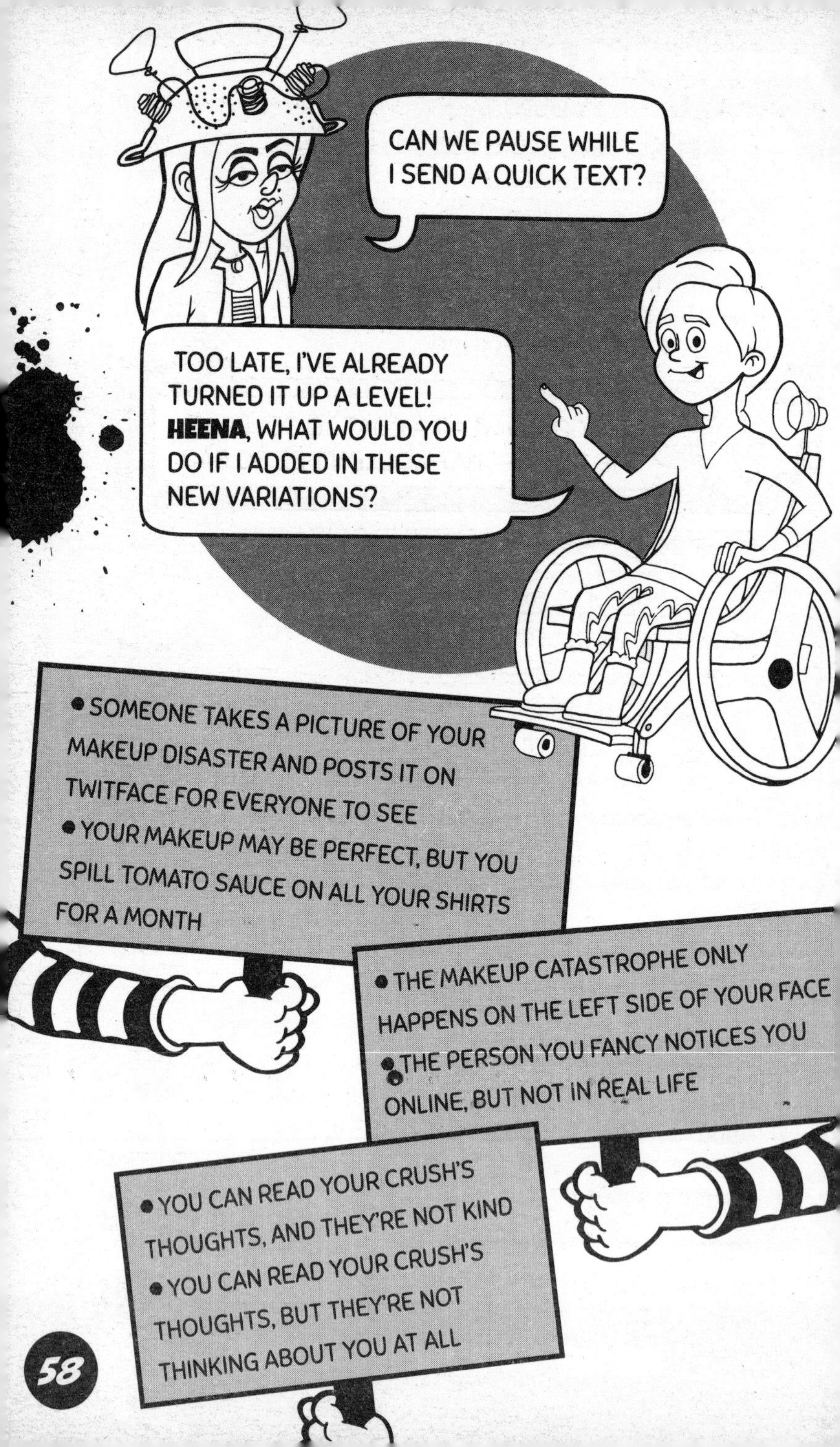

CAN WE PAUSE WHILE I SEND A QUICK TEXT?
TOO LATE, I'VE ALREADY TURNED IT UP A LEVEL! **HEENA**, WHAT WOULD YOU DO IF I ADDED IN THESE NEW VARIATIONS?
• SOMEONE TAKES A PICTURE OF YOUR MAKEUP DISASTER AND POSTS IT ON TWITFACE FOR EVERYONE TO SEE
• YOUR MAKEUP MAY BE PERFECT, BUT YOU SPILL TOMATO SAUCE ON ALL YOUR SHIRTS FOR A MONTH
• THE MAKEUP CATASTROPHE ONLY HAPPENS ON THE LEFT SIDE OF YOUR FACE
• THE PERSON YOU FANCY NOTICES YOU ONLINE, BUT NOT IN REAL LIFE
• YOU CAN READ YOUR CRUSH'S THOUGHTS, AND THEY'RE NOT KIND
• YOU CAN READ YOUR CRUSH'S THOUGHTS, BUT THEY'RE NOT THINKING ABOUT YOU AT ALL

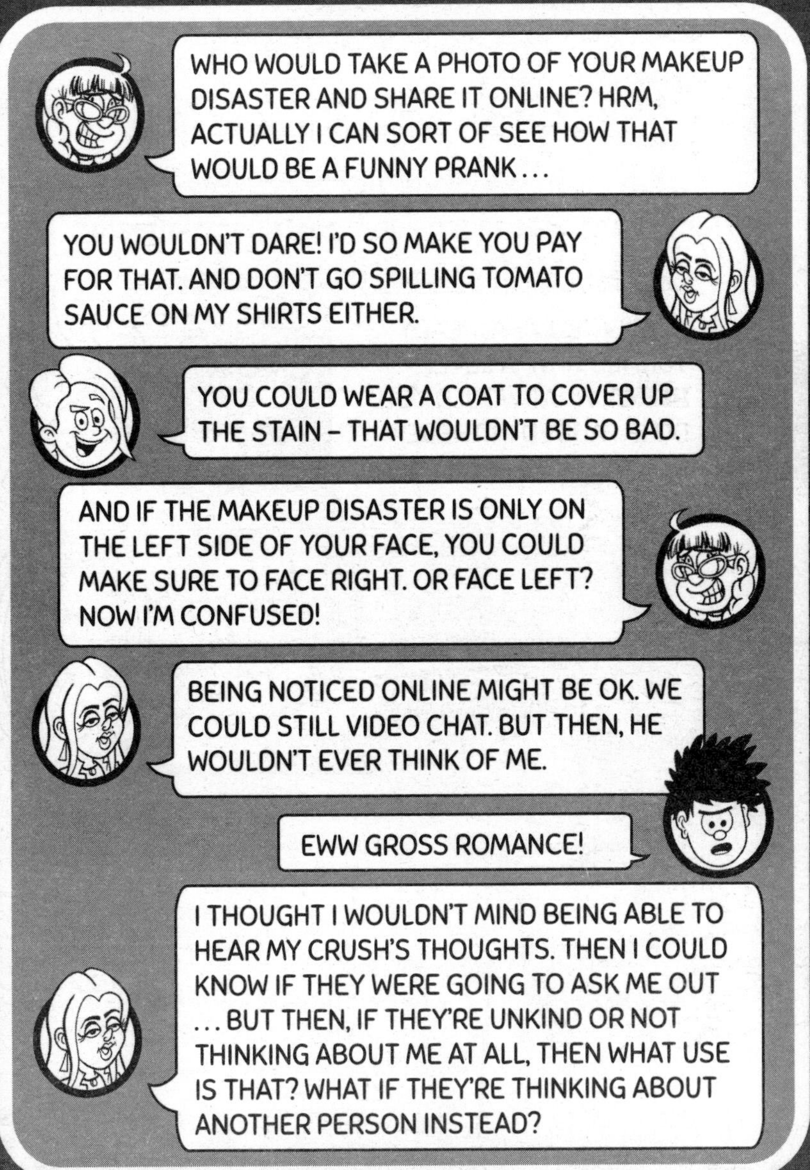
WHO WOULD TAKE A PHOTO OF YOUR MAKEUP DISASTER AND SHARE IT ONLINE? HRM, ACTUALLY I CAN SORT OF SEE HOW THAT WOULD BE A FUNNY PRANK . . .
YOU WOULDN'T DARE! I'D SO MAKE YOU PAY FOR THAT. AND DON'T GO SPILLING TOMATO SAUCE ON MY SHIRTS EITHER.
YOU COULD WEAR A COAT TO COVER UP THE STAIN – THAT WOULDN'T BE SO BAD.
AND IF THE MAKEUP DISASTER IS ONLY ON THE LEFT SIDE OF YOUR FACE, YOU COULD MAKE SURE TO FACE RIGHT. OR FACE LEFT? NOW I'M CONFUSED!
BEING NOTICED ONLINE MIGHT BE OK. WE COULD STILL VIDEO CHAT. BUT THEN, HE WOULDN'T EVER THINK OF ME.
EWW GROSS ROMANCE!
I THOUGHT I WOULDN'T MIND BEING ABLE TO HEAR MY CRUSH'S THOUGHTS. THEN I COULD KNOW IF THEY WERE GOING TO ASK ME OUT . . . BUT THEN, IF THEY'RE UNKIND OR NOT THINKING ABOUT ME AT ALL, THEN WHAT USE IS THAT? WHAT IF THEY'RE THINKING ABOUT ANOTHER PERSON INSTEAD?

WHICH OPTION WOULD YOU CHOOSE WITH ALL THOSE VARIATIONS ADDED INTO THE MIX?

HANI

'My go!' said Hani, blinking his big, puppy-dog eyes. 'Please? Harsha and Heena have had their turns already.'

'We never turn down a willing volunteer,' Rubi laughed.

'This is so cool!' Hani said as Dennis put the MIND reader on his head. 'It's like a video game.'

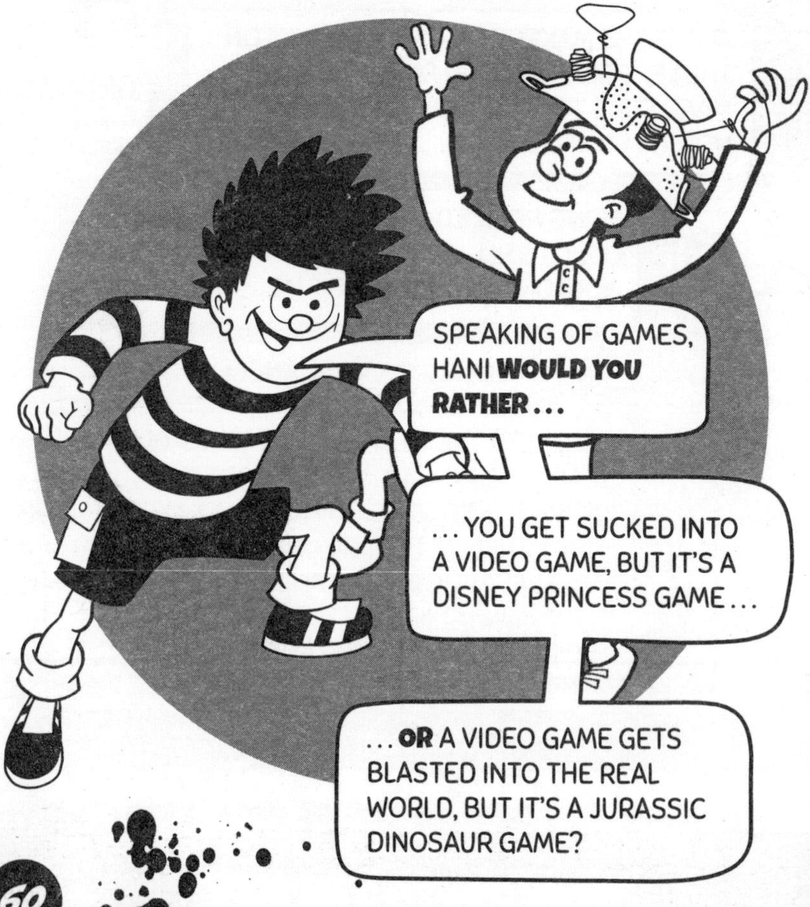

SPEAKING OF GAMES, HANI **WOULD YOU RATHER**...
... YOU GET SUCKED INTO A VIDEO GAME, BUT IT'S A DISNEY PRINCESS GAME...
... **OR** A VIDEO GAME GETS BLASTED INTO THE REAL WORLD, BUT IT'S A JURASSIC DINOSAUR GAME?

WHAT DO HANI'S NUMSKULLS THINK?

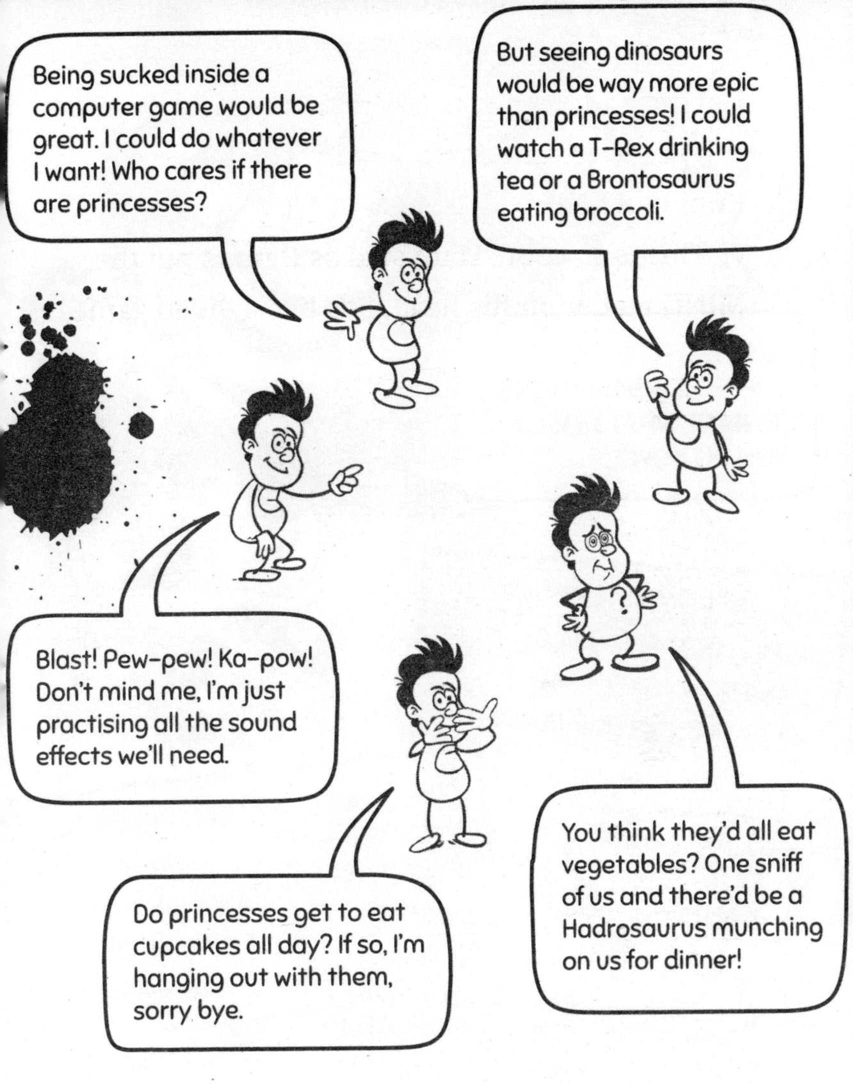

Being sucked inside a computer game would be great. I could do whatever I want! Who cares if there are princesses?
But seeing dinosaurs would be way more epic than princesses! I could watch a T-Rex drinking tea or a Brontosaurus eating broccoli.
Blast! Pew-pew! Ka-pow! Don't mind me, I'm just practising all the sound effects we'll need.
You think they'd all eat vegetables? One sniff of us and there'd be a Hadrosaurus munching on us for dinner!
Do princesses get to eat cupcakes all day? If so, I'm hanging out with them, sorry bye.

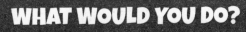

WHAT WOULD YOU DO?

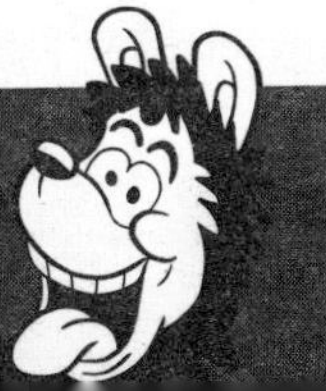

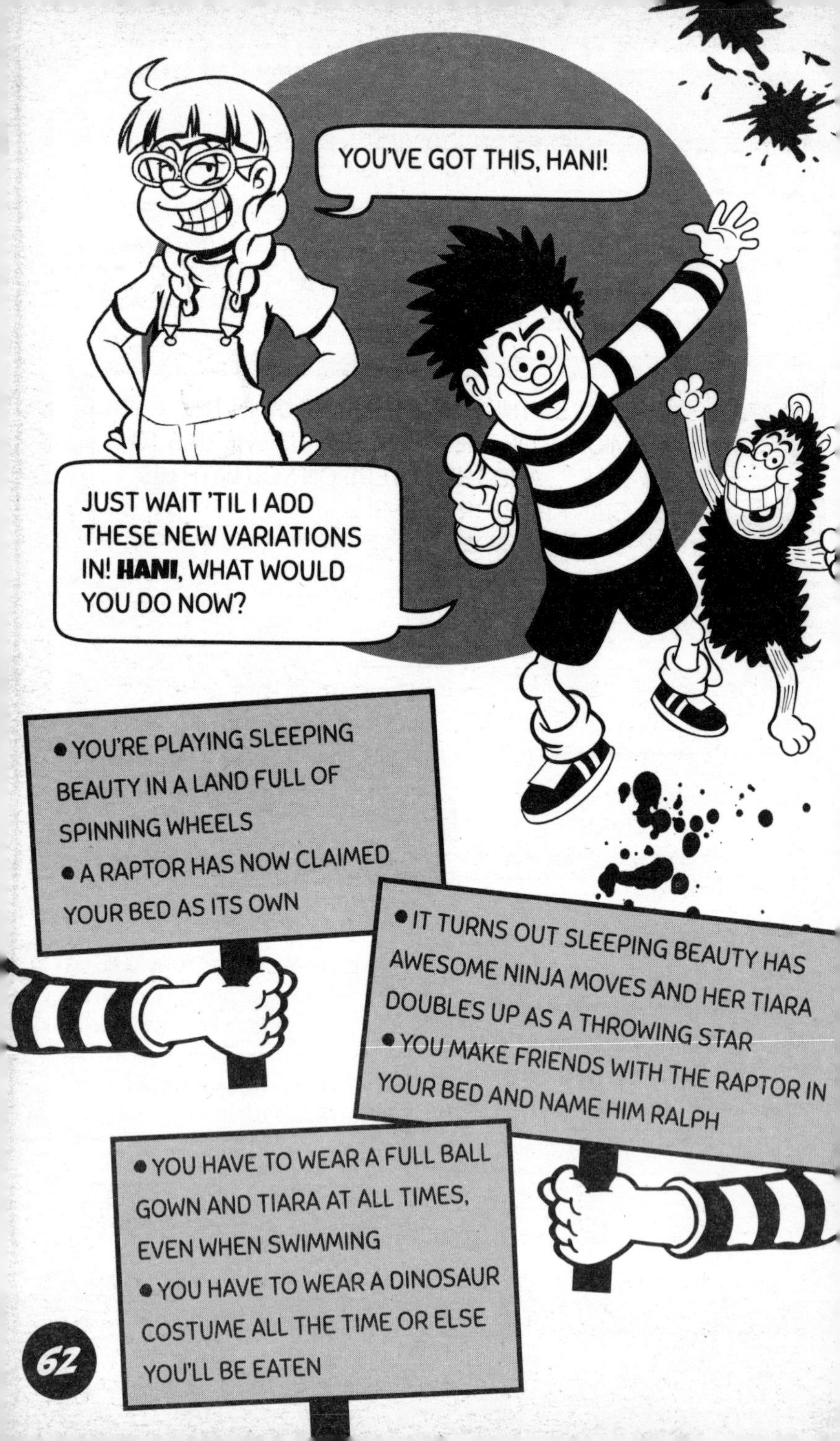
YOU'VE GOT THIS, HANI!
JUST WAIT 'TIL I ADD THESE NEW VARIATIONS IN! **HANI**, WHAT WOULD YOU DO NOW?
• YOU'RE PLAYING SLEEPING BEAUTY IN A LAND FULL OF SPINNING WHEELS
• A RAPTOR HAS NOW CLAIMED YOUR BED AS ITS OWN
• IT TURNS OUT SLEEPING BEAUTY HAS AWESOME NINJA MOVES AND HER TIARA DOUBLES UP AS A THROWING STAR
• YOU MAKE FRIENDS WITH THE RAPTOR IN YOUR BED AND NAME HIM RALPH
• YOU HAVE TO WEAR A FULL BALL GOWN AND TIARA AT ALL TIMES, EVEN WHEN SWIMMING
• YOU HAVE TO WEAR A DINOSAUR COSTUME ALL THE TIME OR ELSE YOU'LL BE EATEN

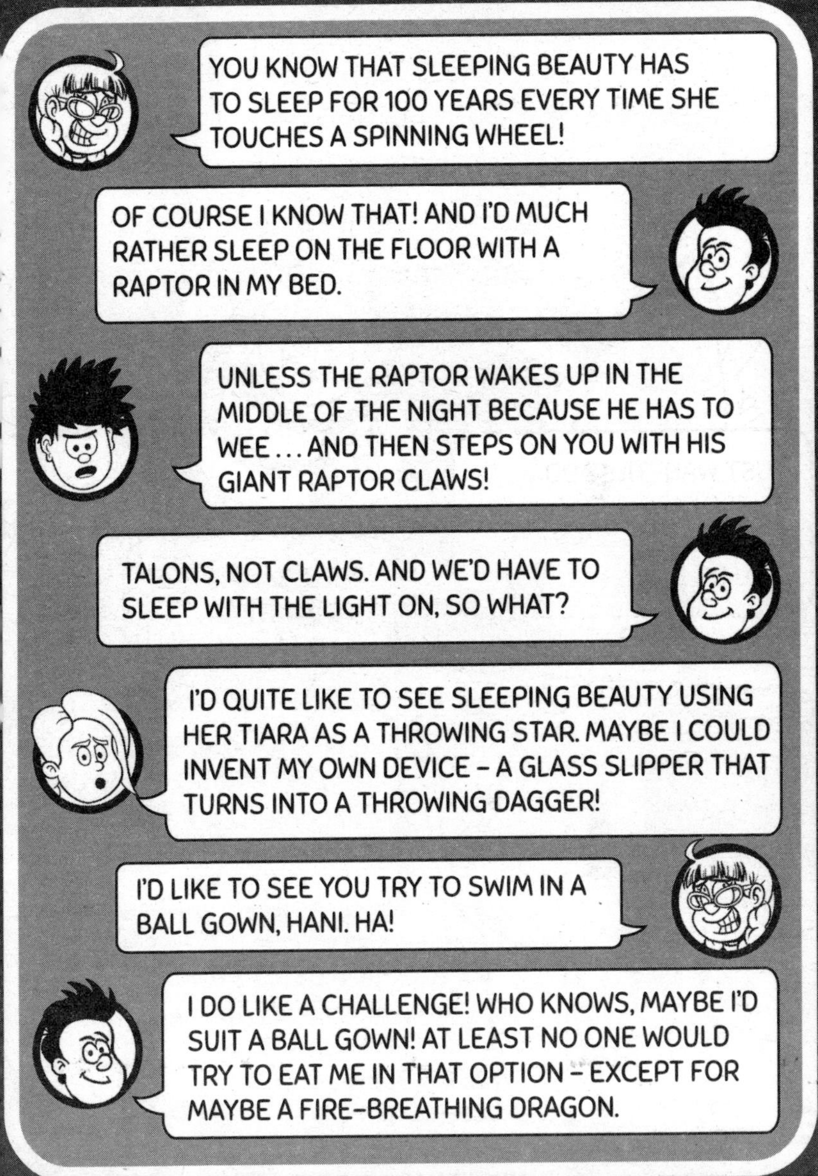
YOU KNOW THAT SLEEPING BEAUTY HAS TO SLEEP FOR 100 YEARS EVERY TIME SHE TOUCHES A SPINNING WHEEL!
OF COURSE I KNOW THAT! AND I'D MUCH RATHER SLEEP ON THE FLOOR WITH A RAPTOR IN MY BED.
UNLESS THE RAPTOR WAKES UP IN THE MIDDLE OF THE NIGHT BECAUSE HE HAS TO WEE . . . AND THEN STEPS ON YOU WITH HIS GIANT RAPTOR CLAWS!
TALONS, NOT CLAWS. AND WE'D HAVE TO SLEEP WITH THE LIGHT ON, SO WHAT?
I'D QUITE LIKE TO SEE SLEEPING BEAUTY USING HER TIARA AS A THROWING STAR. MAYBE I COULD INVENT MY OWN DEVICE – A GLASS SLIPPER THAT TURNS INTO A THROWING DAGGER!
I'D LIKE TO SEE YOU TRY TO SWIM IN A BALL GOWN, HANI. HA!
I DO LIKE A CHALLENGE! WHO KNOWS, MAYBE I'D SUIT A BALL GOWN! AT LEAST NO ONE WOULD TRY TO EAT ME IN THAT OPTION – EXCEPT FOR MAYBE A FIRE-BREATHING DRAGON.

WHICH OPTION WOULD YOU CHOOSE WITH ALL THOSE VARIATIONS ADDED INTO THE MIX?

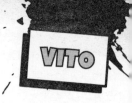

Vito walked past, carrying what looked like a giant hand.

'Hey Vito, what's your project?' Rubi asked.

'It's my Pollution Pointer. I point it at anyone who's a threat to our planet.'

'Cool! Want to try our MIND reader?'

Vito shrugged. 'It's not as cool as my Pollution Pointer, but I'll give it a go!'

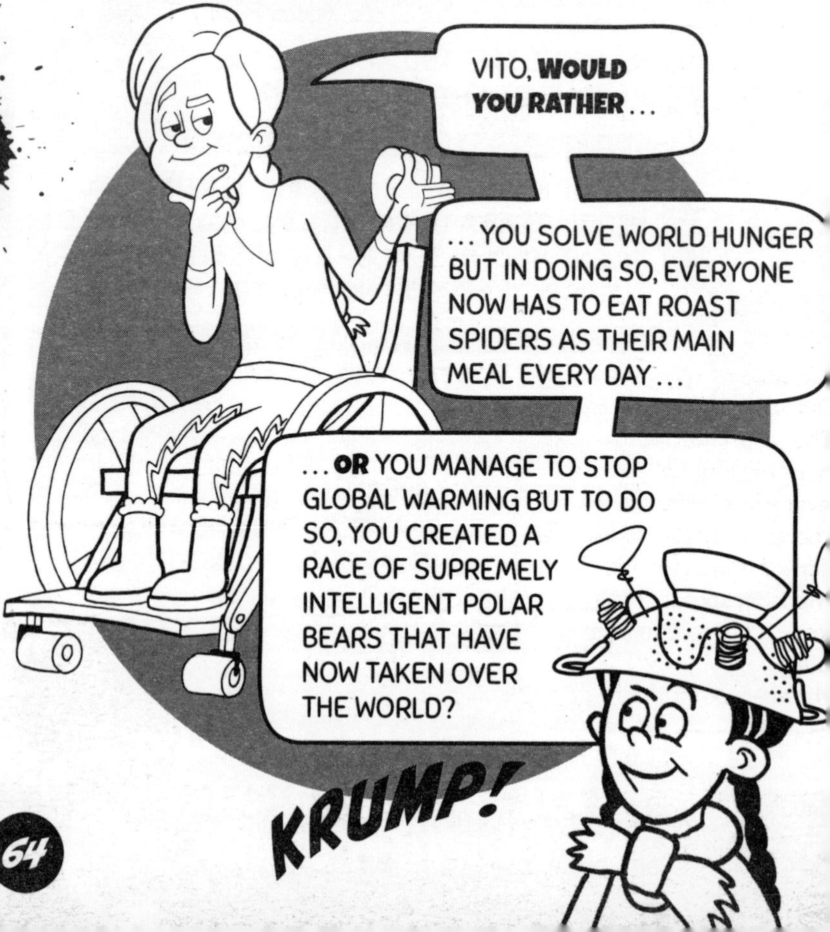
VITO, **WOULD YOU RATHER**...
... YOU SOLVE WORLD HUNGER BUT IN DOING SO, EVERYONE NOW HAS TO EAT ROAST SPIDERS AS THEIR MAIN MEAL EVERY DAY...
... **OR** YOU MANAGE TO STOP GLOBAL WARMING BUT TO DO SO, YOU CREATED A RACE OF SUPREMELY INTELLIGENT POLAR BEARS THAT HAVE NOW TAKEN OVER THE WORLD?
KRUMP!

WHAT DO VITO'S NUMSKULLS THINK?

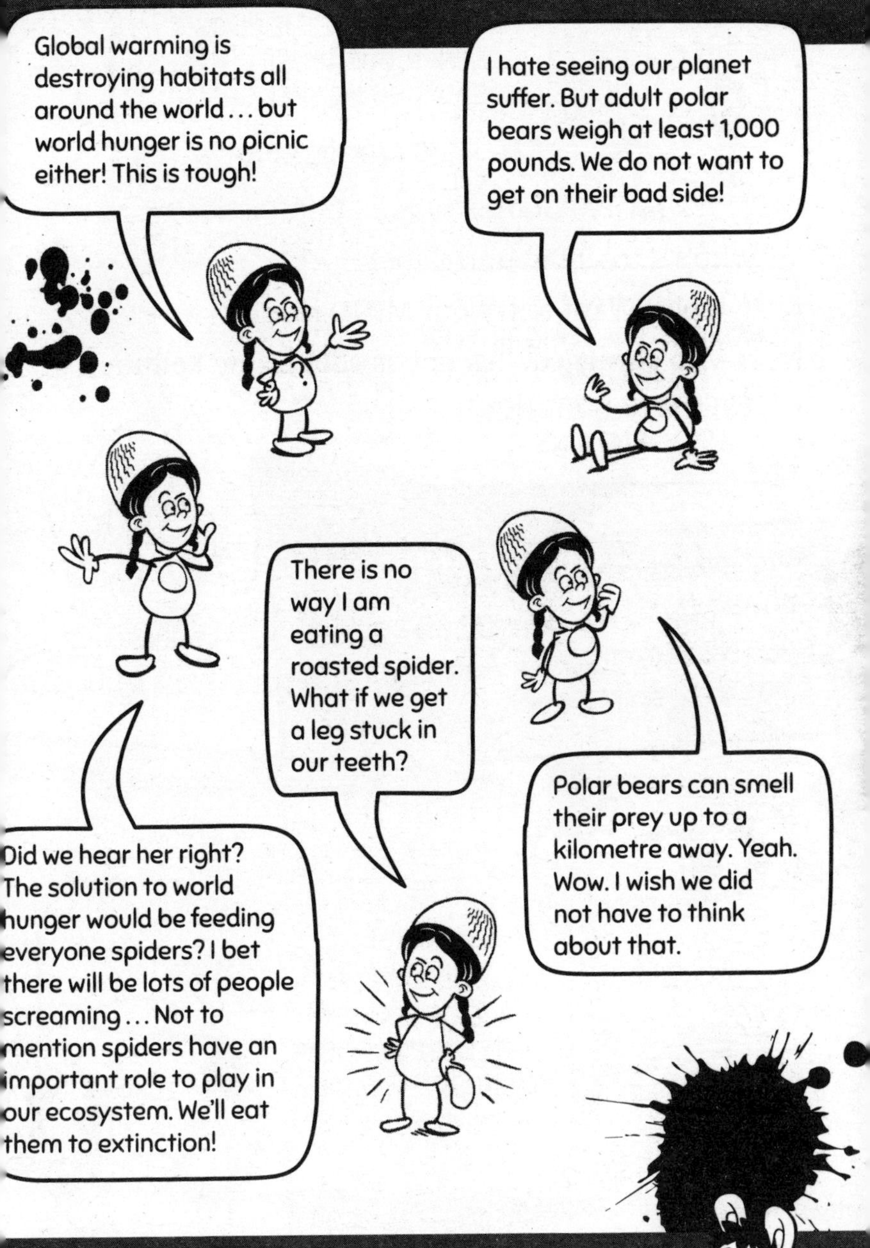
Global warming is destroying habitats all around the world . . . but world hunger is no picnic either! This is tough!
I hate seeing our planet suffer. But adult polar bears weigh at least 1,000 pounds. We do not want to get on their bad side!
Did we hear her right? The solution to world hunger would be feeding everyone spiders? I bet there will be lots of people screaming . . . Not to mention spiders have an important role to play in our ecosystem. We'll eat them to extinction!
There is no way I am eating a roasted spider. What if we get a leg stuck in our teeth?
Polar bears can smell their prey up to a kilometre away. Yeah. Wow. I wish we did not have to think about that.

WHAT WOULD YOU DO?

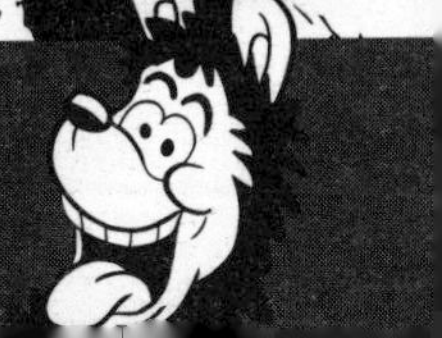

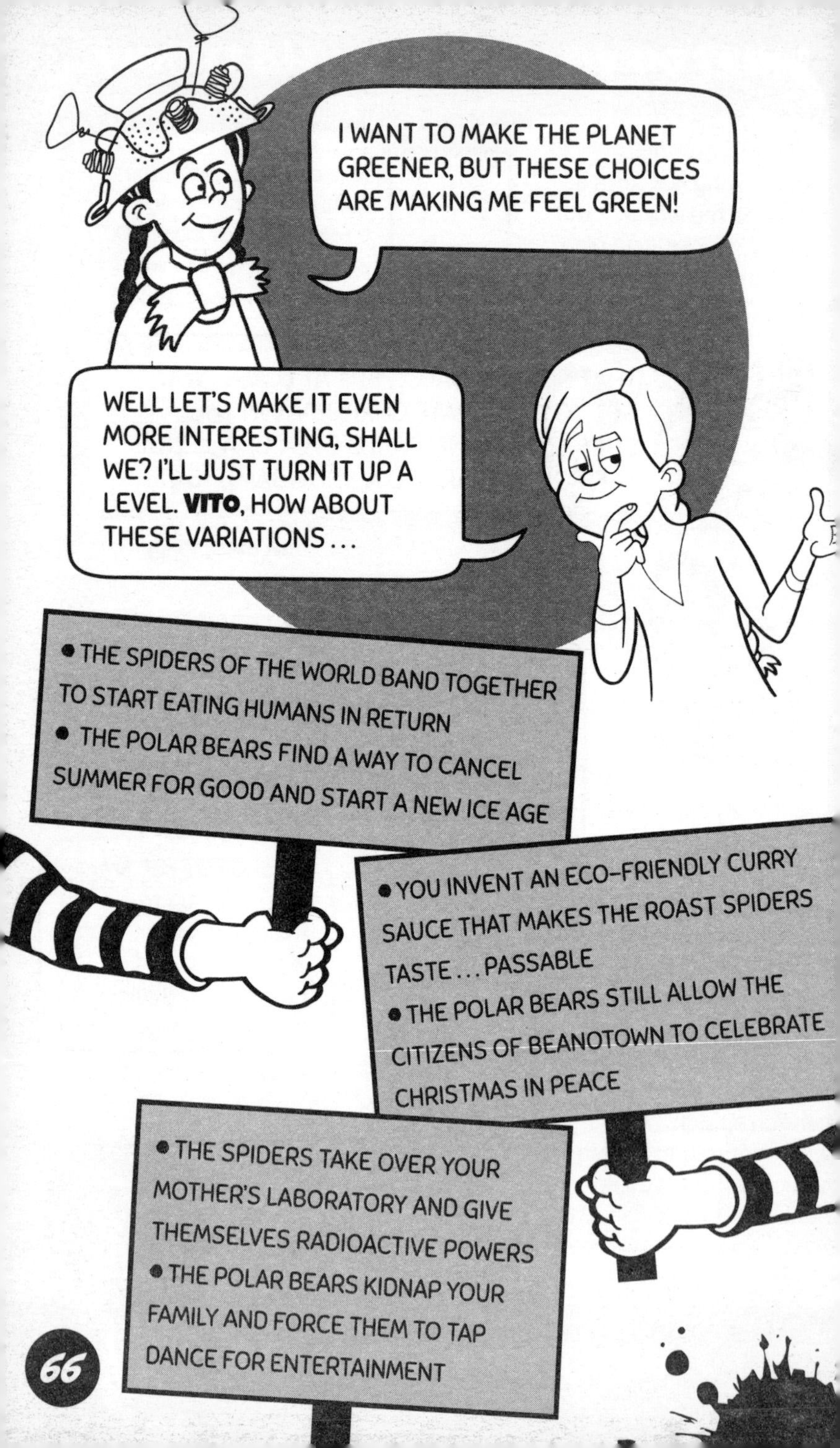
I WANT TO MAKE THE PLANET GREENER, BUT THESE CHOICES ARE MAKING ME FEEL GREEN!
WELL LET'S MAKE IT EVEN MORE INTERESTING, SHALL WE? I'LL JUST TURN IT UP A LEVEL. **VITO**, HOW ABOUT THESE VARIATIONS . . .
• THE SPIDERS OF THE WORLD BAND TOGETHER TO START EATING HUMANS IN RETURN
• THE POLAR BEARS FIND A WAY TO CANCEL SUMMER FOR GOOD AND START A NEW ICE AGE
• YOU INVENT AN ECO-FRIENDLY CURRY SAUCE THAT MAKES THE ROAST SPIDERS TASTE . . . PASSABLE
• THE POLAR BEARS STILL ALLOW THE CITIZENS OF BEANOTOWN TO CELEBRATE CHRISTMAS IN PEACE
• THE SPIDERS TAKE OVER YOUR MOTHER'S LABORATORY AND GIVE THEMSELVES RADIOACTIVE POWERS
• THE POLAR BEARS KIDNAP YOUR FAMILY AND FORCE THEM TO TAP DANCE FOR ENTERTAINMENT

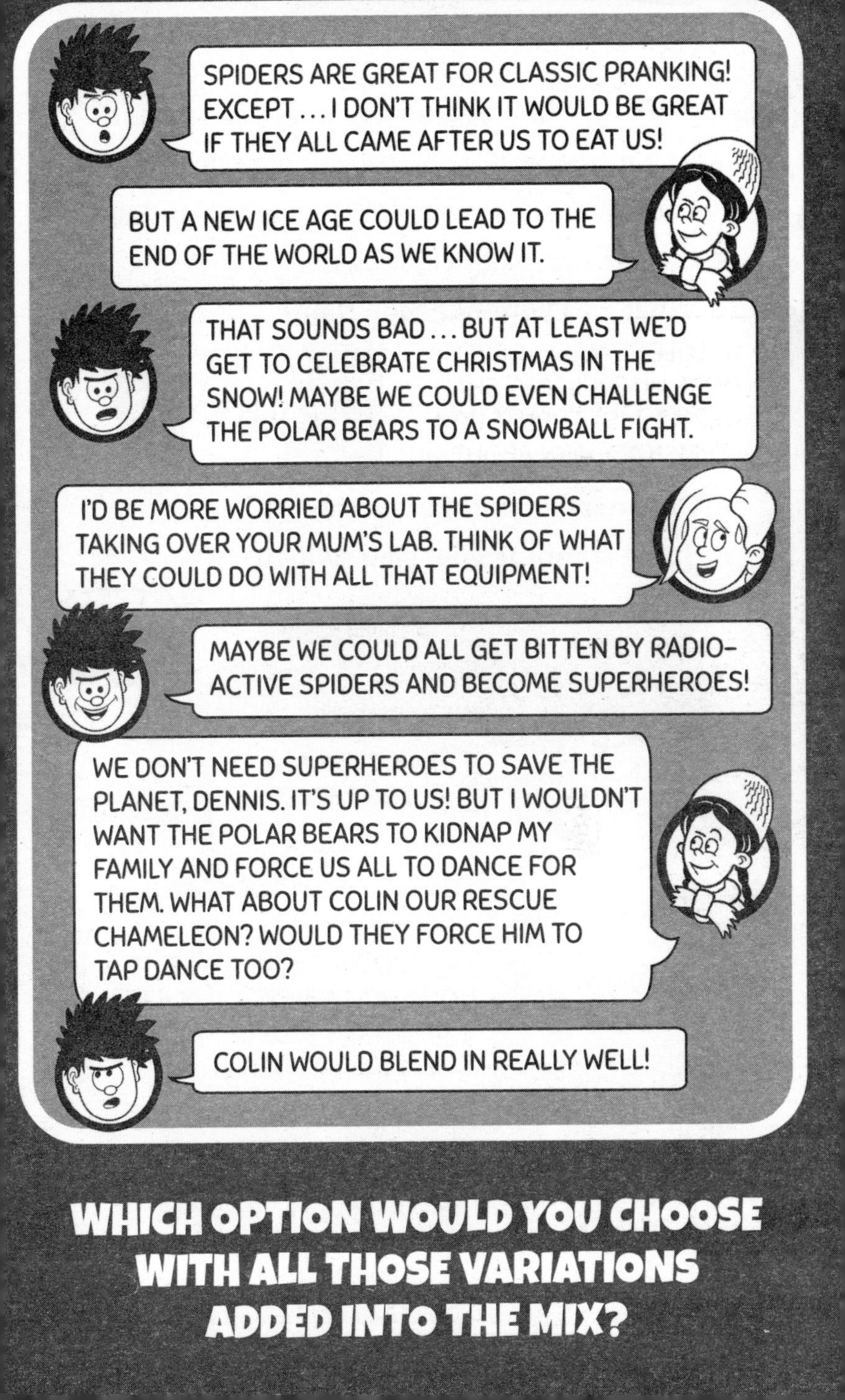
SPIDERS ARE GREAT FOR CLASSIC PRANKING! EXCEPT . . . I DON'T THINK IT WOULD BE GREAT IF THEY ALL CAME AFTER US TO EAT US!
BUT A NEW ICE AGE COULD LEAD TO THE END OF THE WORLD AS WE KNOW IT.
THAT SOUNDS BAD . . . BUT AT LEAST WE'D GET TO CELEBRATE CHRISTMAS IN THE SNOW! MAYBE WE COULD EVEN CHALLENGE THE POLAR BEARS TO A SNOWBALL FIGHT.
I'D BE MORE WORRIED ABOUT THE SPIDERS TAKING OVER YOUR MUM'S LAB. THINK OF WHAT THEY COULD DO WITH ALL THAT EQUIPMENT!
MAYBE WE COULD ALL GET BITTEN BY RADIO-ACTIVE SPIDERS AND BECOME SUPERHEROES!
WE DON'T NEED SUPERHEROES TO SAVE THE PLANET, DENNIS. IT'S UP TO US! BUT I WOULDN'T WANT THE POLAR BEARS TO KIDNAP MY FAMILY AND FORCE US ALL TO DANCE FOR THEM. WHAT ABOUT COLIN OUR RESCUE CHAMELEON? WOULD THEY FORCE HIM TO TAP DANCE TOO?
COLIN WOULD BLEND IN REALLY WELL!

WHICH OPTION WOULD YOU CHOOSE WITH ALL THOSE VARIATIONS ADDED INTO THE MIX?

'So,' Vito asked, 'does each person get a new question, or are you recycling them?'

'Each question on my MIND reader is unique to the person!' Rubi explained.

'What was your question then?'

'Um . . .'

'Wait a minute!' Dennis pointed at Rubi. 'You haven't gone yet!'

'Ok, fine, I'll do it! But be careful with the spinning glib-glob switch!'

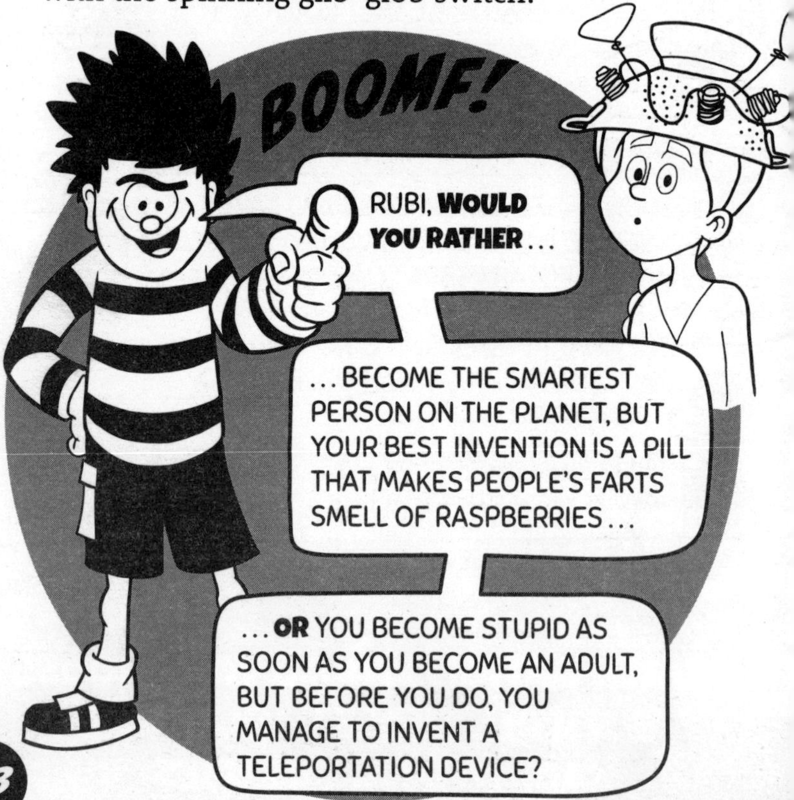
BOOMF!
RUBI, WOULD YOU RATHER . . .
. . . BECOME THE SMARTEST PERSON ON THE PLANET, BUT YOUR BEST INVENTION IS A PILL THAT MAKES PEOPLE'S FARTS SMELL OF RASPBERRIES . . .
. . . OR YOU BECOME STUPID AS SOON AS YOU BECOME AN ADULT, BUT BEFORE YOU DO, YOU MANAGE TO INVENT A TELEPORTATION DEVICE?

WHAT DO RUBI'S NUMSKULLS THINK?

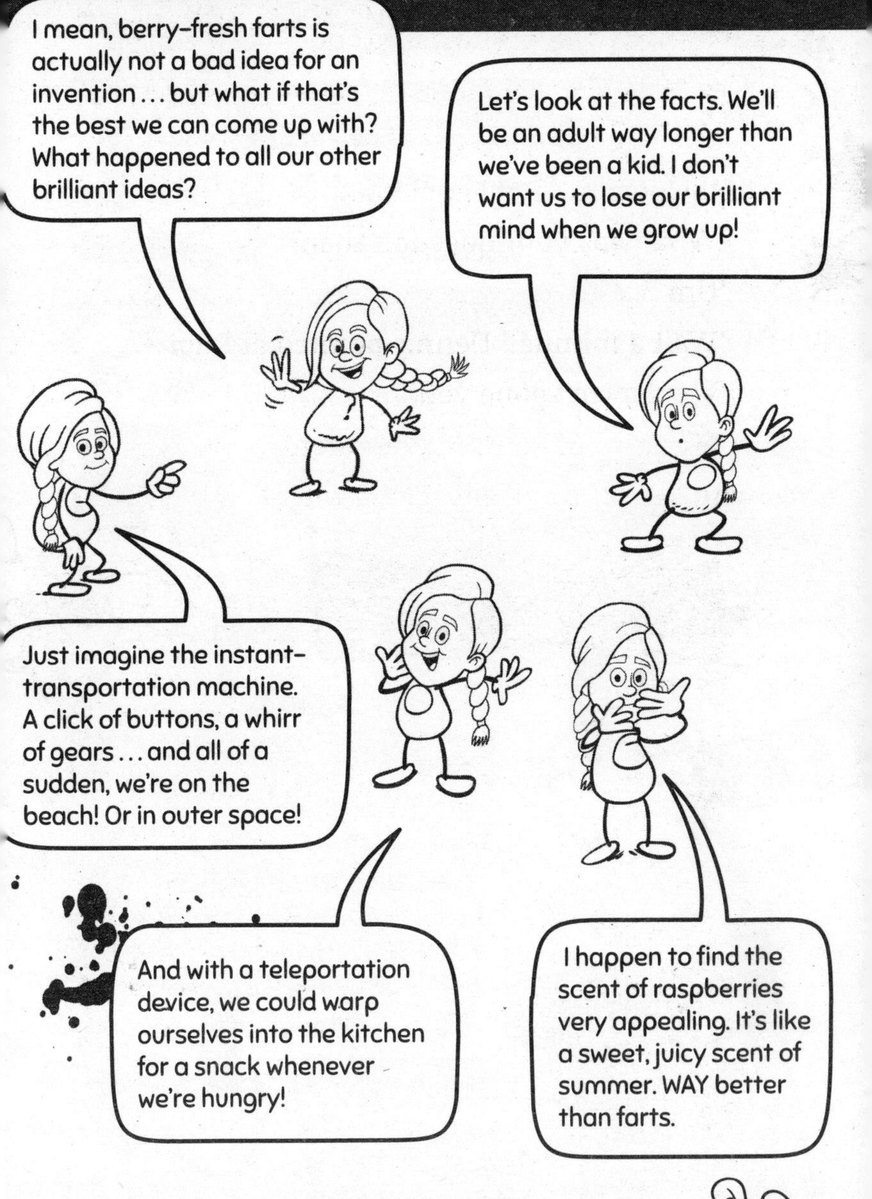
I mean, berry-fresh farts is actually not a bad idea for an invention . . . but what if that's the best we can come up with? What happened to all our other brilliant ideas?
Let's look at the facts. We'll be an adult way longer than we've been a kid. I don't want us to lose our brilliant mind when we grow up!
Just imagine the instant-transportation machine. A click of buttons, a whirr of gears . . . and all of a sudden, we're on the beach! Or in outer space!
And with a teleportation device, we could warp ourselves into the kitchen for a snack whenever we're hungry!
I happen to find the scent of raspberries very appealing. It's like a sweet, juicy scent of summer. WAY better than farts.

WHAT WOULD YOU DO?

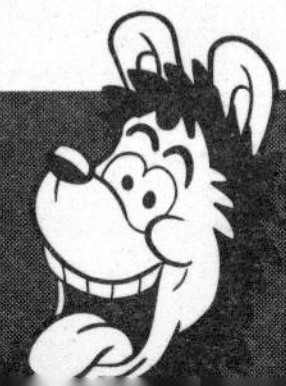

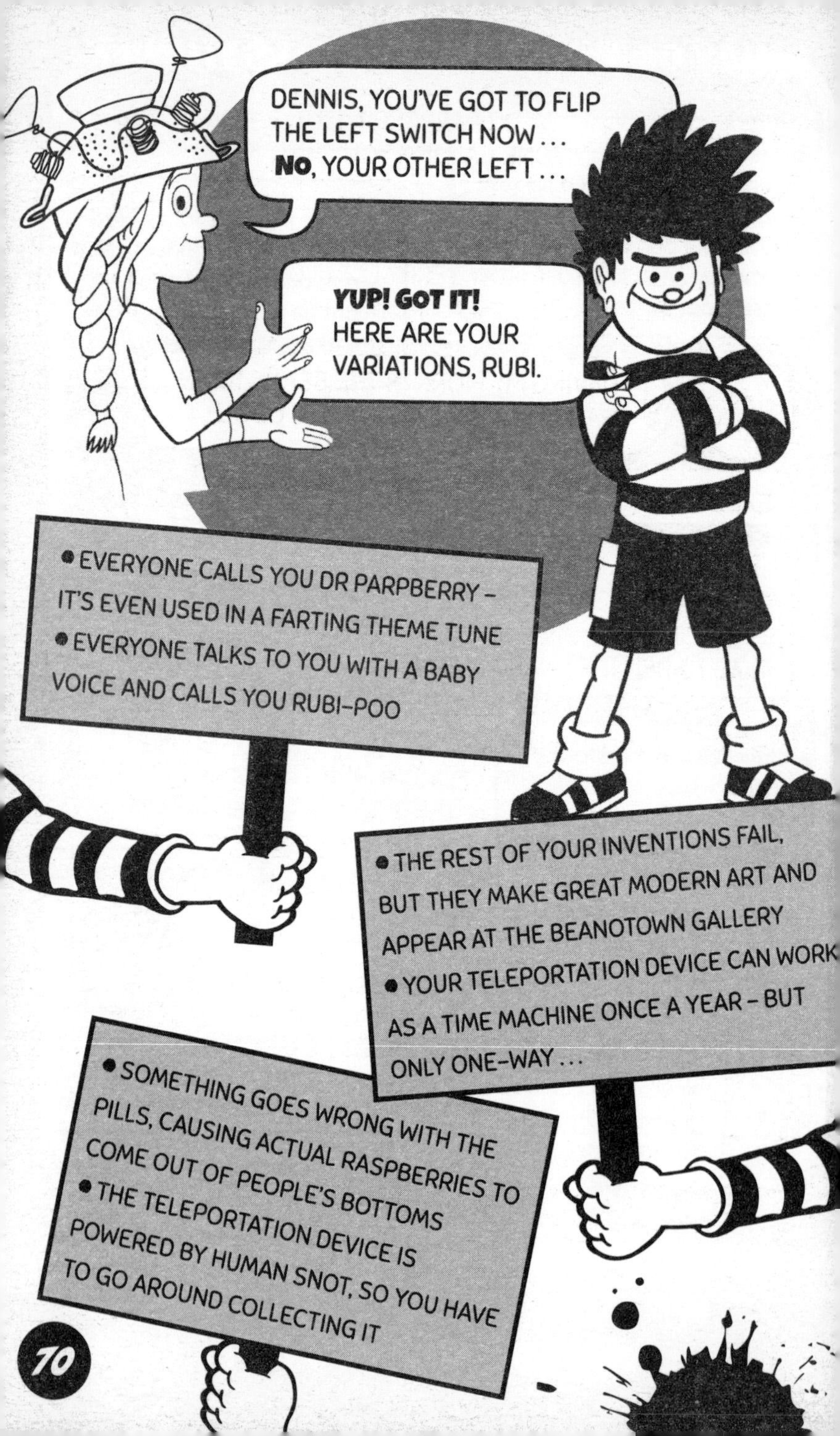

DENNIS, YOU'VE GOT TO FLIP THE LEFT SWITCH NOW ... **NO**, YOUR OTHER LEFT ...
YUP! GOT IT! HERE ARE YOUR VARIATIONS, RUBI.
• EVERYONE CALLS YOU DR PARPBERRY – IT'S EVEN USED IN A FARTING THEME TUNE
• EVERYONE TALKS TO YOU WITH A BABY VOICE AND CALLS YOU RUBI–POO
• THE REST OF YOUR INVENTIONS FAIL, BUT THEY MAKE GREAT MODERN ART AND APPEAR AT THE BEANOTOWN GALLERY
• YOUR TELEPORTATION DEVICE CAN WORK AS A TIME MACHINE ONCE A YEAR – BUT ONLY ONE–WAY ...
• SOMETHING GOES WRONG WITH THE PILLS, CAUSING ACTUAL RASPBERRIES TO COME OUT OF PEOPLE'S BOTTOMS
• THE TELEPORTATION DEVICE IS POWERED BY HUMAN SNOT, SO YOU HAVE TO GO AROUND COLLECTING IT

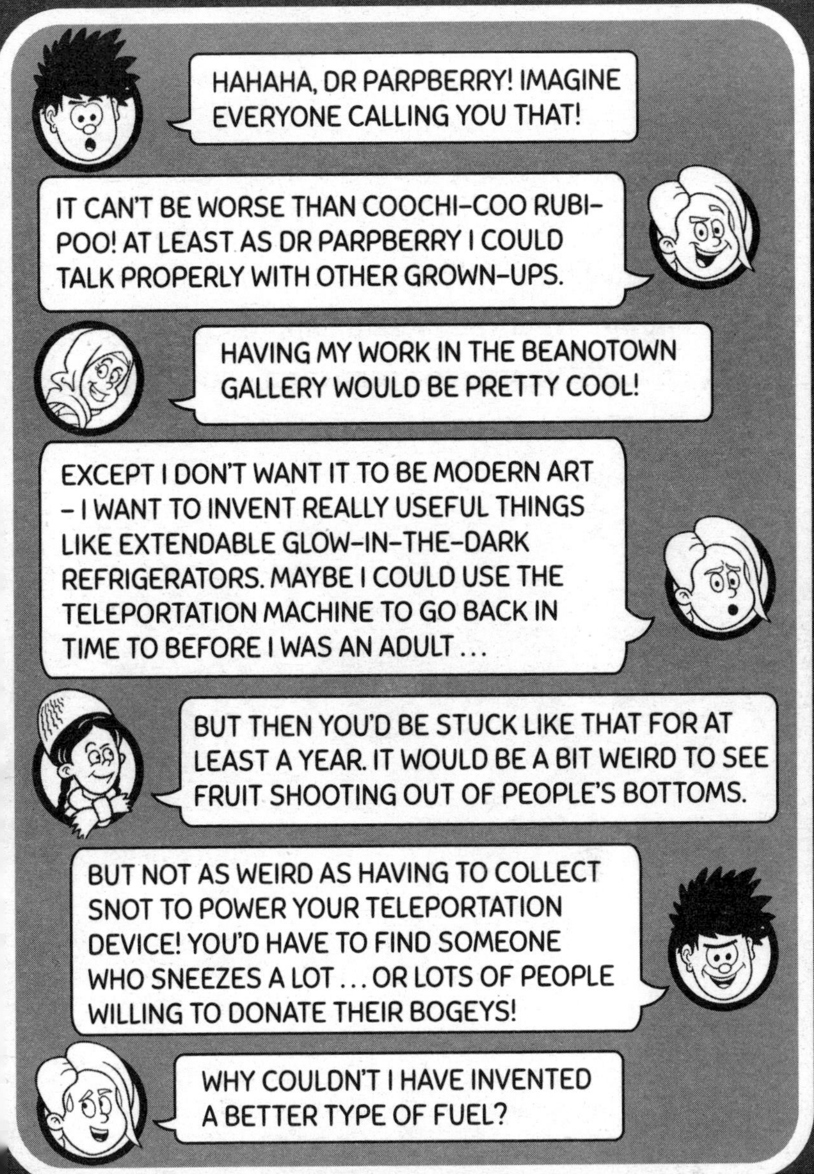
HAHAHA, DR PARPBERRY! IMAGINE EVERYONE CALLING YOU THAT!
IT CAN'T BE WORSE THAN COOCHI-COO RUBI-POO! AT LEAST AS DR PARPBERRY I COULD TALK PROPERLY WITH OTHER GROWN-UPS.
HAVING MY WORK IN THE BEANOTOWN GALLERY WOULD BE PRETTY COOL!
EXCEPT I DON'T WANT IT TO BE MODERN ART – I WANT TO INVENT REALLY USEFUL THINGS LIKE EXTENDABLE GLOW-IN-THE-DARK REFRIGERATORS. MAYBE I COULD USE THE TELEPORTATION MACHINE TO GO BACK IN TIME TO BEFORE I WAS AN ADULT . . .
BUT THEN YOU'D BE STUCK LIKE THAT FOR AT LEAST A YEAR. IT WOULD BE A BIT WEIRD TO SEE FRUIT SHOOTING OUT OF PEOPLE'S BOTTOMS.
BUT NOT AS WEIRD AS HAVING TO COLLECT SNOT TO POWER YOUR TELEPORTATION DEVICE! YOU'D HAVE TO FIND SOMEONE WHO SNEEZES A LOT . . . OR LOTS OF PEOPLE WILLING TO DONATE THEIR BOGEYS!
WHY COULDN'T I HAVE INVENTED A BETTER TYPE OF FUEL?

WHICH OPTION WOULD YOU CHOOSE WITH ALL THOSE VARIATIONS ADDED INTO THE MIX?

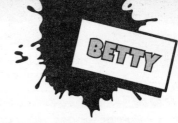

Betty Bhu skipped over.

'What's this?' she asked.

'It's a machine I've invented that can access your numskulls,' Rubi explained.

'I want to try it,' Betty said. 'And then when I'm done, I'll choose the game and you can play.'

'Sorry, Betty, we only have time for the MIND reader today.'

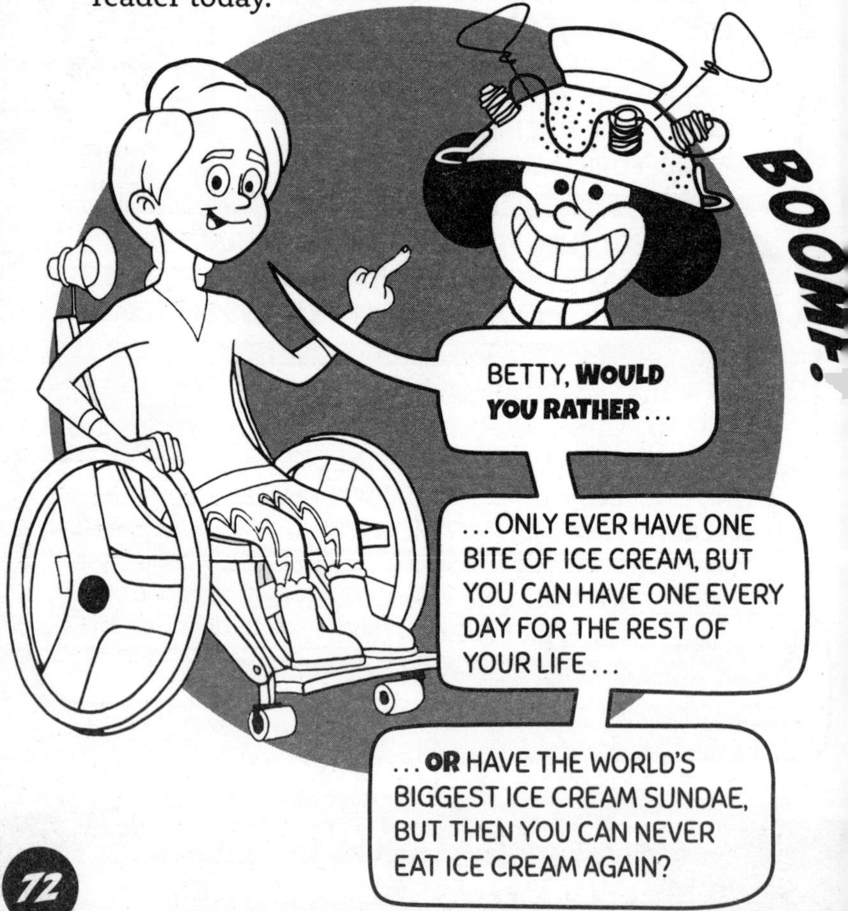
BOOMF
BETTY, **WOULD YOU RATHER** . . .
. . . ONLY EVER HAVE ONE BITE OF ICE CREAM, BUT YOU CAN HAVE ONE EVERY DAY FOR THE REST OF YOUR LIFE . . .
. . . **OR** HAVE THE WORLD'S BIGGEST ICE CREAM SUNDAE, BUT THEN YOU CAN NEVER EAT ICE CREAM AGAIN?

WHAT DO BETTY'S NUMSKULLS THINK?

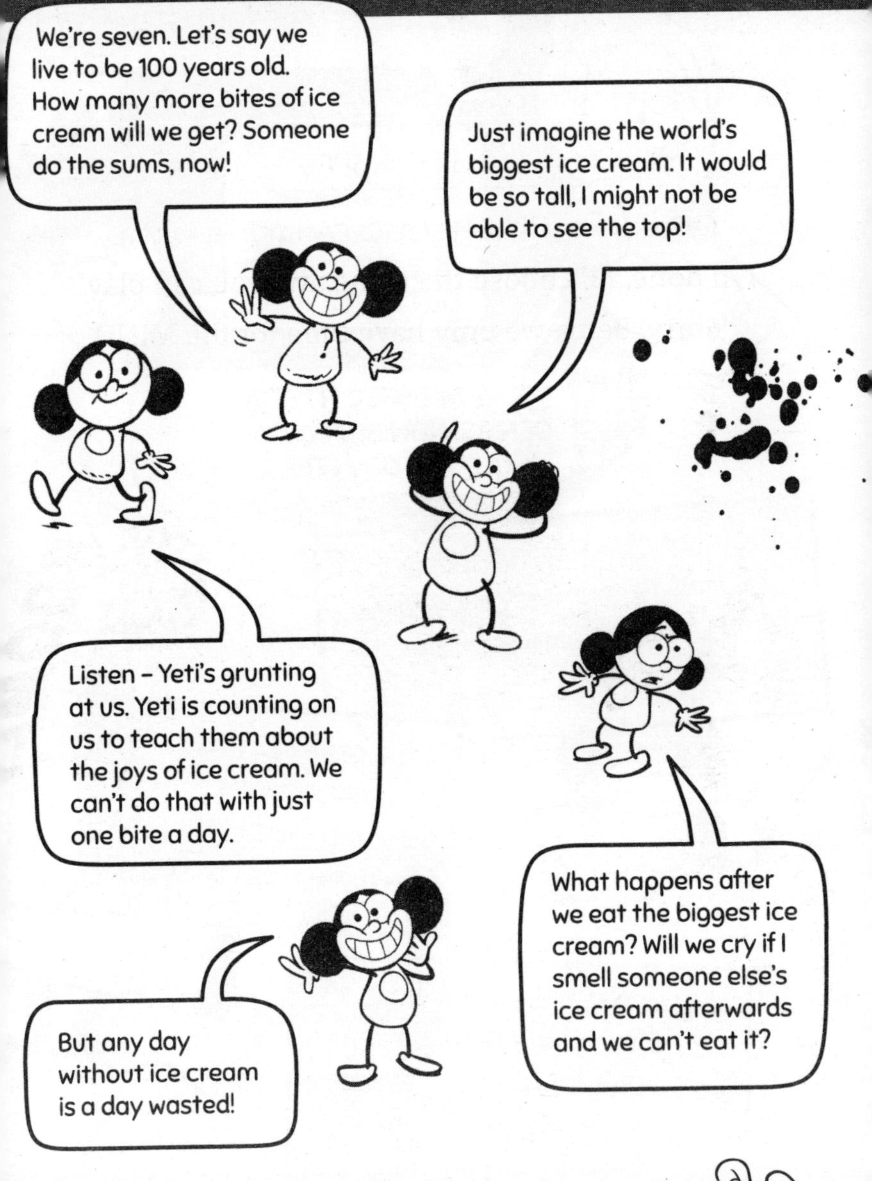
We're seven. Let's say we live to be 100 years old. How many more bites of ice cream will we get? Someone do the sums, now!
Just imagine the world's biggest ice cream. It would be so tall, I might not be able to see the top!
Listen – Yeti's grunting at us. Yeti is counting on us to teach them about the joys of ice cream. We can't do that with just one bite a day.
What happens after we eat the biggest ice cream? Will we cry if I smell someone else's ice cream afterwards and we can't eat it?
But any day without ice cream is a day wasted!

WHAT WOULD YOU DO?

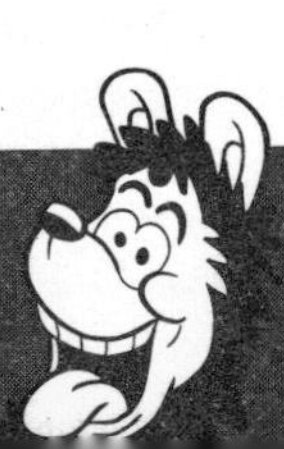

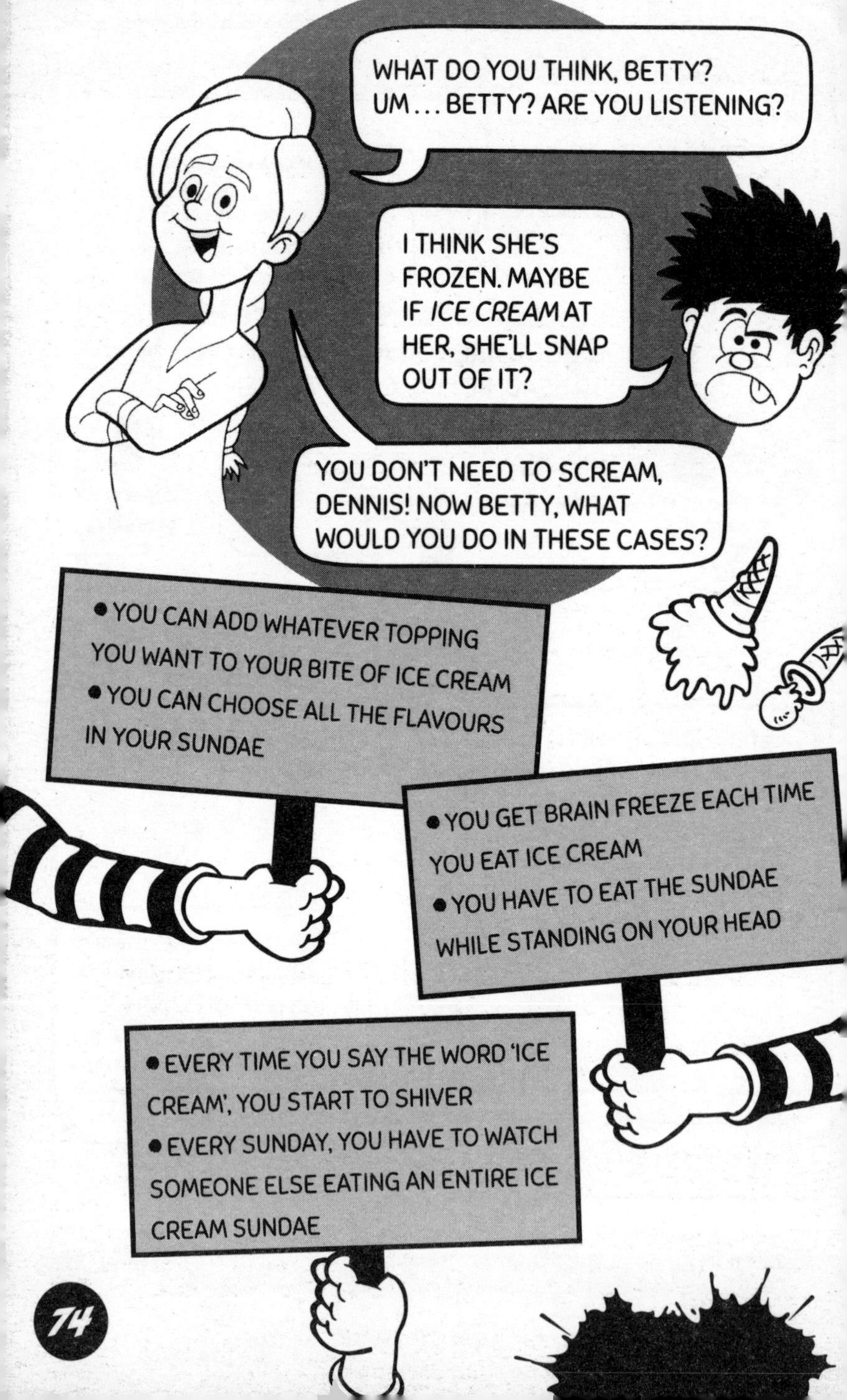
WHAT DO YOU THINK, BETTY? UM... BETTY? ARE YOU LISTENING?
I THINK SHE'S FROZEN. MAYBE IF *ICE CREAM* AT HER, SHE'LL SNAP OUT OF IT?
YOU DON'T NEED TO SCREAM, DENNIS! NOW BETTY, WHAT WOULD YOU DO IN THESE CASES?
• YOU CAN ADD WHATEVER TOPPING YOU WANT TO YOUR BITE OF ICE CREAM
• YOU CAN CHOOSE ALL THE FLAVOURS IN YOUR SUNDAE
• YOU GET BRAIN FREEZE EACH TIME YOU EAT ICE CREAM
• YOU HAVE TO EAT THE SUNDAE WHILE STANDING ON YOUR HEAD
• EVERY TIME YOU SAY THE WORD 'ICE CREAM', YOU START TO SHIVER
• EVERY SUNDAY, YOU HAVE TO WATCH SOMEONE ELSE EATING AN ENTIRE ICE CREAM SUNDAE

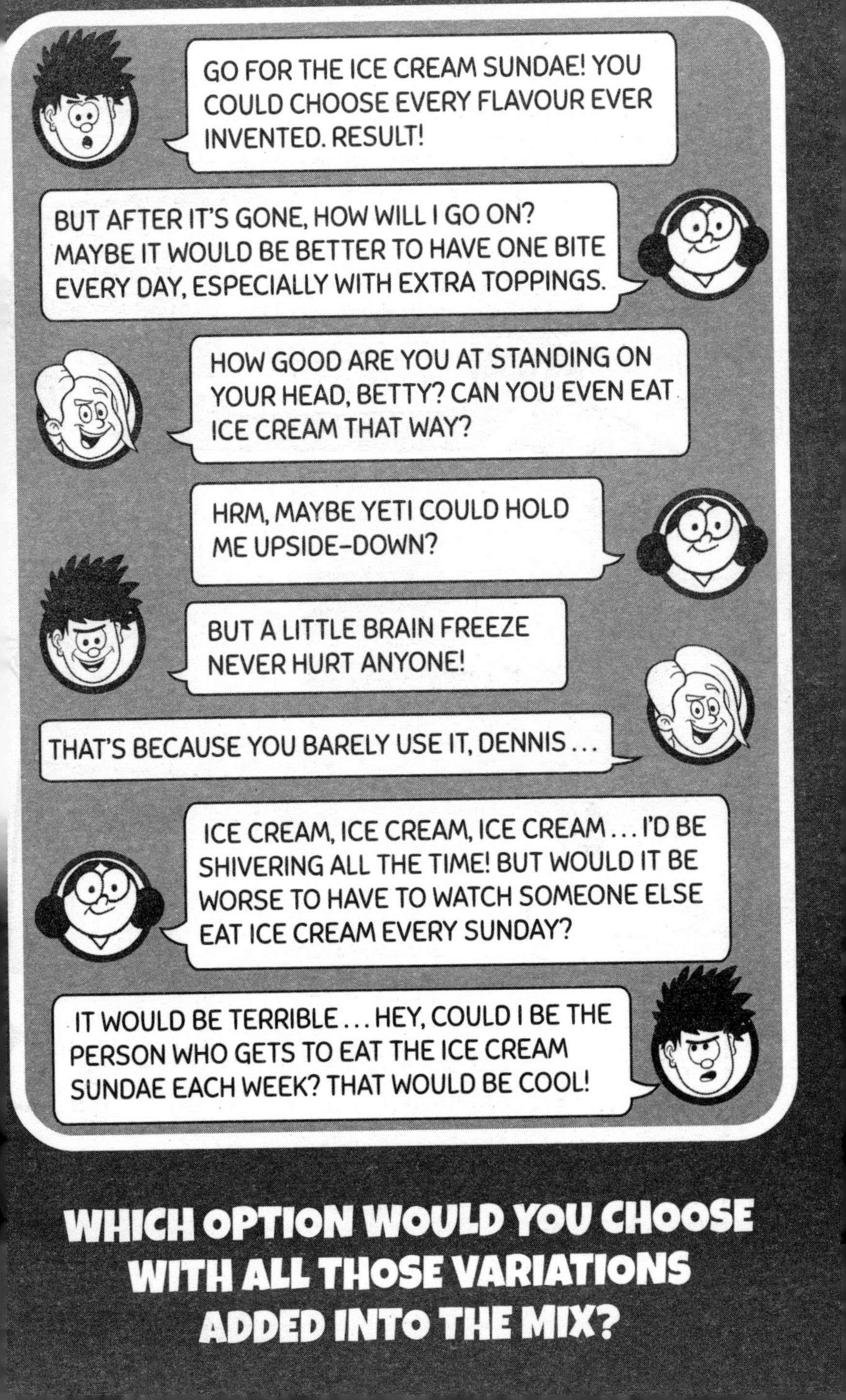
GO FOR THE ICE CREAM SUNDAE! YOU COULD CHOOSE EVERY FLAVOUR EVER INVENTED. RESULT!
BUT AFTER IT'S GONE, HOW WILL I GO ON? MAYBE IT WOULD BE BETTER TO HAVE ONE BITE EVERY DAY, ESPECIALLY WITH EXTRA TOPPINGS.
HOW GOOD ARE YOU AT STANDING ON YOUR HEAD, BETTY? CAN YOU EVEN EAT ICE CREAM THAT WAY?
HRM, MAYBE YETI COULD HOLD ME UPSIDE-DOWN?
BUT A LITTLE BRAIN FREEZE NEVER HURT ANYONE!
THAT'S BECAUSE YOU BARELY USE IT, DENNIS . . .
ICE CREAM, ICE CREAM, ICE CREAM . . . I'D BE SHIVERING ALL THE TIME! BUT WOULD IT BE WORSE TO HAVE TO WATCH SOMEONE ELSE EAT ICE CREAM EVERY SUNDAY?
IT WOULD BE TERRIBLE . . . HEY, COULD I BE THE PERSON WHO GETS TO EAT THE ICE CREAM SUNDAE EACH WEEK? THAT WOULD BE COOL!

WHICH OPTION WOULD YOU CHOOSE WITH ALL THOSE VARIATIONS ADDED INTO THE MIX?

~~YETI~~
AGNES

'Yeti wants a turn!' Betty announced. 'I mean, my cousin Agnes wants a turn!'

'Sure,' Rubi replied, passing the MIND reader over. 'Just try not to get all that long white hair stuck in it . . .'

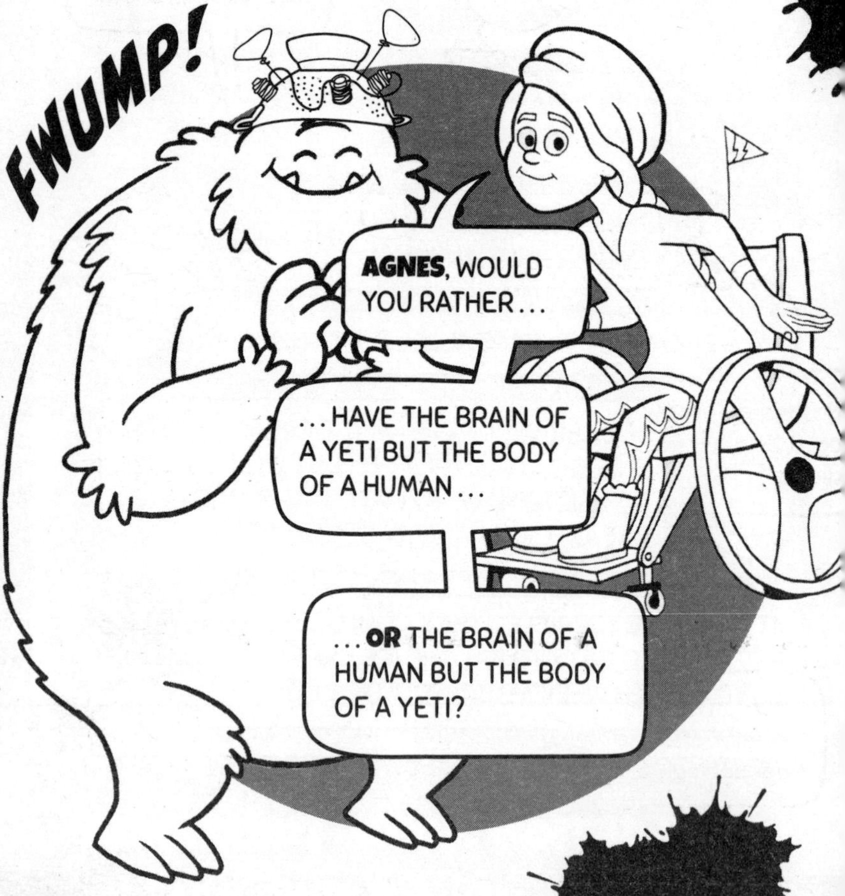
FWUMP!
AGNES, WOULD YOU RATHER . . .
. . . HAVE THE BRAIN OF A YETI BUT THE BODY OF A HUMAN . . .
. . . **OR** THE BRAIN OF A HUMAN BUT THE BODY OF A YETI?

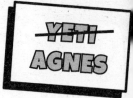

WHAT DO YETI'S NUMSKULLS THINK?

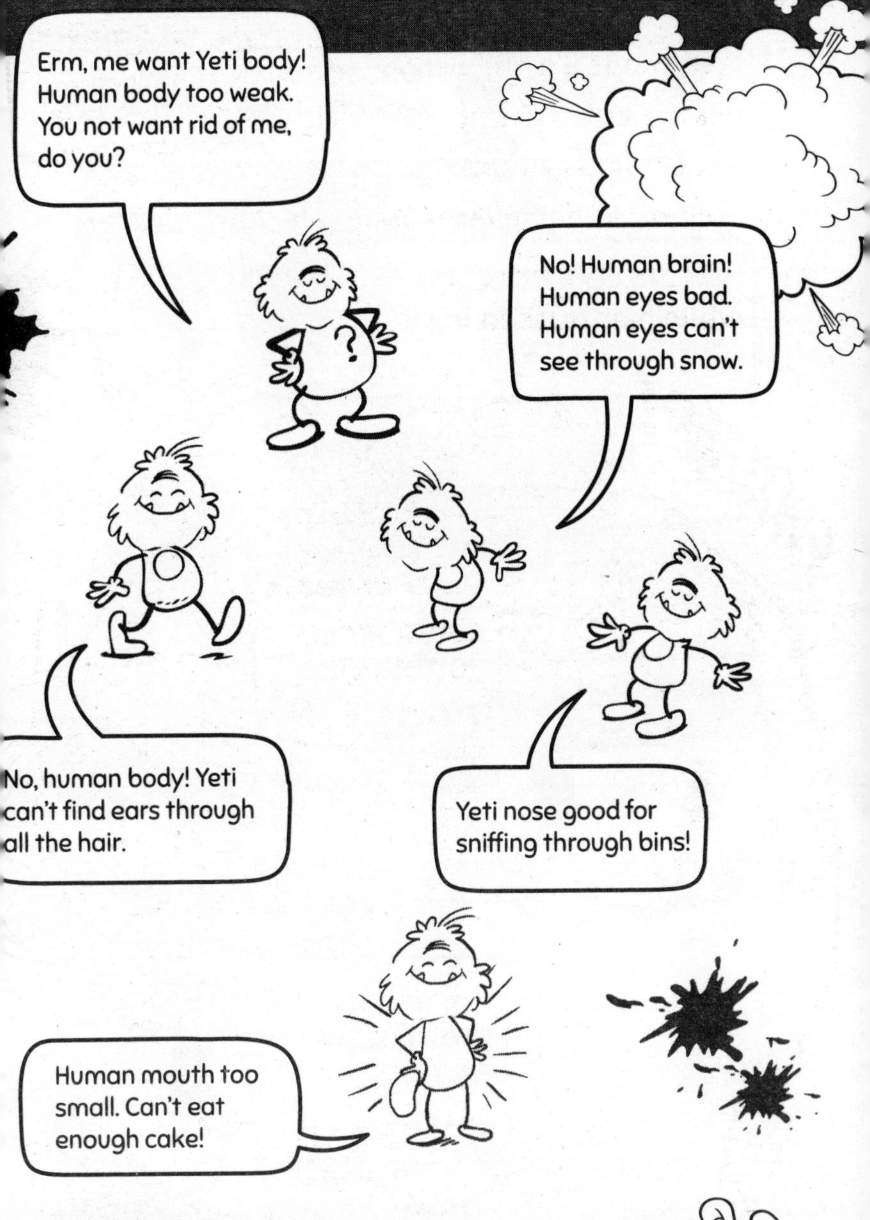
Erm, me want Yeti body! Human body too weak. You not want rid of me, do you?
No! Human brain! Human eyes bad. Human eyes can't see through snow.
No, human body! Yeti can't find ears through all the hair.
Yeti nose good for sniffing through bins!
Human mouth too small. Can't eat enough cake!

WHAT WOULD YOU DO?

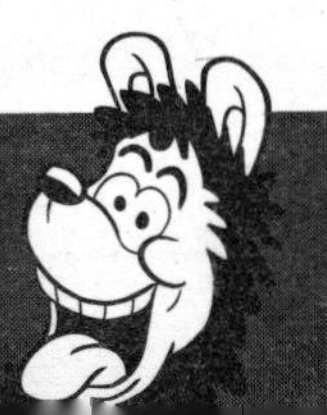

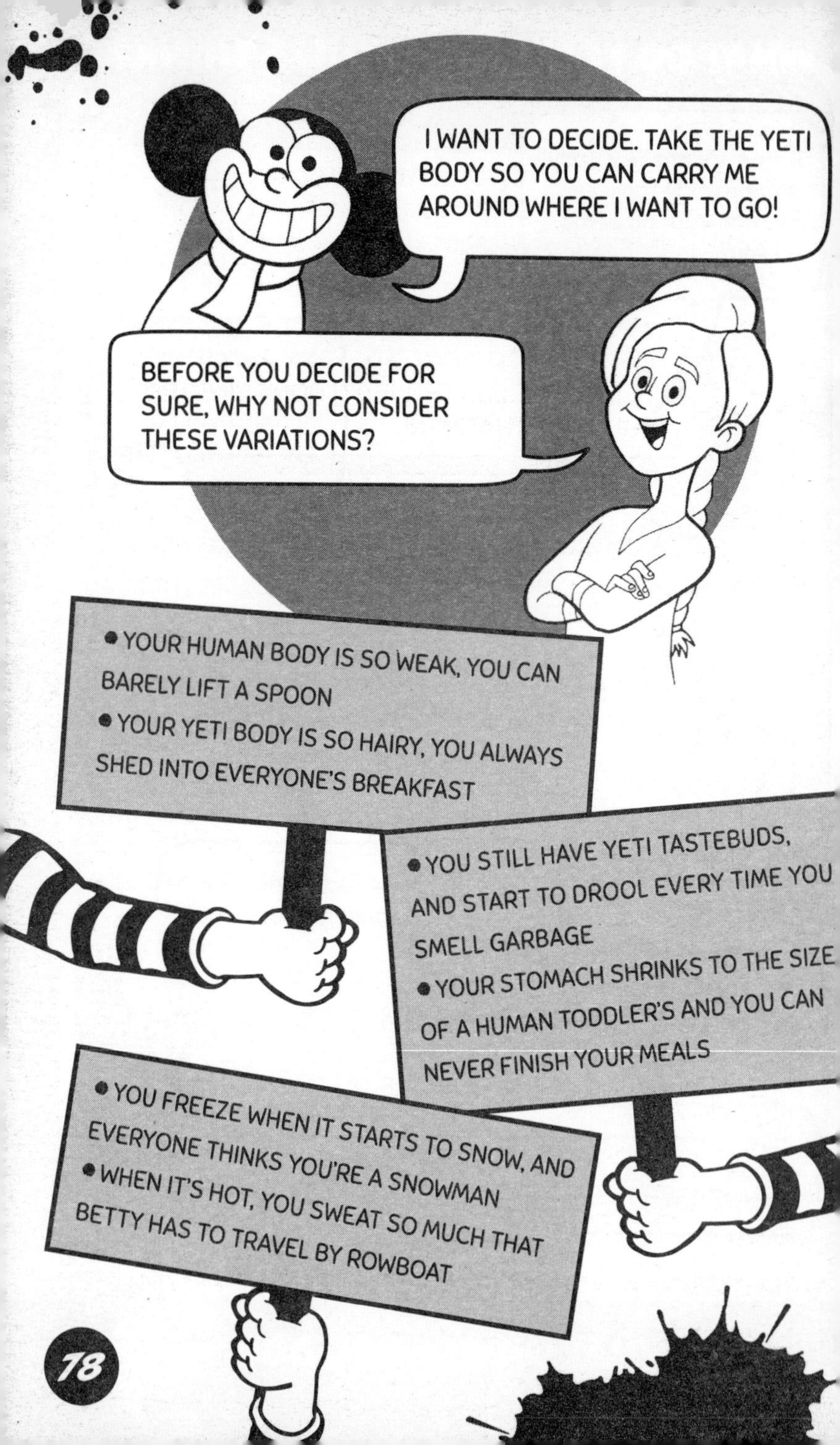
I WANT TO DECIDE. TAKE THE YETI BODY SO YOU CAN CARRY ME AROUND WHERE I WANT TO GO!
BEFORE YOU DECIDE FOR SURE, WHY NOT CONSIDER THESE VARIATIONS?
• YOUR HUMAN BODY IS SO WEAK, YOU CAN BARELY LIFT A SPOON
• YOUR YETI BODY IS SO HAIRY, YOU ALWAYS SHED INTO EVERYONE'S BREAKFAST
• YOU STILL HAVE YETI TASTEBUDS, AND START TO DROOL EVERY TIME YOU SMELL GARBAGE
• YOUR STOMACH SHRINKS TO THE SIZE OF A HUMAN TODDLER'S AND YOU CAN NEVER FINISH YOUR MEALS
• YOU FREEZE WHEN IT STARTS TO SNOW, AND EVERYONE THINKS YOU'RE A SNOWMAN
• WHEN IT'S HOT, YOU SWEAT SO MUCH THAT BETTY HAS TO TRAVEL BY ROWBOAT

NO SHEDDING ON MY WAFFLES! THAT'S MY NEW RULE.

YETI WANTS CAKE FOR BREAKFAST

 WHILE HAIRY CEREAL SOUNDS AWFUL, I WOULDN'T WANT TO STRUGGLE LIFTING EVEN A SPOON INTO MY MOUTH. WHAT ABOUT YETI TASTEBUDS THOUGH? I DON'T LIKE THE SOUND OF THAT MENU

YETI LIKES GARBAGE. SNACKS!

 YEAH, MAYBE YOU WOULD LEARN TO LIKE THAT GRUB! THAT MIGHT BE BETTER THAN NEVER BEING ABLE TO EAT A FULL MEAL – THINK OF THE WASTE! THEN AGAIN, I HAPPEN TO KNOW A DOG WHO WOULD LOVE TO EAT YETI LEFTOVERS.

GNASH!

I CAN ROW A BOAT THROUGH BEANOTOWN NO PROBLEM. BUT I CAN ALSO DRESS YETI UP IN A SPARKLY SCARF – WITH A CARROT FOR A NOSE – EVERY TIME IT SNOWS.

BUT YETI DON'T WANT TO BE FROZEN. YETI READS BOOKS ABOUT SNOWMAN BUT DOESN'T WANT TO BE ONE!

WHICH OPTION WOULD YOU CHOOSE WITH ALL THOSE VARIATIONS ADDED INTO THE MIX?

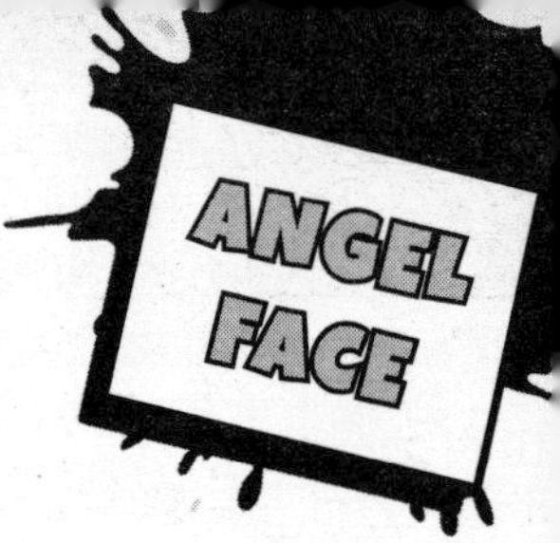
ANGEL FACE

'This looks like a mysterious machine,' Angel Face said as she arrived.

'Want to try it out?' Rubi asked.

'What's in it for me if I do?'

'It's a question all about you,' Rubi replied.

'Yeah . . . OK.'

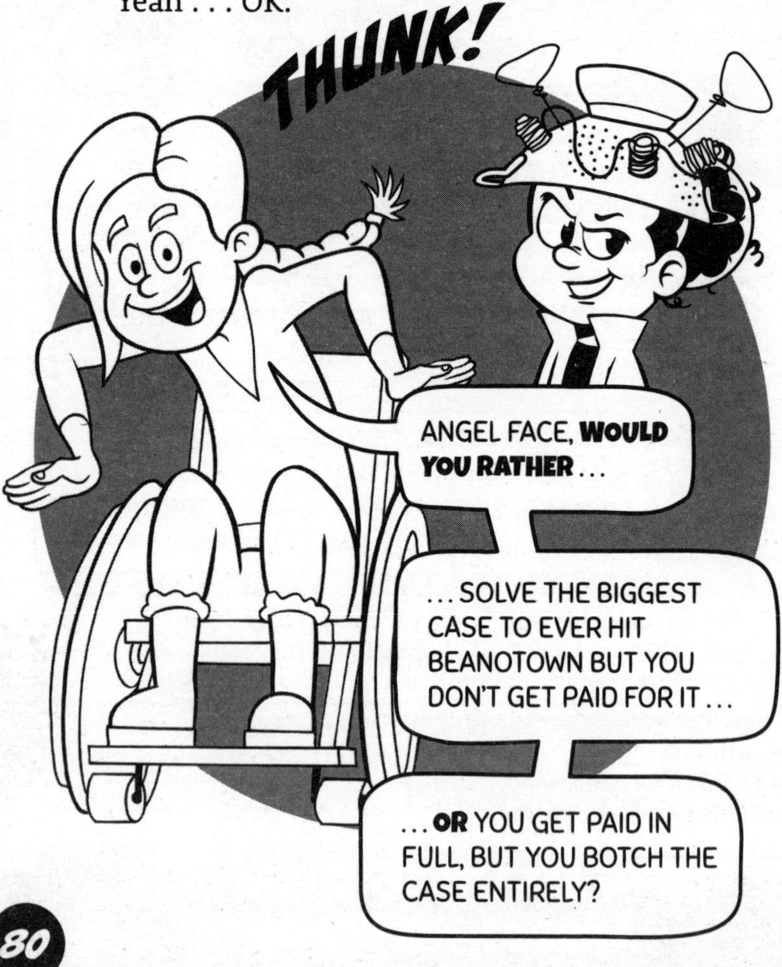
THUNK!
ANGEL FACE, **WOULD YOU RATHER** . . .
. . . SOLVE THE BIGGEST CASE TO EVER HIT BEANOTOWN BUT YOU DON'T GET PAID FOR IT . . .
. . . **OR** YOU GET PAID IN FULL, BUT YOU BOTCH THE CASE ENTIRELY?

WHAT DO ANGEL FACE'S NUMSKULLS THINK?

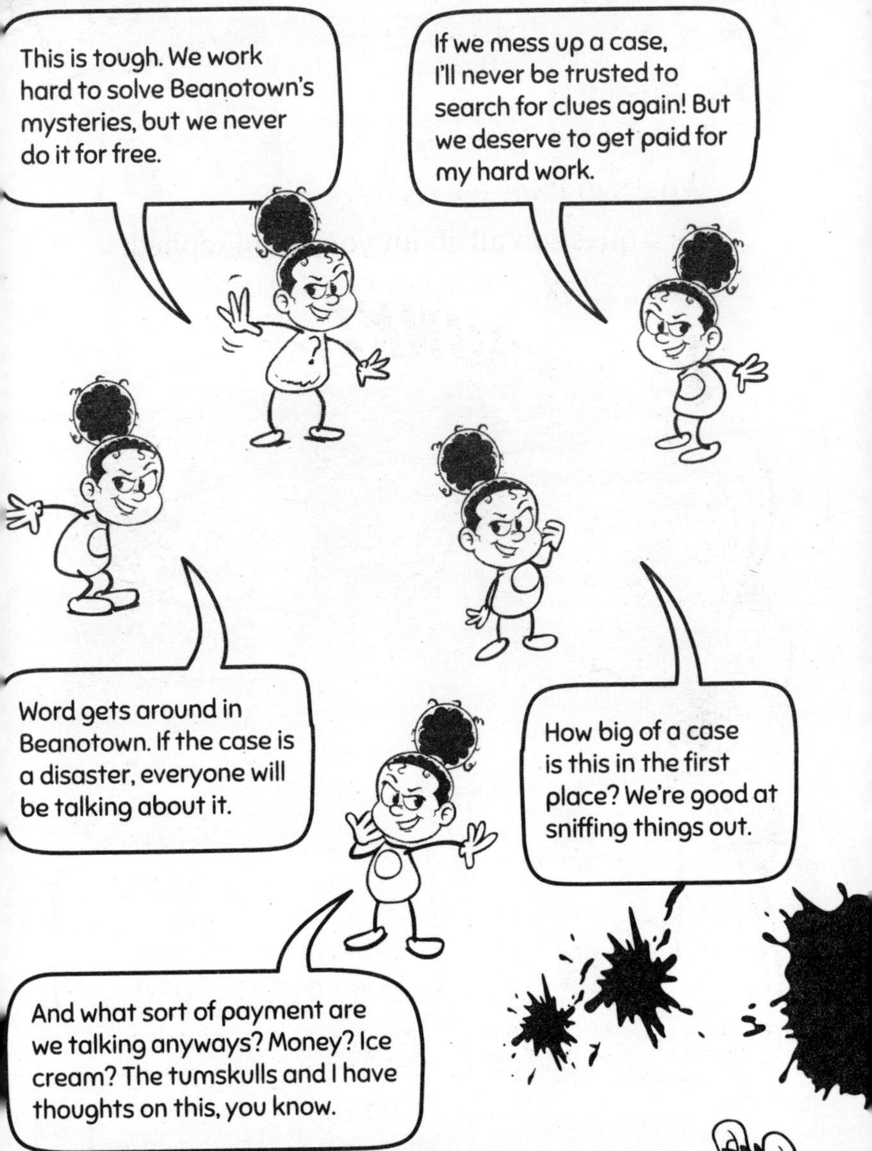

WHAT WOULD YOU DO?

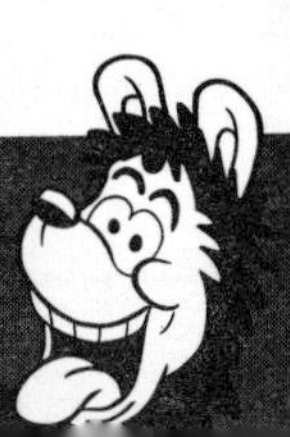

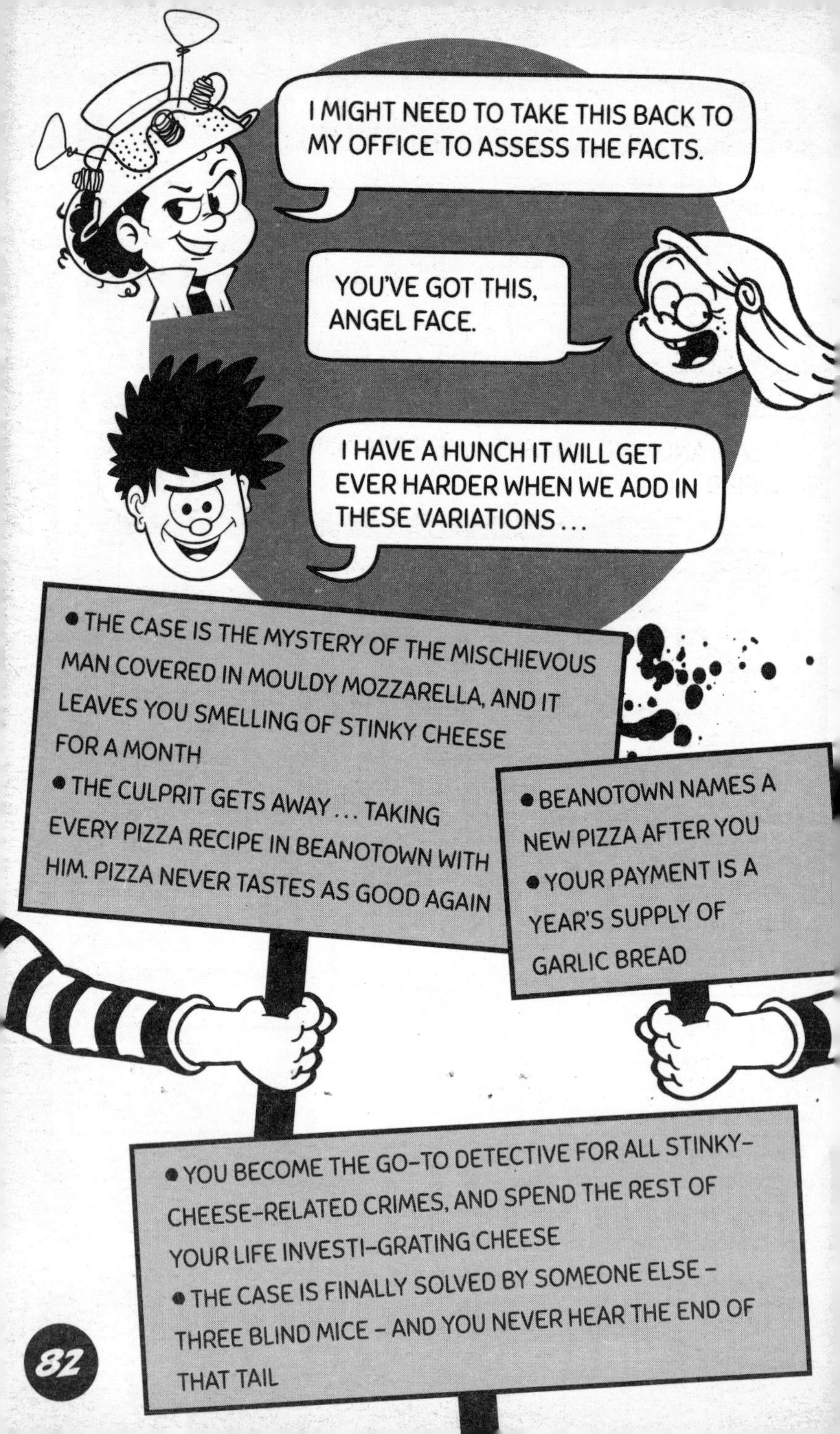
I MIGHT NEED TO TAKE THIS BACK TO MY OFFICE TO ASSESS THE FACTS.
YOU'VE GOT THIS, ANGEL FACE.
I HAVE A HUNCH IT WILL GET EVER HARDER WHEN WE ADD IN THESE VARIATIONS . . .
• THE CASE IS THE MYSTERY OF THE MISCHIEVOUS MAN COVERED IN MOULDY MOZZARELLA, AND IT LEAVES YOU SMELLING OF STINKY CHEESE FOR A MONTH
• THE CULPRIT GETS AWAY . . . TAKING EVERY PIZZA RECIPE IN BEANOTOWN WITH HIM. PIZZA NEVER TASTES AS GOOD AGAIN
• BEANOTOWN NAMES A NEW PIZZA AFTER YOU
• YOUR PAYMENT IS A YEAR'S SUPPLY OF GARLIC BREAD
• YOU BECOME THE GO-TO DETECTIVE FOR ALL STINKY-CHEESE-RELATED CRIMES, AND SPEND THE REST OF YOUR LIFE INVESTI-GRATING CHEESE
• THE CASE IS FINALLY SOLVED BY SOMEONE ELSE – THREE BLIND MICE – AND YOU NEVER HEAR THE END OF THAT TAIL

EWW! STINKY CHEESE? THAT'S *NACHO* FINEST MOMENT, EVEN IF YOU DID SOLVE THE CASE.

IT WOULD STINK UP MY OFFICE!

BUT IF YOU DON'T SOLVE THE CASE, THERE WILL BE NO MORE PIZZA IN BEANOTOWN!

YEAH, AND WHO DOESN'T LIKE PIZZA? ONLY WEIRD–DOUGHS!

'THE ANGEL FACE SUPREME' DOES HAVE A NICE RING TO IT. BUT ENOUGH GARLIC BREAD TO LAST ME AND JENNY ALL YEAR WOULD BE PRETTY SWEET.

YOU BREAD MY MIND.

YOU COULD BECOME FAMOUS IF YOU CRACK THE CASE, BUT YOU'D BE STUCK SOLVING SMELLY CHEESE CRIMES FOR THE REST OF YOUR LIFE.

IN THAT CASE, MAYBE I DON'T WANT TO SOLVE IT . . . BUT WAIT, HOW DID THREE BLIND MICE CRACK A CASE OPEN WHEN I COULDN'T? THEY CAN'T EVEN SEE!

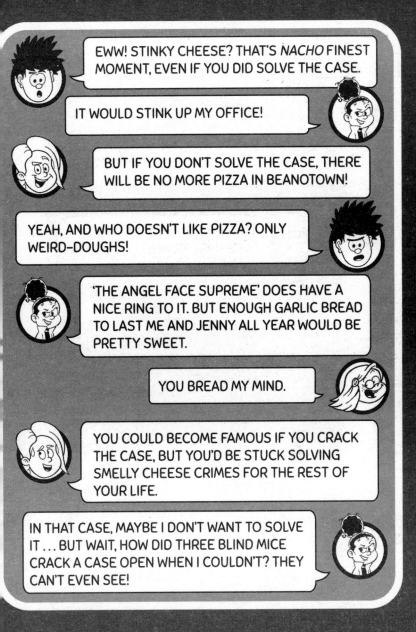

WHICH OPTION WOULD YOU CHOOSE WITH ALL THOSE VARIATIONS ADDED INTO THE MIX?

There was a loud CRASH from behind them.

'Oh, hello!' James called. 'Is this your latest invention? Gosh, I have to check this out!'

'Ok,' Rubi said nervously. 'Just put this on slowly and carefully . . .'

'Like this?' James said, thrusting it haphazardly on his head.

Rubi winced.

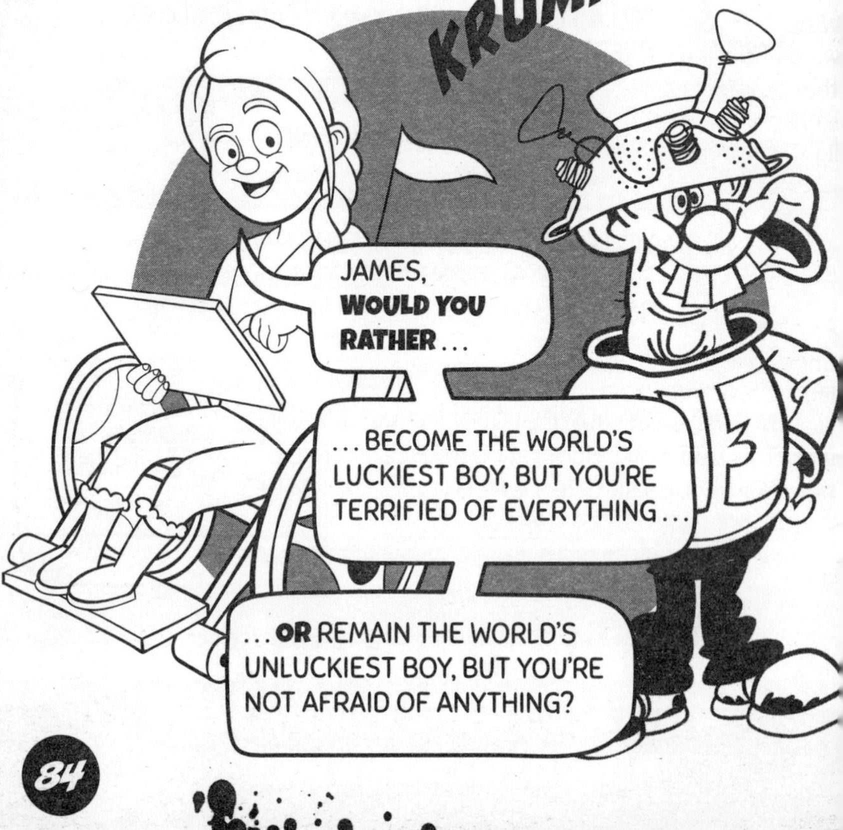
KRUMP!
JAMES, **WOULD YOU RATHER** . . .
. . . BECOME THE WORLD'S LUCKIEST BOY, BUT YOU'RE TERRIFIED OF EVERYTHING . . .
. . . **OR** REMAIN THE WORLD'S UNLUCKIEST BOY, BUT YOU'RE NOT AFRAID OF ANYTHING?

WHAT DO JAMES'S NUMSKULLS THINK?

I think our luck's about to change anyways! Let's just stretch our arms out while we think about that . . .

Look out! We just knocked into the back of Vito . . . who dropped her giant Pollution Pointer on Angel Face's toe. Oh well, could have been worse!

What sorts of things would we be terrified of? Loud thunderstorms? Surely not – I've only been struck by lightning a few times.

I've always wondered if good luck smells as amazing as it sounds. I grow tired of the smell of catastrophe.

Should we choose to live a life without fear? A life where we bite into any sandwich without even checking the filling for pebbles first?

WHAT WOULD YOU DO?

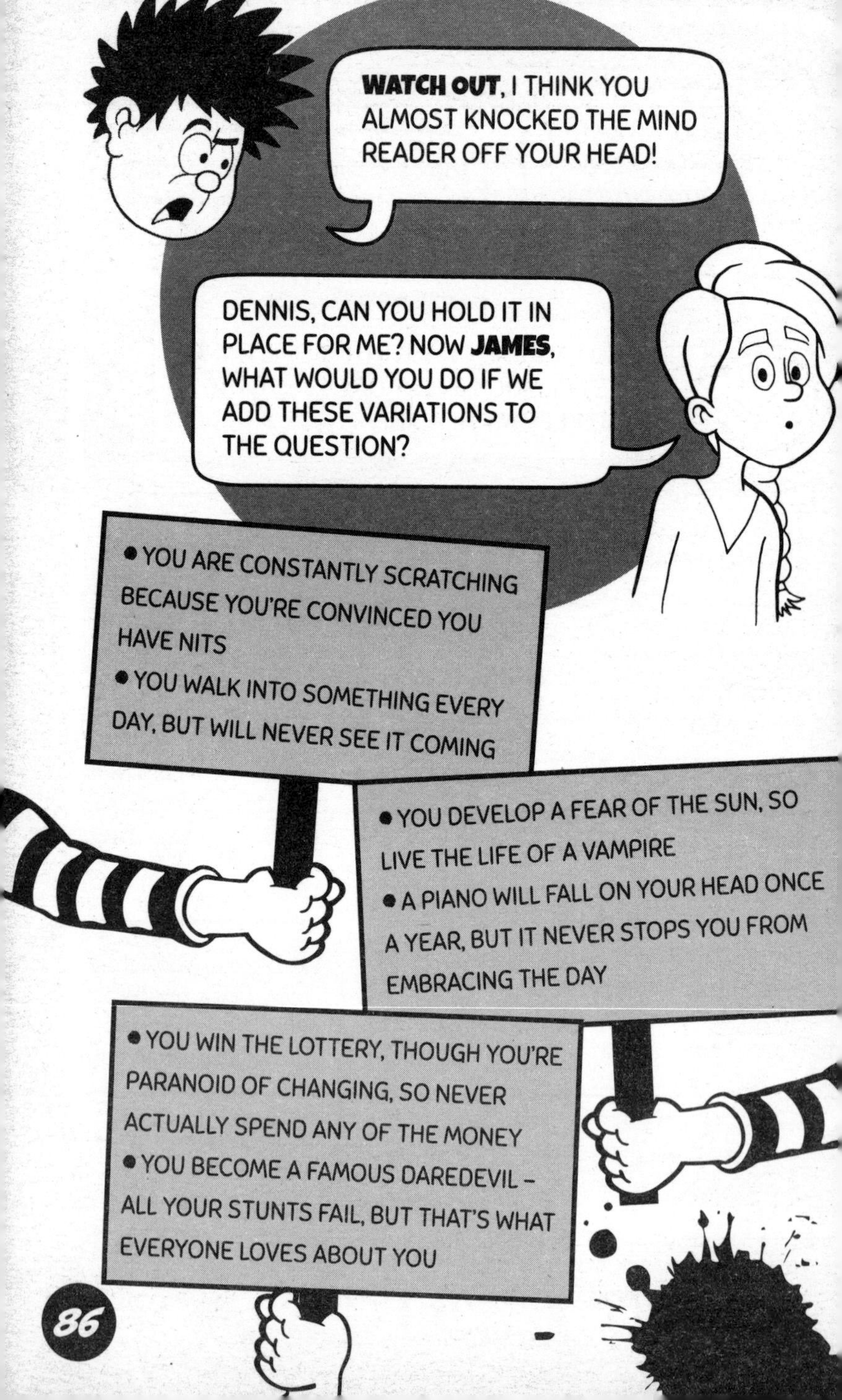
WATCH OUT, I THINK YOU ALMOST KNOCKED THE MIND READER OFF YOUR HEAD!
DENNIS, CAN YOU HOLD IT IN PLACE FOR ME? NOW **JAMES**, WHAT WOULD YOU DO IF WE ADD THESE VARIATIONS TO THE QUESTION?
• YOU ARE CONSTANTLY SCRATCHING BECAUSE YOU'RE CONVINCED YOU HAVE NITS
• YOU WALK INTO SOMETHING EVERY DAY, BUT WILL NEVER SEE IT COMING
• YOU DEVELOP A FEAR OF THE SUN, SO LIVE THE LIFE OF A VAMPIRE
• A PIANO WILL FALL ON YOUR HEAD ONCE A YEAR, BUT IT NEVER STOPS YOU FROM EMBRACING THE DAY
• YOU WIN THE LOTTERY, THOUGH YOU'RE PARANOID OF CHANGING, SO NEVER ACTUALLY SPEND ANY OF THE MONEY
• YOU BECOME A FAMOUS DAREDEVIL – ALL YOUR STUNTS FAIL, BUT THAT'S WHAT EVERYONE LOVES ABOUT YOU

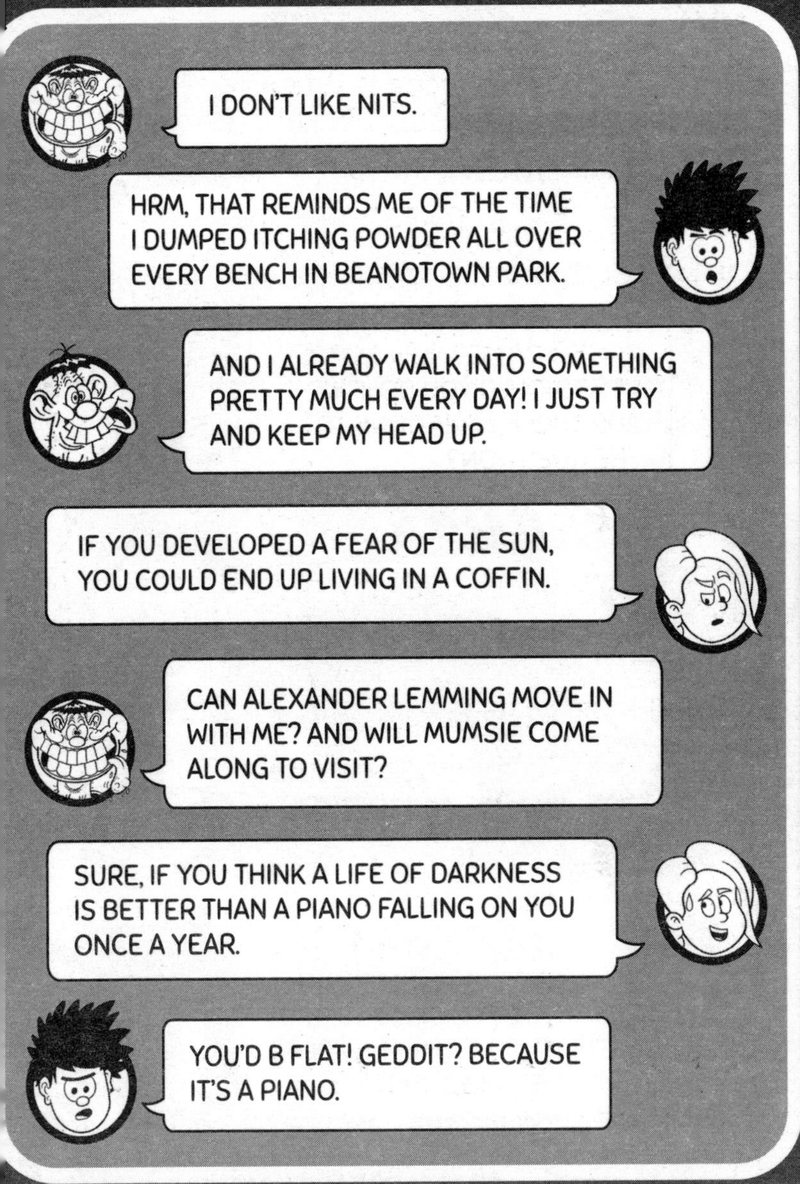
I DON'T LIKE NITS.
HRM, THAT REMINDS ME OF THE TIME I DUMPED ITCHING POWDER ALL OVER EVERY BENCH IN BEANOTOWN PARK.
AND I ALREADY WALK INTO SOMETHING PRETTY MUCH EVERY DAY! I JUST TRY AND KEEP MY HEAD UP.
IF YOU DEVELOPED A FEAR OF THE SUN, YOU COULD END UP LIVING IN A COFFIN.
CAN ALEXANDER LEMMING MOVE IN WITH ME? AND WILL MUMSIE COME ALONG TO VISIT?
SURE, IF YOU THINK A LIFE OF DARKNESS IS BETTER THAN A PIANO FALLING ON YOU ONCE A YEAR.
YOU'D B FLAT! GEDDIT? BECAUSE IT'S A PIANO.

WHICH OPTION WOULD YOU CHOOSE WITH ALL THOSE VARIATIONS ADDED INTO THE MIX?

Roger the Dodger had snuck up without anyone noticing.

'Wow, cool machine!' he said. 'Does it involve any hard work?'

'Building it, yes,' Rubi said. 'Testing it, no.'

'Wanna give it a try?' asked Dennis.

'Sure!'

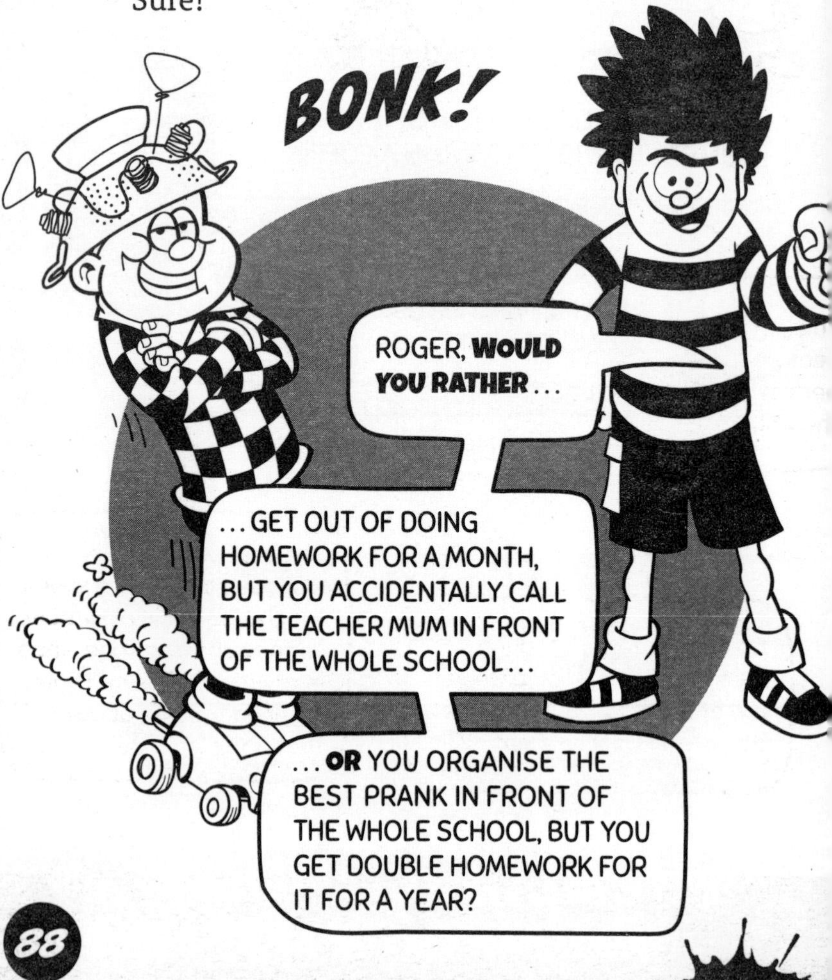
BONK!
ROGER, **WOULD YOU RATHER** . . .
. . . GET OUT OF DOING HOMEWORK FOR A MONTH, BUT YOU ACCIDENTALLY CALL THE TEACHER MUM IN FRONT OF THE WHOLE SCHOOL . . .
. . . **OR** YOU ORGANISE THE BEST PRANK IN FRONT OF THE WHOLE SCHOOL, BUT YOU GET DOUBLE HOMEWORK FOR IT FOR A YEAR?

WHAT DO ROGER'S NUMSKULLS THINK?

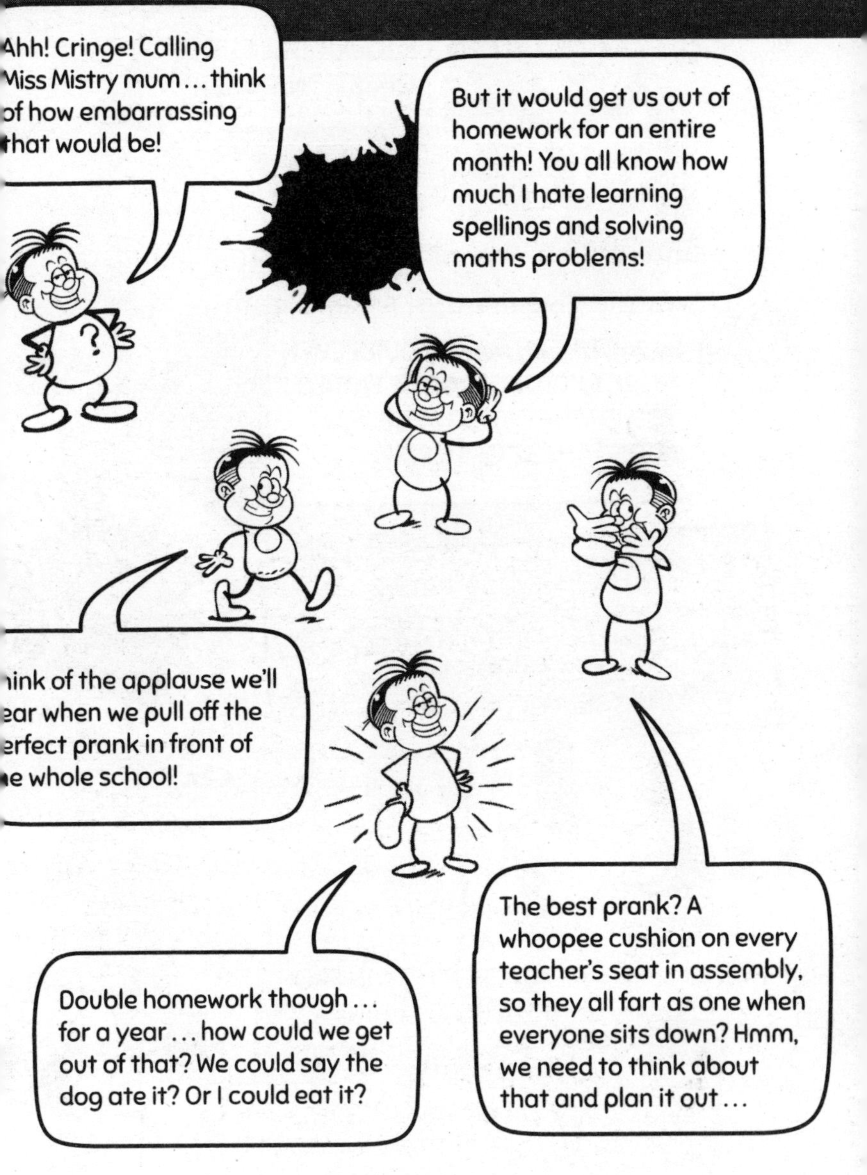
Ahh! Cringe! Calling Miss Mistry mum . . . think of how embarrassing that would be!
But it would get us out of homework for an entire month! You all know how much I hate learning spellings and solving maths problems!
ink of the applause we'll ear when we pull off the erfect prank in front of e whole school!
The best prank? A whoopee cushion on every teacher's seat in assembly, so they all fart as one when everyone sits down? Hmm, we need to think about that and plan it out . . .
Double homework though . . . for a year . . . how could we get out of that? We could say the dog ate it? Or I could eat it?

WHAT WOULD YOU DO?

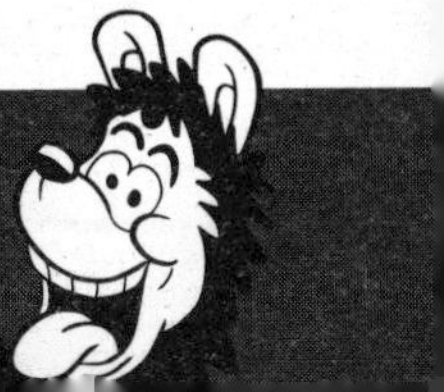

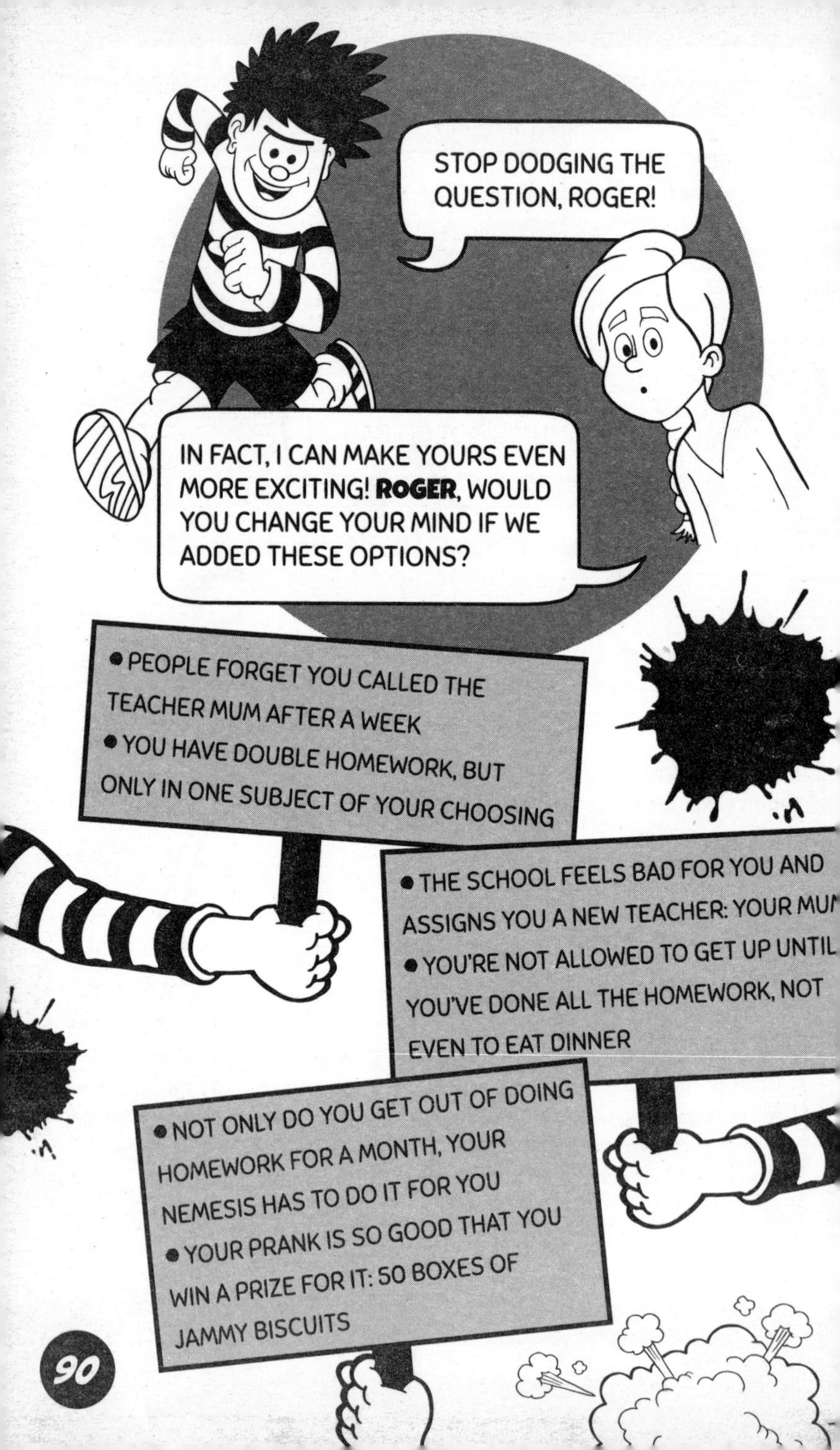
STOP DODGING THE QUESTION, ROGER!
IN FACT, I CAN MAKE YOURS EVEN MORE EXCITING! **ROGER**, WOULD YOU CHANGE YOUR MIND IF WE ADDED THESE OPTIONS?
• PEOPLE FORGET YOU CALLED THE TEACHER MUM AFTER A WEEK
• YOU HAVE DOUBLE HOMEWORK, BUT ONLY IN ONE SUBJECT OF YOUR CHOOSING
• THE SCHOOL FEELS BAD FOR YOU AND ASSIGNS YOU A NEW TEACHER: YOUR MU
• YOU'RE NOT ALLOWED TO GET UP UNTIL YOU'VE DONE ALL THE HOMEWORK, NOT EVEN TO EAT DINNER
• NOT ONLY DO YOU GET OUT OF DOING HOMEWORK FOR A MONTH, YOUR NEMESIS HAS TO DO IT FOR YOU
• YOUR PRANK IS SO GOOD THAT YOU WIN A PRIZE FOR IT: 50 BOXES OF JAMMY BISCUITS

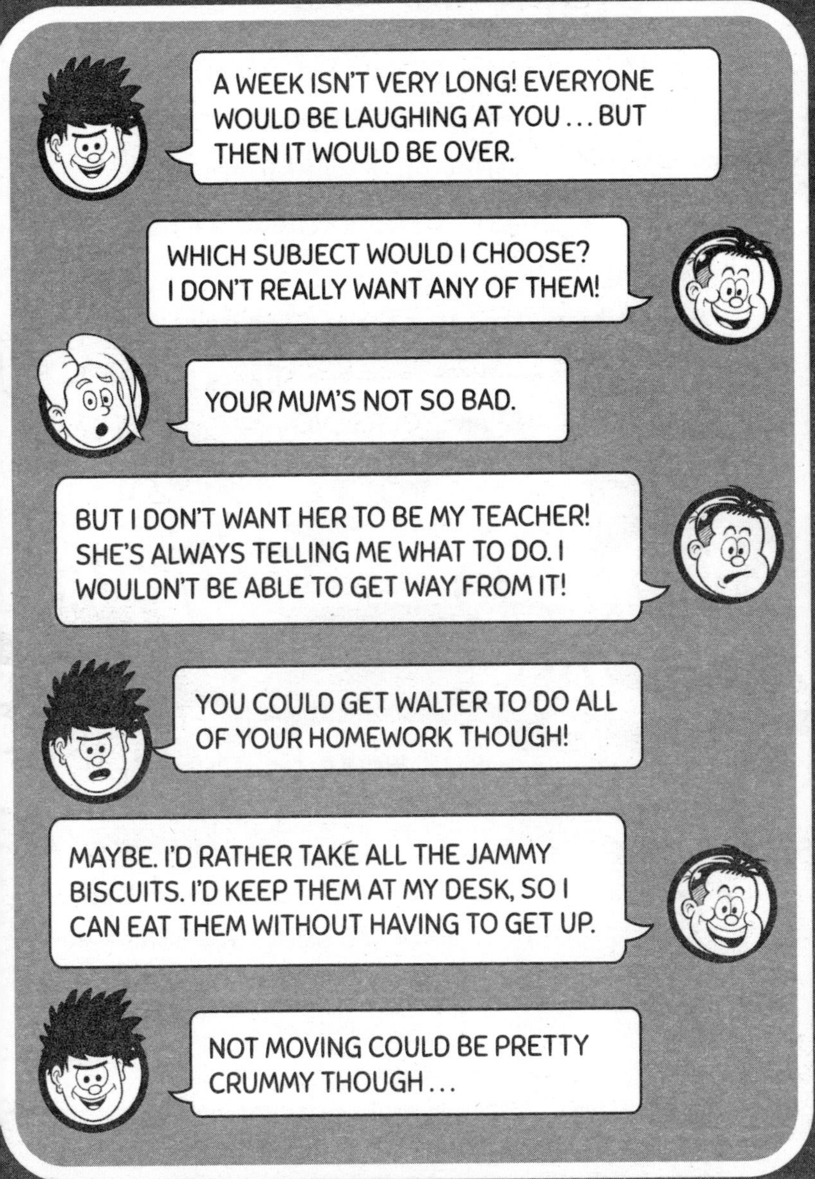
A WEEK ISN'T VERY LONG! EVERYONE WOULD BE LAUGHING AT YOU . . . BUT THEN IT WOULD BE OVER.
WHICH SUBJECT WOULD I CHOOSE? I DON'T REALLY WANT ANY OF THEM!
YOUR MUM'S NOT SO BAD.
BUT I DON'T WANT HER TO BE MY TEACHER! SHE'S ALWAYS TELLING ME WHAT TO DO. I WOULDN'T BE ABLE TO GET WAY FROM IT!
YOU COULD GET WALTER TO DO ALL OF YOUR HOMEWORK THOUGH!
MAYBE. I'D RATHER TAKE ALL THE JAMMY BISCUITS. I'D KEEP THEM AT MY DESK, SO I CAN EAT THEM WITHOUT HAVING TO GET UP.
NOT MOVING COULD BE PRETTY CRUMMY THOUGH . . .

WHICH OPTION WOULD YOU CHOOSE WITH ALL THOSE VARIATIONS ADDED INTO THE MIX?

BILLY WHIZZ

A bred blur whizzed past.

'Hey Billy, want to try out our science project?' Dennis called. 'It's fast becoming a hit!'

Billy Whizz came to a screeching halt. 'OK!'

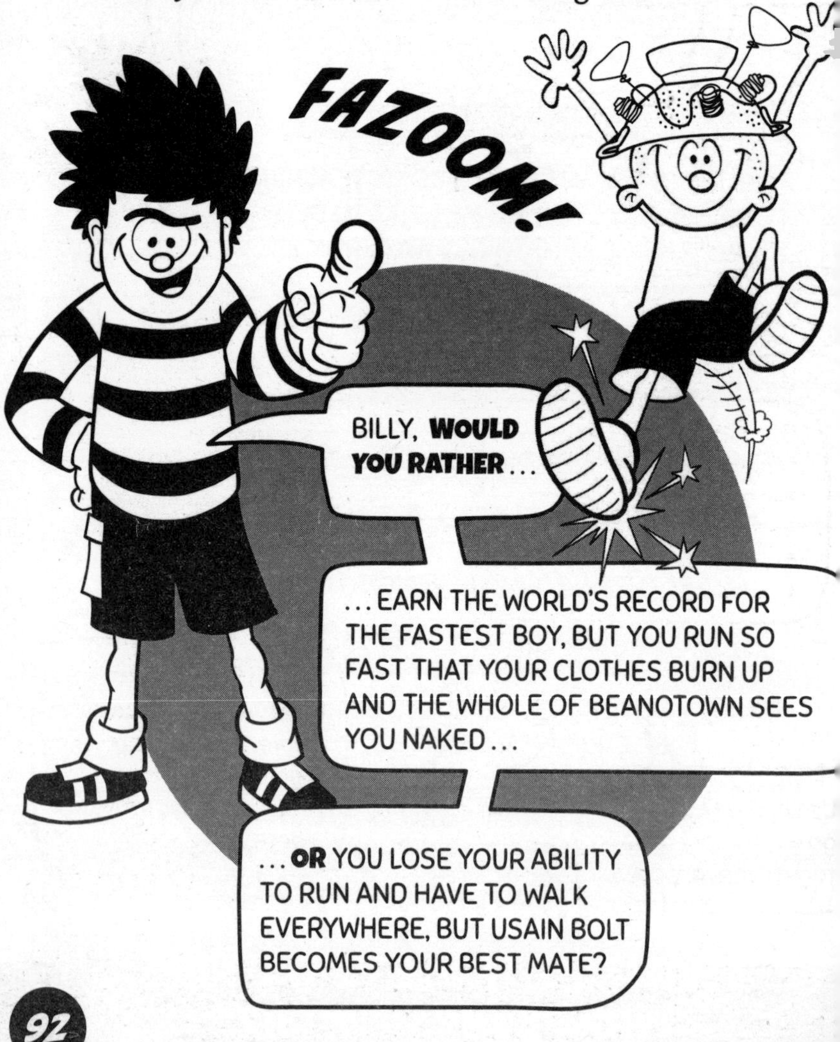

FAZOOM!
BILLY, **WOULD YOU RATHER**...
... EARN THE WORLD'S RECORD FOR THE FASTEST BOY, BUT YOU RUN SO FAST THAT YOUR CLOTHES BURN UP AND THE WHOLE OF BEANOTOWN SEES YOU NAKED...
... **OR** YOU LOSE YOUR ABILITY TO RUN AND HAVE TO WALK EVERYWHERE, BUT USAIN BOLT BECOMES YOUR BEST MATE?

WHAT DO BILLY WHIZZ'S NUMSKULLS THINK?

The entire town would see us naked? That would be so embarrassing! But we could run away quickly. There's a chance they won't see us for more than a second . . .

When she says that our clothes will burn up, does that include our trainers? I would hate to see those go up in flames!

Usain Bolt is my hero! I'd love to listen to him tell us all about his most famous races. And being his best mate would be totally awesome!

If we have to walk everywhere, I'd have more time to stop and sniff the flowers. Wait, what am I saying? I hate flowers!

Usain and I could go out for fast food together every day . . .

WHAT WOULD YOU DO?

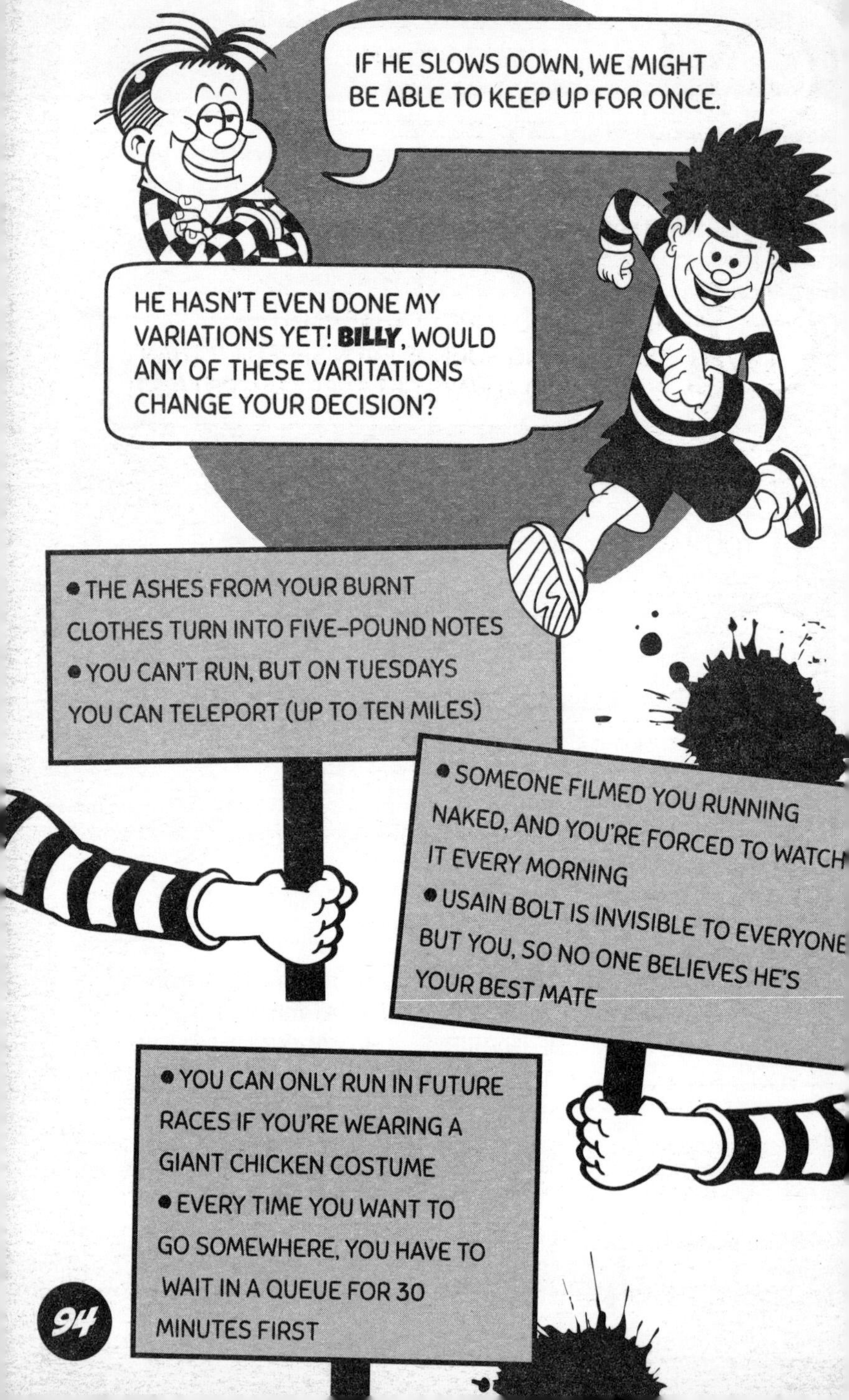

IF HE SLOWS DOWN, WE MIGHT BE ABLE TO KEEP UP FOR ONCE.
HE HASN'T EVEN DONE MY VARIATIONS YET! **BILLY**, WOULD ANY OF THESE VARITATIONS CHANGE YOUR DECISION?
• THE ASHES FROM YOUR BURNT CLOTHES TURN INTO FIVE-POUND NOTES
• YOU CAN'T RUN, BUT ON TUESDAYS YOU CAN TELEPORT (UP TO TEN MILES)
• SOMEONE FILMED YOU RUNNING NAKED, AND YOU'RE FORCED TO WATCH IT EVERY MORNING
• USAIN BOLT IS INVISIBLE TO EVERYONE BUT YOU, SO NO ONE BELIEVES HE'S YOUR BEST MATE
• YOU CAN ONLY RUN IN FUTURE RACES IF YOU'RE WEARING A GIANT CHICKEN COSTUME
• EVERY TIME YOU WANT TO GO SOMEWHERE, YOU HAVE TO WAIT IN A QUEUE FOR 30 MINUTES FIRST

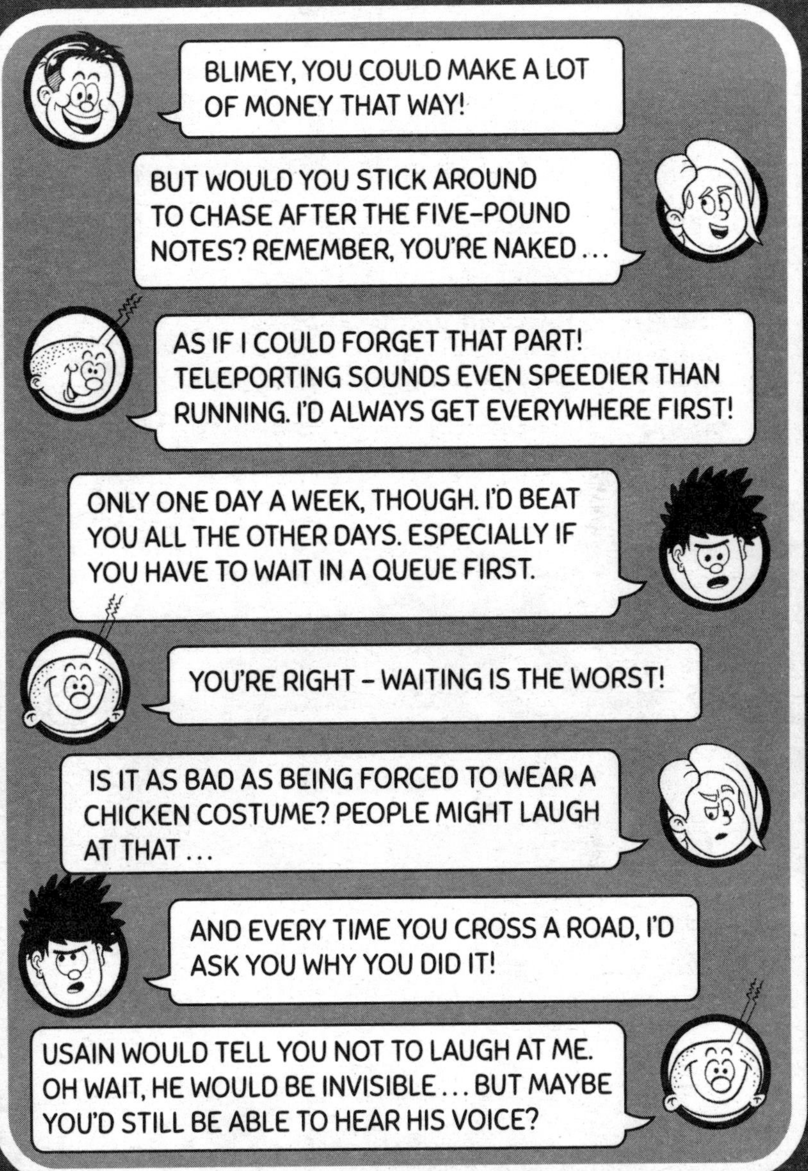
BLIMEY, YOU COULD MAKE A LOT OF MONEY THAT WAY!
BUT WOULD YOU STICK AROUND TO CHASE AFTER THE FIVE-POUND NOTES? REMEMBER, YOU'RE NAKED …
AS IF I COULD FORGET THAT PART! TELEPORTING SOUNDS EVEN SPEEDIER THAN RUNNING. I'D ALWAYS GET EVERYWHERE FIRST!
ONLY ONE DAY A WEEK, THOUGH. I'D BEAT YOU ALL THE OTHER DAYS. ESPECIALLY IF YOU HAVE TO WAIT IN A QUEUE FIRST.
YOU'RE RIGHT – WAITING IS THE WORST!
IS IT AS BAD AS BEING FORCED TO WEAR A CHICKEN COSTUME? PEOPLE MIGHT LAUGH AT THAT …
AND EVERY TIME YOU CROSS A ROAD, I'D ASK YOU WHY YOU DID IT!
USAIN WOULD TELL YOU NOT TO LAUGH AT ME. OH WAIT, HE WOULD BE INVISIBLE … BUT MAYBE YOU'D STILL BE ABLE TO HEAR HIS VOICE?

WHICH OPTION WOULD YOU CHOOSE WITH ALL THOSE VARIATIONS ADDED INTO THE MIX?

DANGEROUS DAN

'Hey, Dan!' Dennis called.

'Hi, Dennis. Are you about to ask me if I'd like to participate in Rubi's MIND control machine?'

'Yeah . . . how did you know?'

'I have my ways,' Dan replied mysteriously.

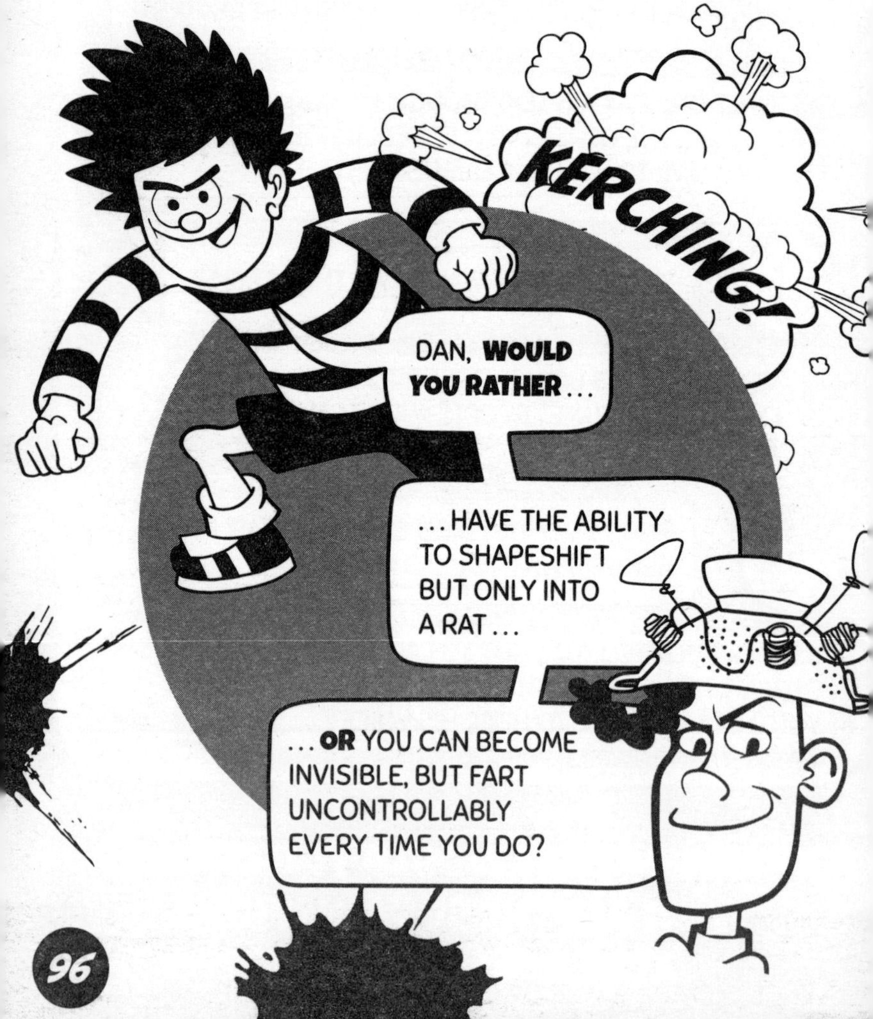
KERCHING!
DAN, **WOULD YOU RATHER** . . .
. . . HAVE THE ABILITY TO SHAPESHIFT BUT ONLY INTO A RAT . . .
. . . **OR** YOU CAN BECOME INVISIBLE, BUT FART UNCONTROLLABLY EVERY TIME YOU DO?

WHAT DO DAN'S NUMSKULLS THINK?

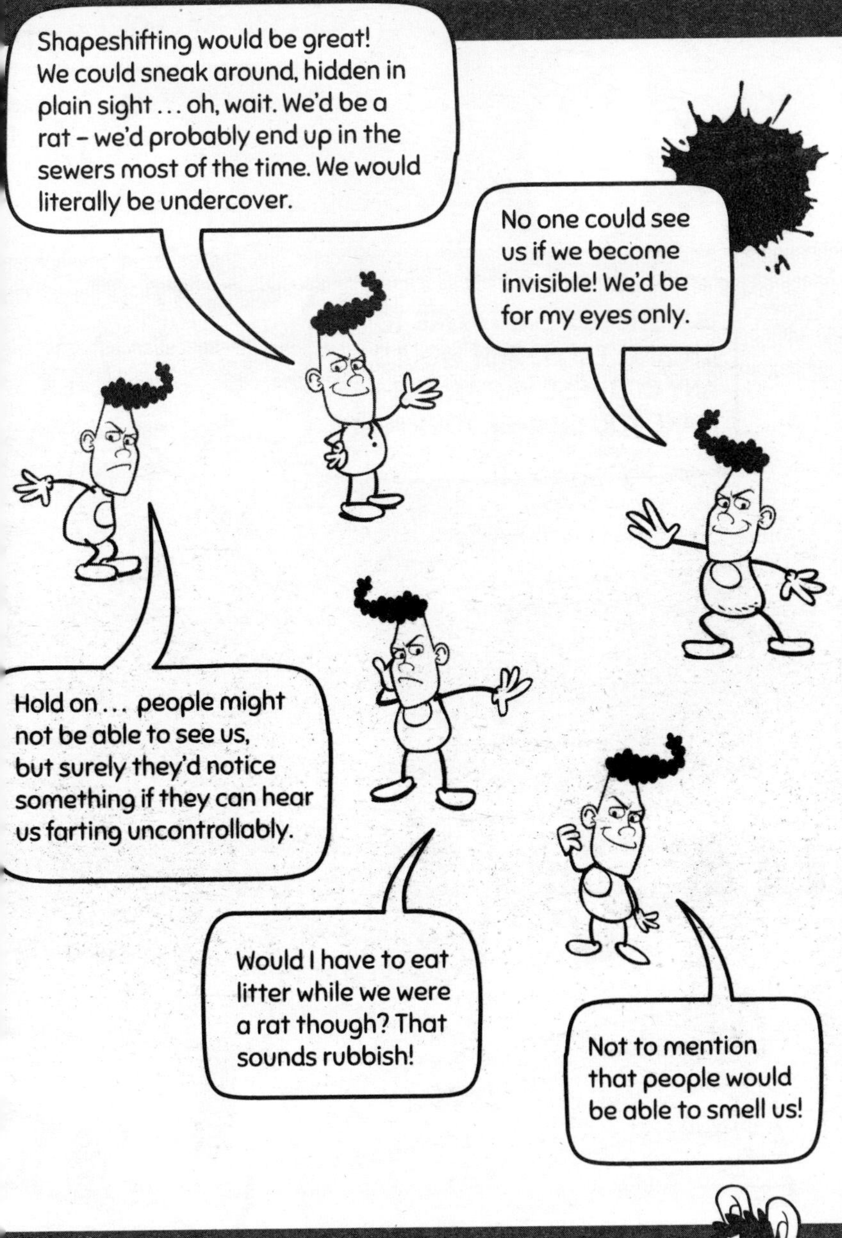

WHAT WOULD YOU DO?

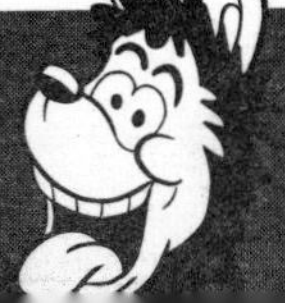

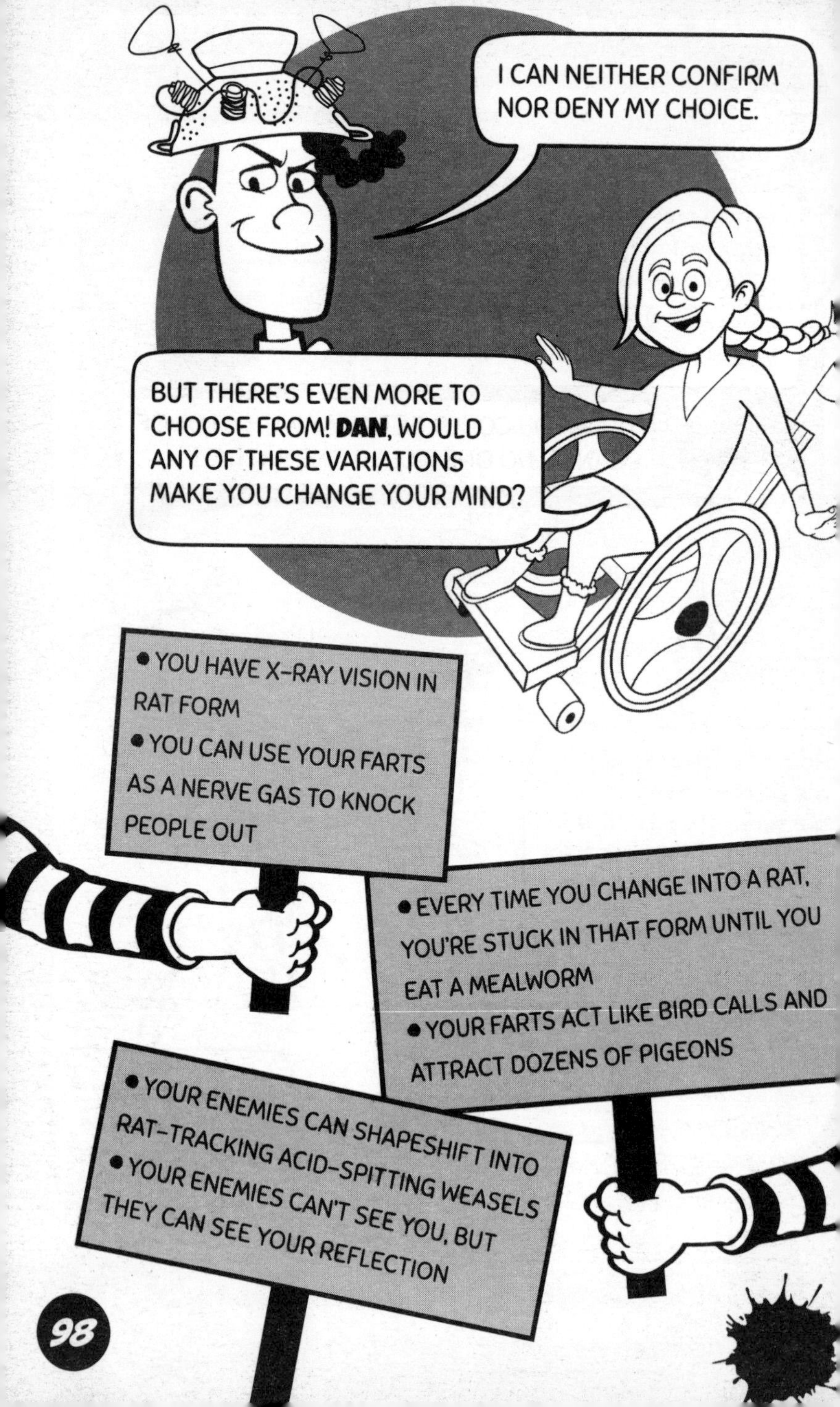
I CAN NEITHER CONFIRM NOR DENY MY CHOICE.
BUT THERE'S EVEN MORE TO CHOOSE FROM! **DAN**, WOULD ANY OF THESE VARIATIONS MAKE YOU CHANGE YOUR MIND?
• YOU HAVE X-RAY VISION IN RAT FORM
• YOU CAN USE YOUR FARTS AS A NERVE GAS TO KNOCK PEOPLE OUT
• EVERY TIME YOU CHANGE INTO A RAT, YOU'RE STUCK IN THAT FORM UNTIL YOU EAT A MEALWORM
• YOUR FARTS ACT LIKE BIRD CALLS AND ATTRACT DOZENS OF PIGEONS
• YOUR ENEMIES CAN SHAPESHIFT INTO RAT-TRACKING ACID-SPITTING WEASELS
• YOUR ENEMIES CAN'T SEE YOU, BUT THEY CAN SEE YOUR REFLECTION

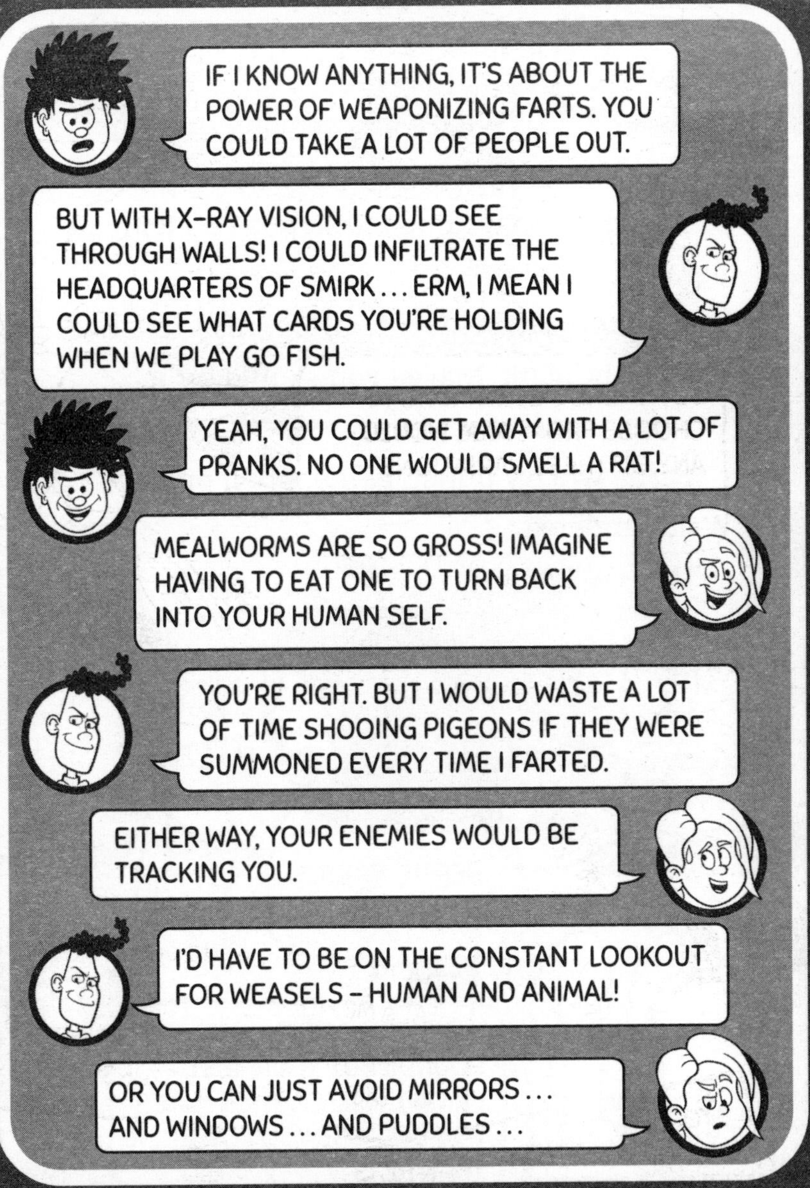
IF I KNOW ANYTHING, IT'S ABOUT THE POWER OF WEAPONIZING FARTS. YOU COULD TAKE A LOT OF PEOPLE OUT.
BUT WITH X-RAY VISION, I COULD SEE THROUGH WALLS! I COULD INFILTRATE THE HEADQUARTERS OF SMIRK . . . ERM, I MEAN I COULD SEE WHAT CARDS YOU'RE HOLDING WHEN WE PLAY GO FISH.
YEAH, YOU COULD GET AWAY WITH A LOT OF PRANKS. NO ONE WOULD SMELL A RAT!
MEALWORMS ARE SO GROSS! IMAGINE HAVING TO EAT ONE TO TURN BACK INTO YOUR HUMAN SELF.
YOU'RE RIGHT. BUT I WOULD WASTE A LOT OF TIME SHOOING PIGEONS IF THEY WERE SUMMONED EVERY TIME I FARTED.
EITHER WAY, YOUR ENEMIES WOULD BE TRACKING YOU.
I'D HAVE TO BE ON THE CONSTANT LOOKOUT FOR WEASELS – HUMAN AND ANIMAL!
OR YOU CAN JUST AVOID MIRRORS . . . AND WINDOWS . . . AND PUDDLES . . .

WHICH OPTION WOULD YOU CHOOSE WITH ALL THOSE VARIATIONS ADDED INTO THE MIX?

'What's this dreadful machine?' Walter sneered. 'It looks like a piece of junk that someone stepped on with an ugly, old shoe.'

'It's Rubi's latest invention,' Dennis explained. 'And it's brilliant. Maybe you should try it, Walter . . . unless you're scared.'

'Bertie will try it first. Bertie, put it on now,' Walter ordered.

'Um, OK Walter!'

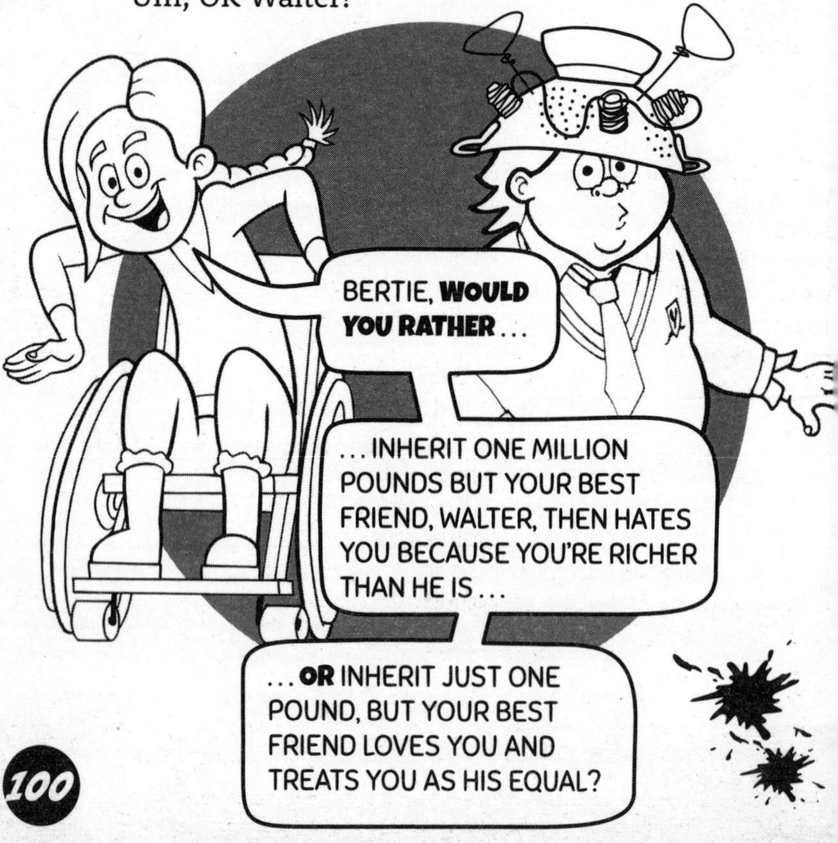
BERTIE, **WOULD YOU RATHER** . . .
. . . INHERIT ONE MILLION POUNDS BUT YOUR BEST FRIEND, WALTER, THEN HATES YOU BECAUSE YOU'RE RICHER THAN HE IS . . .
. . . **OR** INHERIT JUST ONE POUND, BUT YOUR BEST FRIEND LOVES YOU AND TREATS YOU AS HIS EQUAL?

WHAT DO BERTIE'S NUMSKULLS THINK?

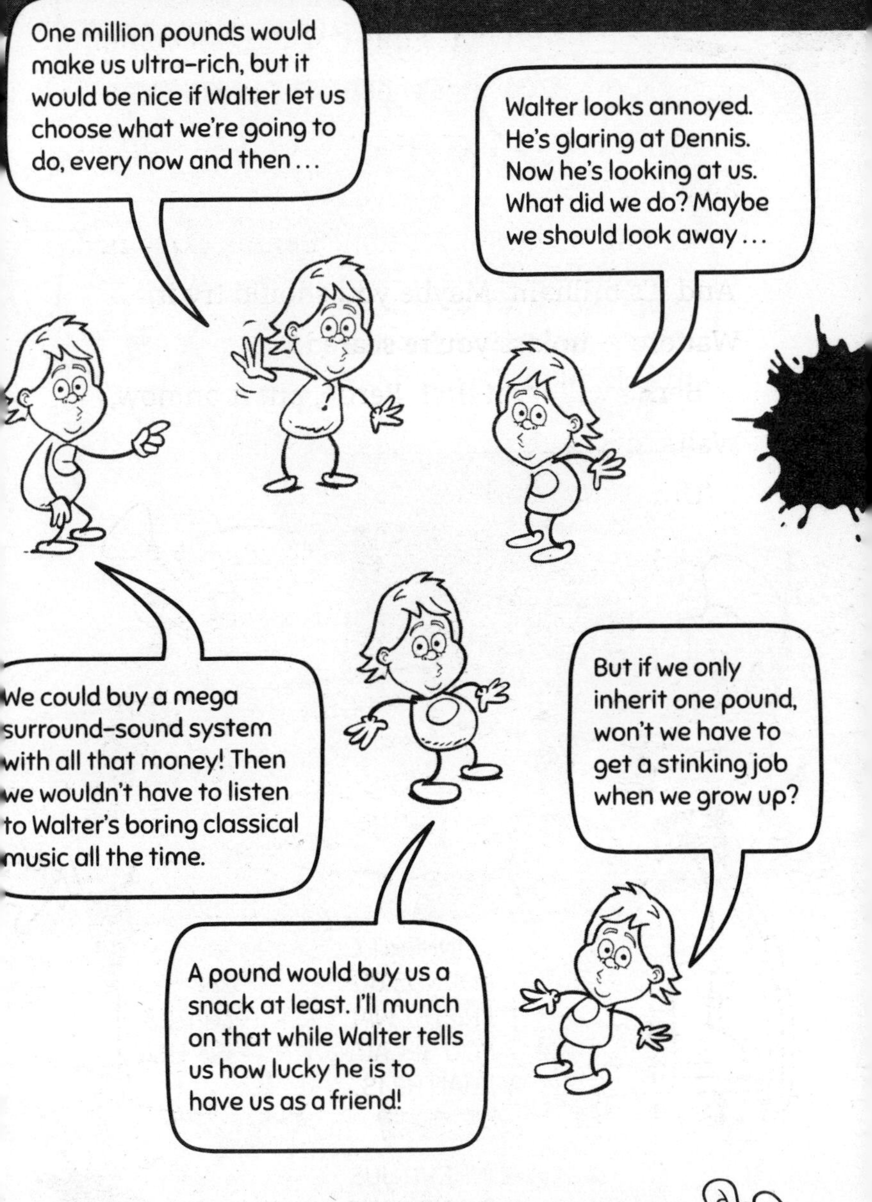
One million pounds would make us ultra-rich, but it would be nice if Walter let us choose what we're going to do, every now and then . . .
Walter looks annoyed. He's glaring at Dennis. Now he's looking at us. What did we do? Maybe we should look away . . .
We could buy a mega surround-sound system with all that money! Then we wouldn't have to listen to Walter's boring classical music all the time.
But if we only inherit one pound, won't we have to get a stinking job when we grow up?
A pound would buy us a snack at least. I'll munch on that while Walter tells us how lucky he is to have us as a friend!

WHAT WOULD YOU DO?

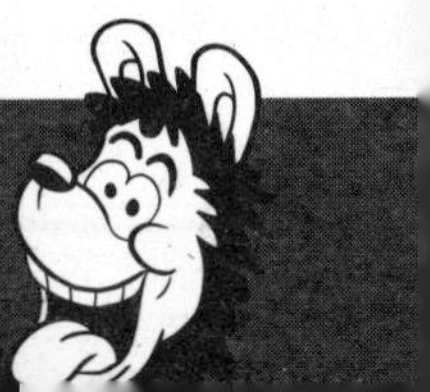

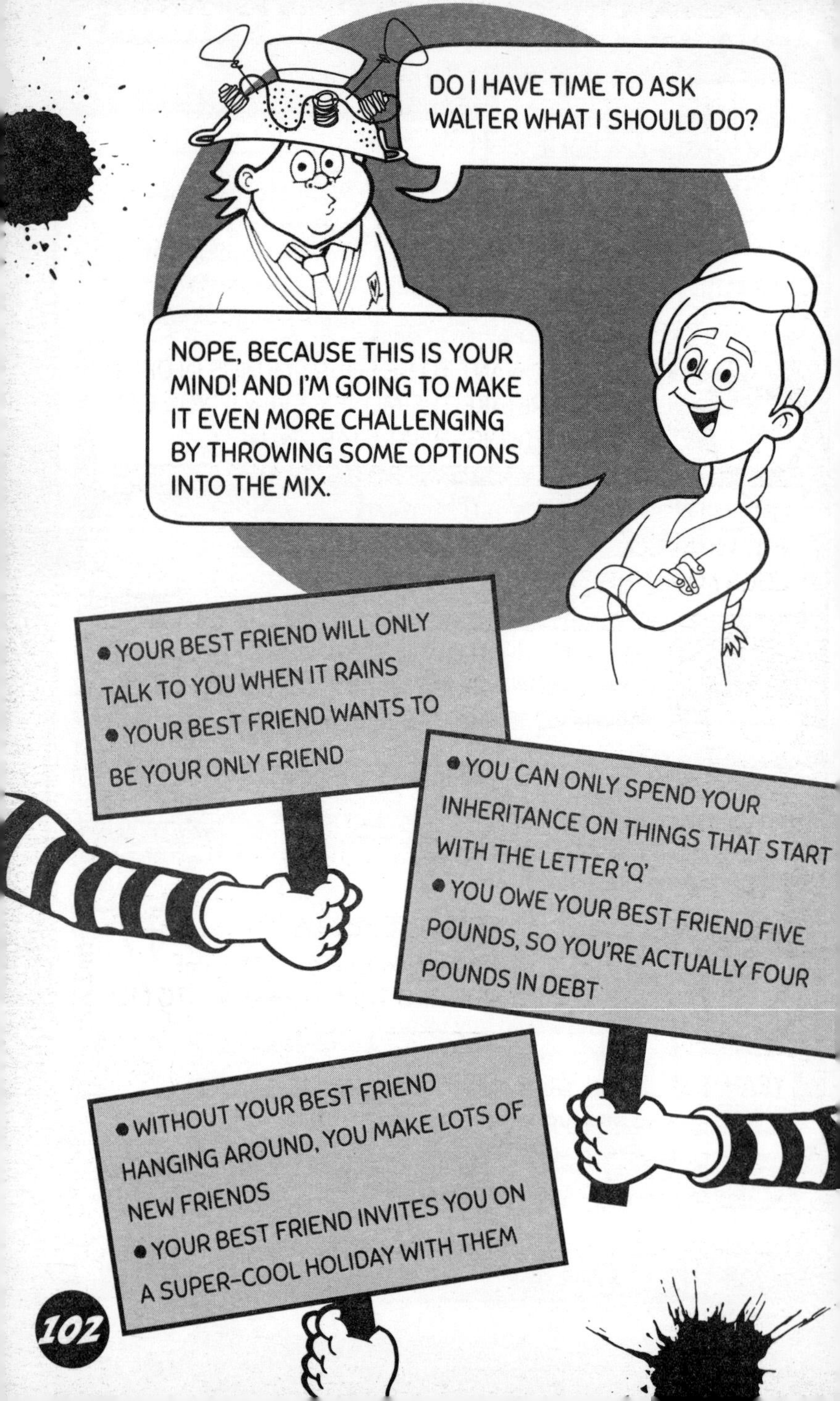
DO I HAVE TIME TO ASK WALTER WHAT I SHOULD DO?
NOPE, BECAUSE THIS IS YOUR MIND! AND I'M GOING TO MAKE IT EVEN MORE CHALLENGING BY THROWING SOME OPTIONS INTO THE MIX.
• YOUR BEST FRIEND WILL ONLY TALK TO YOU WHEN IT RAINS
• YOUR BEST FRIEND WANTS TO BE YOUR ONLY FRIEND
• YOU CAN ONLY SPEND YOUR INHERITANCE ON THINGS THAT START WITH THE LETTER 'Q'
• YOU OWE YOUR BEST FRIEND FIVE POUNDS, SO YOU'RE ACTUALLY FOUR POUNDS IN DEBT
• WITHOUT YOUR BEST FRIEND HANGING AROUND, YOU MAKE LOTS OF NEW FRIENDS
• YOUR BEST FRIEND INVITES YOU ON A SUPER-COOL HOLIDAY WITH THEM

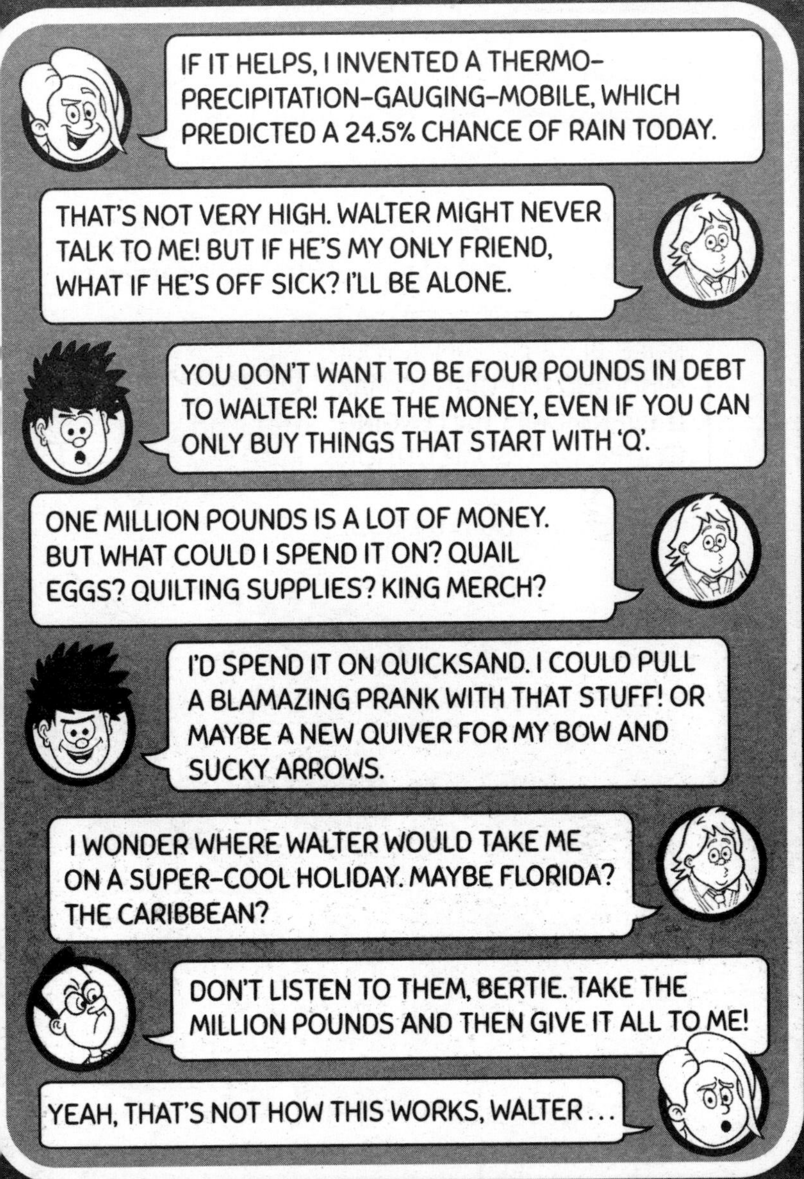
IF IT HELPS, I INVENTED A THERMO-PRECIPITATION-GAUGING-MOBILE, WHICH PREDICTED A 24.5% CHANCE OF RAIN TODAY.
THAT'S NOT VERY HIGH. WALTER MIGHT NEVER TALK TO ME! BUT IF HE'S MY ONLY FRIEND, WHAT IF HE'S OFF SICK? I'LL BE ALONE.
YOU DON'T WANT TO BE FOUR POUNDS IN DEBT TO WALTER! TAKE THE MONEY, EVEN IF YOU CAN ONLY BUY THINGS THAT START WITH 'Q'.
ONE MILLION POUNDS IS A LOT OF MONEY. BUT WHAT COULD I SPEND IT ON? QUAIL EGGS? QUILTING SUPPLIES? KING MERCH?
I'D SPEND IT ON QUICKSAND. I COULD PULL A BLAMAZING PRANK WITH THAT STUFF! OR MAYBE A NEW QUIVER FOR MY BOW AND SUCKY ARROWS.
I WONDER WHERE WALTER WOULD TAKE ME ON A SUPER-COOL HOLIDAY. MAYBE FLORIDA? THE CARIBBEAN?
DON'T LISTEN TO THEM, BERTIE. TAKE THE MILLION POUNDS AND THEN GIVE IT ALL TO ME!
YEAH, THAT'S NOT HOW THIS WORKS, WALTER . . .

WHICH OPTION WOULD YOU CHOOSE WITH ALL THOSE VARIATIONS ADDED INTO THE MIX?

WALTER

'What a childish machine,' said Walter. 'If you really wanted to do something worthwhile, Rubi, you should have invented something that serves me caviar on crackers while shining my shoes.'

'Come on, Walter. You can't pretend you're not at least a teensy bit curious,' Rubi said.

Walter sighed. 'Fine, I'll try your ugly machine, but you'll owe me.'

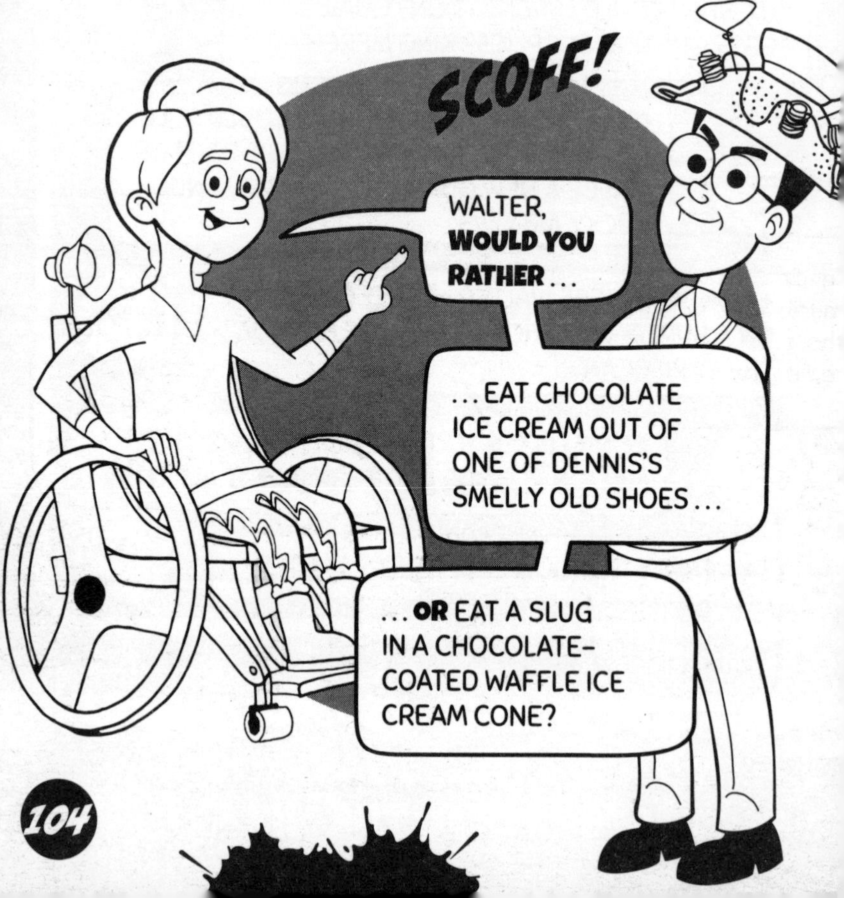
SCOFF!
WALTER, WOULD YOU RATHER ...
... EAT CHOCOLATE ICE CREAM OUT OF ONE OF DENNIS'S SMELLY OLD SHOES ...
... OR EAT A SLUG IN A CHOCOLATE-COATED WAFFLE ICE CREAM CONE?

WHAT DO WALTER'S NUMSKULLS THINK?

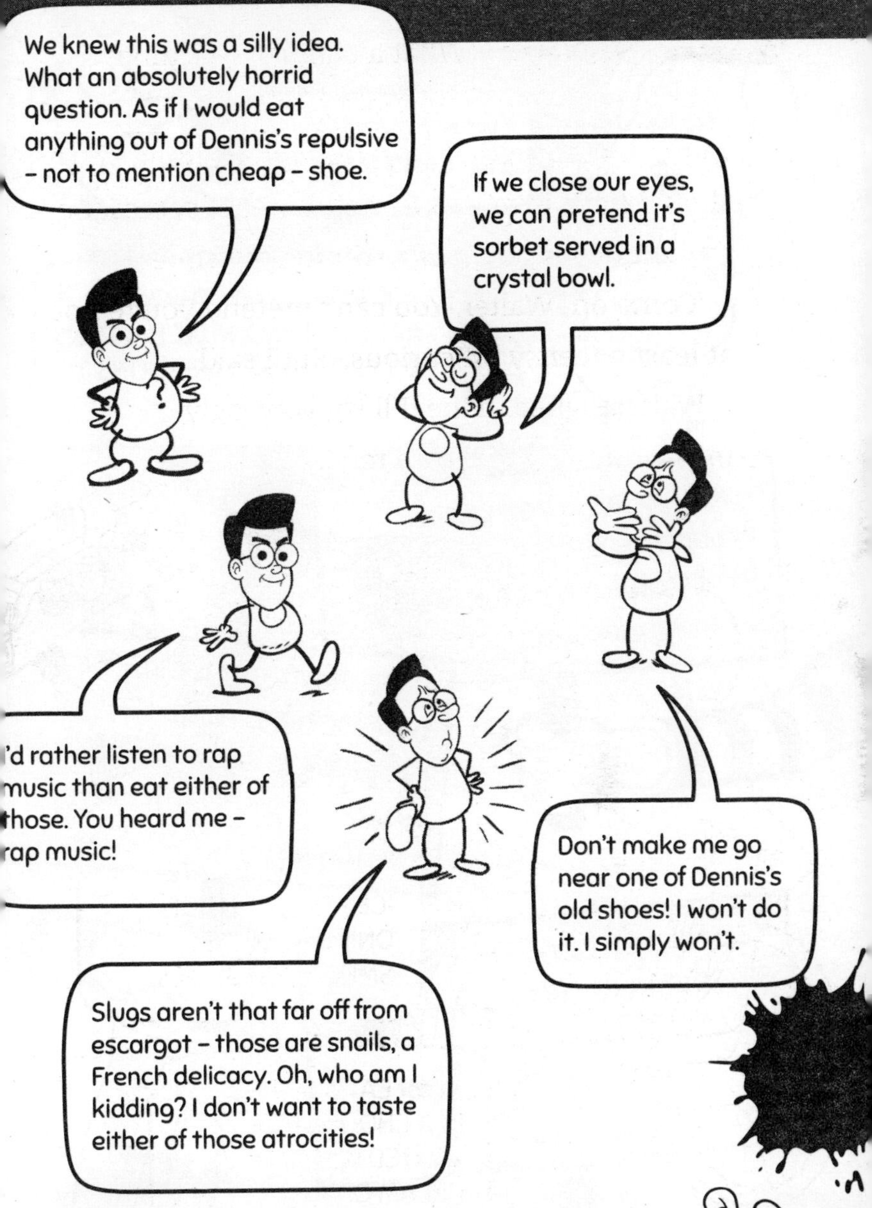
We knew this was a silly idea. What an absolutely horrid question. As if I would eat anything out of Dennis's repulsive – not to mention cheap – shoe.
If we close our eyes, we can pretend it's sorbet served in a crystal bowl.
'd rather listen to rap music than eat either of those. You heard me – rap music!
Don't make me go near one of Dennis's old shoes! I won't do it. I simply won't.
Slugs aren't that far off from escargot – those are snails, a French delicacy. Oh, who am I kidding? I don't want to taste either of those atrocities!

WHAT WOULD YOU DO?

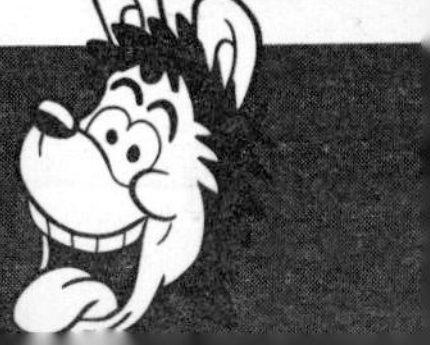

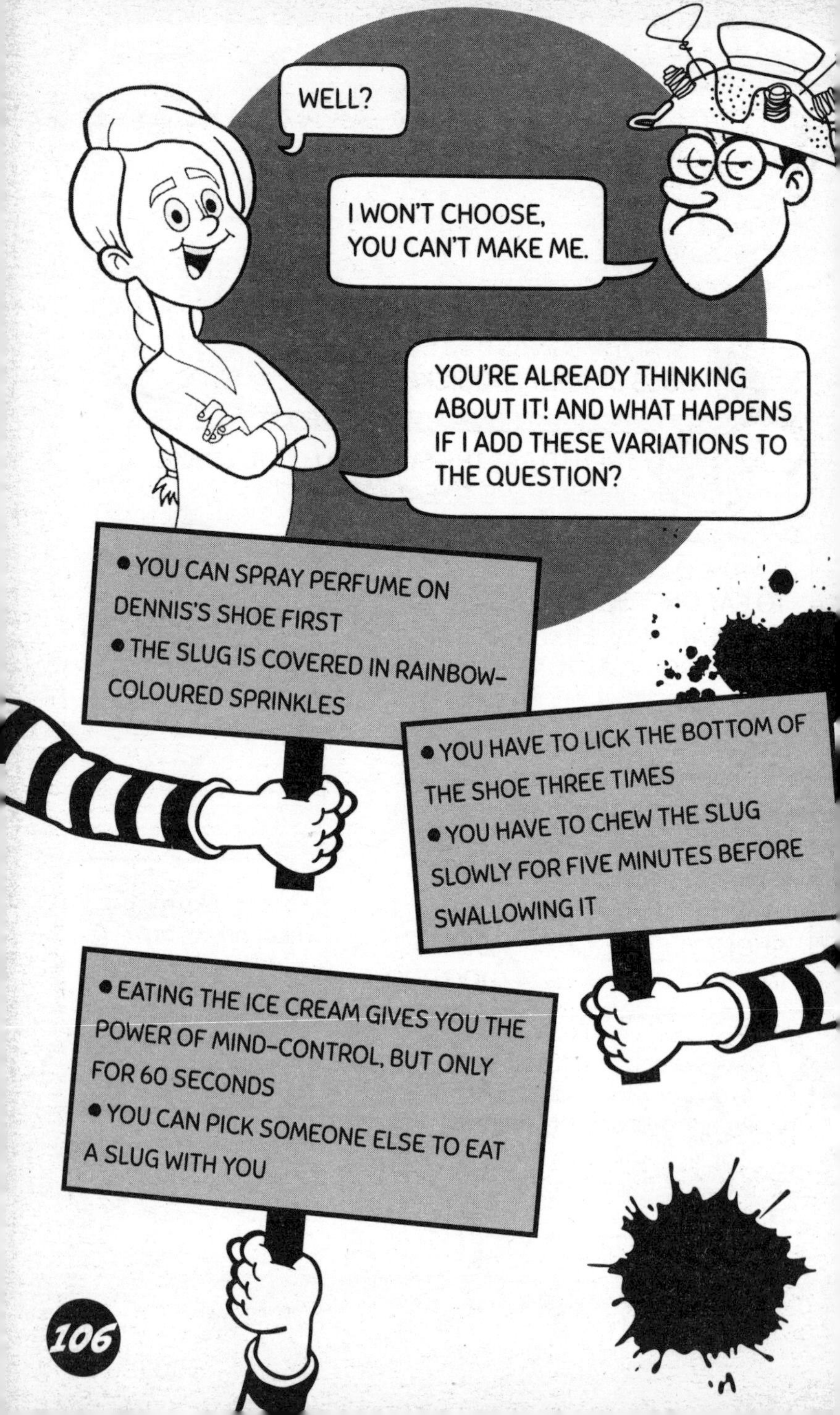
WELL?
I WON'T CHOOSE, YOU CAN'T MAKE ME.
YOU'RE ALREADY THINKING ABOUT IT! AND WHAT HAPPENS IF I ADD THESE VARIATIONS TO THE QUESTION?
• YOU CAN SPRAY PERFUME ON DENNIS'S SHOE FIRST
• THE SLUG IS COVERED IN RAINBOW-COLOURED SPRINKLES
• YOU HAVE TO LICK THE BOTTOM OF THE SHOE THREE TIMES
• YOU HAVE TO CHEW THE SLUG SLOWLY FOR FIVE MINUTES BEFORE SWALLOWING IT
• EATING THE ICE CREAM GIVES YOU THE POWER OF MIND-CONTROL, BUT ONLY FOR 60 SECONDS
• YOU CAN PICK SOMEONE ELSE TO EAT A SLUG WITH YOU

MIND CONTROL . . . NOW YOU'RE TALKING! BUT WHO WOULD I CONTROL FIRST? YOU, DENNIS! NO, YOU RUBI – I'D MAKE YOU INVENT A MACHINE THAT WOULD TIE DENNIS'S ARMS BEHIND HIS BACK – FOREVER!

WELL I AM A GREAT INVENTOR, BUT I'M NOT THAT FAST. 60 SECONDS GOES BY PRETTY QUICKLY!

THEN I'D EAT THE SLUG, SO I COULD MAKE DENNIS HAVE TO EAT ONE TOO!

IT WOULD BE WORTH IT TO SEE YOU HAVE TO EAT ONE FIRST! ESPECIALLY IF YOU HAD TO CHEW IT FOR FIVE WHOLE MINUTES. JUST THINK ABOUT ALL THAT STINKY, SLIMY SLUG JUST SQUISHING AROUND IN YOUR MOUTH.

URGH, THAT'S DISGUSTING!

WOULD YOU RATHER LICK THE BOTTOM OF MY SHOE? YESTERDAY, I ACCIDENTALLY STEPPED IN A BIG, SMELLY PILE OF DOG DOO.

I'M GOING TO TELL MY FATHER ABOUT THIS!

WHICH OPTION WOULD YOU CHOOSE WITH ALL THOSE VARIATIONS ADDED INTO THE MIX?

MISS MISTRY

'Hey Rubi, does the MIND reader work on teachers?' Dennis asked.

'It should work on anyone,' Rubi replied.

'Then let's try it on Miss Mistry,' Dennis said, waving her over.

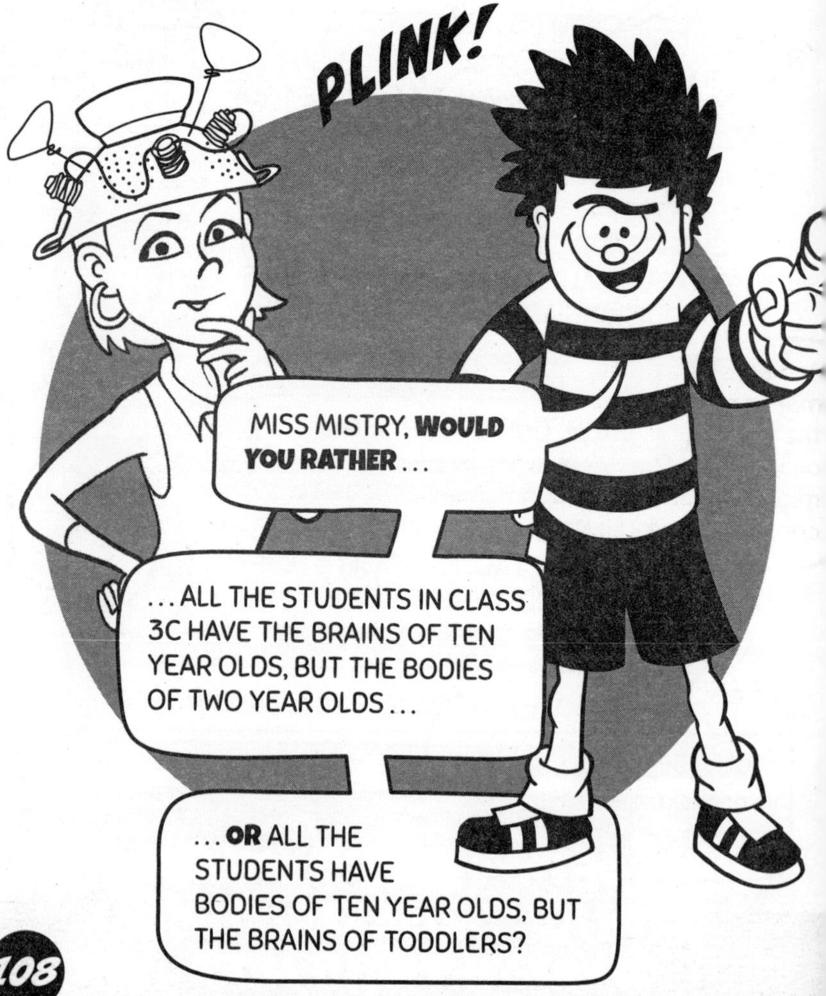
PLINK!
MISS MISTRY, **WOULD YOU RATHER** . . .
. . . ALL THE STUDENTS IN CLASS 3C HAVE THE BRAINS OF TEN YEAR OLDS, BUT THE BODIES OF TWO YEAR OLDS . . .
. . . **OR** ALL THE STUDENTS HAVE BODIES OF TEN YEAR OLDS, BUT THE BRAINS OF TODDLERS?

WHAT DO MISS MISTRY'S NUMSKULLS THINK?

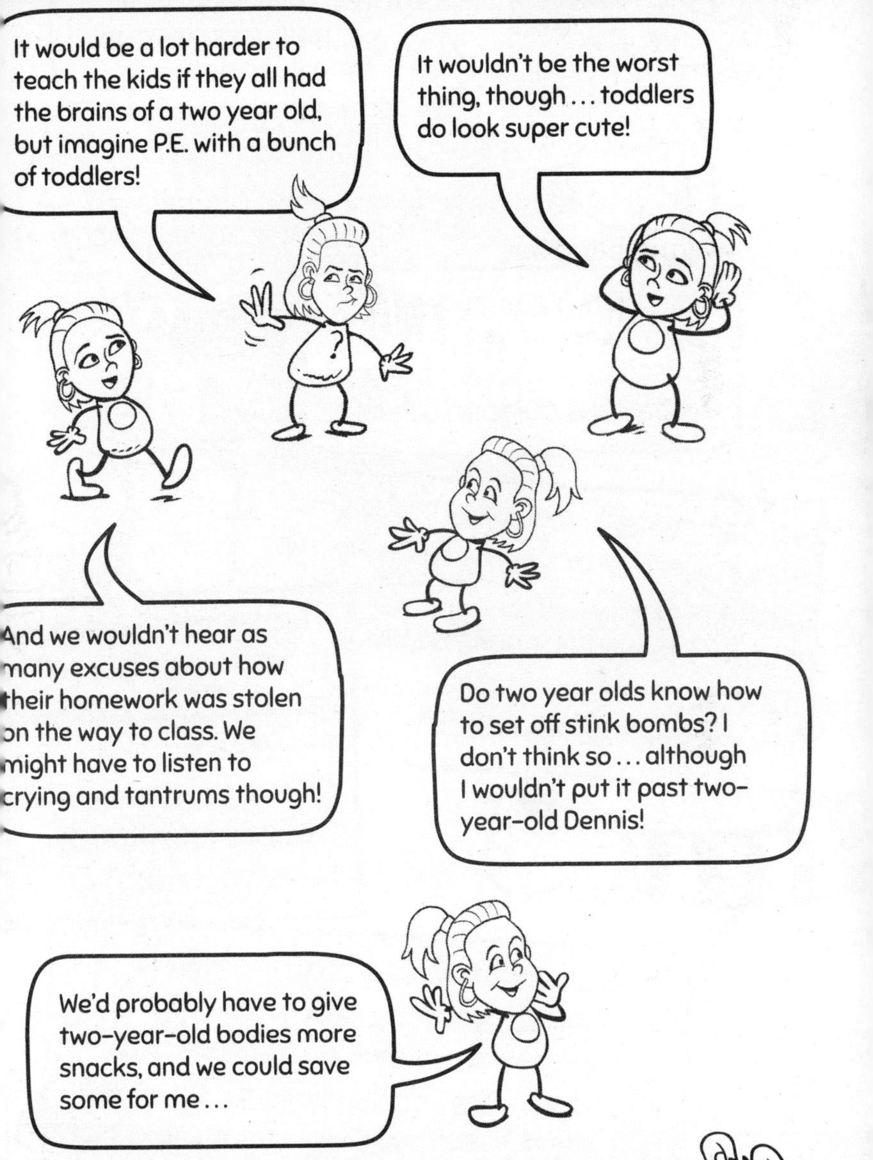
It would be a lot harder to teach the kids if they all had the brains of a two year old, but imagine P.E. with a bunch of toddlers!
It wouldn't be the worst thing, though . . . toddlers do look super cute!
And we wouldn't hear as many excuses about how their homework was stolen on the way to class. We might have to listen to crying and tantrums though!
Do two year olds know how to set off stink bombs? I don't think so . . . although I wouldn't put it past two-year-old Dennis!
We'd probably have to give two-year-old bodies more snacks, and we could save some for me . . .

WHAT WOULD YOU DO?

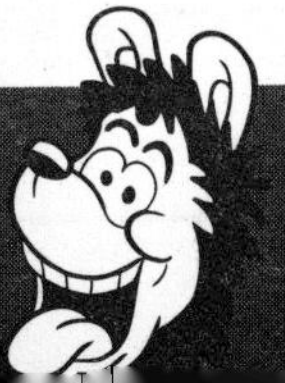

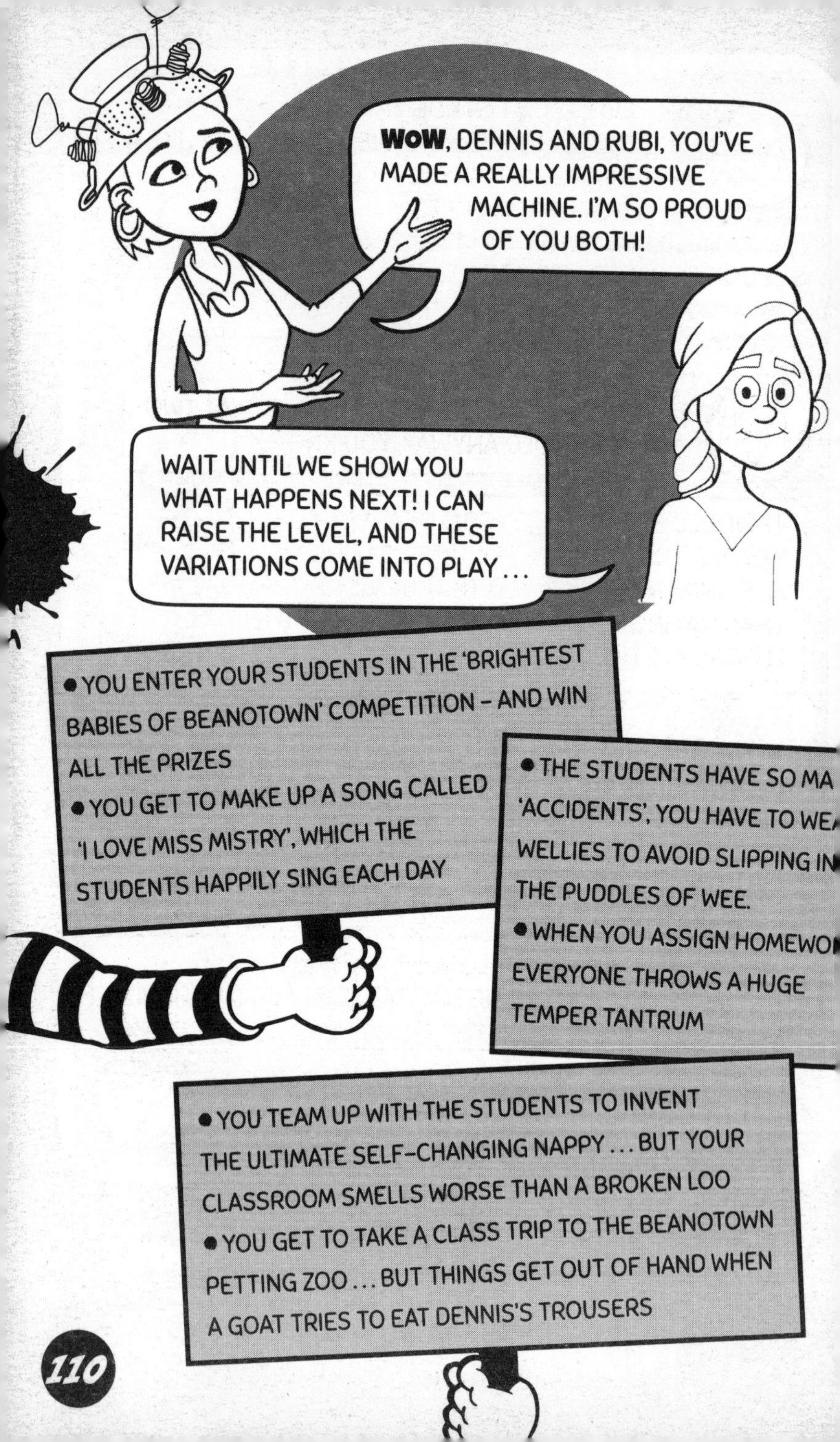
WOW, DENNIS AND RUBI, YOU'VE MADE A REALLY IMPRESSIVE MACHINE. I'M SO PROUD OF YOU BOTH!
WAIT UNTIL WE SHOW YOU WHAT HAPPENS NEXT! I CAN RAISE THE LEVEL, AND THESE VARIATIONS COME INTO PLAY . . .
• YOU ENTER YOUR STUDENTS IN THE 'BRIGHTEST BABIES OF BEANOTOWN' COMPETITION – AND WIN ALL THE PRIZES
• YOU GET TO MAKE UP A SONG CALLED 'I LOVE MISS MISTRY', WHICH THE STUDENTS HAPPILY SING EACH DAY
• THE STUDENTS HAVE SO MA 'ACCIDENTS', YOU HAVE TO WE WELLIES TO AVOID SLIPPING IN THE PUDDLES OF WEE.
• WHEN YOU ASSIGN HOMEWO EVERYONE THROWS A HUGE TEMPER TANTRUM
• YOU TEAM UP WITH THE STUDENTS TO INVENT THE ULTIMATE SELF-CHANGING NAPPY . . . BUT YOUR CLASSROOM SMELLS WORSE THAN A BROKEN LOO
• YOU GET TO TAKE A CLASS TRIP TO THE BEANOTOWN PETTING ZOO . . . BUT THINGS GET OUT OF HAND WHEN A GOAT TRIES TO EAT DENNIS'S TROUSERS

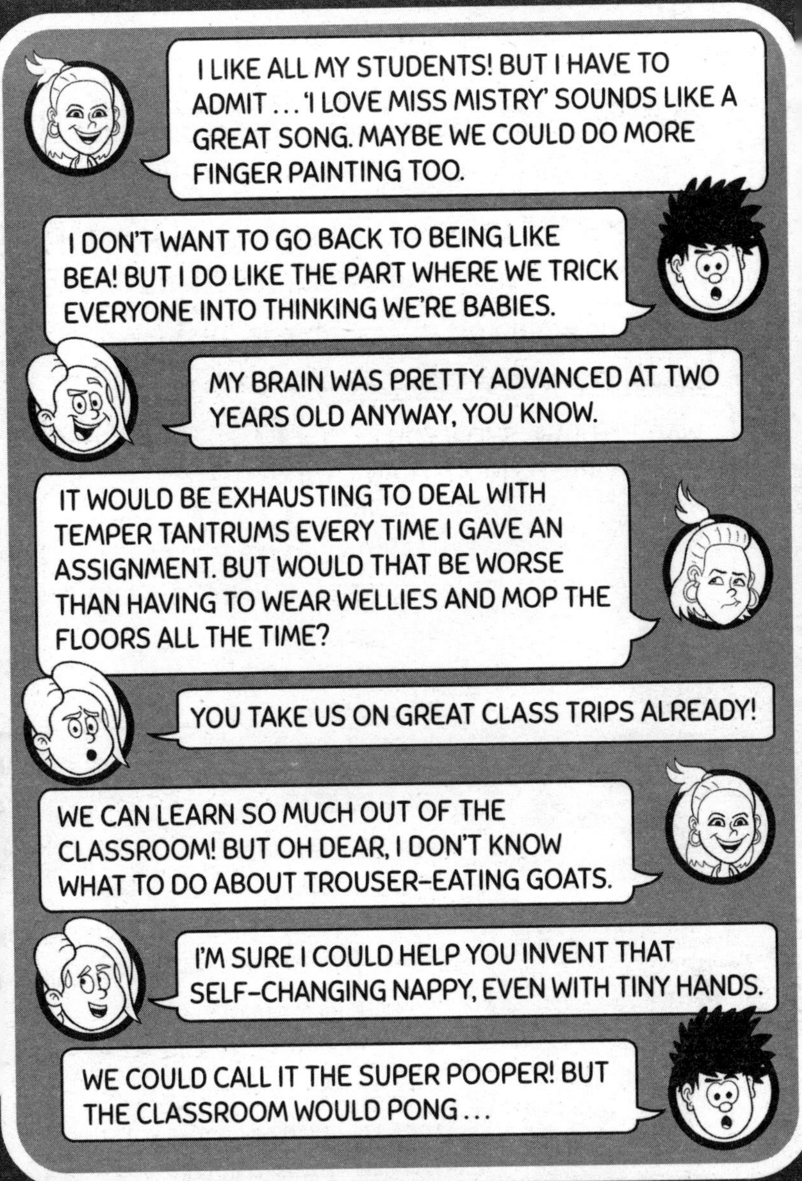
I LIKE ALL MY STUDENTS! BUT I HAVE TO ADMIT . . . 'I LOVE MISS MISTRY' SOUNDS LIKE A GREAT SONG. MAYBE WE COULD DO MORE FINGER PAINTING TOO.
I DON'T WANT TO GO BACK TO BEING LIKE BEA! BUT I DO LIKE THE PART WHERE WE TRICK EVERYONE INTO THINKING WE'RE BABIES.
MY BRAIN WAS PRETTY ADVANCED AT TWO YEARS OLD ANYWAY, YOU KNOW.
IT WOULD BE EXHAUSTING TO DEAL WITH TEMPER TANTRUMS EVERY TIME I GAVE AN ASSIGNMENT. BUT WOULD THAT BE WORSE THAN HAVING TO WEAR WELLIES AND MOP THE FLOORS ALL THE TIME?
YOU TAKE US ON GREAT CLASS TRIPS ALREADY!
WE CAN LEARN SO MUCH OUT OF THE CLASSROOM! BUT OH DEAR, I DON'T KNOW WHAT TO DO ABOUT TROUSER-EATING GOATS.
I'M SURE I COULD HELP YOU INVENT THAT SELF-CHANGING NAPPY, EVEN WITH TINY HANDS.
WE COULD CALL IT THE SUPER POOPER! BUT THE CLASSROOM WOULD PONG . . .

WHICH OPTION WOULD YOU CHOOSE WITH ALL THOSE VARIATIONS ADDED INTO THE MIX?

LORD SNOOTY

'Hello guys,' said Lord Snooty.

'Snooty! I thought you weren't entering this year?' Rubi asked.

'I'm just here to see what my friends are up to. Say, what sort of machine is this?'

'We'll show you!'

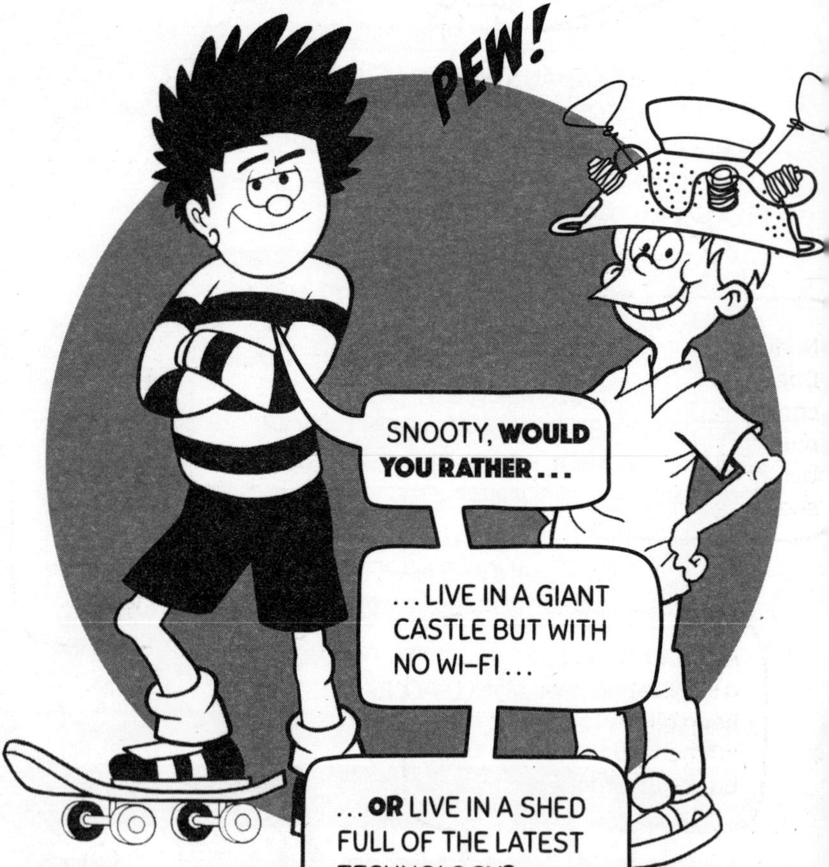

PEW!
SNOOTY, **WOULD YOU RATHER . . .**
. . . LIVE IN A GIANT CASTLE BUT WITH NO WI-FI . . .
. . . **OR** LIVE IN A SHED FULL OF THE LATEST TECHNOLOGY?

WHAT DO LORD SNOOTY'S NUMSKULLS THINK?

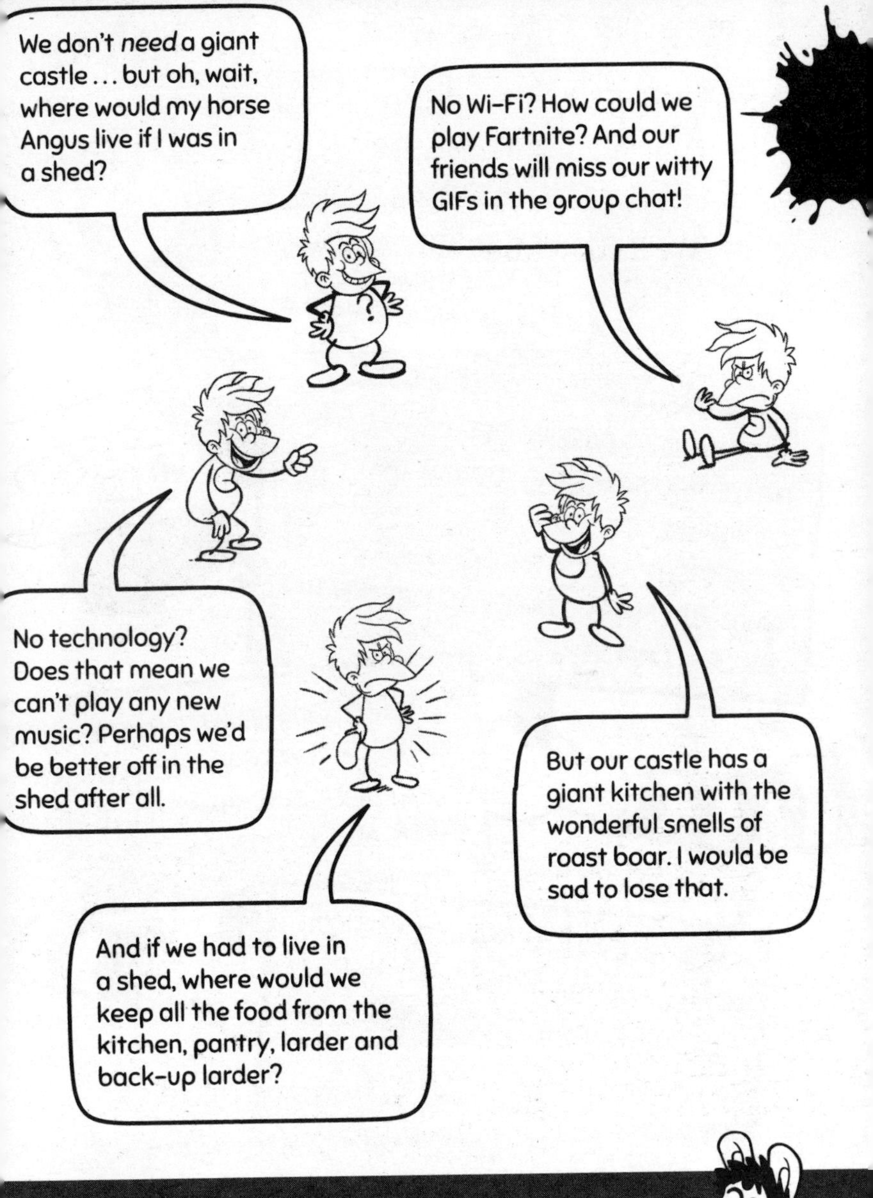
We don't *need* a giant castle . . . but oh, wait, where would my horse Angus live if I was in a shed?
No Wi-Fi? How could we play Fartnite? And our friends will miss our witty GIFs in the group chat!
No technology? Does that mean we can't play any new music? Perhaps we'd be better off in the shed after all.
But our castle has a giant kitchen with the wonderful smells of roast boar. I would be sad to lose that.
And if we had to live in a shed, where would we keep all the food from the kitchen, pantry, larder and back-up larder?

WHAT WOULD YOU DO?

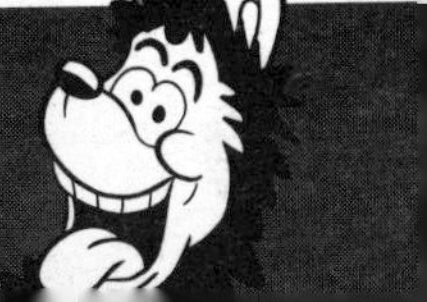

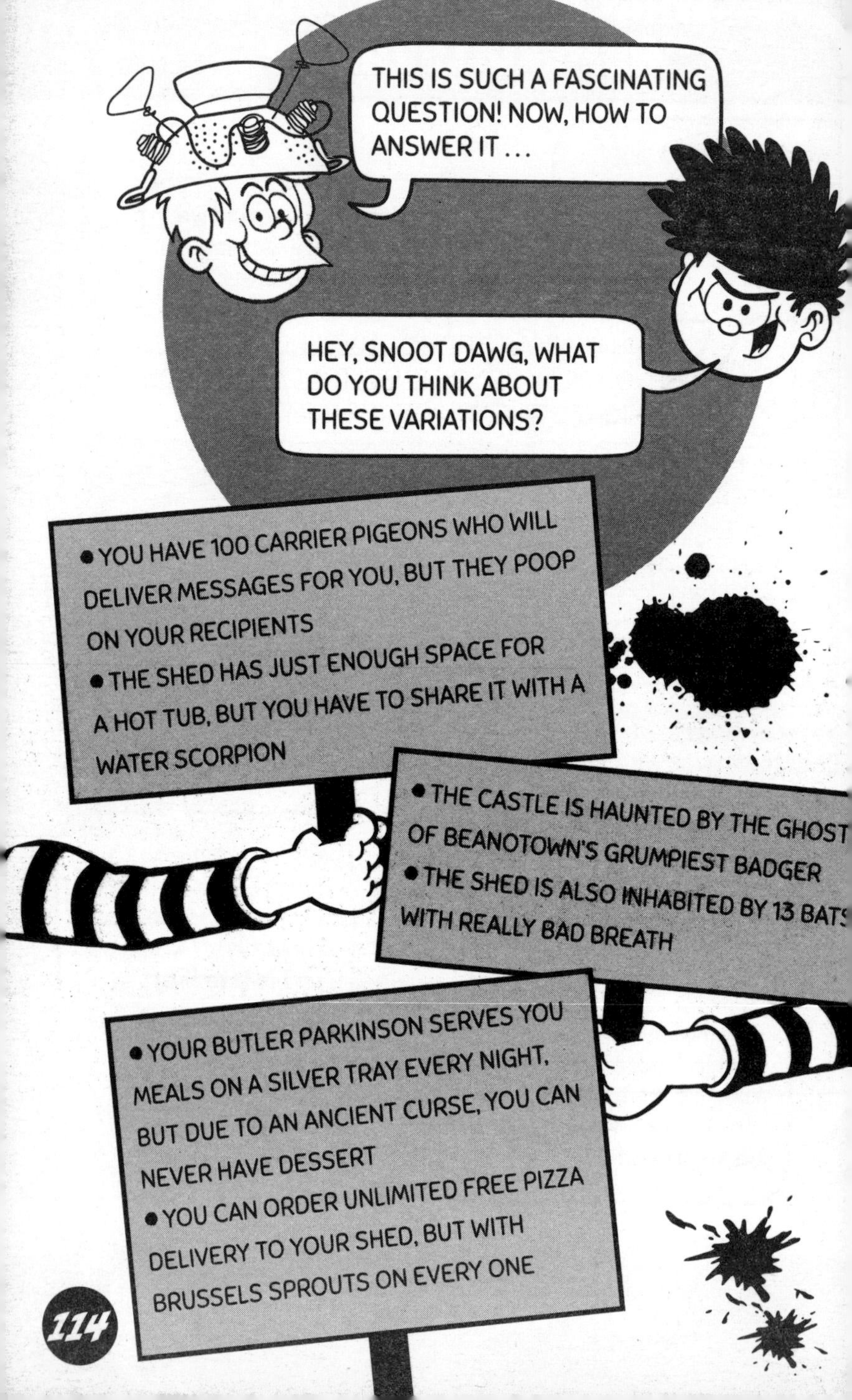

THIS IS SUCH A FASCINATING QUESTION! NOW, HOW TO ANSWER IT . . .
HEY, SNOOT DAWG, WHAT DO YOU THINK ABOUT THESE VARIATIONS?
• YOU HAVE 100 CARRIER PIGEONS WHO WILL DELIVER MESSAGES FOR YOU, BUT THEY POOP ON YOUR RECIPIENTS
• THE SHED HAS JUST ENOUGH SPACE FOR A HOT TUB, BUT YOU HAVE TO SHARE IT WITH A WATER SCORPION
• THE CASTLE IS HAUNTED BY THE GHOST OF BEANOTOWN'S GRUMPIEST BADGER
• THE SHED IS ALSO INHABITED BY 13 BAT WITH REALLY BAD BREATH
• YOUR BUTLER PARKINSON SERVES YOU MEALS ON A SILVER TRAY EVERY NIGHT, BUT DUE TO AN ANCIENT CURSE, YOU CAN NEVER HAVE DESSERT
• YOU CAN ORDER UNLIMITED FREE PIZZA DELIVERY TO YOUR SHED, BUT WITH BRUSSELS SPROUTS ON EVERY ONE

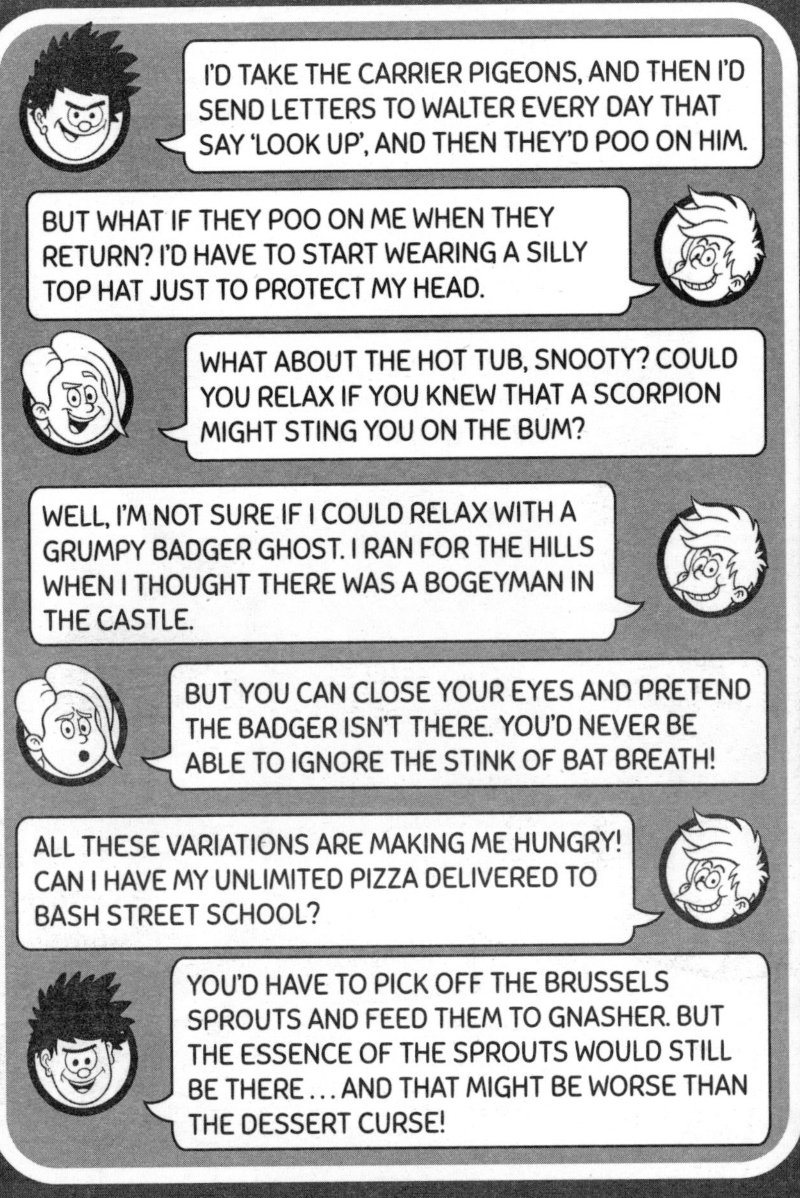
I'D TAKE THE CARRIER PIGEONS, AND THEN I'D SEND LETTERS TO WALTER EVERY DAY THAT SAY 'LOOK UP', AND THEN THEY'D POO ON HIM.
BUT WHAT IF THEY POO ON ME WHEN THEY RETURN? I'D HAVE TO START WEARING A SILLY TOP HAT JUST TO PROTECT MY HEAD.
WHAT ABOUT THE HOT TUB, SNOOTY? COULD YOU RELAX IF YOU KNEW THAT A SCORPION MIGHT STING YOU ON THE BUM?
WELL, I'M NOT SURE IF I COULD RELAX WITH A GRUMPY BADGER GHOST. I RAN FOR THE HILLS WHEN I THOUGHT THERE WAS A BOGEYMAN IN THE CASTLE.
BUT YOU CAN CLOSE YOUR EYES AND PRETEND THE BADGER ISN'T THERE. YOU'D NEVER BE ABLE TO IGNORE THE STINK OF BAT BREATH!
ALL THESE VARIATIONS ARE MAKING ME HUNGRY! CAN I HAVE MY UNLIMITED PIZZA DELIVERED TO BASH STREET SCHOOL?
YOU'D HAVE TO PICK OFF THE BRUSSELS SPROUTS AND FEED THEM TO GNASHER. BUT THE ESSENCE OF THE SPROUTS WOULD STILL BE THERE... AND THAT MIGHT BE WORSE THAN THE DESSERT CURSE!

WHICH OPTION WOULD YOU CHOOSE WITH ALL THOSE VARIATIONS ADDED INTO THE MIX?

DANNY

A ragtag gang of slightly younger kids had wandered over.

'It's Class 2B!' Rubi called.

'What's this?' Danny asked.

'Rubi and I are testing our new machine,' said Dennis.

'I'll go first,' Danny said, grabbing the device.

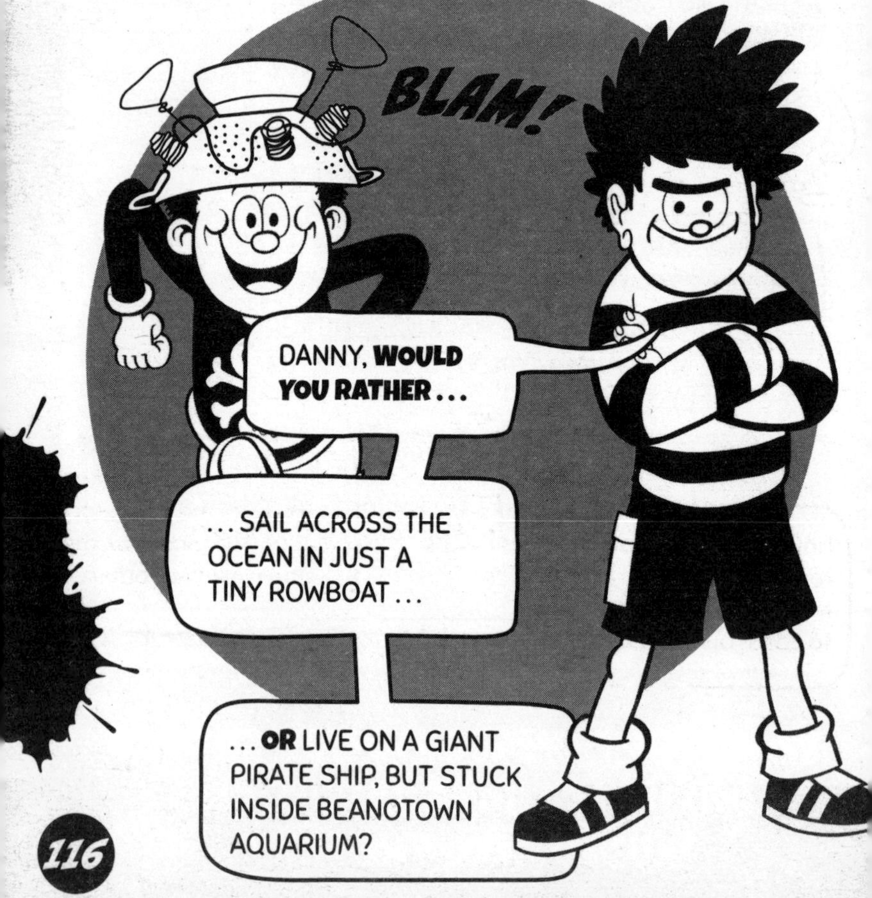
BLAM!
DANNY, **WOULD YOU RATHER . . .**
. . . SAIL ACROSS THE OCEAN IN JUST A TINY ROWBOAT . . .
. . . **OR** LIVE ON A GIANT PIRATE SHIP, BUT STUCK INSIDE BEANOTOWN AQUARIUM?

WHAT DO DANNY'S NUMSKULLS THINK?

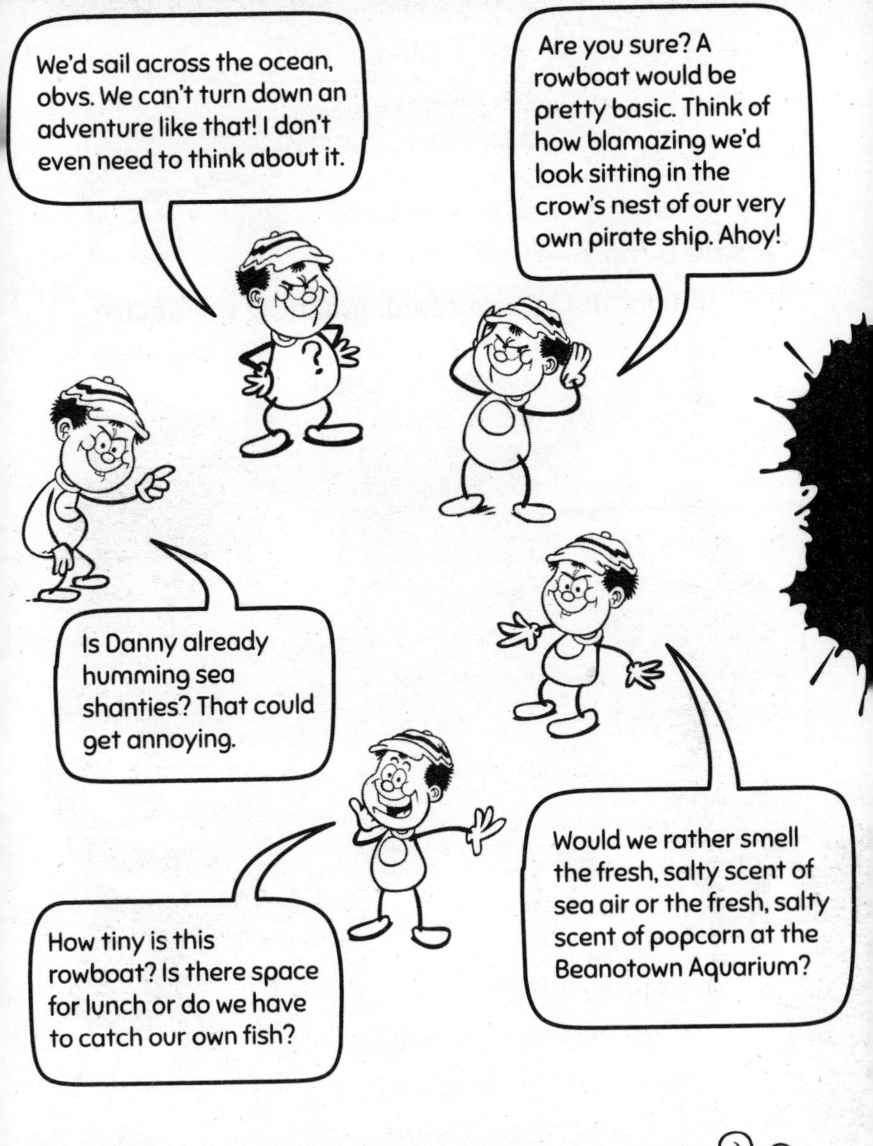

WHAT WOULD YOU DO?

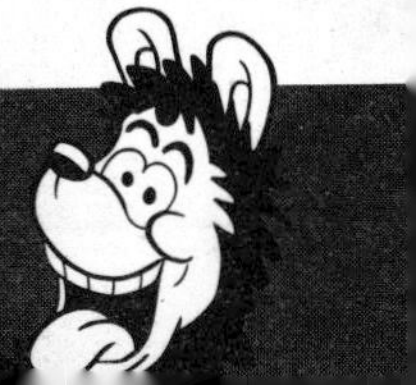

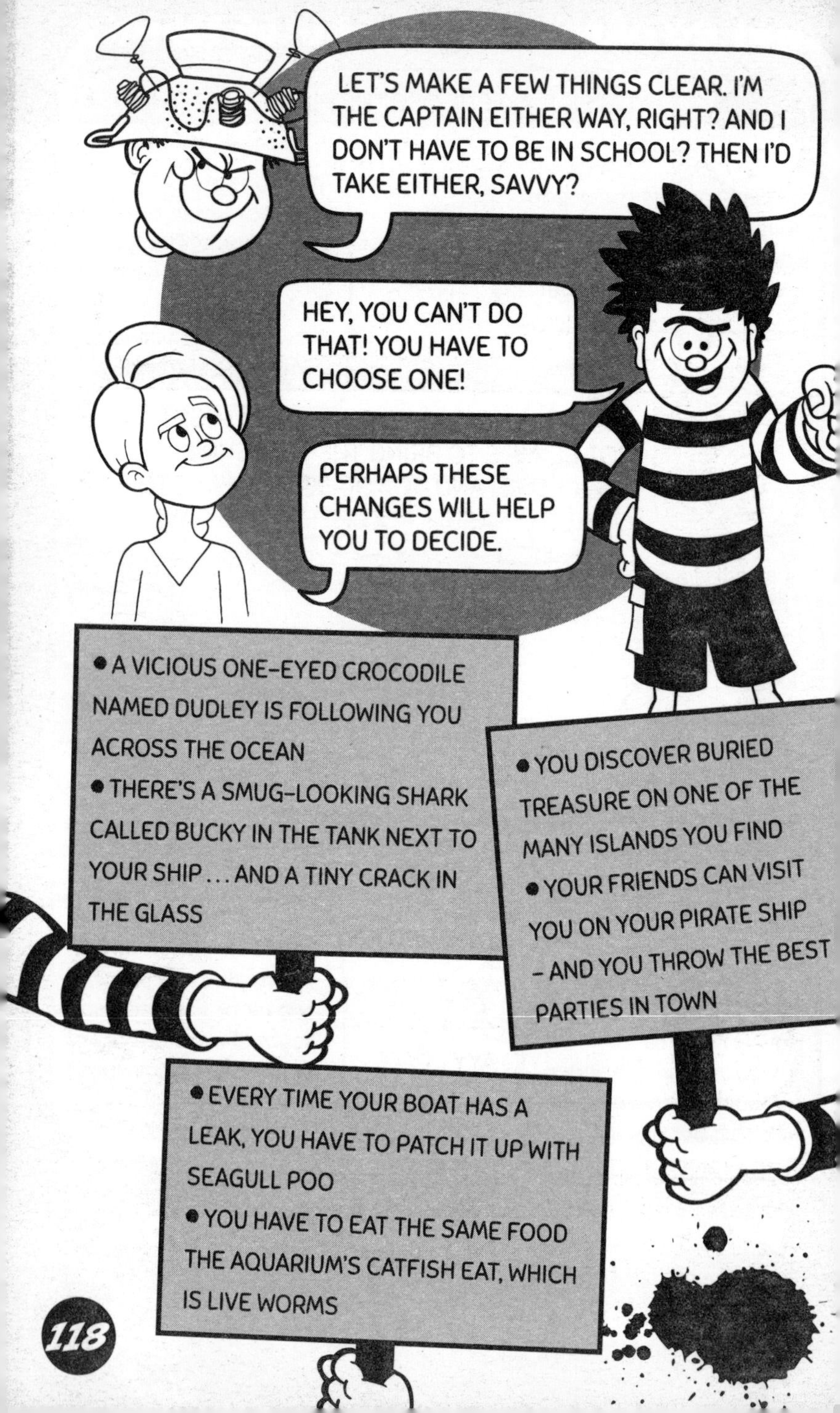
LET'S MAKE A FEW THINGS CLEAR. I'M THE CAPTAIN EITHER WAY, RIGHT? AND I DON'T HAVE TO BE IN SCHOOL? THEN I'D TAKE EITHER, SAVVY?
HEY, YOU CAN'T DO THAT! YOU HAVE TO CHOOSE ONE!
PERHAPS THESE CHANGES WILL HELP YOU TO DECIDE.
• A VICIOUS ONE-EYED CROCODILE NAMED DUDLEY IS FOLLOWING YOU ACROSS THE OCEAN
• THERE'S A SMUG-LOOKING SHARK CALLED BUCKY IN THE TANK NEXT TO YOUR SHIP . . . AND A TINY CRACK IN THE GLASS
• YOU DISCOVER BURIED TREASURE ON ONE OF THE MANY ISLANDS YOU FIND
• YOUR FRIENDS CAN VISIT YOU ON YOUR PIRATE SHIP – AND YOU THROW THE BEST PARTIES IN TOWN
• EVERY TIME YOUR BOAT HAS A LEAK, YOU HAVE TO PATCH IT UP WITH SEAGULL POO
• YOU HAVE TO EAT THE SAME FOOD THE AQUARIUM'S CATFISH EAT, WHICH IS LIVE WORMS

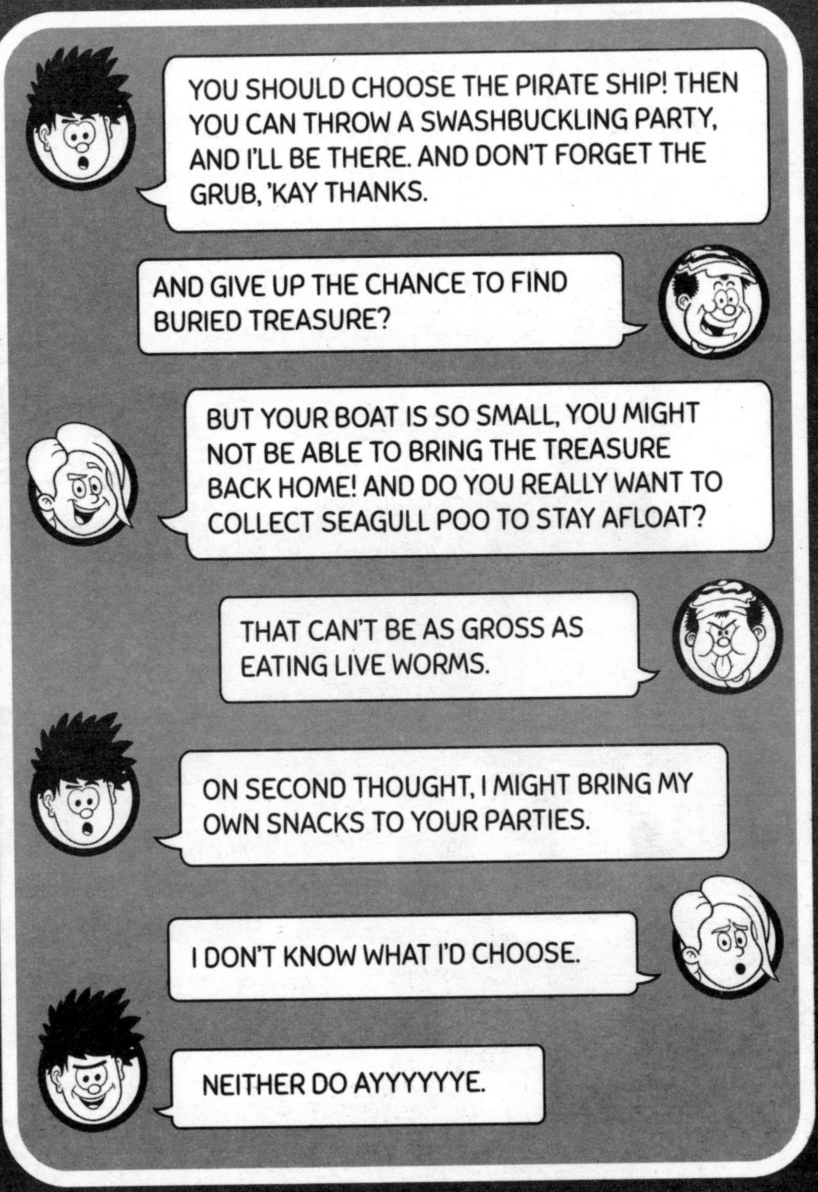
YOU SHOULD CHOOSE THE PIRATE SHIP! THEN YOU CAN THROW A SWASHBUCKLING PARTY, AND I'LL BE THERE. AND DON'T FORGET THE GRUB, 'KAY THANKS.
AND GIVE UP THE CHANCE TO FIND BURIED TREASURE?
BUT YOUR BOAT IS SO SMALL, YOU MIGHT NOT BE ABLE TO BRING THE TREASURE BACK HOME! AND DO YOU REALLY WANT TO COLLECT SEAGULL POO TO STAY AFLOAT?
THAT CAN'T BE AS GROSS AS EATING LIVE WORMS.
ON SECOND THOUGHT, I MIGHT BRING MY OWN SNACKS TO YOUR PARTIES.
I DON'T KNOW WHAT I'D CHOOSE.
NEITHER DO AYYYYYYE.

WHICH OPTION WOULD YOU CHOOSE WITH ALL THOSE VARIATIONS ADDED INTO THE MIX?

SMIFFY

'You should try it, Smiffy,' Danny said. 'Here, wear this helmet thing.'

'Sorry, I don't have time to put this on,' Smiffy explained patiently. 'I'm busy helping Dennis and Rubi test their new experiment.'

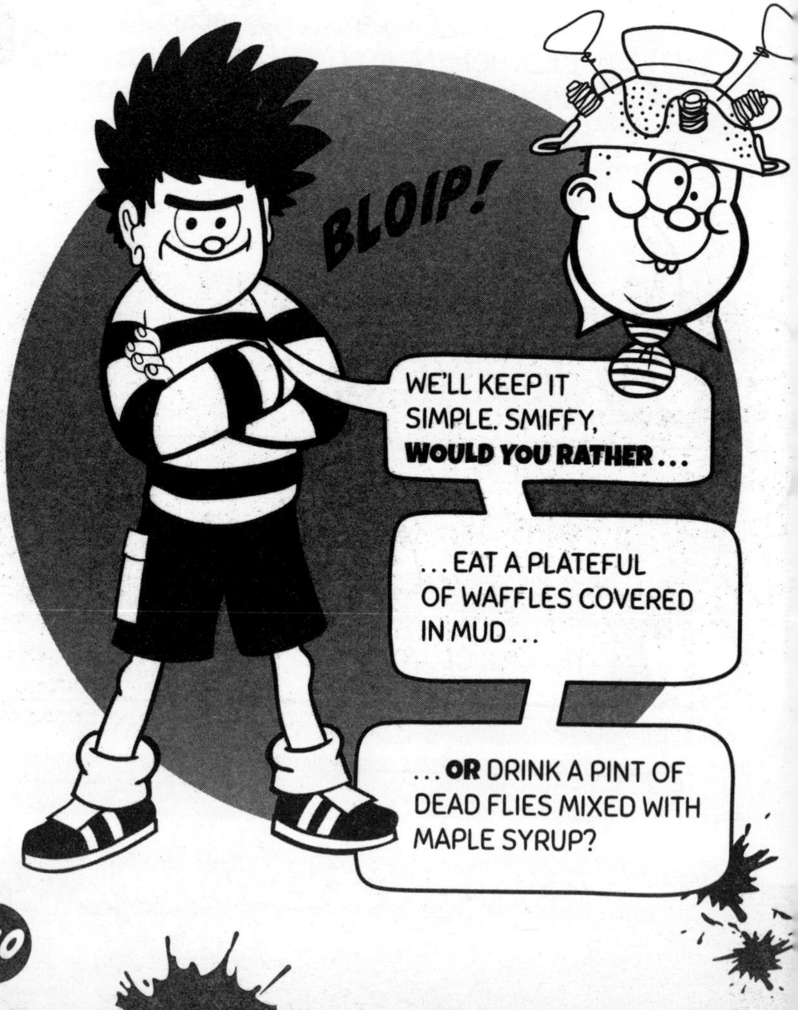
BLOIP!
WE'LL KEEP IT SIMPLE. SMIFFY, **WOULD YOU RATHER...**
...EAT A PLATEFUL OF WAFFLES COVERED IN MUD...
...**OR** DRINK A PINT OF DEAD FLIES MIXED WITH MAPLE SYRUP?

WHAT DO SMIFFY'S NUMSKULLS THINK?

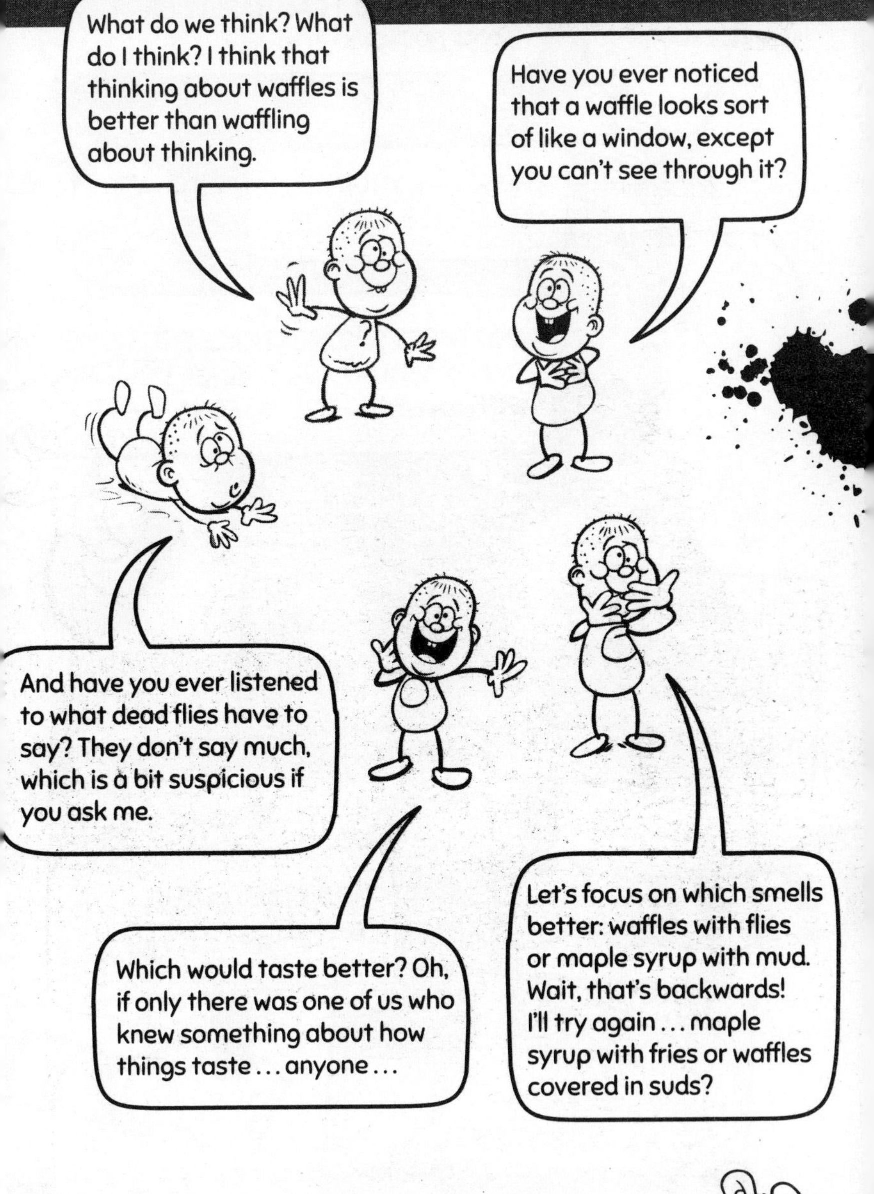
What do we think? What do I think? I think that thinking about waffles is better than waffling about thinking.
Have you ever noticed that a waffle looks sort of like a window, except you can't see through it?
And have you ever listened to what dead flies have to say? They don't say much, which is a bit suspicious if you ask me.
Which would taste better? Oh, if only there was one of us who knew something about how things taste . . . anyone . . .
Let's focus on which smells better: waffles with flies or maple syrup with mud. Wait, that's backwards! I'll try again . . . maple syrup with fries or waffles covered in suds?

WHAT WOULD YOU DO?

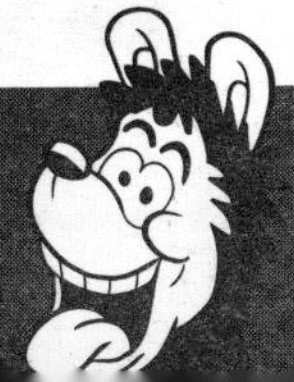

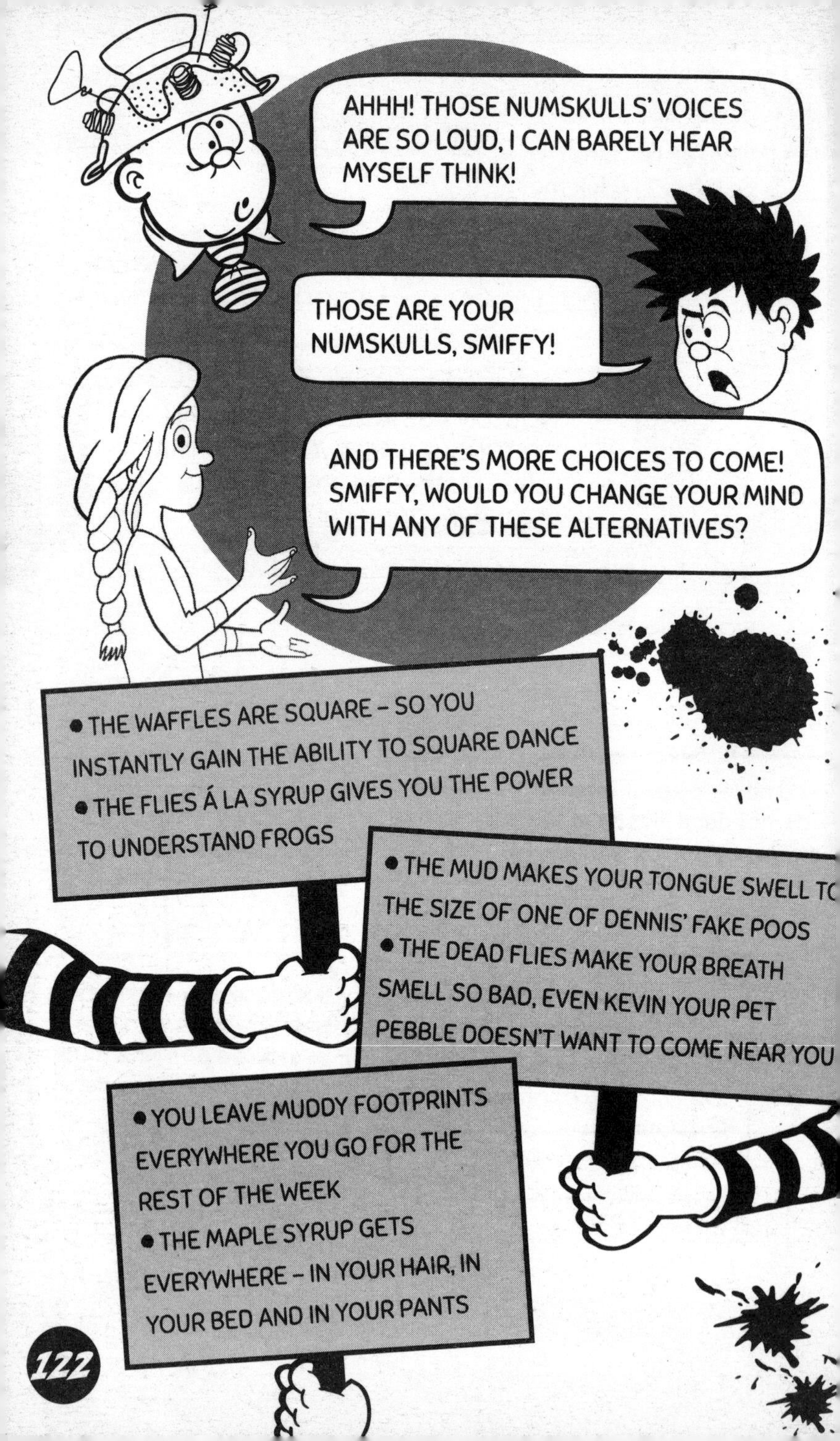
AHHH! THOSE NUMSKULLS' VOICES ARE SO LOUD, I CAN BARELY HEAR MYSELF THINK!
THOSE ARE YOUR NUMSKULLS, SMIFFY!
AND THERE'S MORE CHOICES TO COME! SMIFFY, WOULD YOU CHANGE YOUR MIND WITH ANY OF THESE ALTERNATIVES?
• THE WAFFLES ARE SQUARE – SO YOU INSTANTLY GAIN THE ABILITY TO SQUARE DANCE
• THE FLIES Á LA SYRUP GIVES YOU THE POWER TO UNDERSTAND FROGS
• THE MUD MAKES YOUR TONGUE SWELL TO THE SIZE OF ONE OF DENNIS' FAKE POOS
• THE DEAD FLIES MAKE YOUR BREATH SMELL SO BAD, EVEN KEVIN YOUR PET PEBBLE DOESN'T WANT TO COME NEAR YOU
• YOU LEAVE MUDDY FOOTPRINTS EVERYWHERE YOU GO FOR THE REST OF THE WEEK
• THE MAPLE SYRUP GETS EVERYWHERE – IN YOUR HAIR, IN YOUR BED AND IN YOUR PANTS

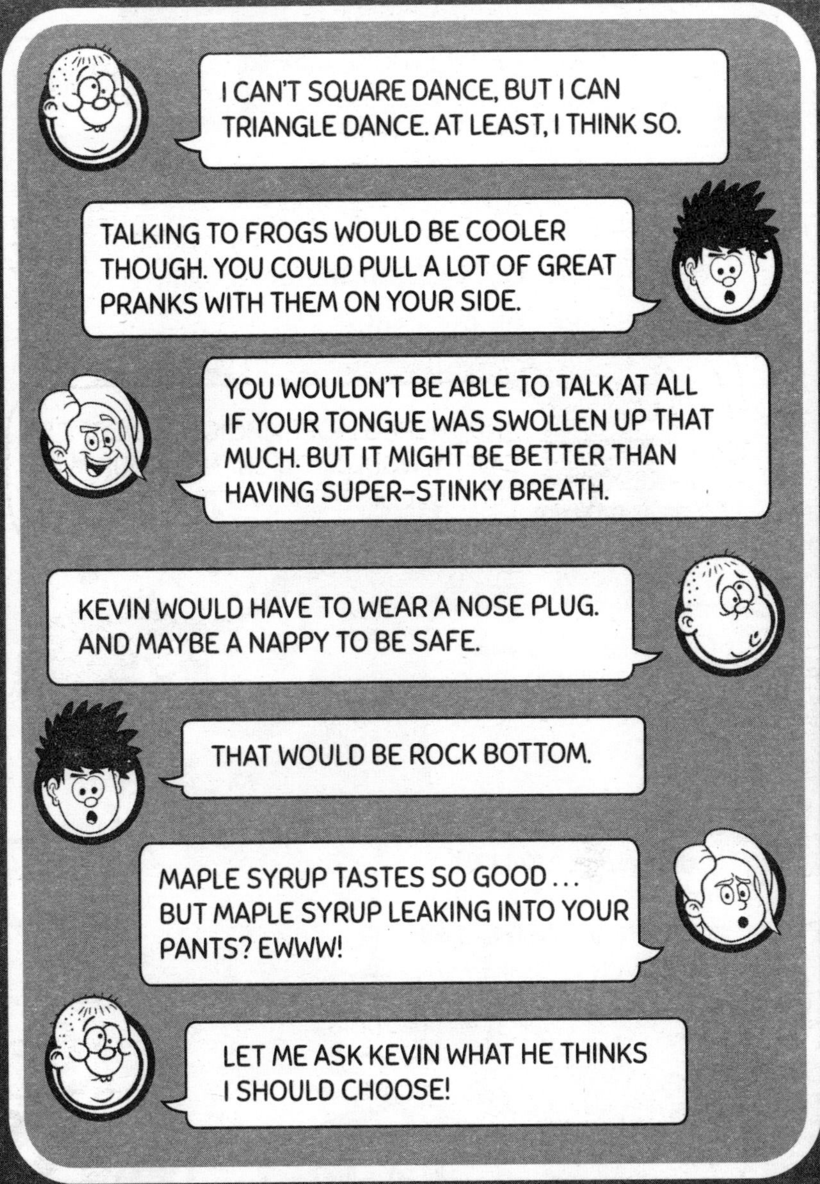
I CAN'T SQUARE DANCE, BUT I CAN TRIANGLE DANCE. AT LEAST, I THINK SO.
TALKING TO FROGS WOULD BE COOLER THOUGH. YOU COULD PULL A LOT OF GREAT PRANKS WITH THEM ON YOUR SIDE.
YOU WOULDN'T BE ABLE TO TALK AT ALL IF YOUR TONGUE WAS SWOLLEN UP THAT MUCH. BUT IT MIGHT BE BETTER THAN HAVING SUPER-STINKY BREATH.
KEVIN WOULD HAVE TO WEAR A NOSE PLUG. AND MAYBE A NAPPY TO BE SAFE.
THAT WOULD BE ROCK BOTTOM.
MAPLE SYRUP TASTES SO GOOD . . . BUT MAPLE SYRUP LEAKING INTO YOUR PANTS? EWWW!
LET ME ASK KEVIN WHAT HE THINKS I SHOULD CHOOSE!

WHICH OPTION WOULD YOU CHOOSE WITH ALL THOSE VARIATIONS ADDED INTO THE MIX?

'It sounds like you're all having a great time over here!' said Freddy. 'Can I have a turn?'

'Sure,' Rubi said. 'Just put the device on, and we'll take you for a spin.'

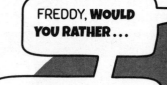

FREDDY, **WOULD YOU RATHER**...

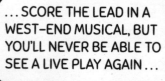

...SCORE THE LEAD IN A WEST-END MUSICAL, BUT YOU'LL NEVER BE ABLE TO SEE A LIVE PLAY AGAIN...

...**OR** HAVE NO TALENT FOR THEATRE AT ALL, BUT YOU CAN SEE A LIVE PLAY WHENEVER YOU LIKE?

SCHLURP!

WHAT DO FREDDY'S NUMSKULLS THINK?

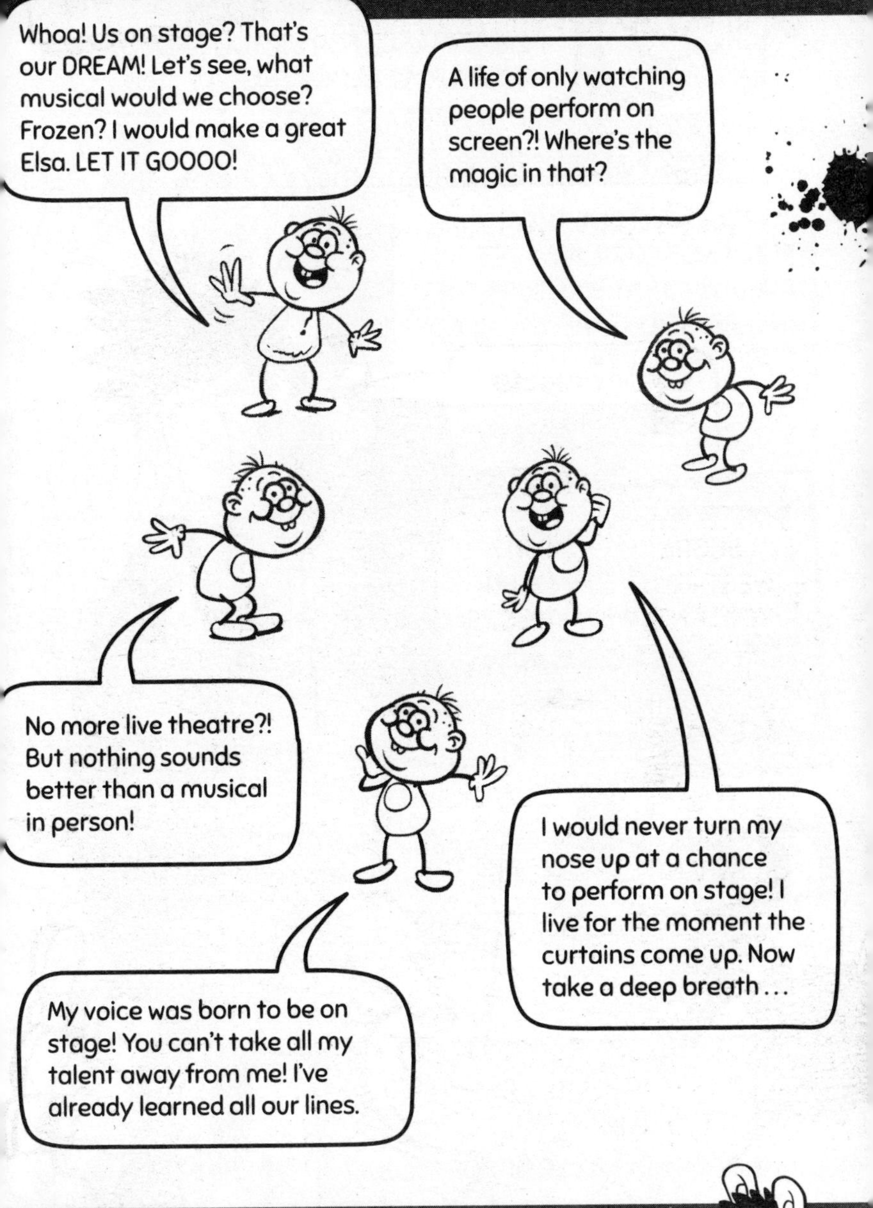
Whoa! Us on stage? That's our DREAM! Let's see, what musical would we choose? Frozen? I would make a great Elsa. LET IT GOOOO!
A life of only watching people perform on screen?! Where's the magic in that?
No more live theatre?! But nothing sounds better than a musical in person!
I would never turn my nose up at a chance to perform on stage! I live for the moment the curtains come up. Now take a deep breath . . .
My voice was born to be on stage! You can't take all my talent away from me! I've already learned all our lines.

WHAT WOULD YOU DO?

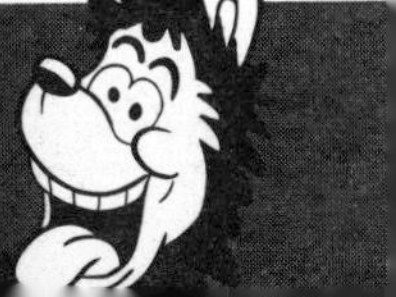

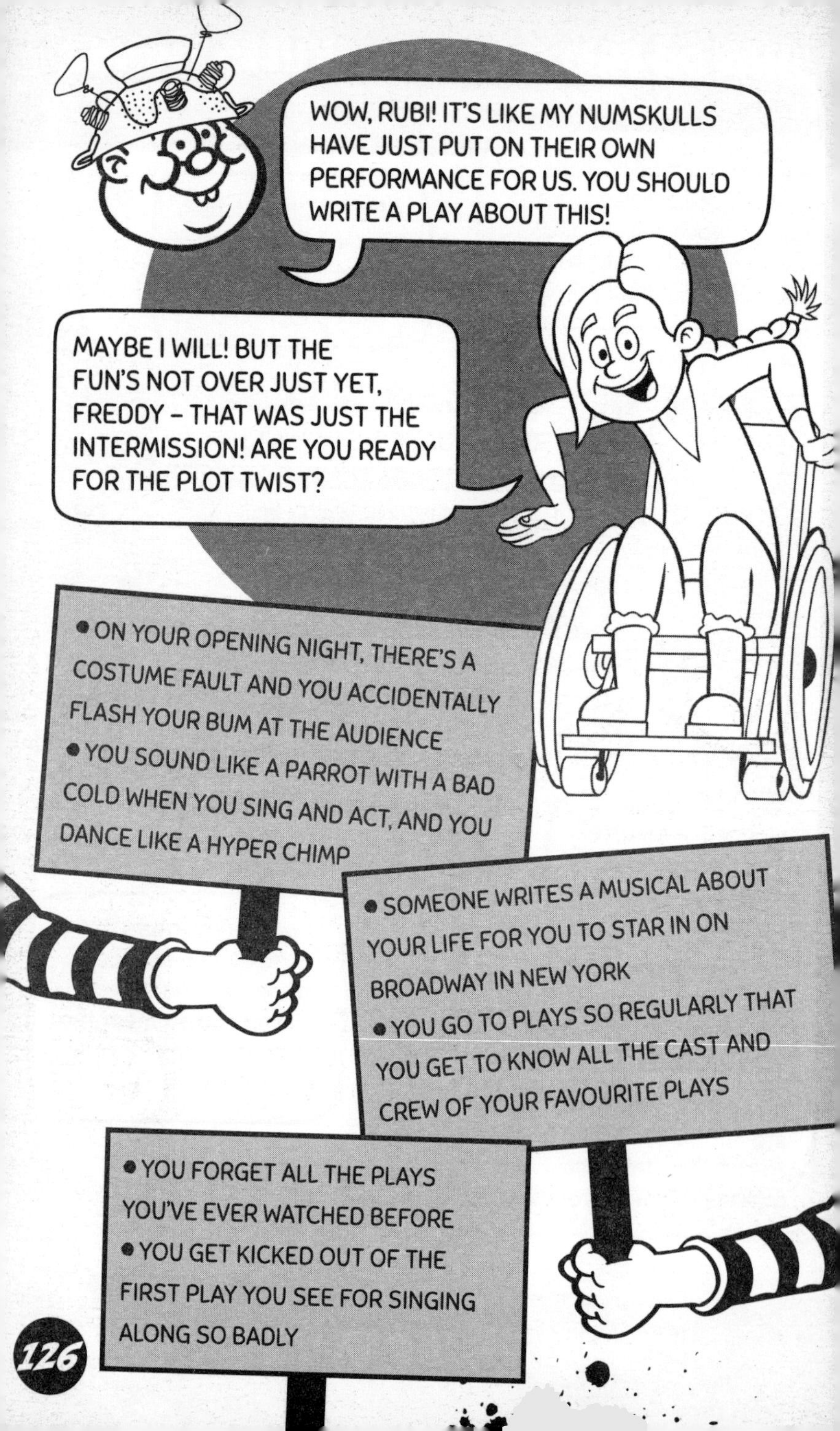
WOW, RUBI! IT'S LIKE MY NUMSKULLS HAVE JUST PUT ON THEIR OWN PERFORMANCE FOR US. YOU SHOULD WRITE A PLAY ABOUT THIS!
MAYBE I WILL! BUT THE FUN'S NOT OVER JUST YET, FREDDY – THAT WAS JUST THE INTERMISSION! ARE YOU READY FOR THE PLOT TWIST?
• ON YOUR OPENING NIGHT, THERE'S A COSTUME FAULT AND YOU ACCIDENTALLY FLASH YOUR BUM AT THE AUDIENCE
• YOU SOUND LIKE A PARROT WITH A BAD COLD WHEN YOU SING AND ACT, AND YOU DANCE LIKE A HYPER CHIMP
• SOMEONE WRITES A MUSICAL ABOUT YOUR LIFE FOR YOU TO STAR IN ON BROADWAY IN NEW YORK
• YOU GO TO PLAYS SO REGULARLY THAT YOU GET TO KNOW ALL THE CAST AND CREW OF YOUR FAVOURITE PLAYS
• YOU FORGET ALL THE PLAYS YOU'VE EVER WATCHED BEFORE
• YOU GET KICKED OUT OF THE FIRST PLAY YOU SEE FOR SINGING ALONG SO BADLY

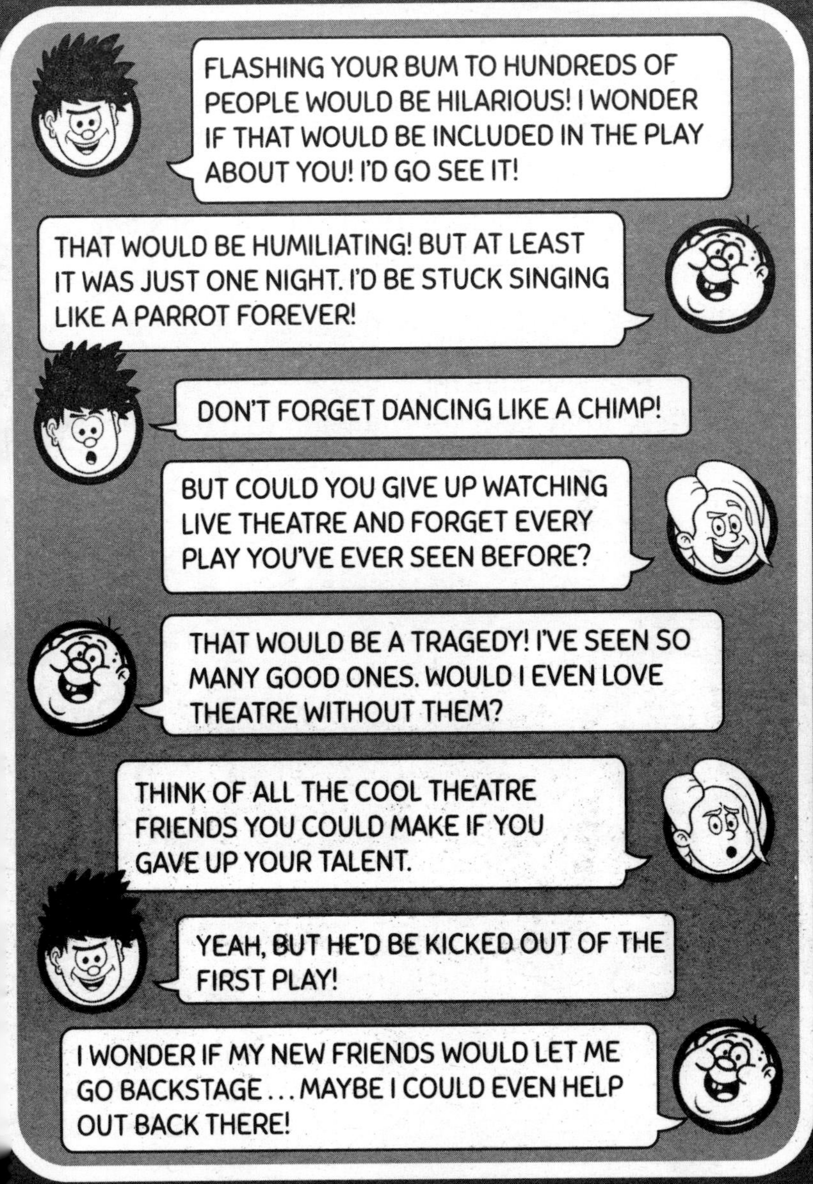
FLASHING YOUR BUM TO HUNDREDS OF PEOPLE WOULD BE HILARIOUS! I WONDER IF THAT WOULD BE INCLUDED IN THE PLAY ABOUT YOU! I'D GO SEE IT!
THAT WOULD BE HUMILIATING! BUT AT LEAST IT WAS JUST ONE NIGHT. I'D BE STUCK SINGING LIKE A PARROT FOREVER!
DON'T FORGET DANCING LIKE A CHIMP!
BUT COULD YOU GIVE UP WATCHING LIVE THEATRE AND FORGET EVERY PLAY YOU'VE EVER SEEN BEFORE?
THAT WOULD BE A TRAGEDY! I'VE SEEN SO MANY GOOD ONES. WOULD I EVEN LOVE THEATRE WITHOUT THEM?
THINK OF ALL THE COOL THEATRE FRIENDS YOU COULD MAKE IF YOU GAVE UP YOUR TALENT.
YEAH, BUT HE'D BE KICKED OUT OF THE FIRST PLAY!
I WONDER IF MY NEW FRIENDS WOULD LET ME GO BACKSTAGE... MAYBE I COULD EVEN HELP OUT BACK THERE!

WHICH OPTION WOULD YOU CHOOSE WITH ALL THOSE VARIATIONS ADDED INTO THE MIX?

CUTHBERT

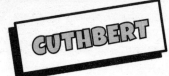

Cuthbert stepped forwards stiffly.

'Your invention is all right,' he said. 'It's not quite as good as this alarm I came up with – it plays a song I composed called *Ode to Mr Teacher* every time he enters the room.'

'Well,' Rubi said, 'do you want to have a go anyway?'

'I suppose so.'

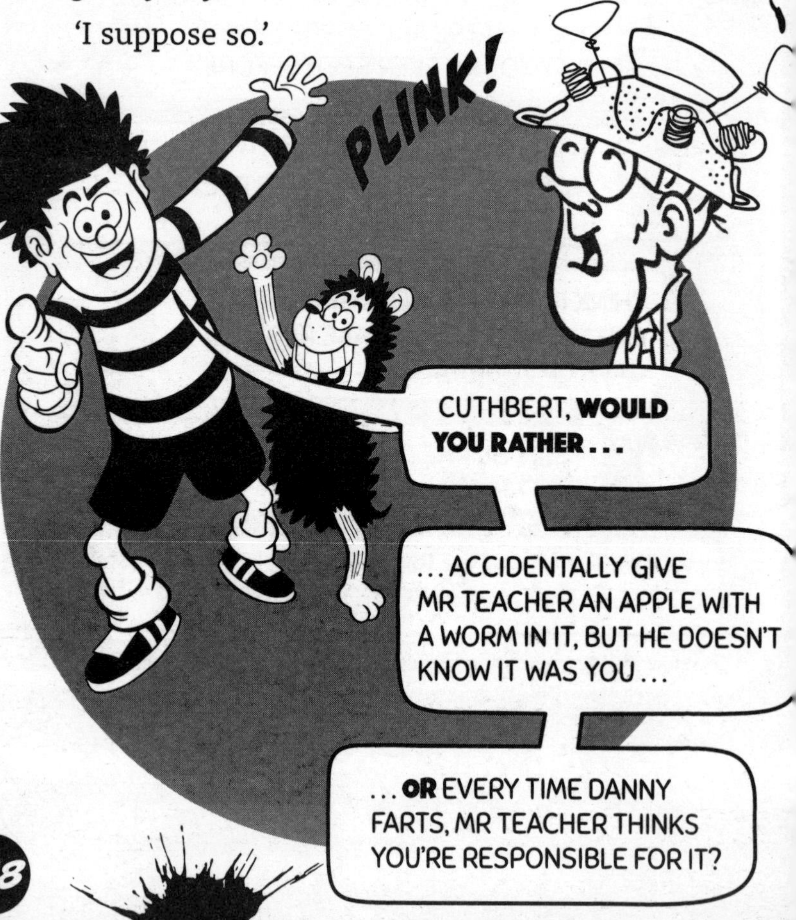

PLINK!
CUTHBERT, **WOULD YOU RATHER . . .**
. . . ACCIDENTALLY GIVE MR TEACHER AN APPLE WITH A WORM IN IT, BUT HE DOESN'T KNOW IT WAS YOU . . .
. . . **OR** EVERY TIME DANNY FARTS, MR TEACHER THINKS YOU'RE RESPONSIBLE FOR IT?

WHAT DO CUTHBERT'S NUMSKULLS THINK?

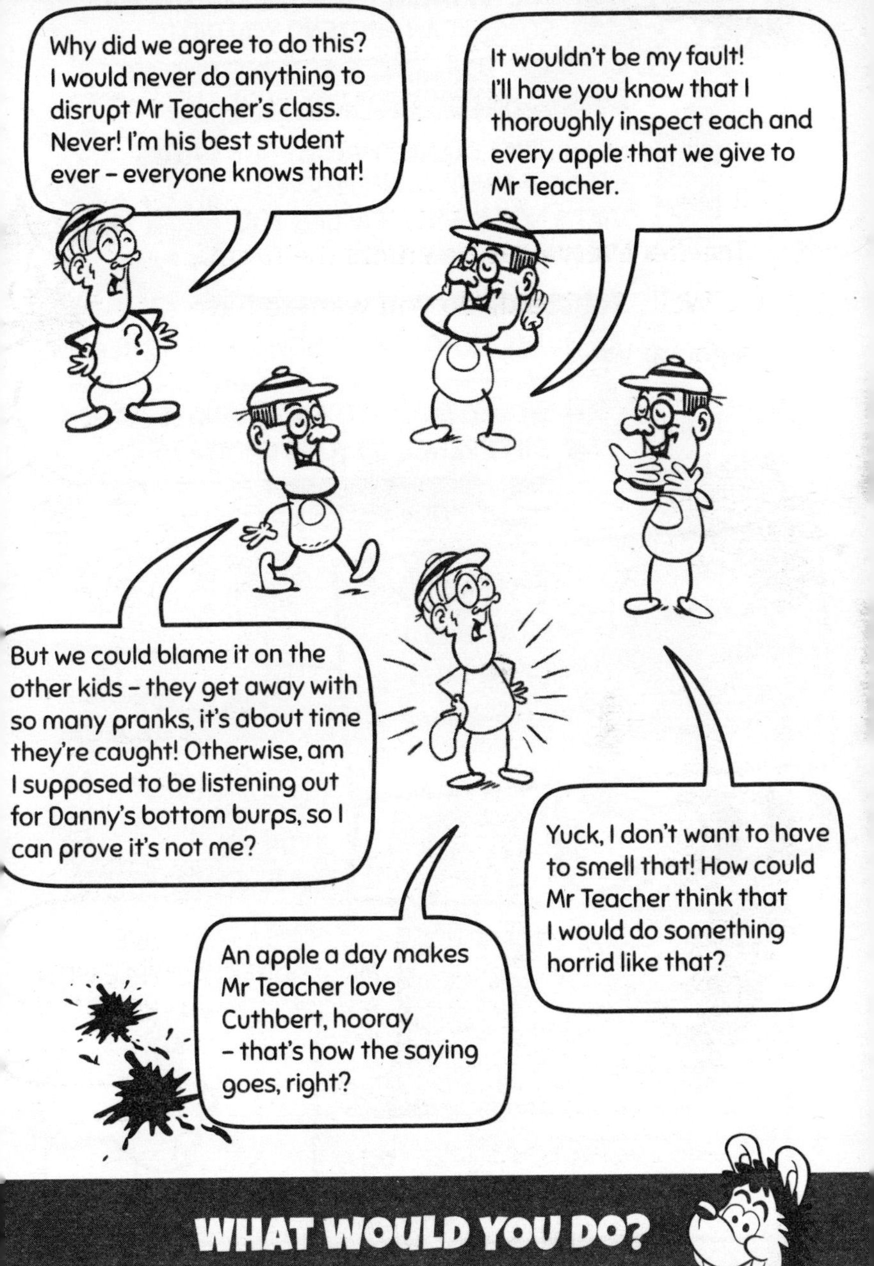
Why did we agree to do this? I would never do anything to disrupt Mr Teacher's class. Never! I'm his best student ever – everyone knows that!
It wouldn't be my fault! I'll have you know that I thoroughly inspect each and every apple that we give to Mr Teacher.
But we could blame it on the other kids – they get away with so many pranks, it's about time they're caught! Otherwise, am I supposed to be listening out for Danny's bottom burps, so I can prove it's not me?
Yuck, I don't want to have to smell that! How could Mr Teacher think that I would do something horrid like that?
An apple a day makes Mr Teacher love Cuthbert, hooray – that's how the saying goes, right?

WHAT WOULD YOU DO?

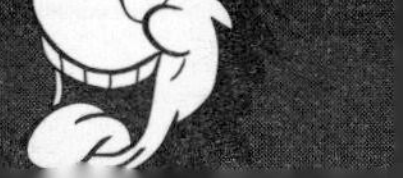

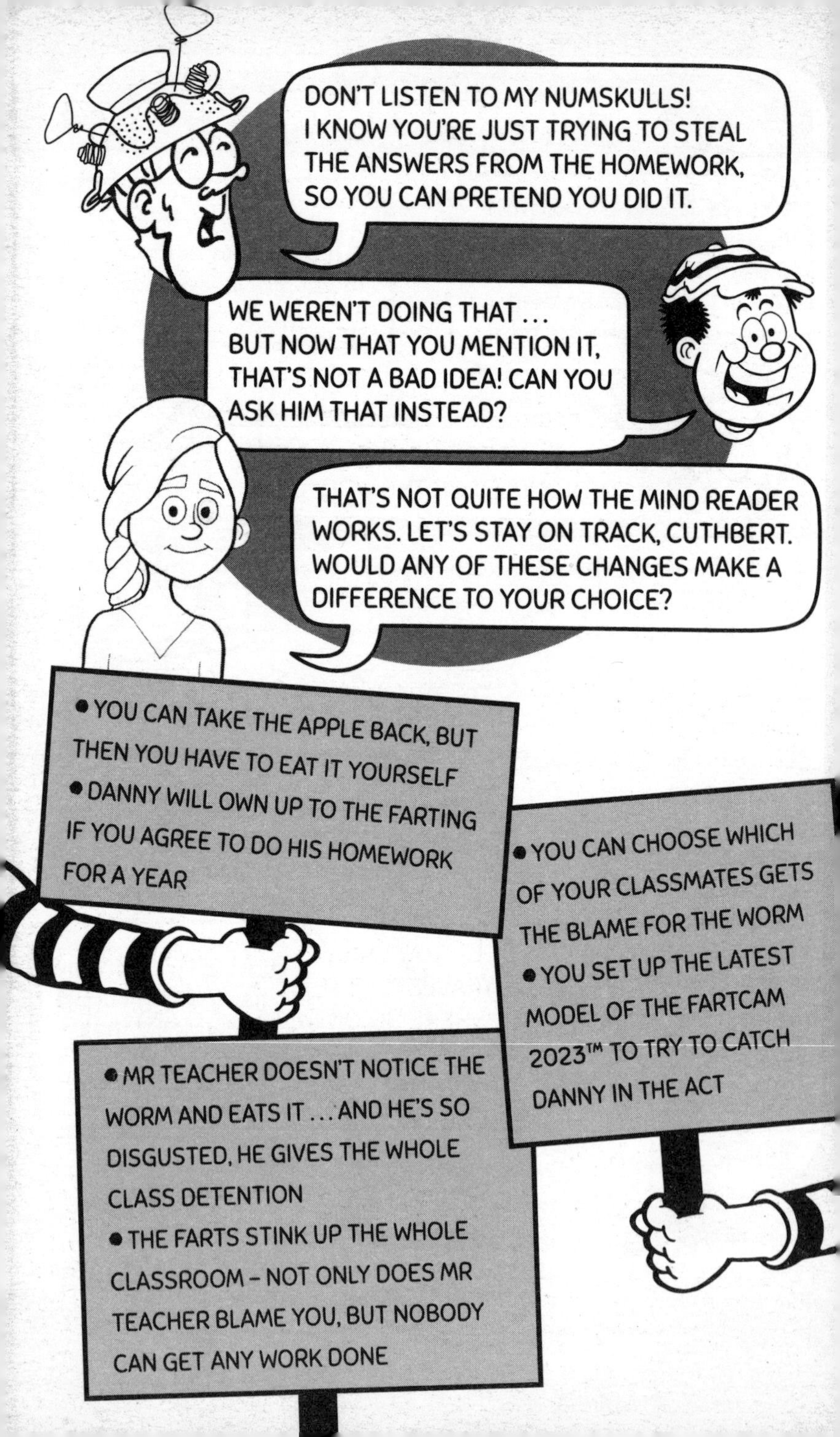
DON'T LISTEN TO MY NUMSKULLS! I KNOW YOU'RE JUST TRYING TO STEAL THE ANSWERS FROM THE HOMEWORK, SO YOU CAN PRETEND YOU DID IT.
WE WEREN'T DOING THAT . . . BUT NOW THAT YOU MENTION IT, THAT'S NOT A BAD IDEA! CAN YOU ASK HIM THAT INSTEAD?
THAT'S NOT QUITE HOW THE MIND READER WORKS. LET'S STAY ON TRACK, CUTHBERT. WOULD ANY OF THESE CHANGES MAKE A DIFFERENCE TO YOUR CHOICE?
• YOU CAN TAKE THE APPLE BACK, BUT THEN YOU HAVE TO EAT IT YOURSELF
• DANNY WILL OWN UP TO THE FARTING IF YOU AGREE TO DO HIS HOMEWORK FOR A YEAR
• YOU CAN CHOOSE WHICH OF YOUR CLASSMATES GETS THE BLAME FOR THE WORM
• YOU SET UP THE LATEST MODEL OF THE FARTCAM 2023™ TO TRY TO CATCH DANNY IN THE ACT
• MR TEACHER DOESN'T NOTICE THE WORM AND EATS IT . . . AND HE'S SO DISGUSTED, HE GIVES THE WHOLE CLASS DETENTION
• THE FARTS STINK UP THE WHOLE CLASSROOM – NOT ONLY DOES MR TEACHER BLAME YOU, BUT NOBODY CAN GET ANY WORK DONE

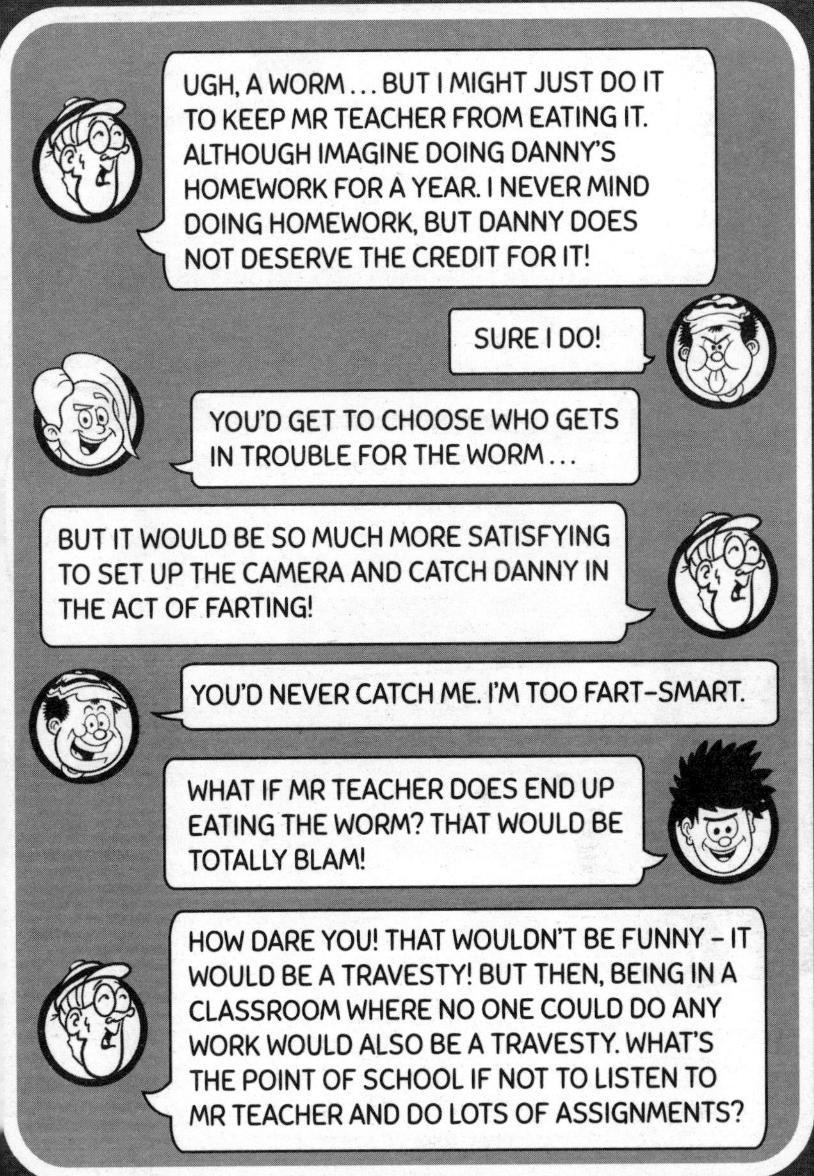
UGH, A WORM . . . BUT I MIGHT JUST DO IT TO KEEP MR TEACHER FROM EATING IT. ALTHOUGH IMAGINE DOING DANNY'S HOMEWORK FOR A YEAR. I NEVER MIND DOING HOMEWORK, BUT DANNY DOES NOT DESERVE THE CREDIT FOR IT!
SURE I DO!
YOU'D GET TO CHOOSE WHO GETS IN TROUBLE FOR THE WORM . . .
BUT IT WOULD BE SO MUCH MORE SATISFYING TO SET UP THE CAMERA AND CATCH DANNY IN THE ACT OF FARTING!
YOU'D NEVER CATCH ME. I'M TOO FART–SMART.
WHAT IF MR TEACHER DOES END UP EATING THE WORM? THAT WOULD BE TOTALLY BLAM!
HOW DARE YOU! THAT WOULDN'T BE FUNNY – IT WOULD BE A TRAVESTY! BUT THEN, BEING IN A CLASSROOM WHERE NO ONE COULD DO ANY WORK WOULD ALSO BE A TRAVESTY. WHAT'S THE POINT OF SCHOOL IF NOT TO LISTEN TO MR TEACHER AND DO LOTS OF ASSIGNMENTS?

WHICH OPTION WOULD YOU CHOOSE WITH ALL THOSE VARIATIONS ADDED INTO THE MIX?

'I'm next,' called Sidney.

'No, *I'm* next,' Toots said, pushing her twin aside. 'I was born first, so I get to go first. That's a scientific fact, and this project is for science after all.'

'Fine, but I'm going *right after you*,' Sidney grumbled.

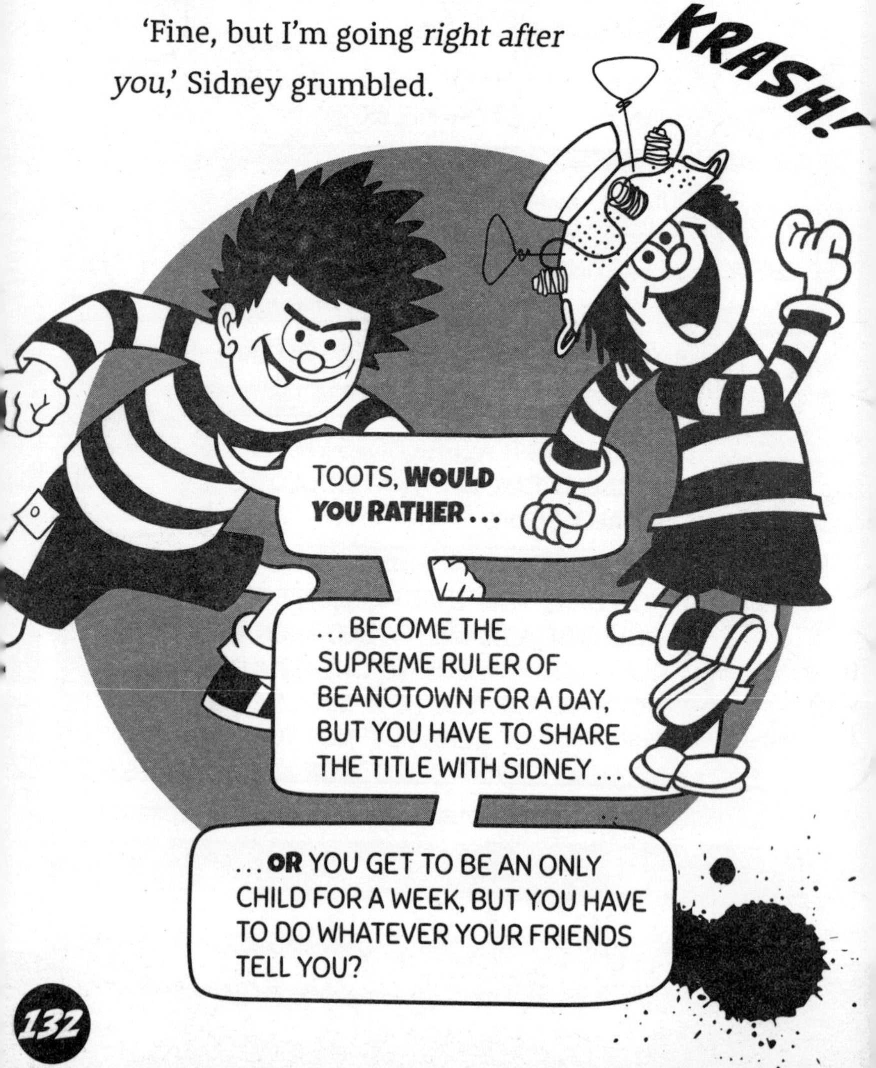
KRASH!
TOOTS, **WOULD YOU RATHER . . .**
. . . BECOME THE SUPREME RULER OF BEANOTOWN FOR A DAY, BUT YOU HAVE TO SHARE THE TITLE WITH SIDNEY . . .
. . . **OR** YOU GET TO BE AN ONLY CHILD FOR A WEEK, BUT YOU HAVE TO DO WHATEVER YOUR FRIENDS TELL YOU?

WHAT DO TOOTS' NUMSKULLS THINK?

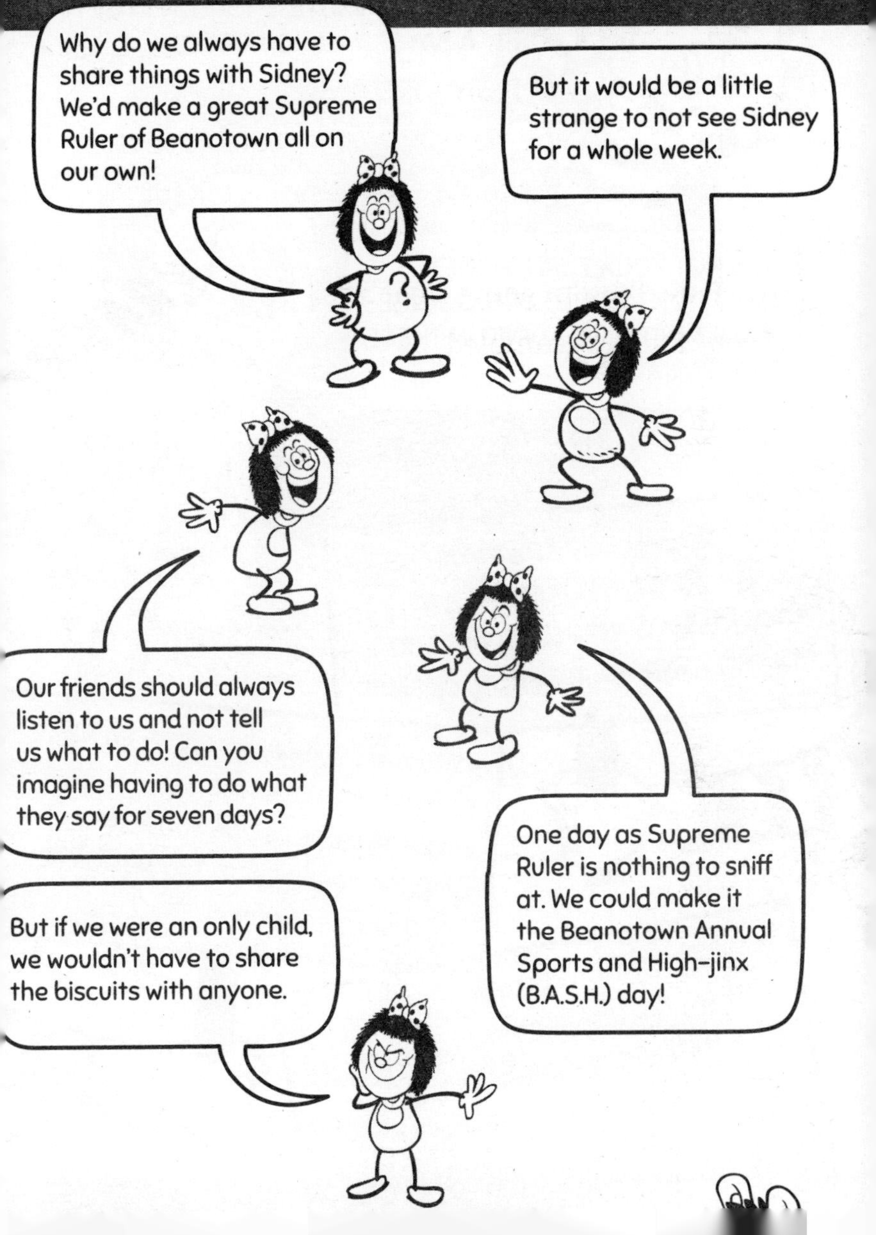
Why do we always have to share things with Sidney? We'd make a great Supreme Ruler of Beanotown all on our own!
But it would be a little strange to not see Sidney for a whole week.
Our friends should always listen to us and not tell us what to do! Can you imagine having to do what they say for seven days?
One day as Supreme Ruler is nothing to sniff at. We could make it the Beanotown Annual Sports and High-jinx (B.A.S.H.) day!
But if we were an only child, we wouldn't have to share the biscuits with anyone.

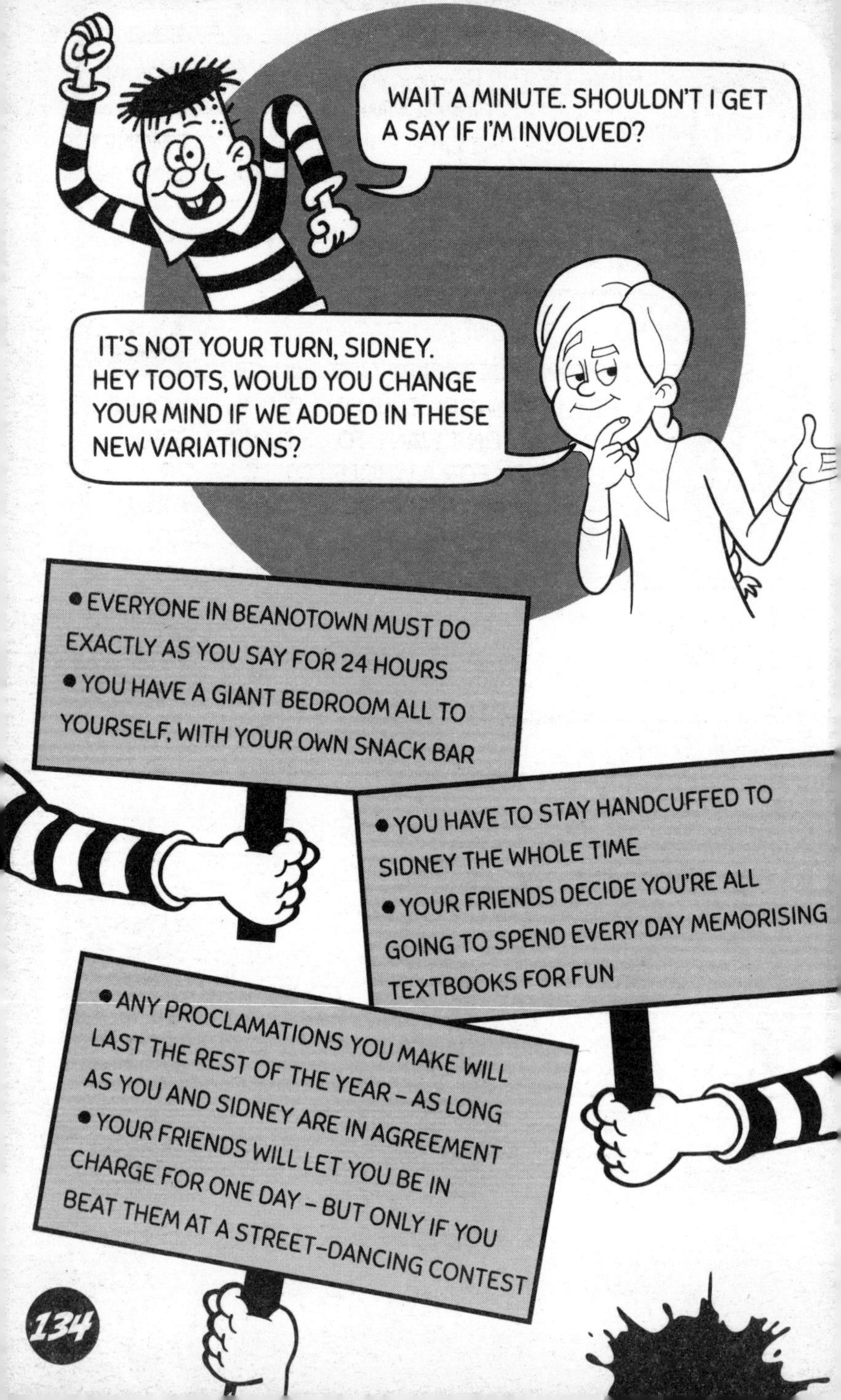
WAIT A MINUTE. SHOULDN'T I GET A SAY IF I'M INVOLVED?
IT'S NOT YOUR TURN, SIDNEY. HEY TOOTS, WOULD YOU CHANGE YOUR MIND IF WE ADDED IN THESE NEW VARIATIONS?
• EVERYONE IN BEANOTOWN MUST DO EXACTLY AS YOU SAY FOR 24 HOURS
• YOU HAVE A GIANT BEDROOM ALL TO YOURSELF, WITH YOUR OWN SNACK BAR
• YOU HAVE TO STAY HANDCUFFED TO SIDNEY THE WHOLE TIME
• YOUR FRIENDS DECIDE YOU'RE ALL GOING TO SPEND EVERY DAY MEMORISING TEXTBOOKS FOR FUN
• ANY PROCLAMATIONS YOU MAKE WILL LAST THE REST OF THE YEAR – AS LONG AS YOU AND SIDNEY ARE IN AGREEMENT
• YOUR FRIENDS WILL LET YOU BE IN CHARGE FOR ONE DAY – BUT ONLY IF YOU BEAT THEM AT A STREET-DANCING CONTEST

THINK OF THE POWER YOU'D HAVE AS SUPREME RULER. YOU COULD COMMAND ANYONE TO DO ANYTHING, LIKE GIVE YOU THEIR POCKET MONEY OR SMASH A MUD PIE INTO THEIR OWN FACE.

BUT THAT'S ONLY FOR ONE DAY. WHY WOULDN'T YOU TAKE THE BEDROOM TO YOURSELF WITH BUILT-IN SNACK BAR?

HEY, I CAN WORK THIS ONE OUT ON MY OWN! I KNOW I DON'T WANT TO BE HANDCUFFED TO SIDNEY FOR A WHOLE DAY. I'D NEVER HAVE A MOMENT TO MYSELF, AND IT WOULD MAKE USING MY CATAPULT REALLY HARD.

BUT WHAT IF WE TRICKED YOU INTO HAVING TO MEMORISE ONE OF YOUR TEXTBOOKS? THAT WOULD BE A FUNNY PRANK.

THIS IS WHY I'D BE AN ONLY CHILD FOR A WEEK!

BUT ... BUT ... I'M SURE WE COULD COME UP WITH GREAT PROCLAMATIONS FOR BEANOTOWN TOGETHER.

AND I'M SURE THAT I COULD BEAT YOU ALL AT A STREET-DANCING COMPETITION. THEN YOU'D HAVE TO DO WHAT I SAY - SO THERE!

WHICH OPTION WOULD YOU CHOOSE WITH ALL THOSE VARIATIONS ADDED INTO THE MIX?

SIDNEY

'I still can't believe Toots got to go before me,' Sidney complained.

'You can have your turn now, Sidney,' Rubi offered diplomatically.

Sidney eagerly grabbed the MIND reader from his sister's head.

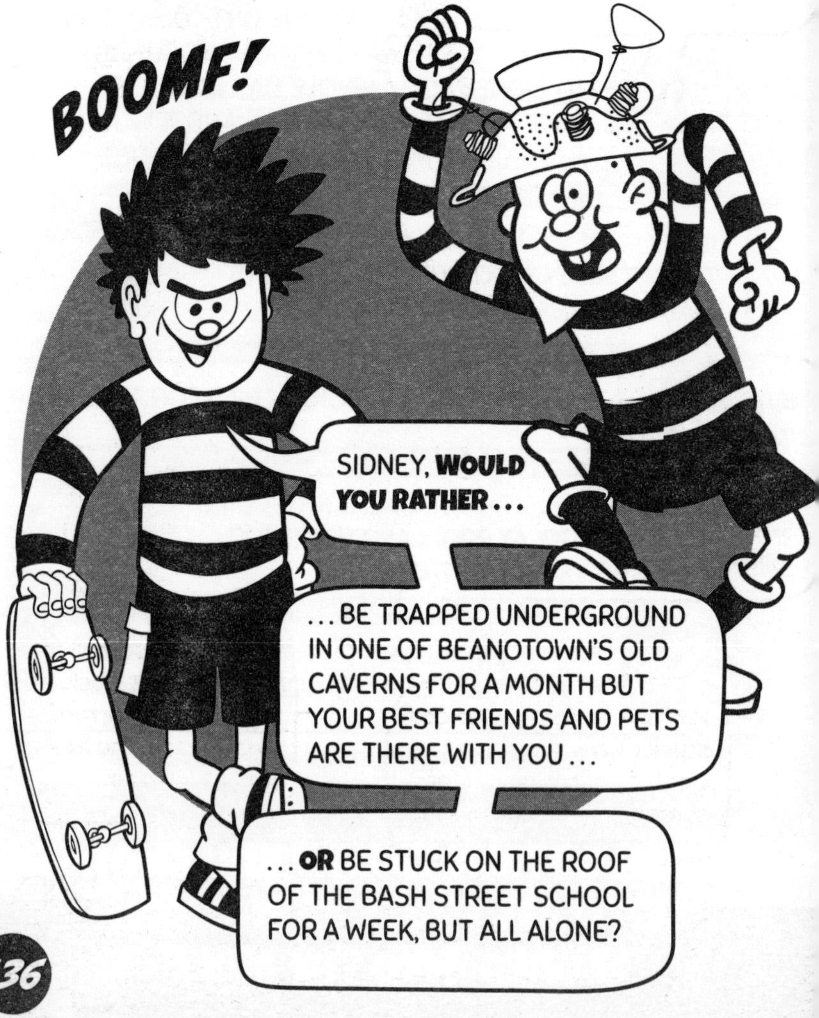

BOOMF!
SIDNEY, **WOULD YOU RATHER ...**
... BE TRAPPED UNDERGROUND IN ONE OF BEANOTOWN'S OLD CAVERNS FOR A MONTH BUT YOUR BEST FRIENDS AND PETS ARE THERE WITH YOU ...
... **OR** BE STUCK ON THE ROOF OF THE BASH STREET SCHOOL FOR A WEEK, BUT ALL ALONE?

WHAT DO SIDNEY'S NUMSKULLS THINK?

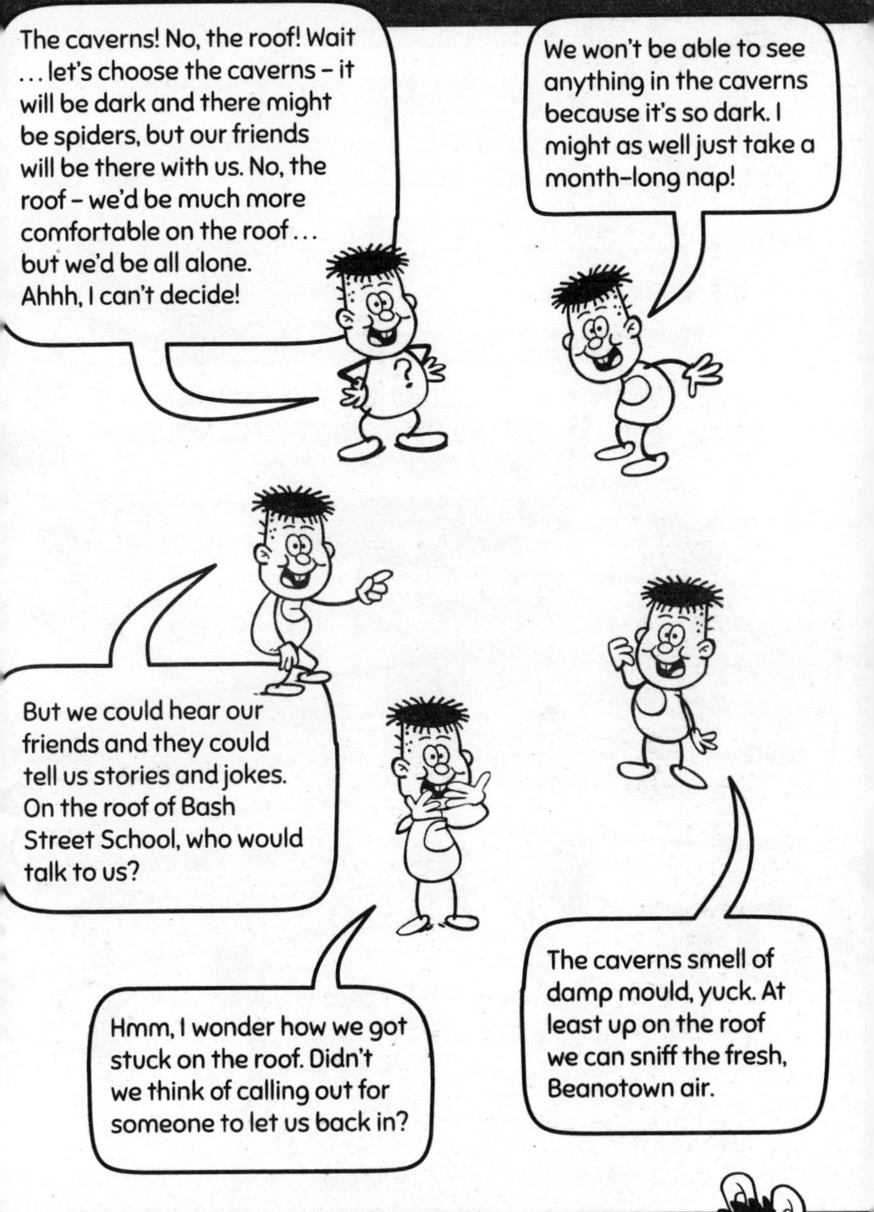
The caverns! No, the roof! Wait ... let's choose the caverns – it will be dark and there might be spiders, but our friends will be there with us. No, the roof – we'd be much more comfortable on the roof ... but we'd be all alone. Ahhh, I can't decide!
?
We won't be able to see anything in the caverns because it's so dark. I might as well just take a month-long nap!
But we could hear our friends and they could tell us stories and jokes. On the roof of Bash Street School, who would talk to us?
Hmm, I wonder how we got stuck on the roof. Didn't we think of calling out for someone to let us back in?
The caverns smell of damp mould, yuck. At least up on the roof we can sniff the fresh, Beanotown air.

WHAT WOULD YOU DO?

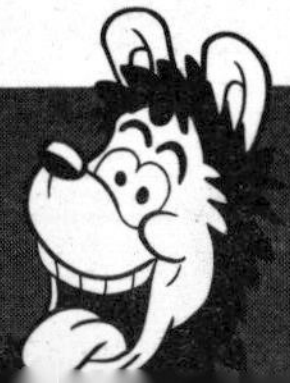

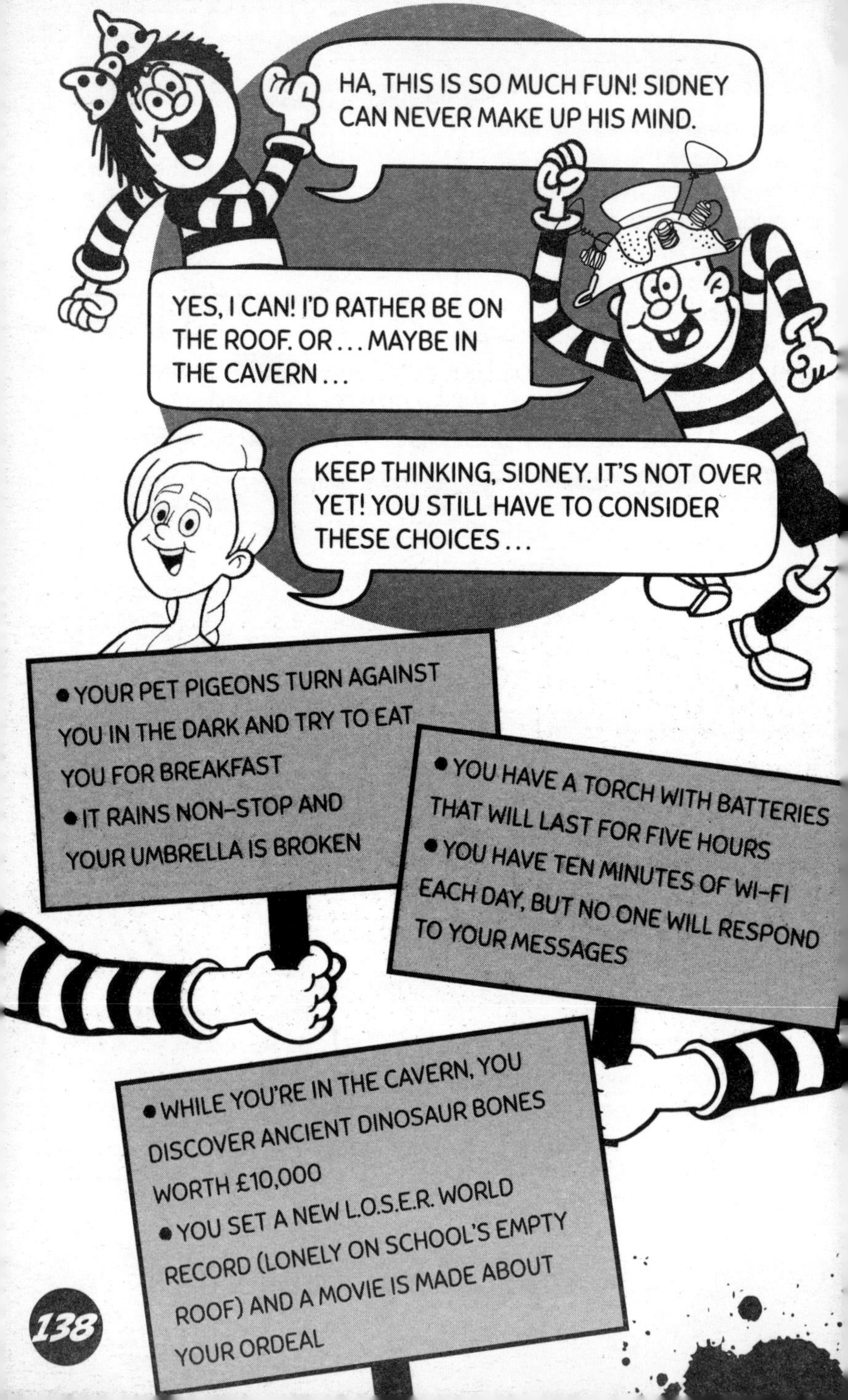
HA, THIS IS SO MUCH FUN! SIDNEY CAN NEVER MAKE UP HIS MIND.
YES, I CAN! I'D RATHER BE ON THE ROOF. OR . . . MAYBE IN THE CAVERN . . .
KEEP THINKING, SIDNEY. IT'S NOT OVER YET! YOU STILL HAVE TO CONSIDER THESE CHOICES . . .
• YOUR PET PIGEONS TURN AGAINST YOU IN THE DARK AND TRY TO EAT YOU FOR BREAKFAST
• IT RAINS NON-STOP AND YOUR UMBRELLA IS BROKEN
• YOU HAVE A TORCH WITH BATTERIES THAT WILL LAST FOR FIVE HOURS
• YOU HAVE TEN MINUTES OF WI-FI EACH DAY, BUT NO ONE WILL RESPOND TO YOUR MESSAGES
• WHILE YOU'RE IN THE CAVERN, YOU DISCOVER ANCIENT DINOSAUR BONES WORTH £10,000
• YOU SET A NEW L.O.S.E.R. WORLD RECORD (LONELY ON SCHOOL'S EMPTY ROOF) AND A MOVIE IS MADE ABOUT YOUR ORDEAL

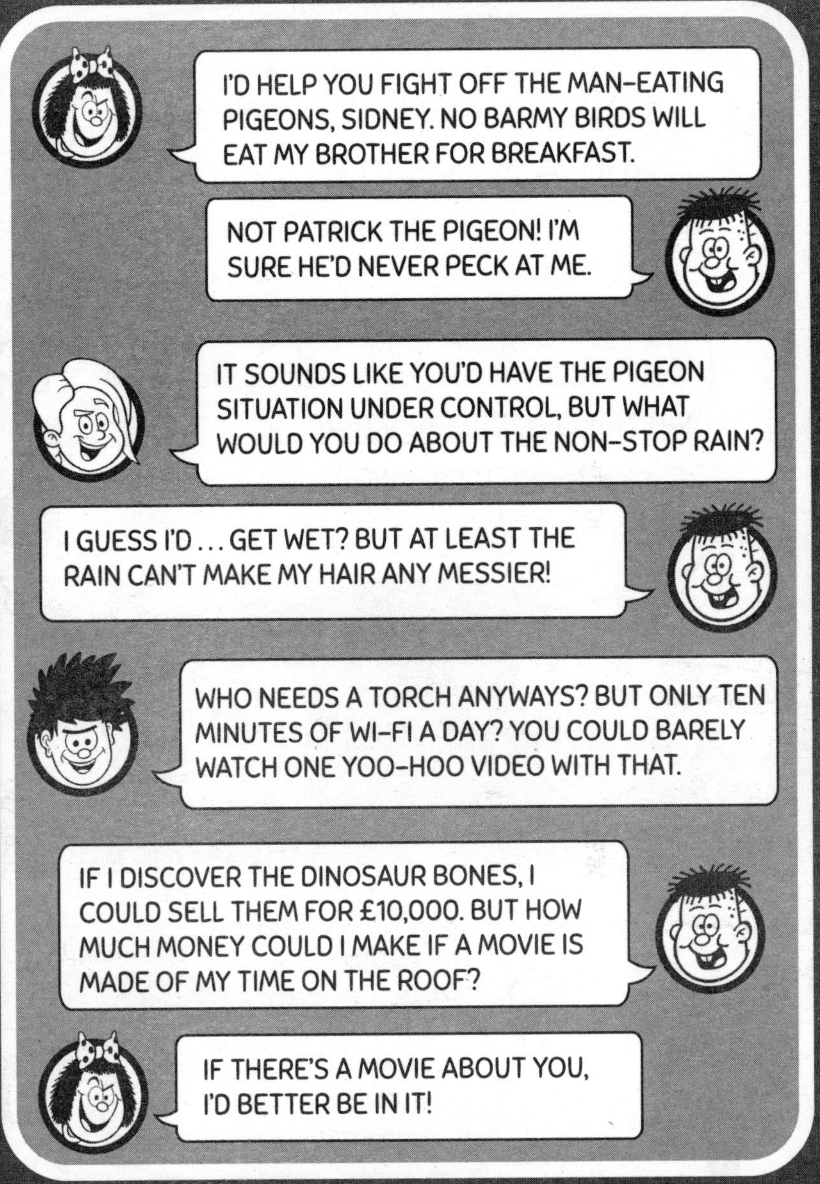
I'D HELP YOU FIGHT OFF THE MAN-EATING PIGEONS, SIDNEY. NO BARMY BIRDS WILL EAT MY BROTHER FOR BREAKFAST.
NOT PATRICK THE PIGEON! I'M SURE HE'D NEVER PECK AT ME.
IT SOUNDS LIKE YOU'D HAVE THE PIGEON SITUATION UNDER CONTROL, BUT WHAT WOULD YOU DO ABOUT THE NON-STOP RAIN?
I GUESS I'D . . . GET WET? BUT AT LEAST THE RAIN CAN'T MAKE MY HAIR ANY MESSIER!
WHO NEEDS A TORCH ANYWAYS? BUT ONLY TEN MINUTES OF WI-FI A DAY? YOU COULD BARELY WATCH ONE YOO-HOO VIDEO WITH THAT.
IF I DISCOVER THE DINOSAUR BONES, I COULD SELL THEM FOR £10,000. BUT HOW MUCH MONEY COULD I MAKE IF A MOVIE IS MADE OF MY TIME ON THE ROOF?
IF THERE'S A MOVIE ABOUT YOU, I'D BETTER BE IN IT!

WHICH OPTION WOULD YOU CHOOSE WITH ALL THOSE VARIATIONS ADDED INTO THE MIX?

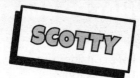

All of a sudden, an alarm sounded on Rubi's control panel.

'What is that?' Scotty asked. 'That alarm is louder than I am!'

Rubi twisted a nozzle, sighing loudly. 'That's just your tie, Scotty. It got caught in the MIND reader! Hold on, I'll pull it free.'

'Oh, ok. Glad you spotted the problem. When you fix it, can I have a go?'

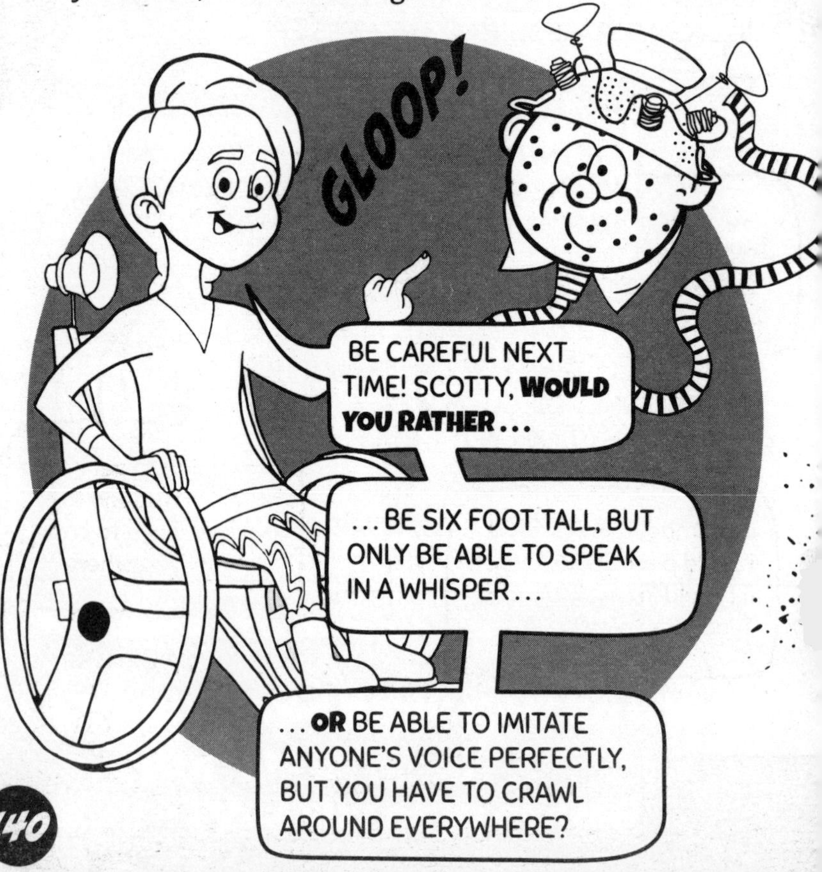
GLOOP!
BE CAREFUL NEXT TIME! SCOTTY, **WOULD YOU RATHER . . .**
. . . BE SIX FOOT TALL, BUT ONLY BE ABLE TO SPEAK IN A WHISPER . . .
. . . **OR** BE ABLE TO IMITATE ANYONE'S VOICE PERFECTLY, BUT YOU HAVE TO CRAWL AROUND EVERYWHERE?

WHAT DO SCOTTY'S NUMSKULLS THINK?

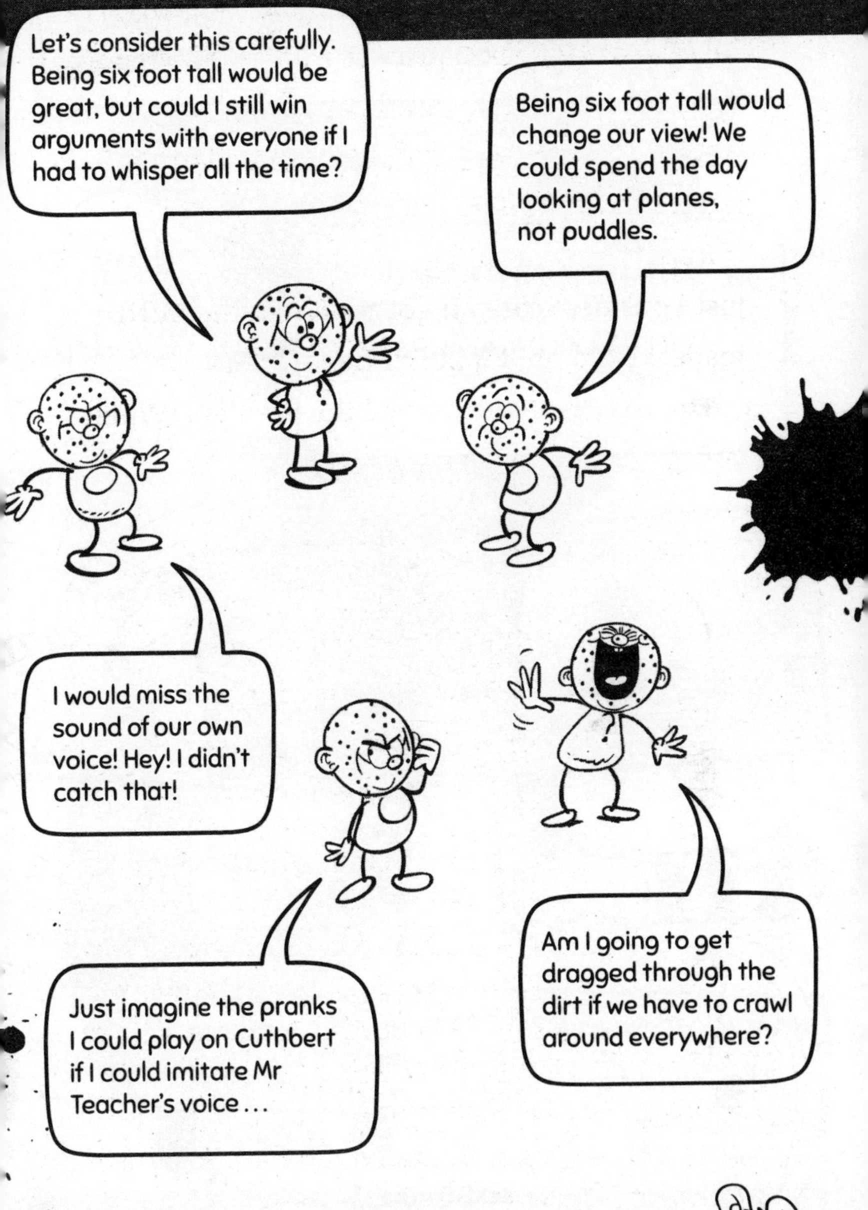

Let's consider this carefully. Being six foot tall would be great, but could I still win arguments with everyone if I had to whisper all the time?
Being six foot tall would change our view! We could spend the day looking at planes, not puddles.
I would miss the sound of our own voice! Hey! I didn't catch that!
Am I going to get dragged through the dirt if we have to crawl around everywhere?
Just imagine the pranks I could play on Cuthbert if I could imitate Mr Teacher's voice . . .

WHAT WOULD YOU DO?

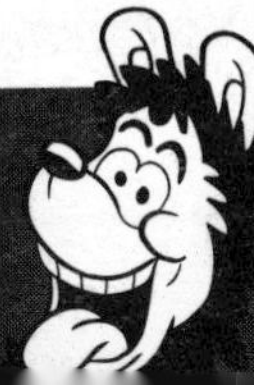

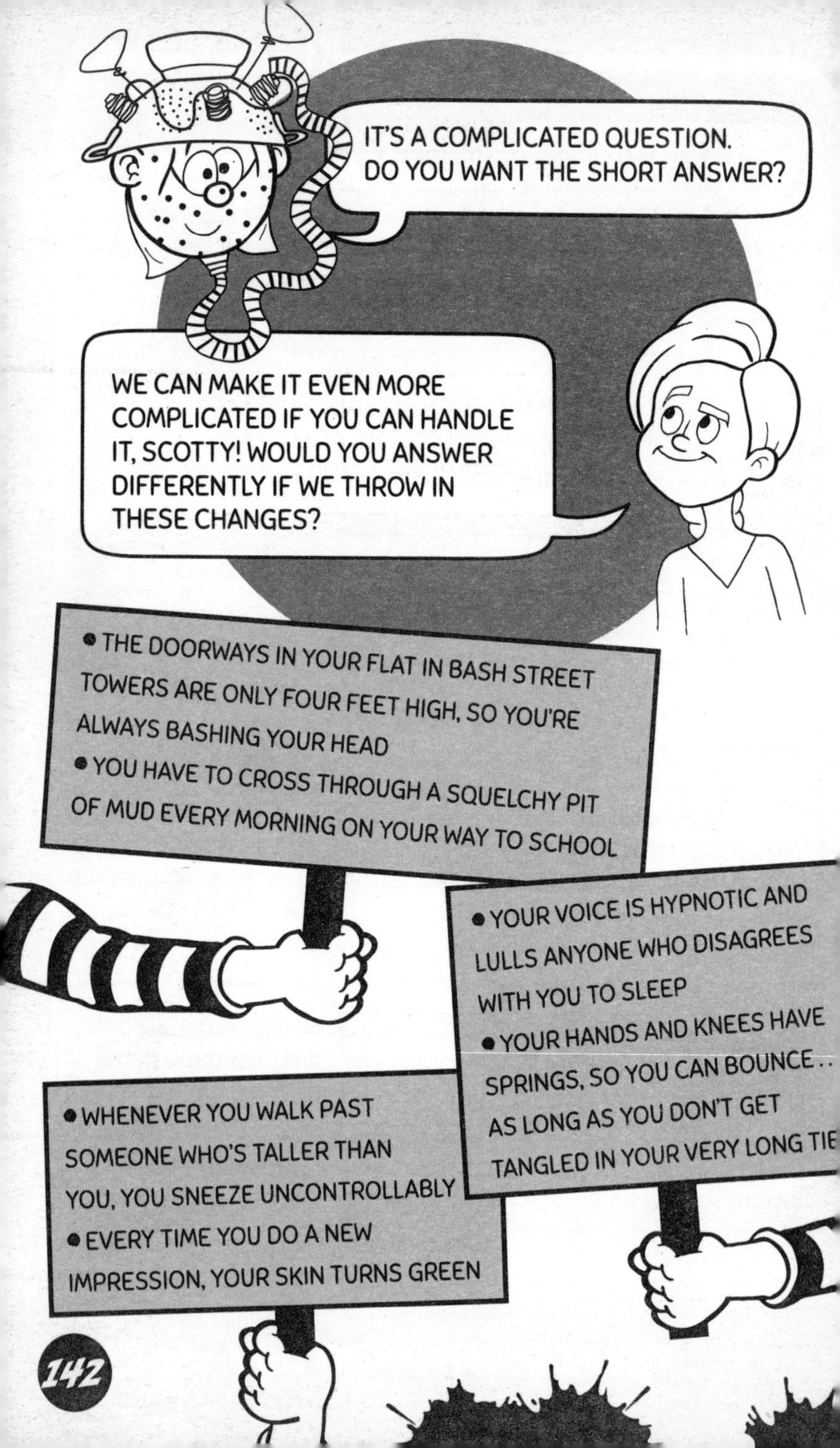

IT'S A COMPLICATED QUESTION. DO YOU WANT THE SHORT ANSWER?
WE CAN MAKE IT EVEN MORE COMPLICATED IF YOU CAN HANDLE IT, SCOTTY! WOULD YOU ANSWER DIFFERENTLY IF WE THROW IN THESE CHANGES?
• THE DOORWAYS IN YOUR FLAT IN BASH STREET TOWERS ARE ONLY FOUR FEET HIGH, SO YOU'RE ALWAYS BASHING YOUR HEAD
• YOU HAVE TO CROSS THROUGH A SQUELCHY PIT OF MUD EVERY MORNING ON YOUR WAY TO SCHOOL
• YOUR VOICE IS HYPNOTIC AND LULLS ANYONE WHO DISAGREES WITH YOU TO SLEEP
• YOUR HANDS AND KNEES HAVE SPRINGS, SO YOU CAN BOUNCE... AS LONG AS YOU DON'T GET TANGLED IN YOUR VERY LONG TIE
• WHENEVER YOU WALK PAST SOMEONE WHO'S TALLER THAN YOU, YOU SNEEZE UNCONTROLLABLY
• EVERY TIME YOU DO A NEW IMPRESSION, YOUR SKIN TURNS GREEN

BASHING YOUR HEAD IS NO FUN. YOU'D HAVE TO REMEMBER TO DUCK!

I'VE NEVER BASHED MY HEAD ON A DOORWAY BEFORE ... SO THANKS FOR THAT HEADS UP.

YOU'D HAVE SUCH A HEADACHE! BUT SURELY IT WOULDN'T BE AS BAD AS CRAWLING THROUGH A MUD PIT EVERY DAY.

I DON'T KNOW IF I AGREE, RUBI. HEY! THAT MEANS I COULD USE MY HYPNOTIC VOICE POWERS TO PUT YOU TO SLEEP!

YOU COULD PUT MR TEACHER TO SLEEP EVERY DAY! OR TAKE THE SPRINGS ON YOUR HANDS. THEY'D MAKE YOU SO GOOD AT SPORTS, YOU MIGHT EVEN SCORE A GOAL AGAINST ME ONE DAY.

YOU GUYS KNOW I LIVE ON THE EIGHTH STOREY, RIGHT? SO I'D HAVE TO MOVE, OR I'D BE SNEEZING ALL THE TIME.

I WANT TO SEE YOUR SKIN TURN GREEN WITH YOUR VOICE IMPRESSIONS. YOU'D LOOK LIKE A BOGEYMAN!

WHICH OPTION WOULD YOU CHOOSE WITH ALL THOSE VARIATIONS ADDED INTO THE MIX?

WILFRID

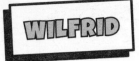

Toots pushed someone else forwards for a go.

'Wilfrid, is that you?' Rubi asked.

'No,' came a voice from inside the jumper.

'Oh, go on Wilfrid,' Danny said. 'We've all done it.'

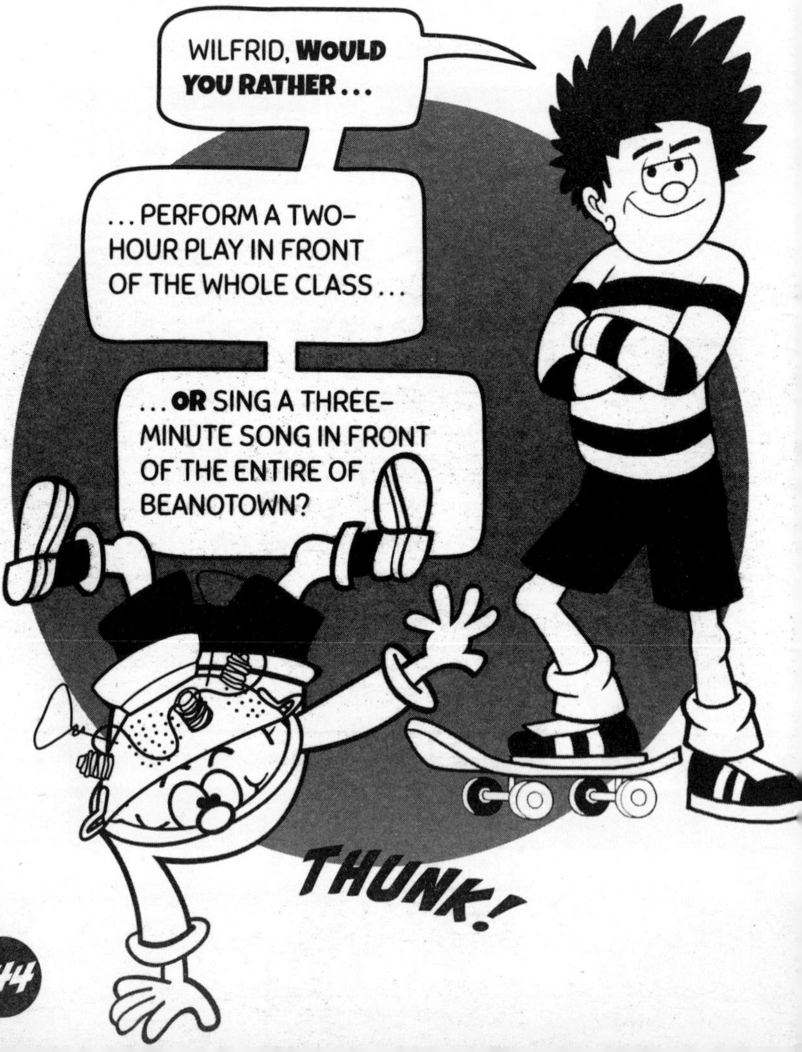
WILFRID, **WOULD YOU RATHER . . .**
. . . PERFORM A TWO-HOUR PLAY IN FRONT OF THE WHOLE CLASS . . .
. . . **OR** SING A THREE-MINUTE SONG IN FRONT OF THE ENTIRE OF BEANOTOWN?
THUNK!

WHAT DO WILFRID'S NUMSKULLS THINK?

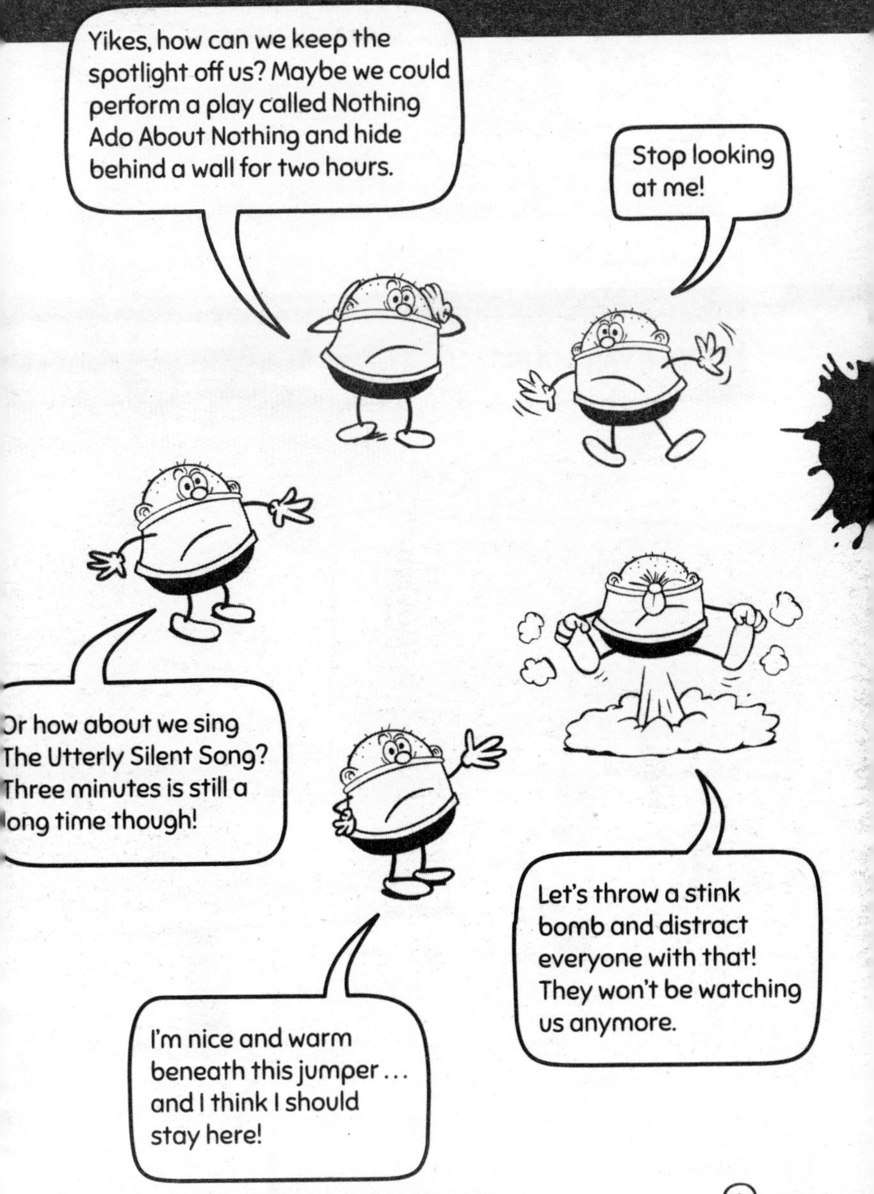
Yikes, how can we keep the spotlight off us? Maybe we could perform a play called Nothing Ado About Nothing and hide behind a wall for two hours.
Stop looking at me!
Or how about we sing The Utterly Silent Song? Three minutes is still a ong time though!
Let's throw a stink bomb and distract everyone with that! They won't be watching us anymore.
I'm nice and warm beneath this jumper . . . and I think I should stay here!

WHAT WOULD YOU DO?

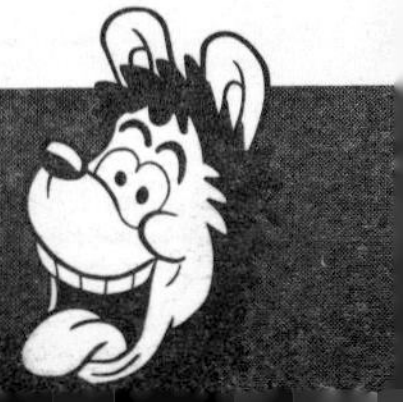

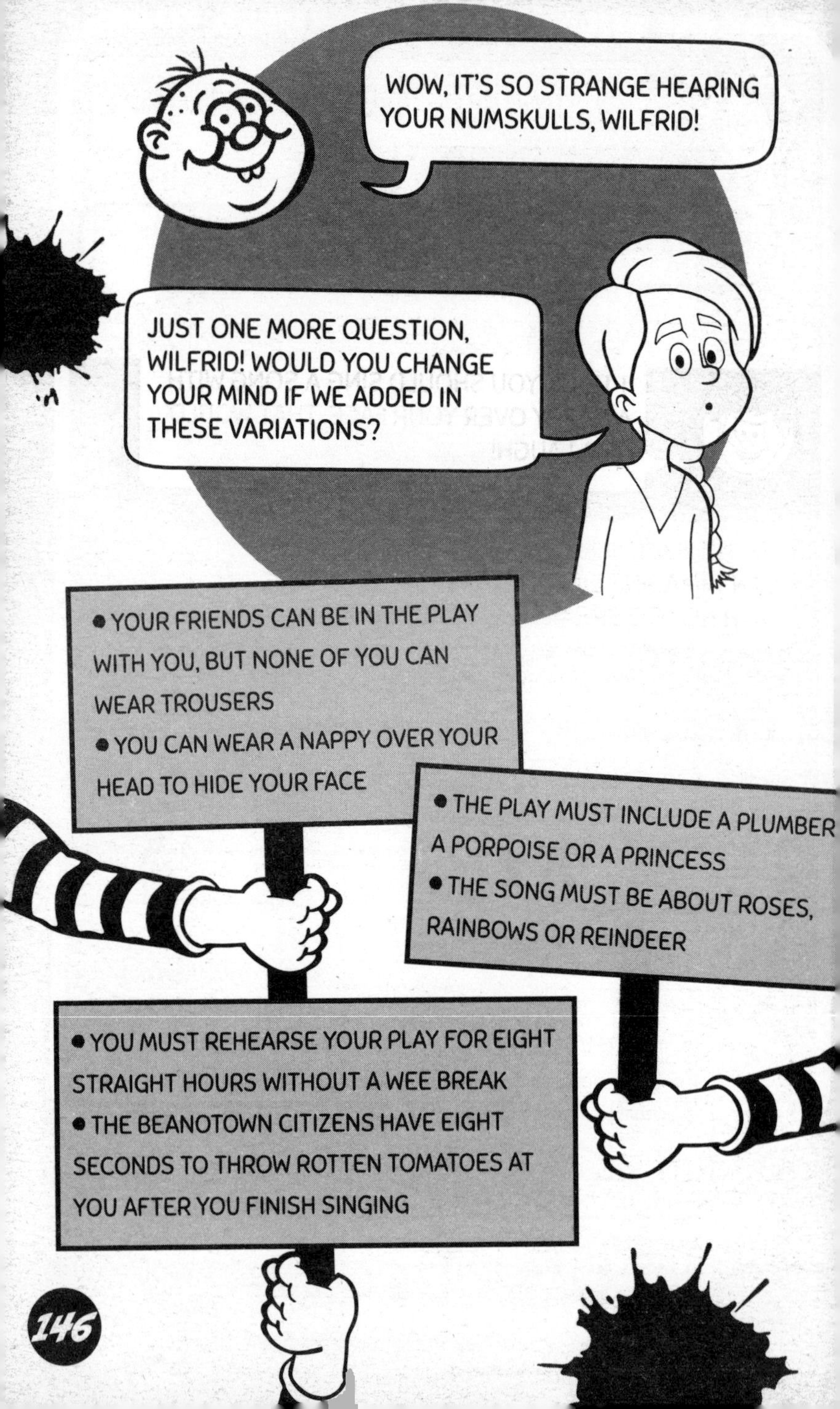
WOW, IT'S SO STRANGE HEARING YOUR NUMSKULLS, WILFRID!
JUST ONE MORE QUESTION, WILFRID! WOULD YOU CHANGE YOUR MIND IF WE ADDED IN THESE VARIATIONS?
• YOUR FRIENDS CAN BE IN THE PLAY WITH YOU, BUT NONE OF YOU CAN WEAR TROUSERS
• YOU CAN WEAR A NAPPY OVER YOUR HEAD TO HIDE YOUR FACE
• THE PLAY MUST INCLUDE A PLUMBER A PORPOISE OR A PRINCESS
• THE SONG MUST BE ABOUT ROSES, RAINBOWS OR REINDEER
• YOU MUST REHEARSE YOUR PLAY FOR EIGHT STRAIGHT HOURS WITHOUT A WEE BREAK
• THE BEANOTOWN CITIZENS HAVE EIGHT SECONDS TO THROW ROTTEN TOMATOES AT YOU AFTER YOU FINISH SINGING

I'LL STAND UP ON STAGE WITH YOU, WILFRID.

THANKS, TOOTS. MAYBE WE CAN DO A PLAY ABOUT MAGIC TRICKS, AND YOU CAN MAKE ME DISAPPEAR!

I THINK YOU SHOULD SING A SONG WITH A NAPPY OVER YOUR FACE. THAT WOULD BE A LAUGH!

I DON'T WANT A NAPPY ON MY HEAD! BUT I CAN'T IMAGINE EIGHT HOURS OF REHEARSAL WITH NO LOO BREAKS.

AT LEAST YOU'D HAVE A NAPPY!

THAT COULD END BADLY. BUT MAYBE NOT AS BADLY AS GIVING BEANOTOWN THE CHANCE TO THROW ROTTEN TOMATOES. I WOULDN'T WANT TO BE COVERED FROM MY HEAD TO-MA-TOES IN TOMATOES.

HRM, YES, THAT WOULD BE SOUP-ER BAD! MAYBE YOU SHOULD DO THIS ONE, DENNIS.

WHICH OPTION WOULD YOU CHOOSE WITH ALL THOSE VARIATIONS ADDED INTO THE MIX?

PLUG

Plug turned to look at the other kids from Class 2B. 'Thanks for saving the most strikingly handsome of us for last,' he said with a toothy grin.

'Who?' Dennis asked, puzzled.

'Ha ha, Dennis. Rubi, you can hook me up now,' Plug continued.

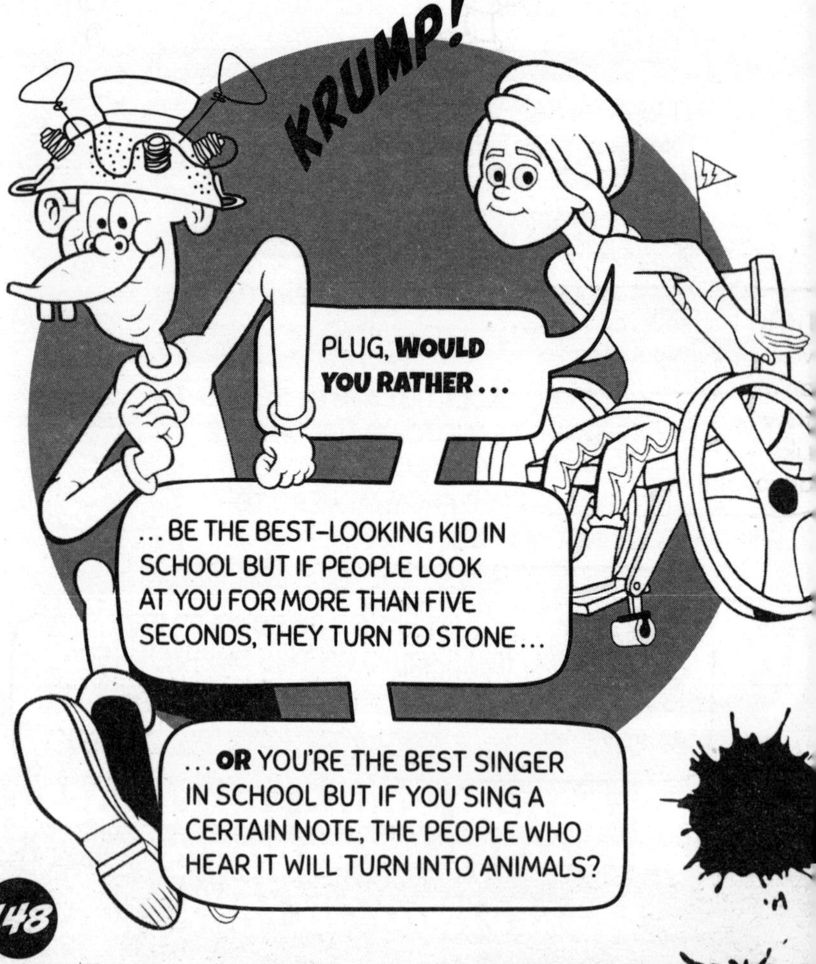

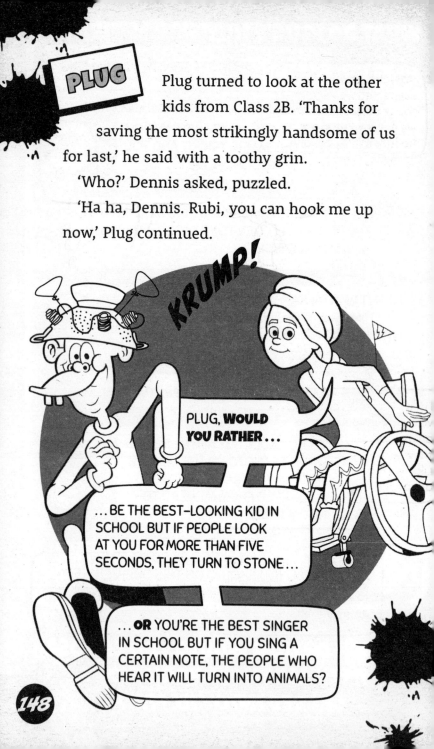

KRUMP!
PLUG, **WOULD YOU RATHER**...
...BE THE BEST-LOOKING KID IN SCHOOL BUT IF PEOPLE LOOK AT YOU FOR MORE THAN FIVE SECONDS, THEY TURN TO STONE...
...**OR** YOU'RE THE BEST SINGER IN SCHOOL BUT IF YOU SING A CERTAIN NOTE, THE PEOPLE WHO HEAR IT WILL TURN INTO ANIMALS?

WHAT DO PLUG'S NUMSKULLS THINK?

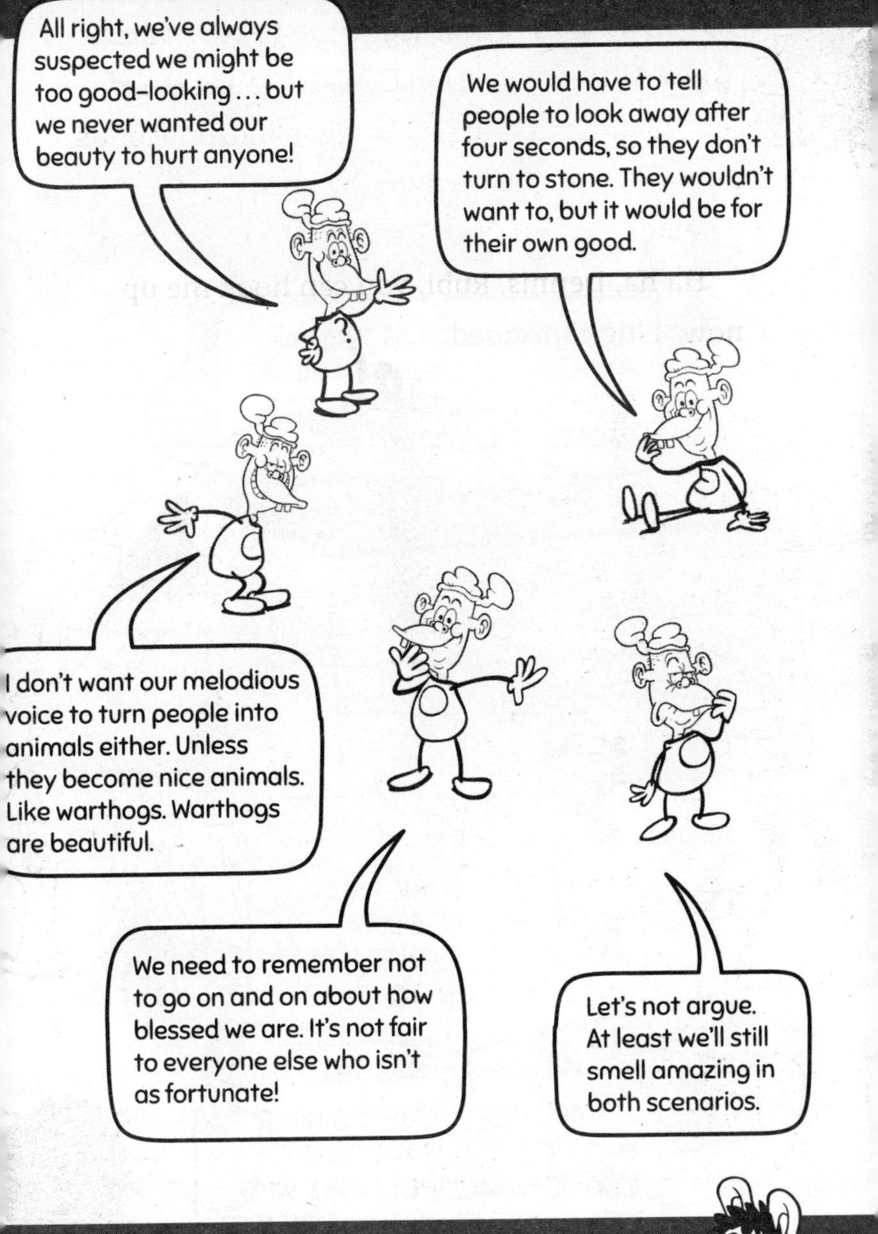
All right, we've always suspected we might be too good-looking ... but we never wanted our beauty to hurt anyone!
We would have to tell people to look away after four seconds, so they don't turn to stone. They wouldn't want to, but it would be for their own good.
I don't want our melodious voice to turn people into animals either. Unless they become nice animals. Like warthogs. Warthogs are beautiful.
We need to remember not to go on and on about how blessed we are. It's not fair to everyone else who isn't as fortunate!
Let's not argue. At least we'll still smell amazing in both scenarios.

WHAT WOULD YOU DO?

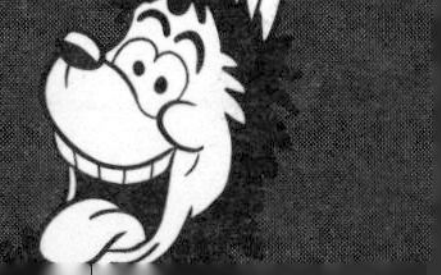

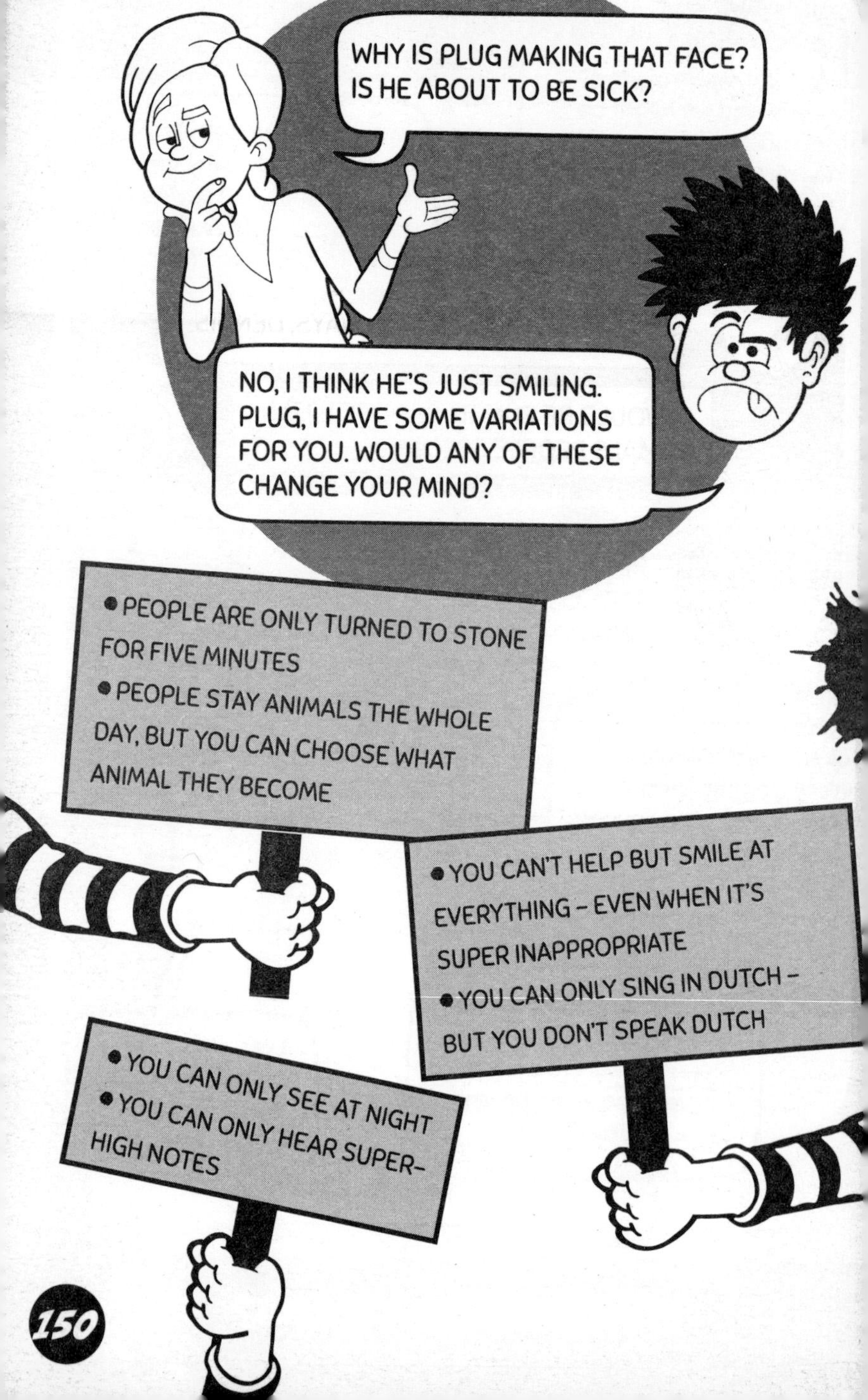

WHY IS PLUG MAKING THAT FACE? IS HE ABOUT TO BE SICK?
NO, I THINK HE'S JUST SMILING. PLUG, I HAVE SOME VARIATIONS FOR YOU. WOULD ANY OF THESE CHANGE YOUR MIND?
• PEOPLE ARE ONLY TURNED TO STONE FOR FIVE MINUTES
• PEOPLE STAY ANIMALS THE WHOLE DAY, BUT YOU CAN CHOOSE WHAT ANIMAL THEY BECOME
• YOU CAN'T HELP BUT SMILE AT EVERYTHING – EVEN WHEN IT'S SUPER INAPPROPRIATE
• YOU CAN ONLY SING IN DUTCH – BUT YOU DON'T SPEAK DUTCH
• YOU CAN ONLY SEE AT NIGHT
• YOU CAN ONLY HEAR SUPER-HIGH NOTES

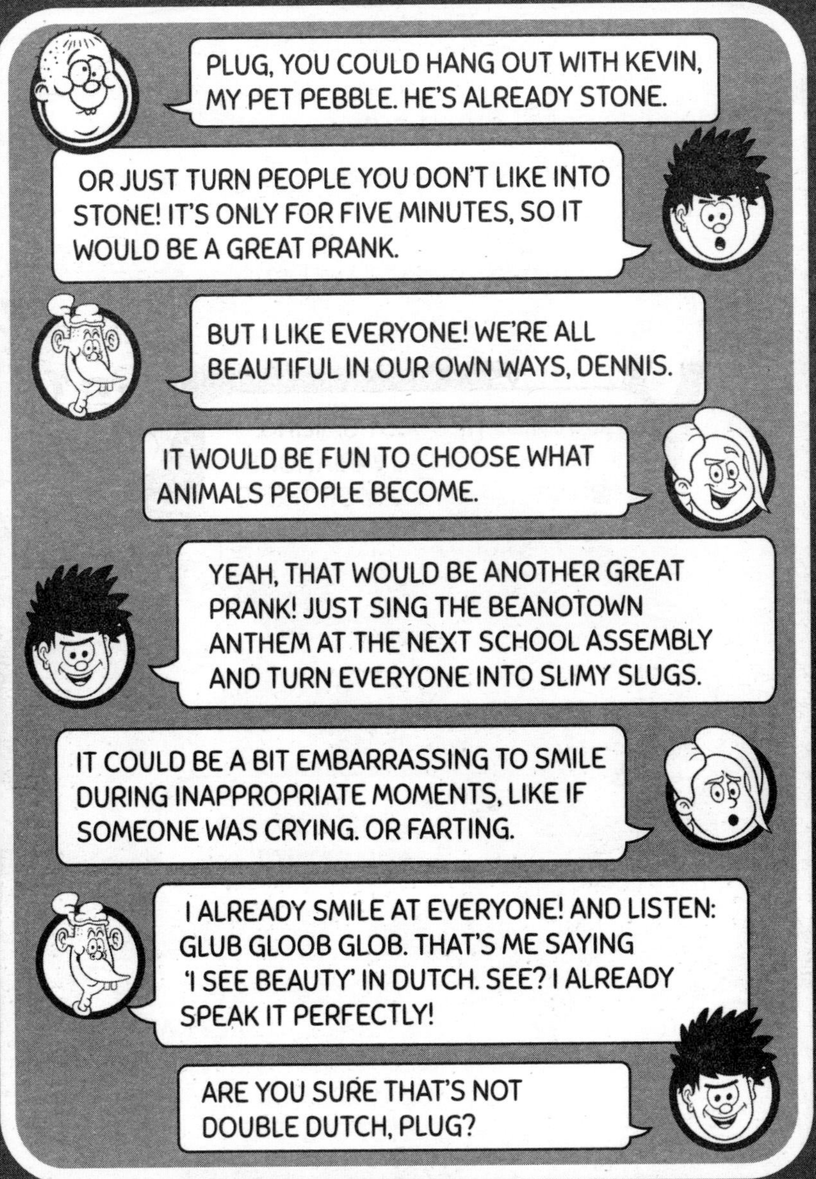
PLUG, YOU COULD HANG OUT WITH KEVIN, MY PET PEBBLE. HE'S ALREADY STONE.
OR JUST TURN PEOPLE YOU DON'T LIKE INTO STONE! IT'S ONLY FOR FIVE MINUTES, SO IT WOULD BE A GREAT PRANK.
BUT I LIKE EVERYONE! WE'RE ALL BEAUTIFUL IN OUR OWN WAYS, DENNIS.
IT WOULD BE FUN TO CHOOSE WHAT ANIMALS PEOPLE BECOME.
YEAH, THAT WOULD BE ANOTHER GREAT PRANK! JUST SING THE BEANOTOWN ANTHEM AT THE NEXT SCHOOL ASSEMBLY AND TURN EVERYONE INTO SLIMY SLUGS.
IT COULD BE A BIT EMBARRASSING TO SMILE DURING INAPPROPRIATE MOMENTS, LIKE IF SOMEONE WAS CRYING. OR FARTING.
I ALREADY SMILE AT EVERYONE! AND LISTEN: GLUB GLOOB GLOB. THAT'S ME SAYING 'I SEE BEAUTY' IN DUTCH. SEE? I ALREADY SPEAK IT PERFECTLY!
ARE YOU SURE THAT'S NOT DOUBLE DUTCH, PLUG?

WHICH OPTION WOULD YOU CHOOSE WITH ALL THOSE VARIATIONS ADDED INTO THE MIX?

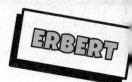

'May I go next?' Erbert asked.

'Sure, Erbert,' Dennis replied. 'Just put this device on . . .'

'Ok,' said Erbert, picking up Dennis's shoe and putting it on his head.

'Wait a minute,' Rubi sighed. 'Dennis, can you set this up?'

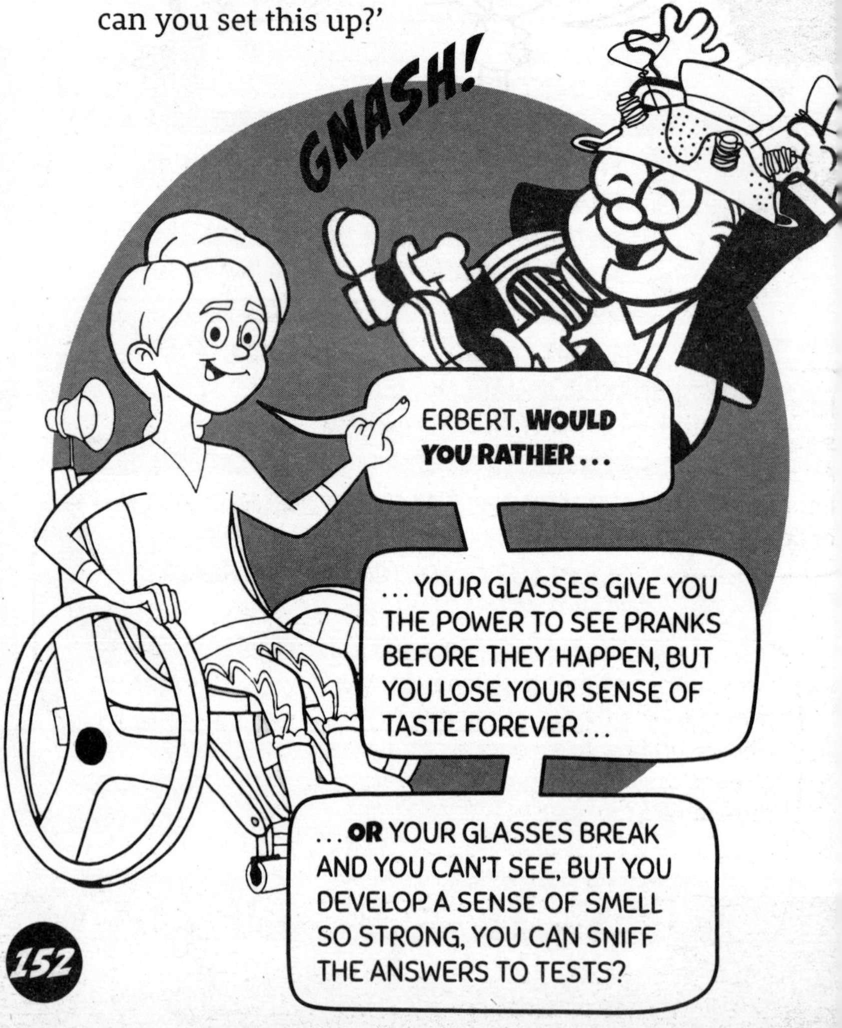
GNASH!
ERBERT, **WOULD YOU RATHER . . .**
. . . YOUR GLASSES GIVE YOU THE POWER TO SEE PRANKS BEFORE THEY HAPPEN, BUT YOU LOSE YOUR SENSE OF TASTE FOREVER . . .
. . . **OR** YOUR GLASSES BREAK AND YOU CAN'T SEE, BUT YOU DEVELOP A SENSE OF SMELL SO STRONG, YOU CAN SNIFF THE ANSWERS TO TESTS?

WHAT DO ERBERT'S NUMSKULLS THINK?

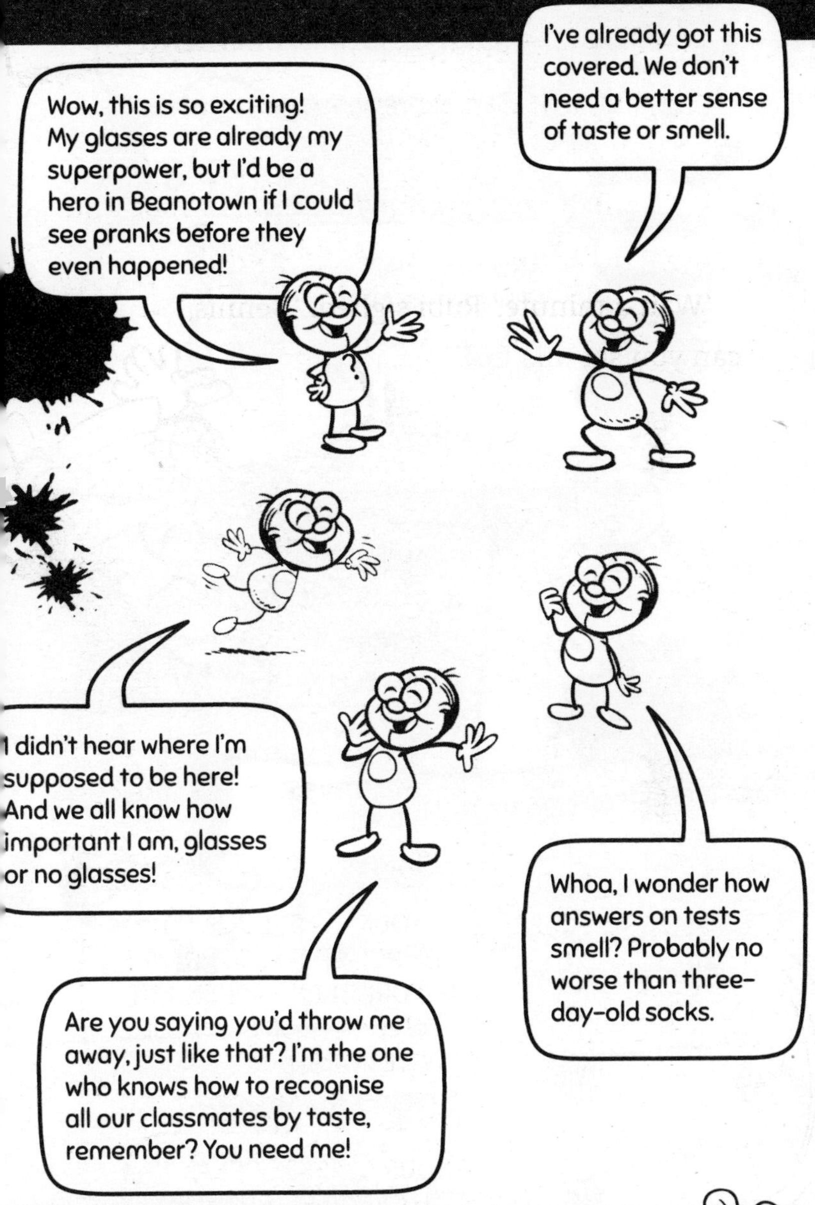
Wow, this is so exciting! My glasses are already my superpower, but I'd be a hero in Beanotown if I could see pranks before they even happened!
I've already got this covered. We don't need a better sense of taste or smell.
I didn't hear where I'm supposed to be here! And we all know how important I am, glasses or no glasses!
Whoa, I wonder how answers on tests smell? Probably no worse than three-day-old socks.
Are you saying you'd throw me away, just like that? I'm the one who knows how to recognise all our classmates by taste, remember? You need me!

WHAT WOULD YOU DO?

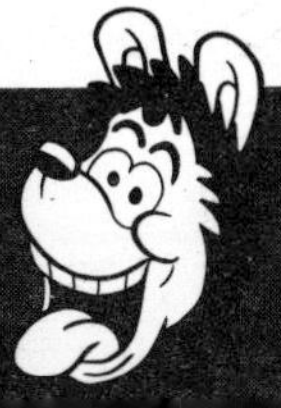

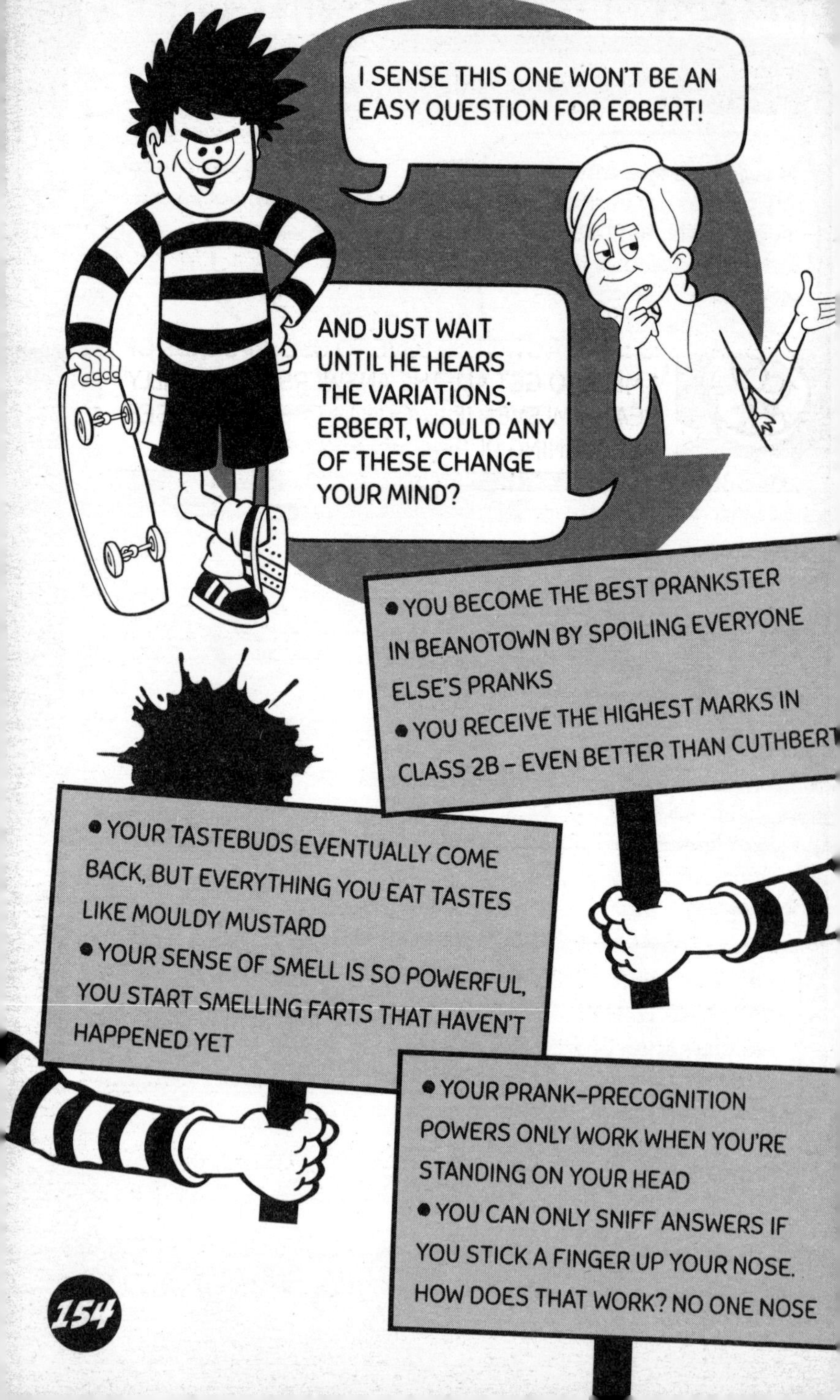
I SENSE THIS ONE WON'T BE AN EASY QUESTION FOR ERBERT!
AND JUST WAIT UNTIL HE HEARS THE VARIATIONS. ERBERT, WOULD ANY OF THESE CHANGE YOUR MIND?
• YOU BECOME THE BEST PRANKSTER IN BEANOTOWN BY SPOILING EVERYONE ELSE'S PRANKS
• YOU RECEIVE THE HIGHEST MARKS IN CLASS 2B – EVEN BETTER THAN CUTHBERT
• YOUR TASTEBUDS EVENTUALLY COME BACK, BUT EVERYTHING YOU EAT TASTES LIKE MOULDY MUSTARD
• YOUR SENSE OF SMELL IS SO POWERFUL, YOU START SMELLING FARTS THAT HAVEN'T HAPPENED YET
• YOUR PRANK–PRECOGNITION POWERS ONLY WORK WHEN YOU'RE STANDING ON YOUR HEAD
• YOU CAN ONLY SNIFF ANSWERS IF YOU STICK A FINGER UP YOUR NOSE. HOW DOES THAT WORK? NO ONE NOSE

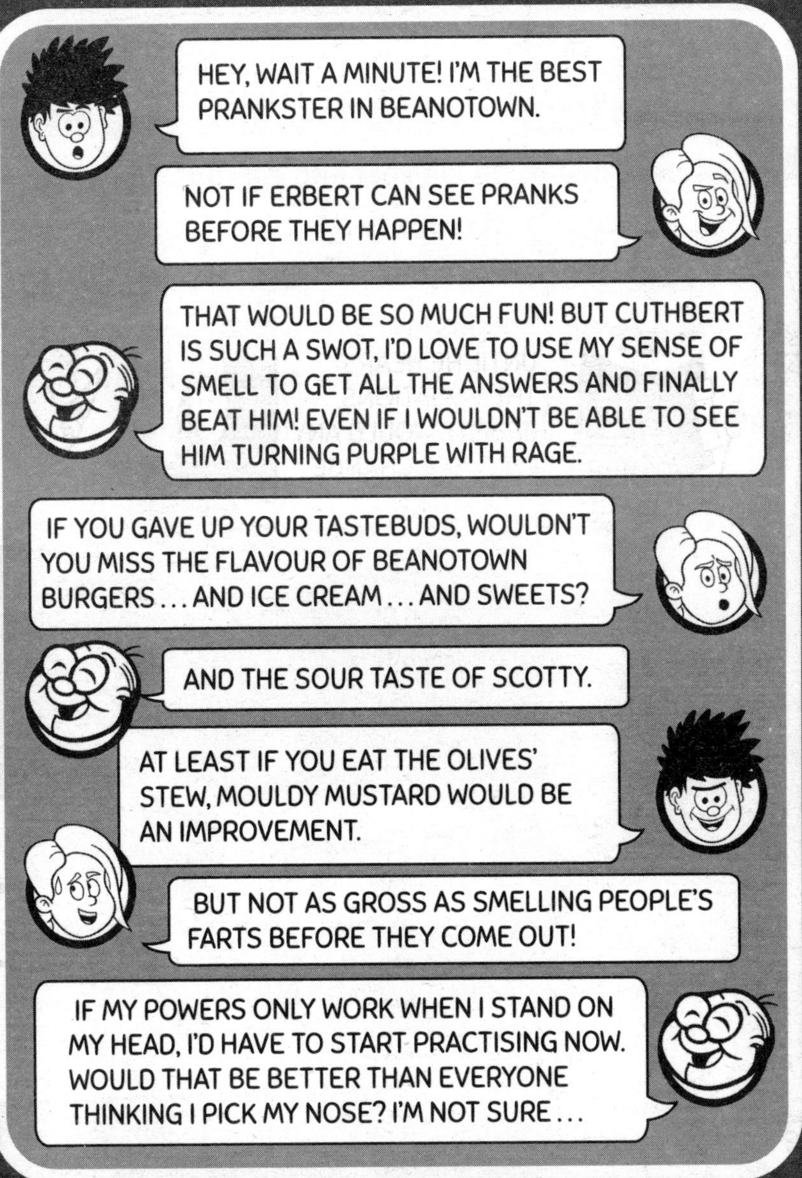
HEY, WAIT A MINUTE! I'M THE BEST PRANKSTER IN BEANOTOWN.
NOT IF ERBERT CAN SEE PRANKS BEFORE THEY HAPPEN!
THAT WOULD BE SO MUCH FUN! BUT CUTHBERT IS SUCH A SWOT, I'D LOVE TO USE MY SENSE OF SMELL TO GET ALL THE ANSWERS AND FINALLY BEAT HIM! EVEN IF I WOULDN'T BE ABLE TO SEE HIM TURNING PURPLE WITH RAGE.
IF YOU GAVE UP YOUR TASTEBUDS, WOULDN'T YOU MISS THE FLAVOUR OF BEANOTOWN BURGERS . . . AND ICE CREAM . . . AND SWEETS?
AND THE SOUR TASTE OF SCOTTY.
AT LEAST IF YOU EAT THE OLIVES' STEW, MOULDY MUSTARD WOULD BE AN IMPROVEMENT.
BUT NOT AS GROSS AS SMELLING PEOPLE'S FARTS BEFORE THEY COME OUT!
IF MY POWERS ONLY WORK WHEN I STAND ON MY HEAD, I'D HAVE TO START PRACTISING NOW. WOULD THAT BE BETTER THAN EVERYONE THINKING I PICK MY NOSE? I'M NOT SURE . . .

WHICH OPTION WOULD YOU CHOOSE WITH ALL THOSE VARIATIONS ADDED INTO THE MIX?

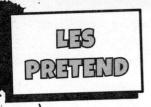

LES PRETEND

Les Pretend walked by, wearing a lab coat and six rolls of loo roll taped to his head.

'Oh, hi, Les!' Rubi said. 'Want to try our MIND reader?'

'I'm not Les. I'm the famous scientist Albert Einstein, here in Beanotown to learn about science! But, sure – I bet this machine will help us understand the universe better!'

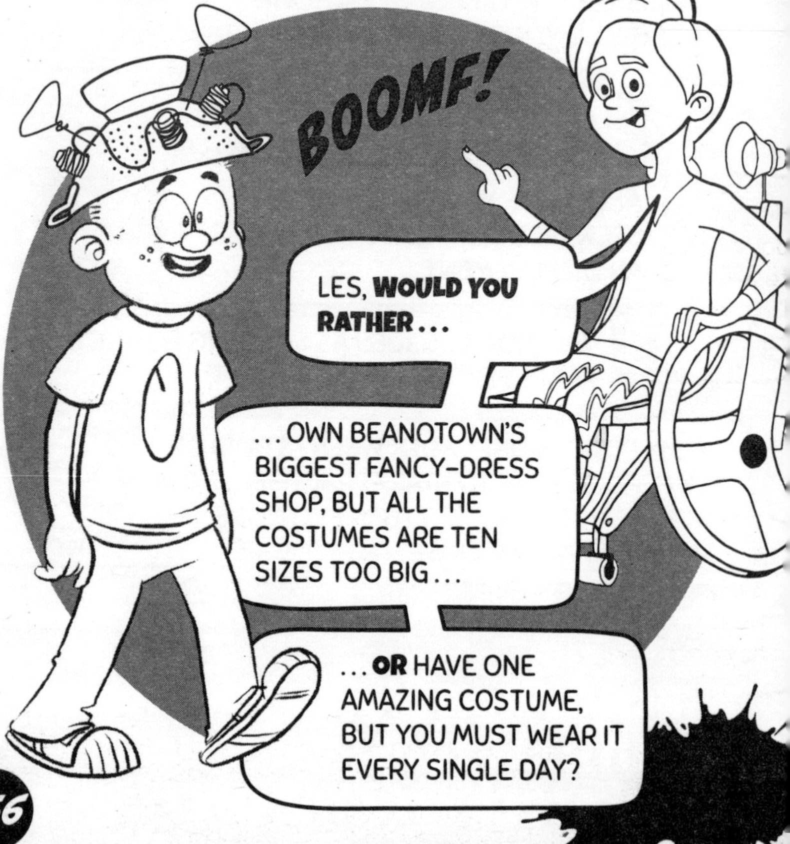

BOOMF!
LES, **WOULD YOU RATHER . . .**
. . . OWN BEANOTOWN'S BIGGEST FANCY-DRESS SHOP, BUT ALL THE COSTUMES ARE TEN SIZES TOO BIG . . .
. . . **OR** HAVE ONE AMAZING COSTUME, BUT YOU MUST WEAR IT EVERY SINGLE DAY?

WHAT DO LES'S NUMSKULLS THINK?

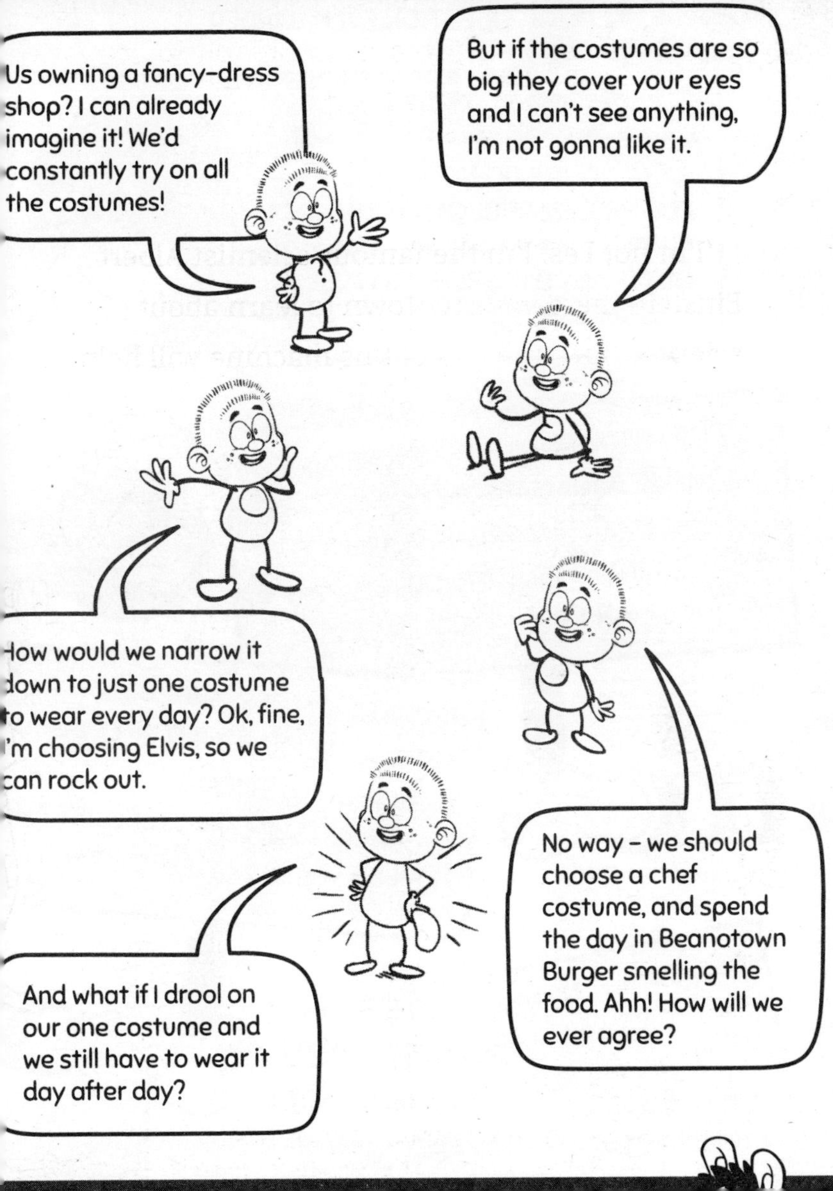
Us owning a fancy-dress shop? I can already imagine it! We'd constantly try on all the costumes!
But if the costumes are so big they cover your eyes and I can't see anything, I'm not gonna like it.
How would we narrow it down to just one costume to wear every day? Ok, fine, I'm choosing Elvis, so we can rock out.
No way – we should choose a chef costume, and spend the day in Beanotown Burger smelling the food. Ahh! How will we ever agree?
And what if I drool on our one costume and we still have to wear it day after day?

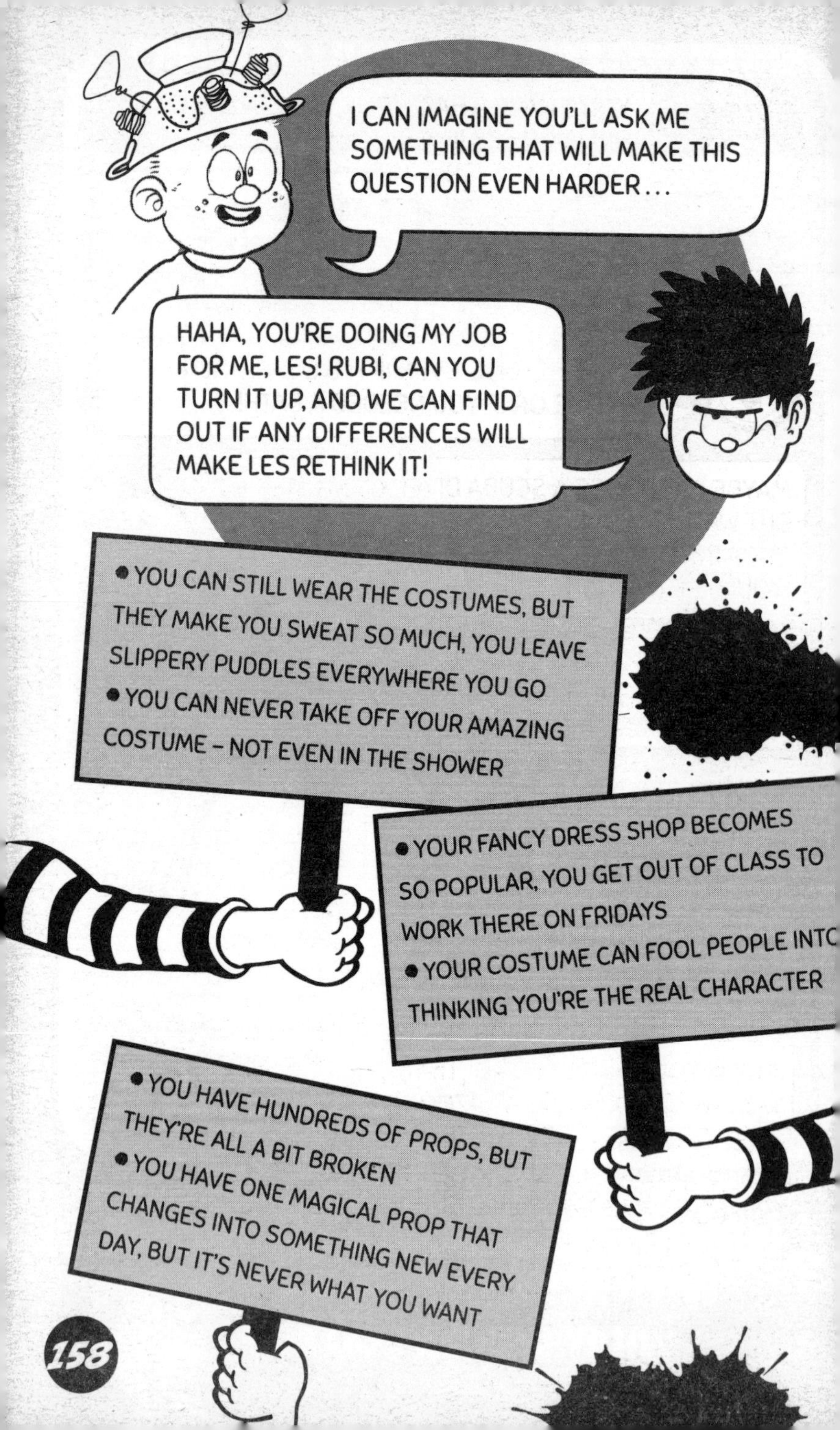
I CAN IMAGINE YOU'LL ASK ME SOMETHING THAT WILL MAKE THIS QUESTION EVEN HARDER...
HAHA, YOU'RE DOING MY JOB FOR ME, LES! RUBI, CAN YOU TURN IT UP, AND WE CAN FIND OUT IF ANY DIFFERENCES WILL MAKE LES RETHINK IT!
• YOU CAN STILL WEAR THE COSTUMES, BUT THEY MAKE YOU SWEAT SO MUCH, YOU LEAVE SLIPPERY PUDDLES EVERYWHERE YOU GO
• YOU CAN NEVER TAKE OFF YOUR AMAZING COSTUME – NOT EVEN IN THE SHOWER
• YOUR FANCY DRESS SHOP BECOMES SO POPULAR, YOU GET OUT OF CLASS TO WORK THERE ON FRIDAYS
• YOUR COSTUME CAN FOOL PEOPLE INTO THINKING YOU'RE THE REAL CHARACTER
• YOU HAVE HUNDREDS OF PROPS, BUT THEY'RE ALL A BIT BROKEN
• YOU HAVE ONE MAGICAL PROP THAT CHANGES INTO SOMETHING NEW EVERY DAY, BUT IT'S NEVER WHAT YOU WANT

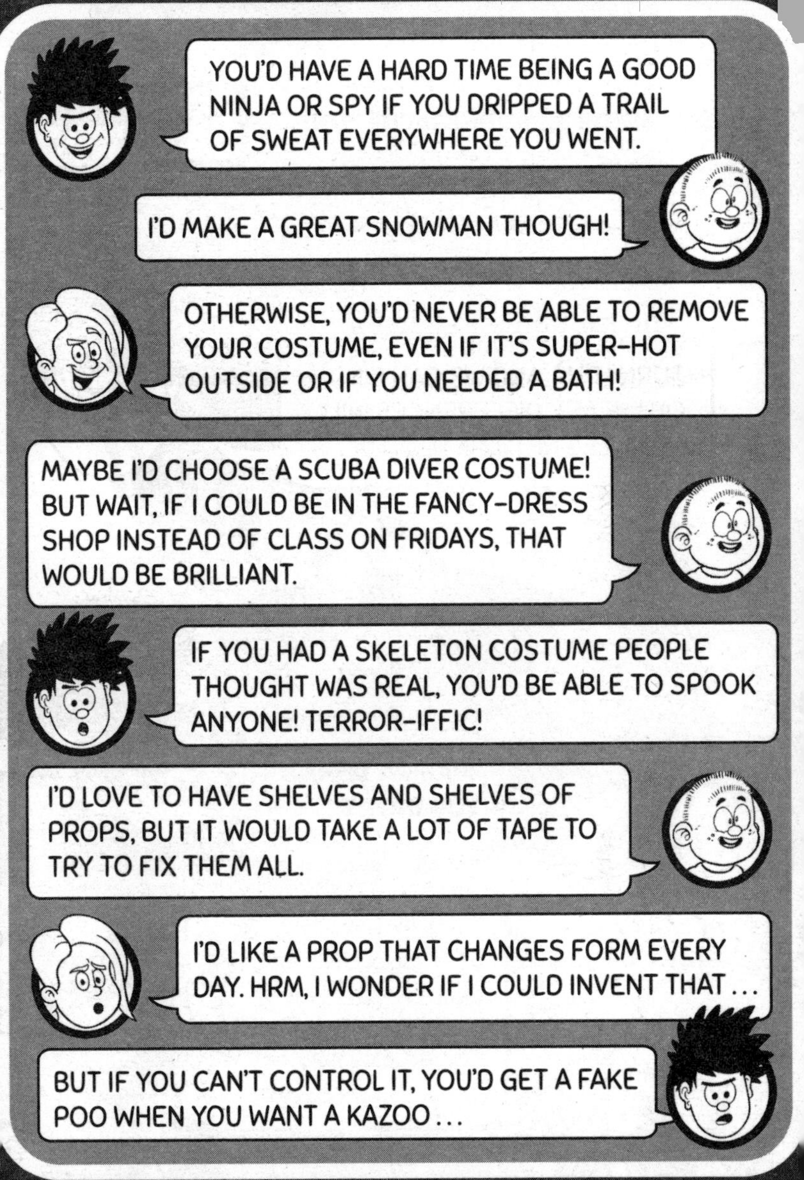
YOU'D HAVE A HARD TIME BEING A GOOD NINJA OR SPY IF YOU DRIPPED A TRAIL OF SWEAT EVERYWHERE YOU WENT.
I'D MAKE A GREAT SNOWMAN THOUGH!
OTHERWISE, YOU'D NEVER BE ABLE TO REMOVE YOUR COSTUME, EVEN IF IT'S SUPER-HOT OUTSIDE OR IF YOU NEEDED A BATH!
MAYBE I'D CHOOSE A SCUBA DIVER COSTUME! BUT WAIT, IF I COULD BE IN THE FANCY-DRESS SHOP INSTEAD OF CLASS ON FRIDAYS, THAT WOULD BE BRILLIANT.
IF YOU HAD A SKELETON COSTUME PEOPLE THOUGHT WAS REAL, YOU'D BE ABLE TO SPOOK ANYONE! TERROR-IFFIC!
I'D LOVE TO HAVE SHELVES AND SHELVES OF PROPS, BUT IT WOULD TAKE A LOT OF TAPE TO TRY TO FIX THEM ALL.
I'D LIKE A PROP THAT CHANGES FORM EVERY DAY. HRM, I WONDER IF I COULD INVENT THAT . . .
BUT IF YOU CAN'T CONTROL IT, YOU'D GET A FAKE POO WHEN YOU WANT A KAZOO . . .

WHICH OPTION WOULD YOU CHOOSE WITH ALL THOSE VARIATIONS ADDED INTO THE MIX?

MAHIRA

'Hey Mahira,' Rubi called, 'will you try out my latest invention?'

'Sure,' Mahira replied, barely taking her eyes off the football she was kicking. '1047, 1048, 1049 . . .' she muttered to herself.

'Be careful with your ball,' Dennis warned. 'Rubi spent weeks making this.'

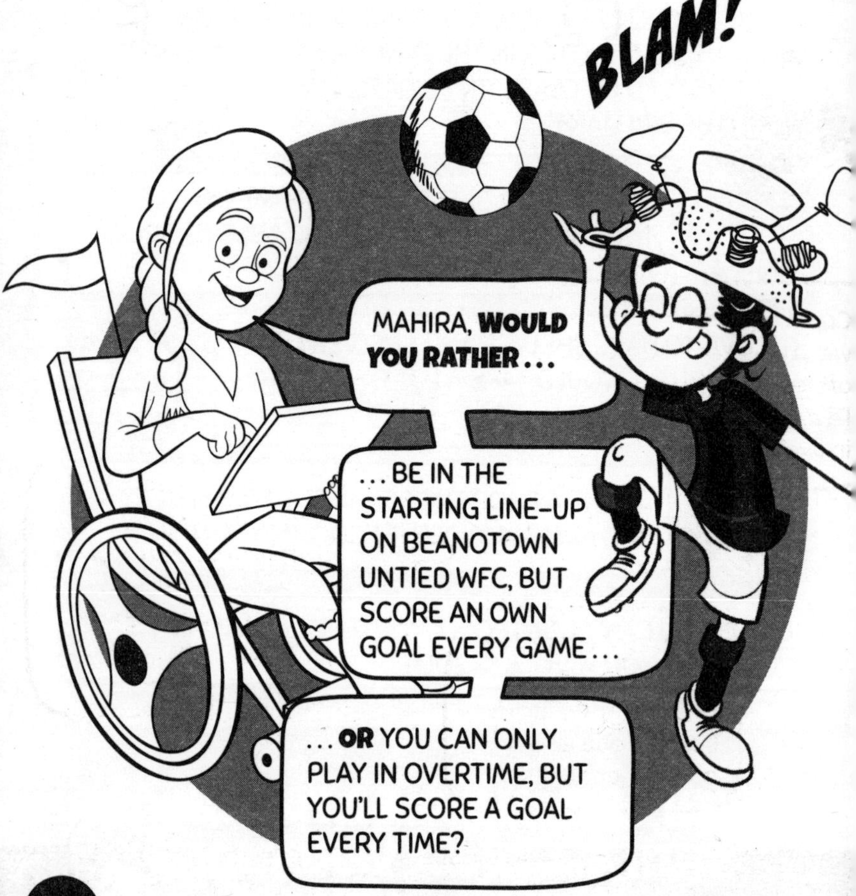
BLAM!
MAHIRA, **WOULD YOU RATHER . . .**
. . . BE IN THE STARTING LINE-UP ON BEANOTOWN UNTIED WFC, BUT SCORE AN OWN GOAL EVERY GAME . . .
. . . **OR** YOU CAN ONLY PLAY IN OVERTIME, BUT YOU'LL SCORE A GOAL EVERY TIME?

WHAT DO MAHIRA'S NUMSKULLS THINK?

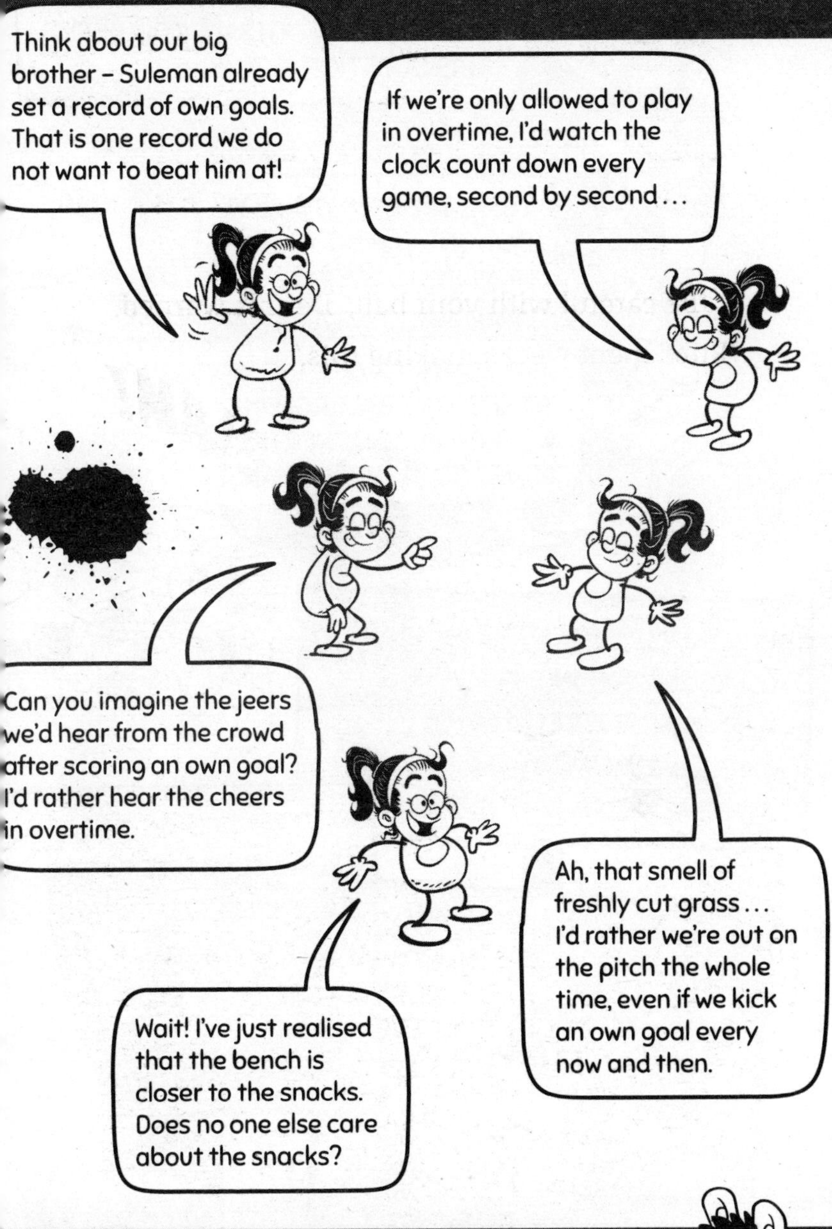
Think about our big brother – Suleman already set a record of own goals. That is one record we do not want to beat him at!
If we're only allowed to play in overtime, I'd watch the clock count down every game, second by second . . .
Can you imagine the jeers we'd hear from the crowd after scoring an own goal? I'd rather hear the cheers in overtime.
Ah, that smell of freshly cut grass . . . I'd rather we're out on the pitch the whole time, even if we kick an own goal every now and then.
Wait! I've just realised that the bench is closer to the snacks. Does no one else care about the snacks?

WHAT WOULD YOU DO?

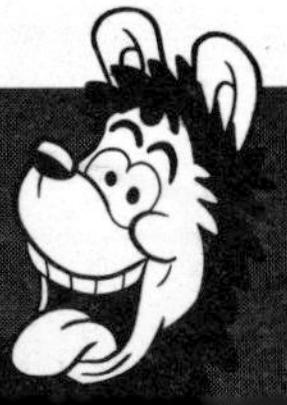

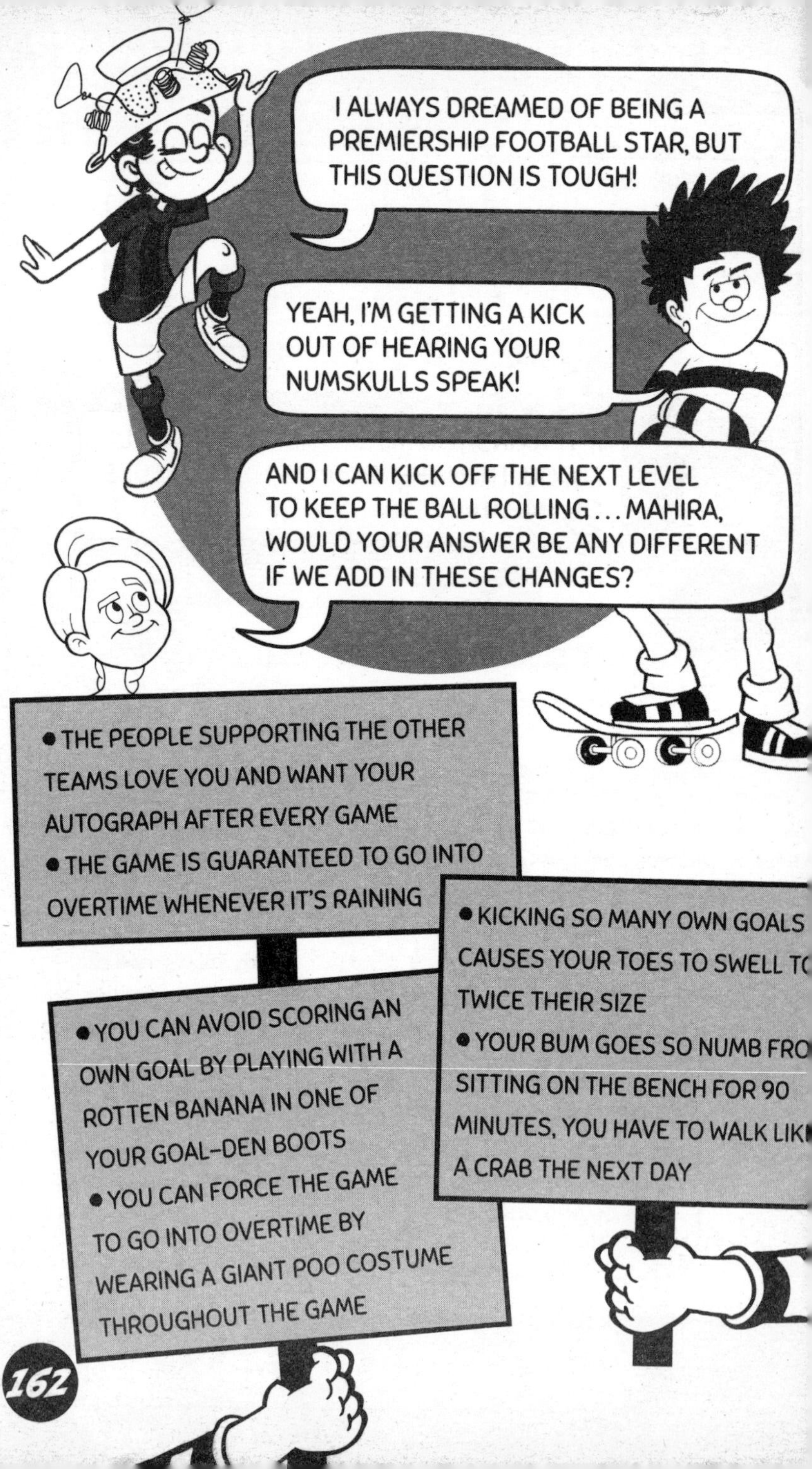

I ALWAYS DREAMED OF BEING A PREMIERSHIP FOOTBALL STAR, BUT THIS QUESTION IS TOUGH!
YEAH, I'M GETTING A KICK OUT OF HEARING YOUR NUMSKULLS SPEAK!
AND I CAN KICK OFF THE NEXT LEVEL TO KEEP THE BALL ROLLING . . . MAHIRA, WOULD YOUR ANSWER BE ANY DIFFERENT IF WE ADD IN THESE CHANGES?
• THE PEOPLE SUPPORTING THE OTHER TEAMS LOVE YOU AND WANT YOUR AUTOGRAPH AFTER EVERY GAME
• THE GAME IS GUARANTEED TO GO INTO OVERTIME WHENEVER IT'S RAINING
• KICKING SO MANY OWN GOALS CAUSES YOUR TOES TO SWELL T TWICE THEIR SIZE
• YOUR BUM GOES SO NUMB FRO SITTING ON THE BENCH FOR 90 MINUTES, YOU HAVE TO WALK LIK A CRAB THE NEXT DAY
• YOU CAN AVOID SCORING AN OWN GOAL BY PLAYING WITH A ROTTEN BANANA IN ONE OF YOUR GOAL-DEN BOOTS
• YOU CAN FORCE THE GAME TO GO INTO OVERTIME BY WEARING A GIANT POO COSTUME THROUGHOUT THE GAME

I'LL GET SO MUCH BETTER IF I CAN PLAY MORE. I DON'T WANT TO LET MY TEAMMATES DOWN, THOUGH. AND I DON'T THINK THEY'D BE HAPPY IF I STARTED SIGNING AUTOGRAPHS FOR THE OPPOSITION'S FANS.

IT RAINS A LOT IN BEANOTOWN, SO YOU COULD END UP PLAYING QUITE A BIT.

IF IT RAINS TOO MUCH, THE PITCHES WILL FLOOD. THEN THEY'LL HAVE TO SEND SUBS ON. HAHAHA! GET IT?

I DON'T WANT SWOLLEN TOES.

BUT WHAT ABOUT HAVING A NUMB BUM? A NUMB BUM WOULD MAKE ANYONE GLUM!

AT LEAST THE SWELLING WOULD PROBABLY GO DOWN AT SOME POINT. ON THE OTHER HAND, NO ONE WOULD EVER FORGET IF YOU WORE A GIANT POO COSTUME.

THAT WOULD BE SO EMBARRASSING . . . BUT I CAN'T IMAGINE PUTTING A ROTTEN BANANA INSIDE ONE OF MY BOOTS.

IT WOULD BE SO SQUISHY AND SLIMY!

WHICH OPTION WOULD YOU CHOOSE WITH ALL THOSE VARIATIONS ADDED INTO THE MIX?

OLIVE

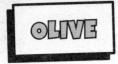

'Hey, Rubi, would the MIND reader work on two people at once?' Dennis asked.

'I don't think so,' Rubi replied. 'Why?'

'I think we should ask the Olives to try it out!'

'You can go,' said Olive Pratt, pushing Olive Spratt forwards with her wooden spoon.

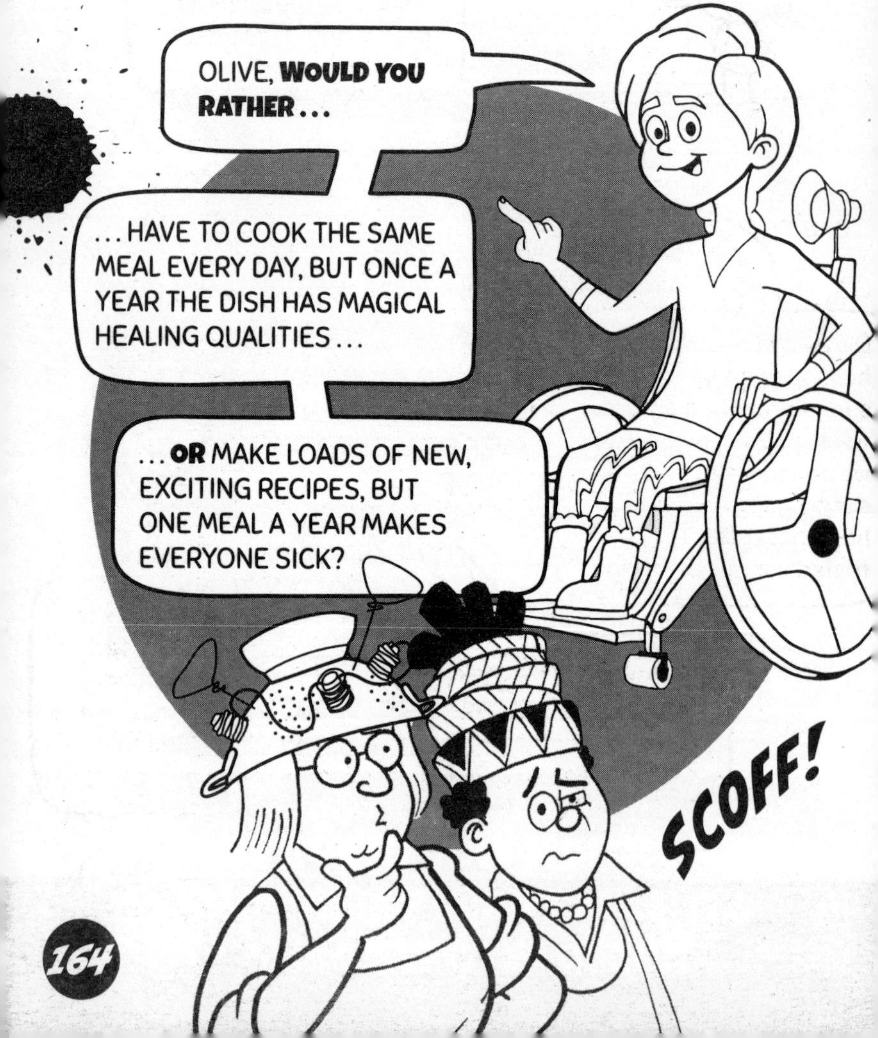

OLIVE, **WOULD YOU RATHER ...**
... HAVE TO COOK THE SAME MEAL EVERY DAY, BUT ONCE A YEAR THE DISH HAS MAGICAL HEALING QUALITIES ...
... **OR** MAKE LOADS OF NEW, EXCITING RECIPES, BUT ONE MEAL A YEAR MAKES EVERYONE SICK?
SCOFF!

WHAT DO OLIVE'S NUMSKULLS THINK?

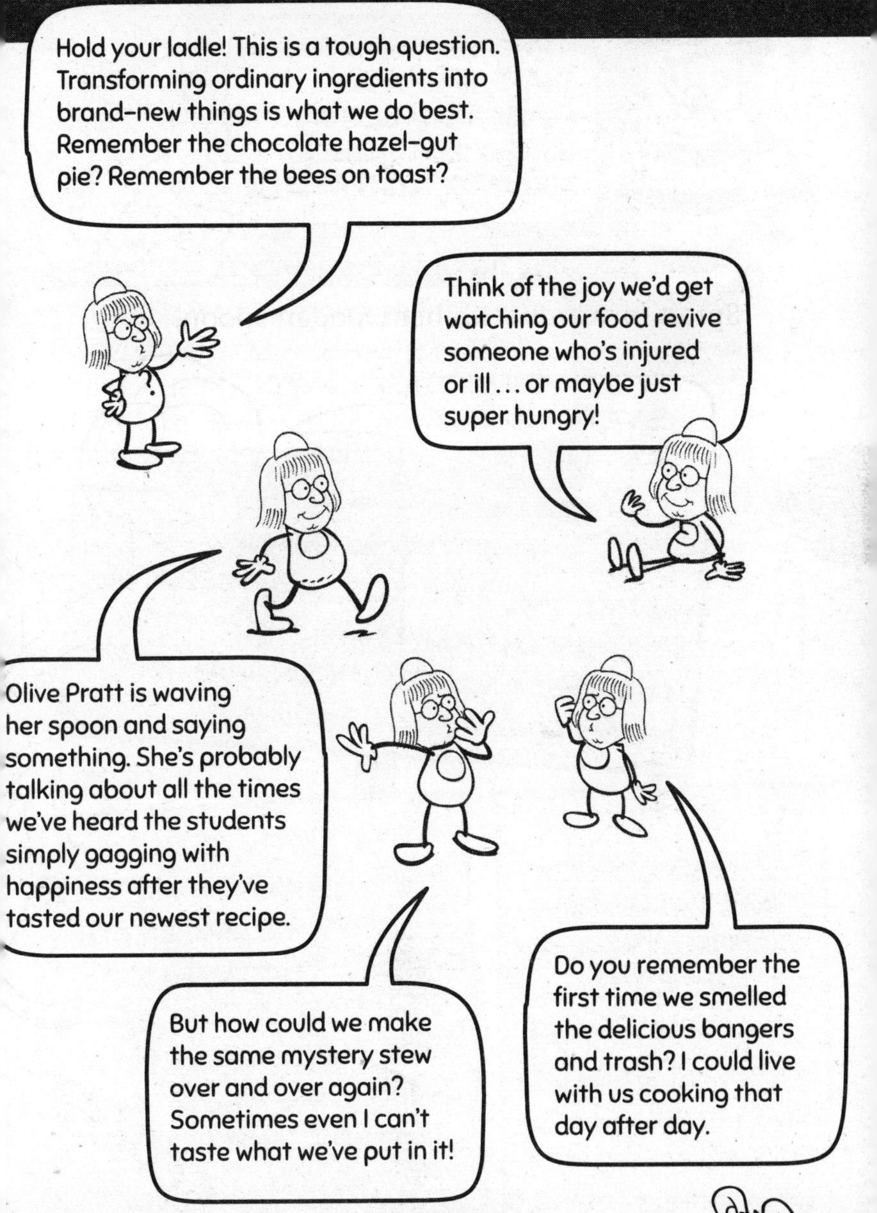
Hold your ladle! This is a tough question. Transforming ordinary ingredients into brand-new things is what we do best. Remember the chocolate hazel-gut pie? Remember the bees on toast?
Think of the joy we'd get watching our food revive someone who's injured or ill . . . or maybe just super hungry!
Olive Pratt is waving her spoon and saying something. She's probably talking about all the times we've heard the students simply gagging with happiness after they've tasted our newest recipe.
But how could we make the same mystery stew over and over again? Sometimes even I can't taste what we've put in it!
Do you remember the first time we smelled the delicious bangers and trash? I could live with us cooking that day after day.

WHAT WOULD YOU DO?

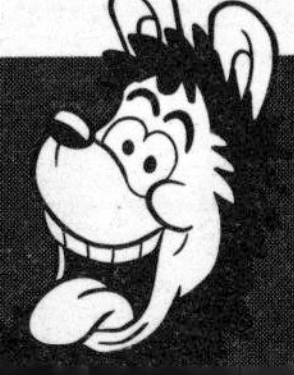

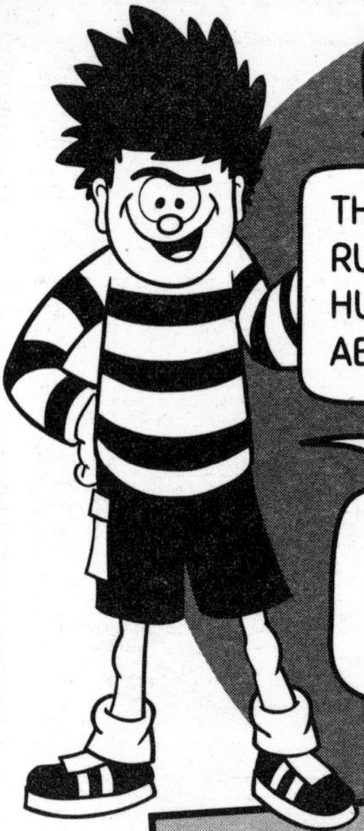

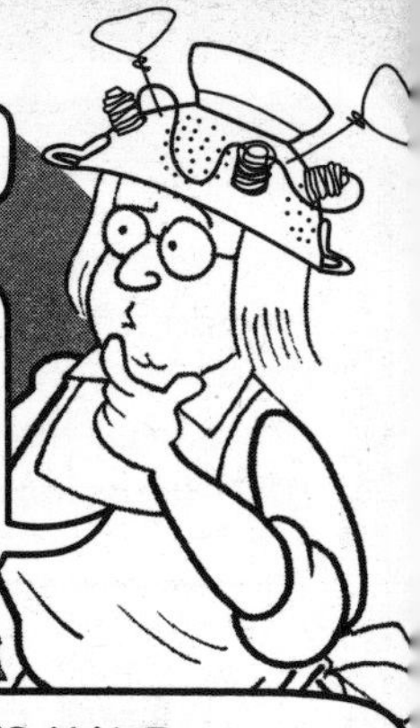

WHAT'S THAT SOUND?

THAT'S MY STOMACH RUMBLING. I'M GETTING HUNGRY JUST THINKING ABOUT THE MYSTERY STEW.

ERR . . . THERE'S NO TIME TO MAKE MYSTERY STEW RIGHT NOW, BECAUSE I NEED TO ASK IF ANY OF THESE VARIATIONS WOULD CHANGE YOUR MIND . . .

- YOU GET SO FAST AT MAKING YOUR SIGNATURE DISH, YOU CAN COOK WITH ONE HAND WHILE PLAYING BEANOBASH ON YOUR PHONE WITH THE OTHER
- YOU INVENT A NEW RECIPE THAT GETS NOTICED BY CELEBRITY CHEF PAUL BEANOWOOD

- THE MAGICAL HEALING DISH ONLY WORKS ON CHILDREN – IT CAUSES ADULTS, INCLUDING ALL THE TEACHERS, TO GROW THICK HAIR ON THEIR KNUCKLES
- THE SICKNESS DISH ONLY MAKES ADULTS SICK, AND MAKES ALL THE CHILDREN HYPERACTIVE ALL DAY

- YOU BECOME SO BORED WITH THE ONE RECIPE, IT MAKES YOU WANT TO CRY INTO IT (AND WHY NOT – MAYBE THAT WILL CHANGE THE FLAVOUR!)
- THE INGREDIENTS FOR YOUR NEW DISHES BECOME INCREASINGLY DIFFICULT TO TRACK DOWN, AND YOU NEARLY LOSE AN EYE WHILE COLLECTING PUS FROM A PUKING PIG

YOU KNOW YOU CAN ONLY TRULY BECOME A MASTER OF A SIGNATURE DISH BY COOKING IT 10,000 TIMES.

DENNIS, ARE YOU SURE YOU THOUGHT THIS THROUGH? I CAN'T HANDLE 10,000 DINNERS OF MYSTERY STEW!

IF PAUL BEANOWOOD LIKES YOUR NEWEST FANCY RECIPE, MAYBE IT DOESN'T MATTER IF THE STUDENTS WON'T TRY IT? HE'S DISHY!

STUDENTS CAN BE SO CLOSED-MINDED SOMETIMES. WHAT'S WRONG WITH PUKING PIG PUS PIES? I WOULDN'T WANT TO GET INJURED COLLECTING INGREDIENTS THOUGH.

YEAH, THE BEANOTOWN HOSPITAL FOOD IS TERRIBLE.

UM, I CAN THINK OF WORSE FOOD ... BUT COOKING A DISH EVERY YEAR THAT HEALS CHILDREN WOULD BE COOL!

NOT AS COOL AS SEEING MRS CREECHER GROW HAIRY KNUCKLES.

DON'T BE SILLY, DENNIS. THAT WOULD NEVER HAPPEN! I DID ONE TIME MAKE A LIVE, SLIMY TOAD IN THE HOLE AND A FEW STUDENTS DEVELOPED WARTS ... BUT I'M SURE THAT WAS JUST A COINCIDENCE.

WHICH OPTION WOULD YOU CHOOSE WITH ALL THOSE VARIATIONS ADDED INTO THE MIX?

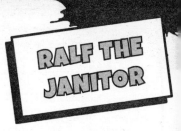

RALF THE JANITOR

Ralf the Janitor walked past carrying his mop and looking very tired.

'What a day,' he sighed. 'First, Billie Whizz invents a rocket-powered skateboard and leaves tyre marks all over the school. Then Calamity James wants to try it, but he gets dizzy and throws up all over the floor. Before I can get to it, Winston walks through it . . . I've spent the last hour cleaning up vomit cat prints.'

'You need a break,' Dennis offered. 'Try this!'

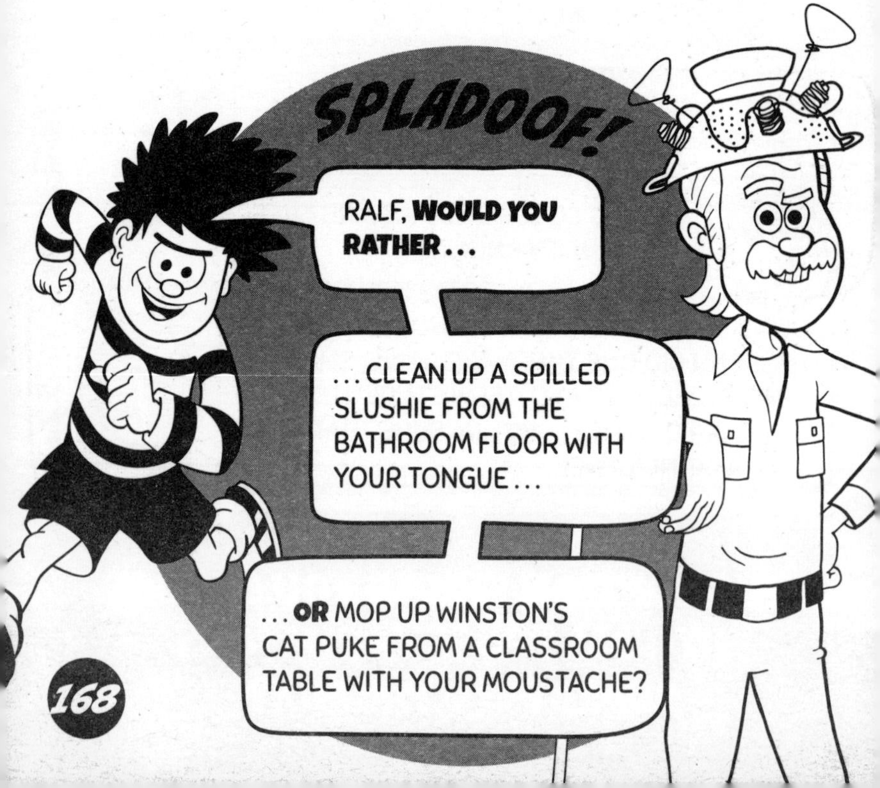
SPLADOOF!
RALF, WOULD YOU RATHER . . .
. . . CLEAN UP A SPILLED SLUSHIE FROM THE BATHROOM FLOOR WITH YOUR TONGUE . . .
. . . OR MOP UP WINSTON'S CAT PUKE FROM A CLASSROOM TABLE WITH YOUR MOUSTACHE?

WHAT DO RALF'S NUMSKULLS THINK?

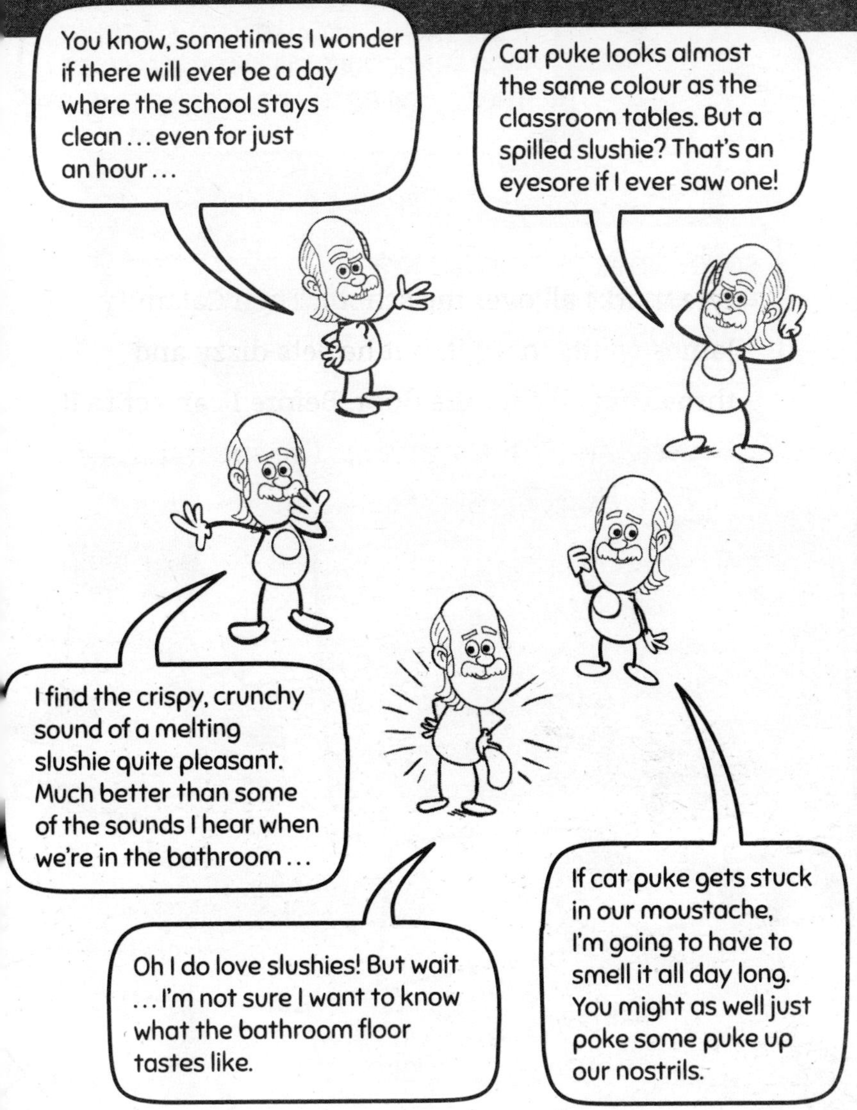

WHAT WOULD YOU DO?

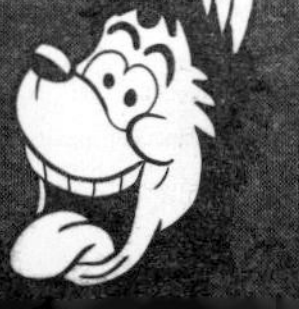

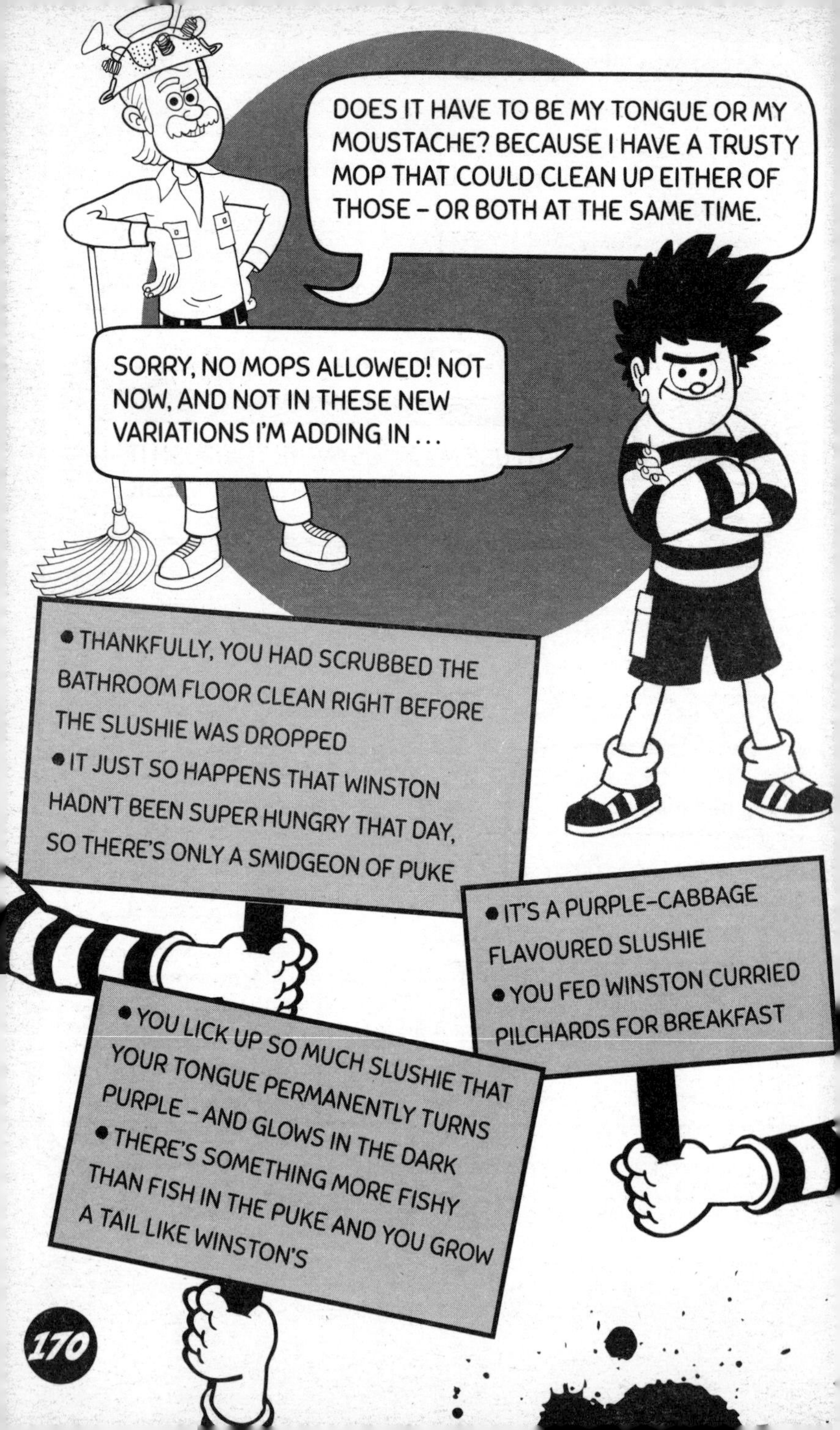
DOES IT HAVE TO BE MY TONGUE OR MY MOUSTACHE? BECAUSE I HAVE A TRUSTY MOP THAT COULD CLEAN UP EITHER OF THOSE – OR BOTH AT THE SAME TIME.
SORRY, NO MOPS ALLOWED! NOT NOW, AND NOT IN THESE NEW VARIATIONS I'M ADDING IN . . .
• THANKFULLY, YOU HAD SCRUBBED THE BATHROOM FLOOR CLEAN RIGHT BEFORE THE SLUSHIE WAS DROPPED
• IT JUST SO HAPPENS THAT WINSTON HADN'T BEEN SUPER HUNGRY THAT DAY, SO THERE'S ONLY A SMIDGEON OF PUKE
• IT'S A PURPLE-CABBAGE FLAVOURED SLUSHIE
• YOU FED WINSTON CURRIED PILCHARDS FOR BREAKFAST
• YOU LICK UP SO MUCH SLUSHIE THAT YOUR TONGUE PERMANENTLY TURNS PURPLE – AND GLOWS IN THE DARK
• THERE'S SOMETHING MORE FISHY THAN FISH IN THE PUKE AND YOU GROW A TAIL LIKE WINSTON'S

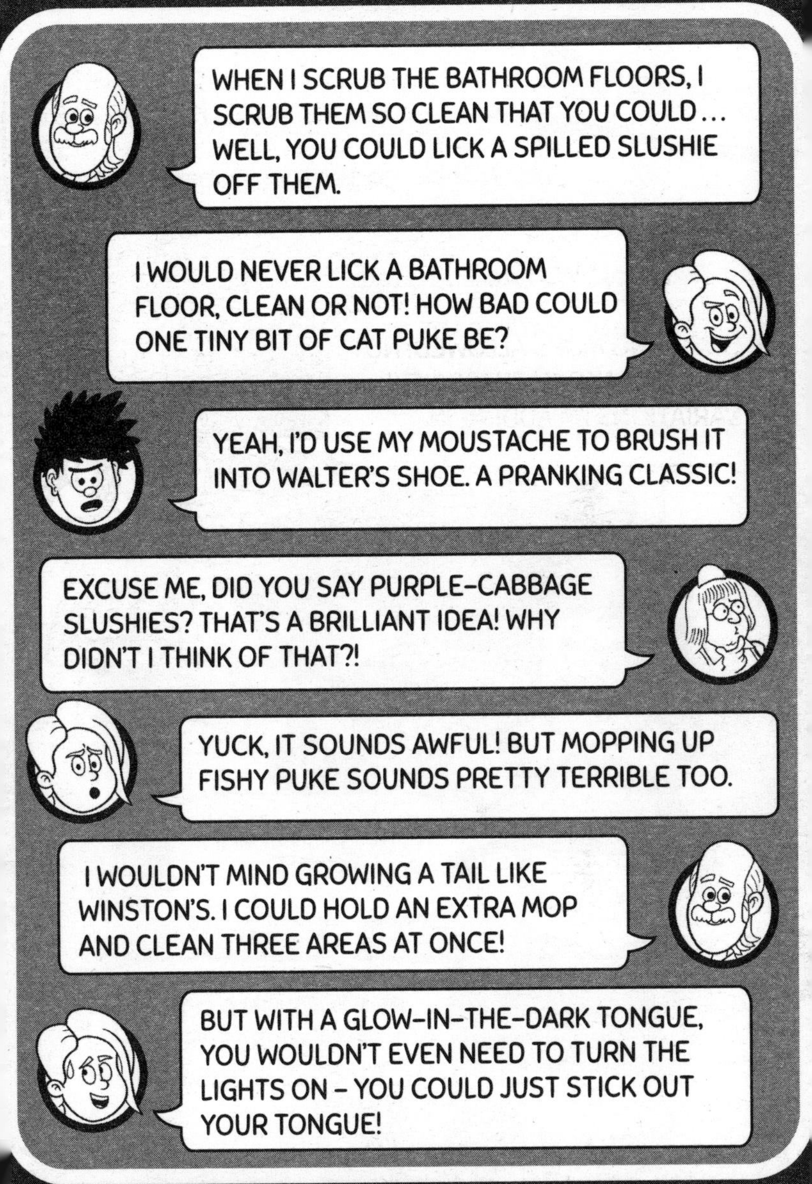
WHEN I SCRUB THE BATHROOM FLOORS, I SCRUB THEM SO CLEAN THAT YOU COULD… WELL, YOU COULD LICK A SPILLED SLUSHIE OFF THEM.
I WOULD NEVER LICK A BATHROOM FLOOR, CLEAN OR NOT! HOW BAD COULD ONE TINY BIT OF CAT PUKE BE?
YEAH, I'D USE MY MOUSTACHE TO BRUSH IT INTO WALTER'S SHOE. A PRANKING CLASSIC!
EXCUSE ME, DID YOU SAY PURPLE-CABBAGE SLUSHIES? THAT'S A BRILLIANT IDEA! WHY DIDN'T I THINK OF THAT?!
YUCK, IT SOUNDS AWFUL! BUT MOPPING UP FISHY PUKE SOUNDS PRETTY TERRIBLE TOO.
I WOULDN'T MIND GROWING A TAIL LIKE WINSTON'S. I COULD HOLD AN EXTRA MOP AND CLEAN THREE AREAS AT ONCE!
BUT WITH A GLOW-IN-THE-DARK TONGUE, YOU WOULDN'T EVEN NEED TO TURN THE LIGHTS ON – YOU COULD JUST STICK OUT YOUR TONGUE!

WHICH OPTION WOULD YOU CHOOSE WITH ALL THOSE VARIATIONS ADDED INTO THE MIX?

WINSTON

'Winston probably wants to try my MIND reader too, doesn't he?' Rubi asked.

'Meow?' Winston replied.

'I'm sure that means yes,' Dennis said confidently, strapping the helmet to the school cat.

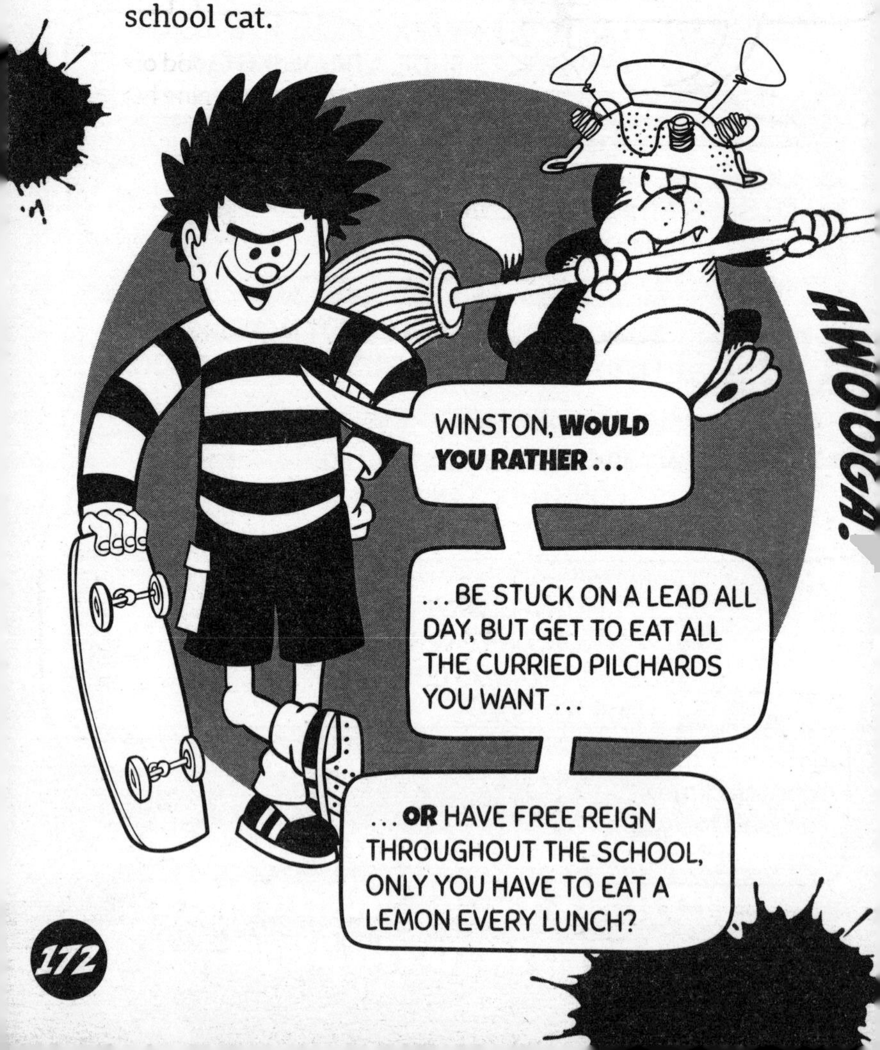
WINSTON, **WOULD YOU RATHER . . .**
. . . BE STUCK ON A LEAD ALL DAY, BUT GET TO EAT ALL THE CURRIED PILCHARDS YOU WANT . . .
. . . **OR** HAVE FREE REIGN THROUGHOUT THE SCHOOL, ONLY YOU HAVE TO EAT A LEMON EVERY LUNCH?
AWOOGA.

WHAT DO WINSTON'S NUMSKULLS THINK?

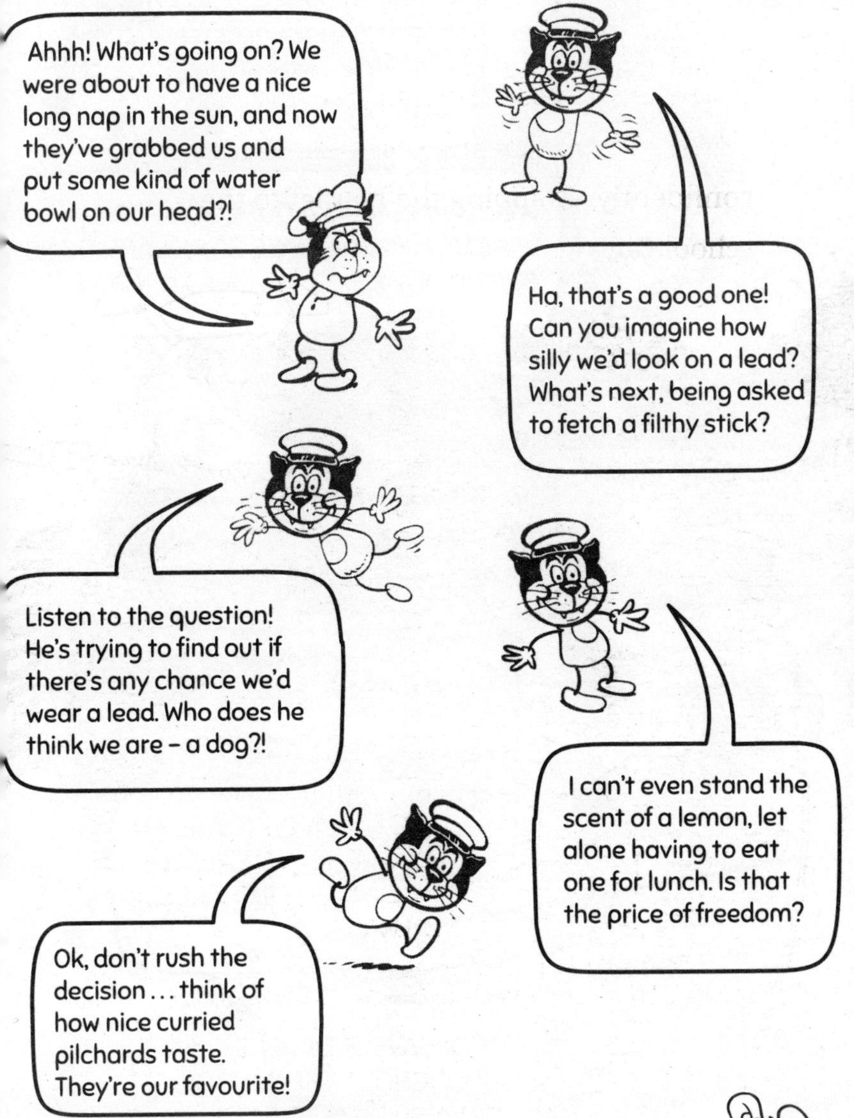
Ahhh! What's going on? We were about to have a nice long nap in the sun, and now they've grabbed us and put some kind of water bowl on our head?!
Ha, that's a good one! Can you imagine how silly we'd look on a lead? What's next, being asked to fetch a filthy stick?
Listen to the question! He's trying to find out if there's any chance we'd wear a lead. Who does he think we are – a dog?!
I can't even stand the scent of a lemon, let alone having to eat one for lunch. Is that the price of freedom?
Ok, don't rush the decision . . . think of how nice curried pilchards taste. They're our favourite!

WHAT WOULD YOU DO?

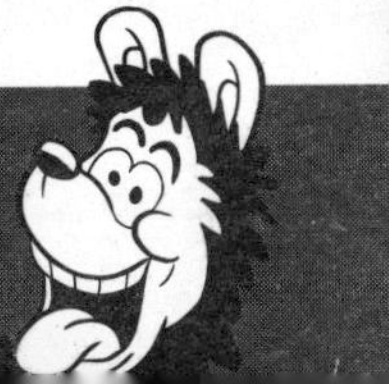

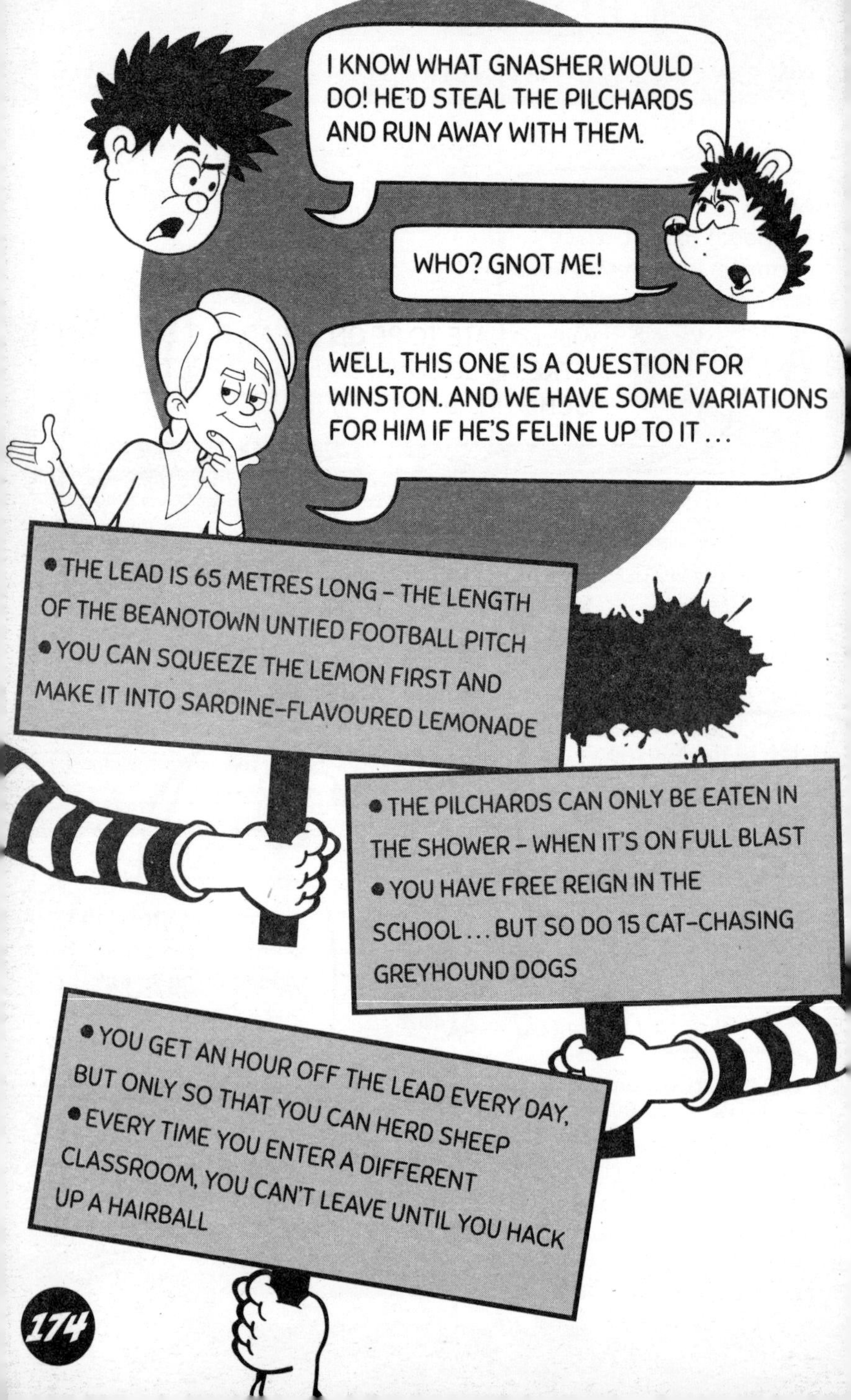
I KNOW WHAT GNASHER WOULD DO! HE'D STEAL THE PILCHARDS AND RUN AWAY WITH THEM.
WHO? GNOT ME!
WELL, THIS ONE IS A QUESTION FOR WINSTON. AND WE HAVE SOME VARIATIONS FOR HIM IF HE'S FELINE UP TO IT . . .
• THE LEAD IS 65 METRES LONG – THE LENGTH OF THE BEANOTOWN UNTIED FOOTBALL PITCH
• YOU CAN SQUEEZE THE LEMON FIRST AND MAKE IT INTO SARDINE-FLAVOURED LEMONADE
• THE PILCHARDS CAN ONLY BE EATEN IN THE SHOWER – WHEN IT'S ON FULL BLAST
• YOU HAVE FREE REIGN IN THE SCHOOL . . . BUT SO DO 15 CAT-CHASING GREYHOUND DOGS
• YOU GET AN HOUR OFF THE LEAD EVERY DAY, BUT ONLY SO THAT YOU CAN HERD SHEEP
• EVERY TIME YOU ENTER A DIFFERENT CLASSROOM, YOU CAN'T LEAVE UNTIL YOU HACK UP A HAIRBALL

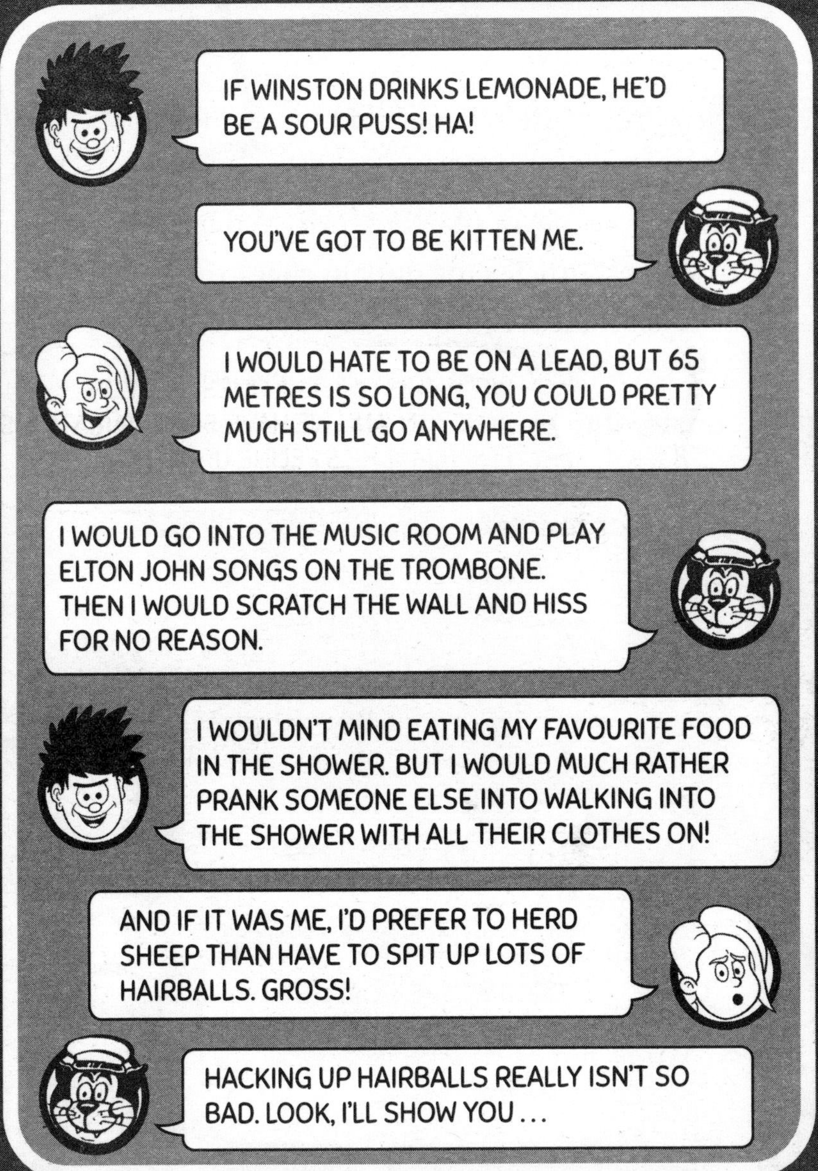
IF WINSTON DRINKS LEMONADE, HE'D BE A SOUR PUSS! HA!
YOU'VE GOT TO BE KITTEN ME.
I WOULD HATE TO BE ON A LEAD, BUT 65 METRES IS SO LONG, YOU COULD PRETTY MUCH STILL GO ANYWHERE.
I WOULD GO INTO THE MUSIC ROOM AND PLAY ELTON JOHN SONGS ON THE TROMBONE. THEN I WOULD SCRATCH THE WALL AND HISS FOR NO REASON.
I WOULDN'T MIND EATING MY FAVOURITE FOOD IN THE SHOWER. BUT I WOULD MUCH RATHER PRANK SOMEONE ELSE INTO WALKING INTO THE SHOWER WITH ALL THEIR CLOTHES ON!
AND IF IT WAS ME, I'D PREFER TO HERD SHEEP THAN HAVE TO SPIT UP LOTS OF HAIRBALLS. GROSS!
HACKING UP HAIRBALLS REALLY ISN'T SO BAD. LOOK, I'LL SHOW YOU . . .

WHICH OPTION WOULD YOU CHOOSE WITH ALL THOSE VARIATIONS ADDED INTO THE MIX?

WILBUR BROWN

'Now this is interesting,' said Wilbur Brown, walking over with Walter. 'As mayor of Beanotown and boss of WilburCorp, it's my duty to check this out.'

'It is?' Rubi asked.

'It's a MIND reader, isn't it? I need to see if I can use it to control you all . . . I mean, I want to support the growing minds of Beanotown's youths, of course.'

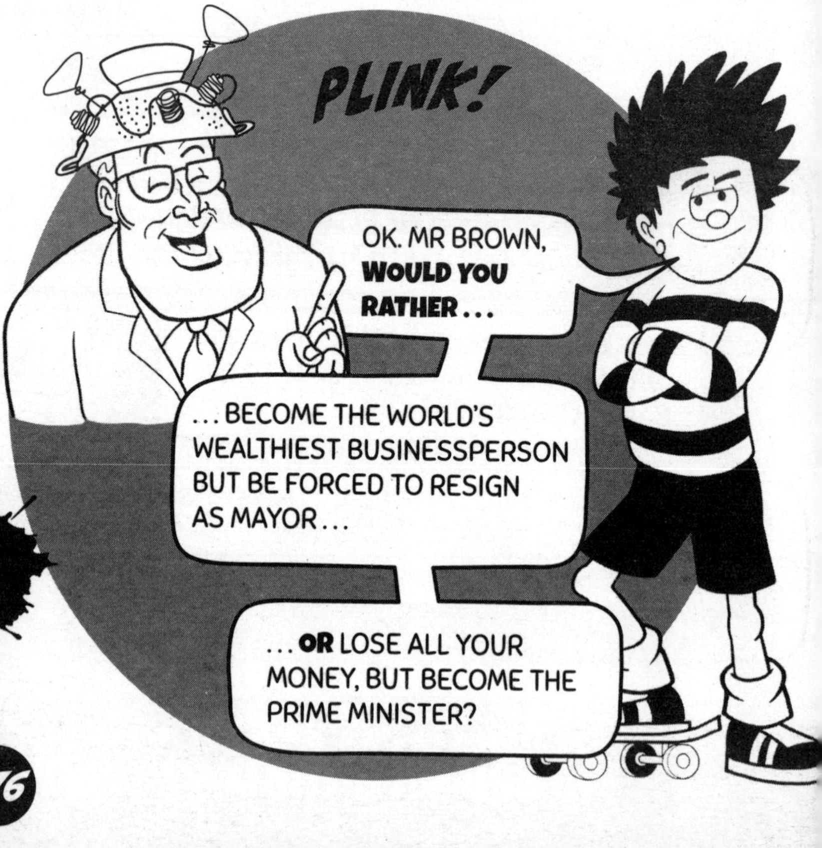

PLINK!
OK. MR BROWN, **WOULD YOU RATHER . . .**
. . . BECOME THE WORLD'S WEALTHIEST BUSINESSPERSON BUT BE FORCED TO RESIGN AS MAYOR . . .
. . . **OR** LOSE ALL YOUR MONEY, BUT BECOME THE PRIME MINISTER?

WHAT DO WILBUR'S NUMSKULLS THINK?

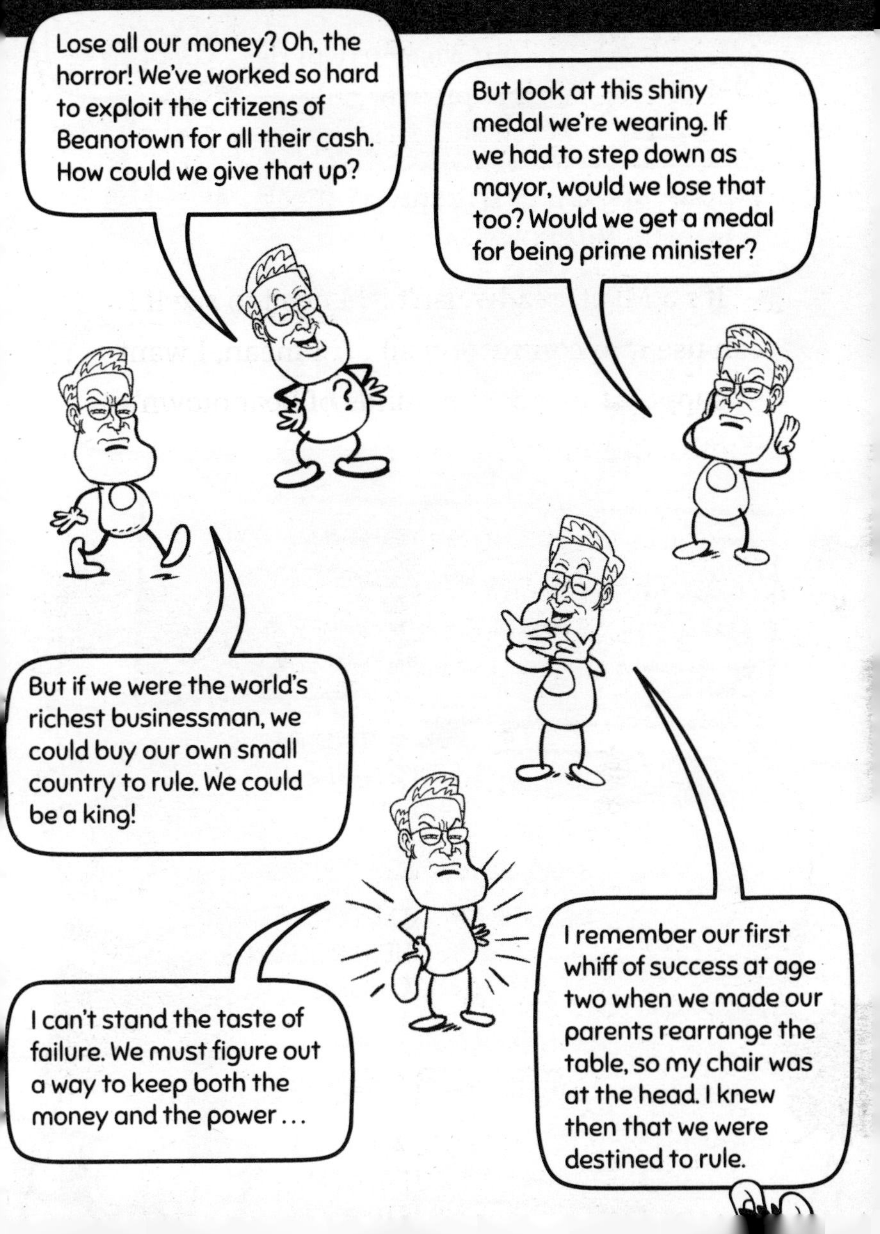
Lose all our money? Oh, the horror! We've worked so hard to exploit the citizens of Beanotown for all their cash. How could we give that up?
But look at this shiny medal we're wearing. If we had to step down as mayor, would we lose that too? Would we get a medal for being prime minister?
But if we were the world's richest businessman, we could buy our own small country to rule. We could be a king!
I remember our first whiff of success at age two when we made our parents rearrange the table, so my chair was at the head. I knew then that we were destined to rule.
I can't stand the taste of failure. We must figure out a way to keep both the money and the power . . .

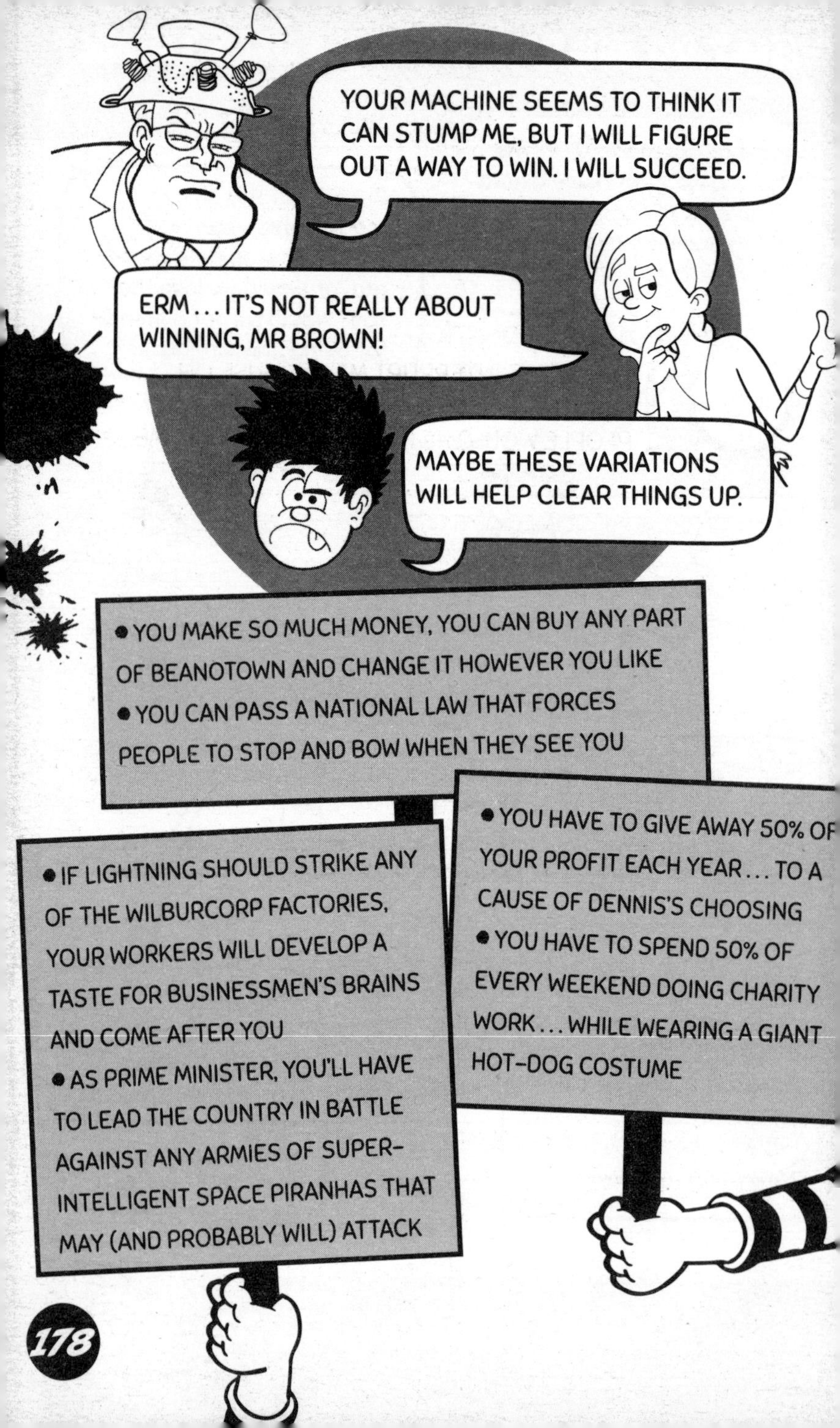
YOUR MACHINE SEEMS TO THINK IT CAN STUMP ME, BUT I WILL FIGURE OUT A WAY TO WIN. I WILL SUCCEED.
ERM . . . IT'S NOT REALLY ABOUT WINNING, MR BROWN!
MAYBE THESE VARIATIONS WILL HELP CLEAR THINGS UP.
• YOU MAKE SO MUCH MONEY, YOU CAN BUY ANY PART OF BEANOTOWN AND CHANGE IT HOWEVER YOU LIKE
• YOU CAN PASS A NATIONAL LAW THAT FORCES PEOPLE TO STOP AND BOW WHEN THEY SEE YOU
• IF LIGHTNING SHOULD STRIKE ANY OF THE WILBURCORP FACTORIES, YOUR WORKERS WILL DEVELOP A TASTE FOR BUSINESSMEN'S BRAINS AND COME AFTER YOU
• AS PRIME MINISTER, YOU'LL HAVE TO LEAD THE COUNTRY IN BATTLE AGAINST ANY ARMIES OF SUPER-INTELLIGENT SPACE PIRANHAS THAT MAY (AND PROBABLY WILL) ATTACK
• YOU HAVE TO GIVE AWAY 50% OF YOUR PROFIT EACH YEAR . . . TO A CAUSE OF DENNIS'S CHOOSING
• YOU HAVE TO SPEND 50% OF EVERY WEEKEND DOING CHARITY WORK . . . WHILE WEARING A GIANT HOT-DOG COSTUME

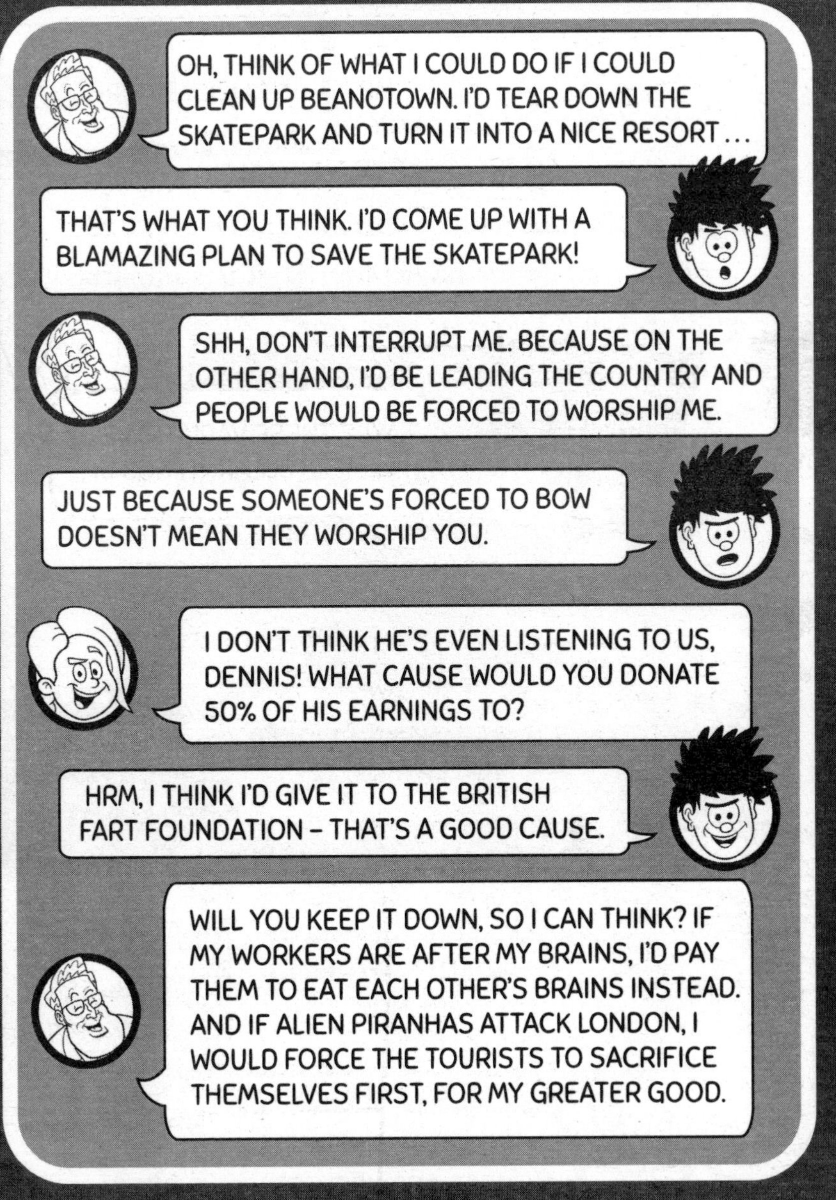
OH, THINK OF WHAT I COULD DO IF I COULD CLEAN UP BEANOTOWN. I'D TEAR DOWN THE SKATEPARK AND TURN IT INTO A NICE RESORT . . .
THAT'S WHAT YOU THINK. I'D COME UP WITH A BLAMAZING PLAN TO SAVE THE SKATEPARK!
SHH, DON'T INTERRUPT ME. BECAUSE ON THE OTHER HAND, I'D BE LEADING THE COUNTRY AND PEOPLE WOULD BE FORCED TO WORSHIP ME.
JUST BECAUSE SOMEONE'S FORCED TO BOW DOESN'T MEAN THEY WORSHIP YOU.
I DON'T THINK HE'S EVEN LISTENING TO US, DENNIS! WHAT CAUSE WOULD YOU DONATE 50% OF HIS EARNINGS TO?
HRM, I THINK I'D GIVE IT TO THE BRITISH FART FOUNDATION – THAT'S A GOOD CAUSE.
WILL YOU KEEP IT DOWN, SO I CAN THINK? IF MY WORKERS ARE AFTER MY BRAINS, I'D PAY THEM TO EAT EACH OTHER'S BRAINS INSTEAD. AND IF ALIEN PIRANHAS ATTACK LONDON, I WOULD FORCE THE TOURISTS TO SACRIFICE THEMSELVES FIRST, FOR MY GREATER GOOD.

WHICH OPTION WOULD YOU CHOOSE WITH ALL THOSE VARIATIONS ADDED INTO THE MIX?

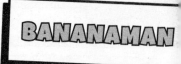

'Rubi, look. Bananaman is here! We have got to try it on him!' Dennis said. 'Bananaman! Over here!'

'Ahh, what do we have here? That is a bananas contraption if I've ever seen one.'

'It's our MIND reader, want to give it a go?'

'Oh, I don't know . . .'

'Don't worry, it's perfectly safe.' Dennis plonked the contraption on Bananaman's head before he could say no.

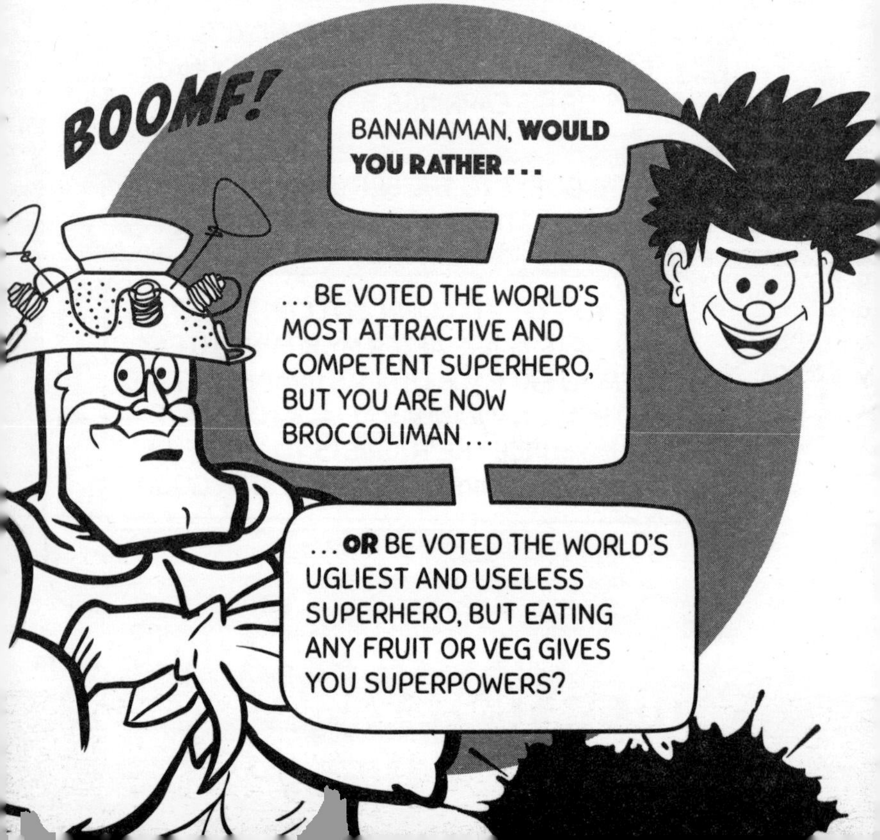
BOOMF!
BANANAMAN, **WOULD YOU RATHER . . .**
. . . BE VOTED THE WORLD'S MOST ATTRACTIVE AND COMPETENT SUPERHERO, BUT YOU ARE NOW BROCCOLIMAN . . .
. . . **OR** BE VOTED THE WORLD'S UGLIEST AND USELESS SUPERHERO, BUT EATING ANY FRUIT OR VEG GIVES YOU SUPERPOWERS?

WHAT DO BANANAMAN'S NUMSKULLS THINK?

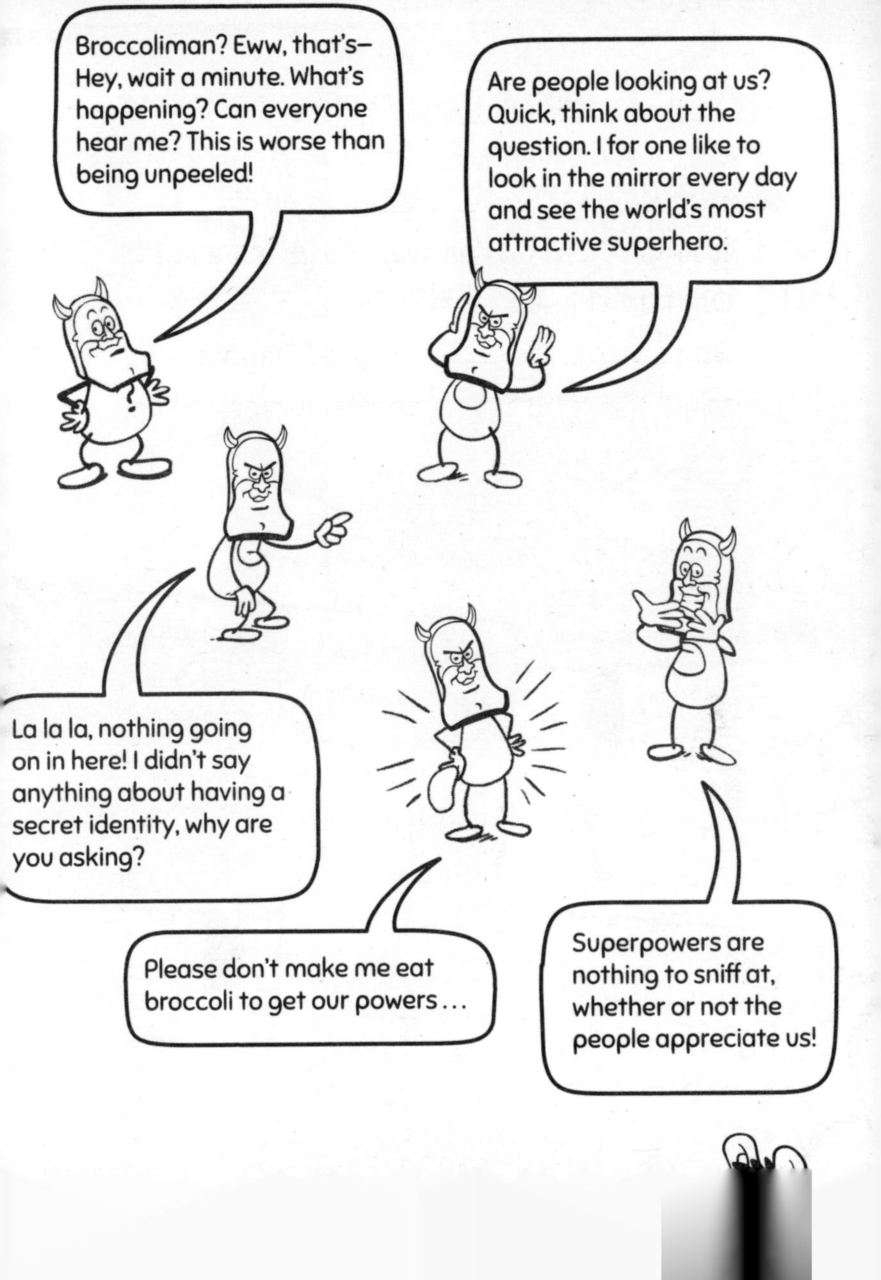

Broccoliman? Eww, that's– Hey, wait a minute. What's happening? Can everyone hear me? This is worse than being unpeeled!
Are people looking at us? Quick, think about the question. I for one like to look in the mirror every day and see the world's most attractive superhero.
La la la, nothing going on in here! I didn't say anything about having a secret identity, why are you asking?
Please don't make me eat broccoli to get our powers . . .
Superpowers are nothing to sniff at, whether or not the people appreciate us!

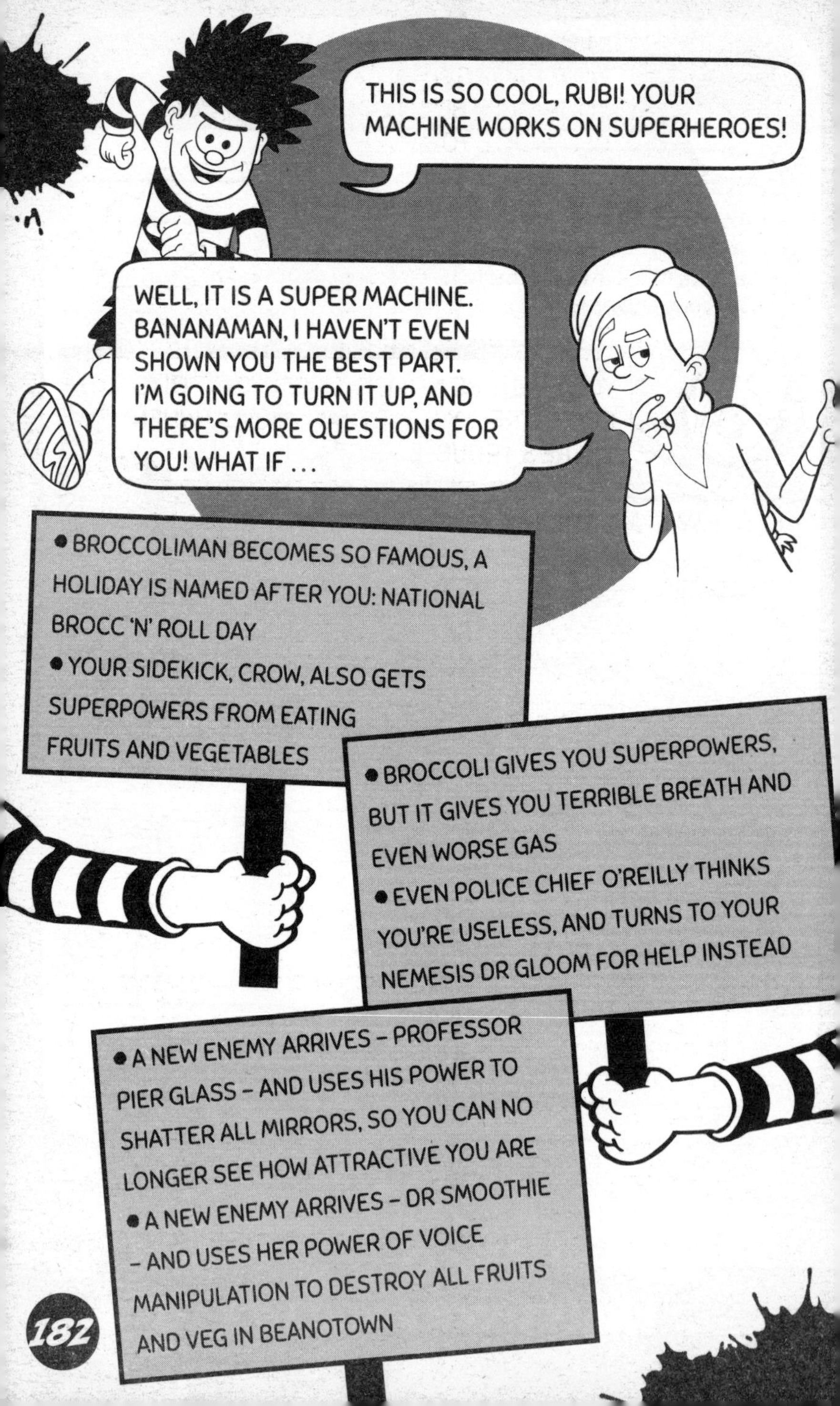
THIS IS SO COOL, RUBI! YOUR MACHINE WORKS ON SUPERHEROES!
WELL, IT IS A SUPER MACHINE. BANANAMAN, I HAVEN'T EVEN SHOWN YOU THE BEST PART. I'M GOING TO TURN IT UP, AND THERE'S MORE QUESTIONS FOR YOU! WHAT IF . . .
• BROCCOLIMAN BECOMES SO FAMOUS, A HOLIDAY IS NAMED AFTER YOU: NATIONAL BROCC 'N' ROLL DAY
• YOUR SIDEKICK, CROW, ALSO GETS SUPERPOWERS FROM EATING FRUITS AND VEGETABLES
• BROCCOLI GIVES YOU SUPERPOWERS, BUT IT GIVES YOU TERRIBLE BREATH AND EVEN WORSE GAS
• EVEN POLICE CHIEF O'REILLY THINKS YOU'RE USELESS, AND TURNS TO YOUR NEMESIS DR GLOOM FOR HELP INSTEAD
• A NEW ENEMY ARRIVES – PROFESSOR PIER GLASS – AND USES HIS POWER TO SHATTER ALL MIRRORS, SO YOU CAN NO LONGER SEE HOW ATTRACTIVE YOU ARE
• A NEW ENEMY ARRIVES – DR SMOOTHIE – AND USES HER POWER OF VOICE MANIPULATION TO DESTROY ALL FRUITS AND VEG IN BEANOTOWN

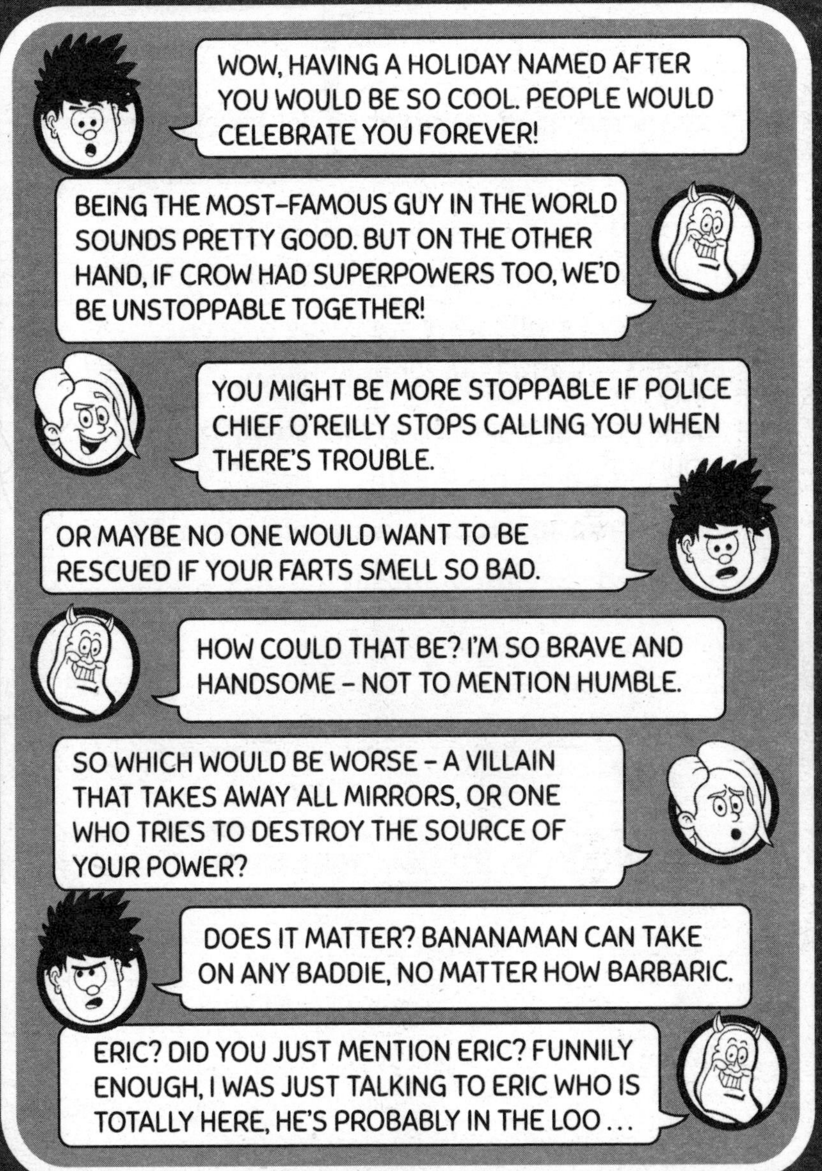
WOW, HAVING A HOLIDAY NAMED AFTER YOU WOULD BE SO COOL. PEOPLE WOULD CELEBRATE YOU FOREVER!
BEING THE MOST-FAMOUS GUY IN THE WORLD SOUNDS PRETTY GOOD. BUT ON THE OTHER HAND, IF CROW HAD SUPERPOWERS TOO, WE'D BE UNSTOPPABLE TOGETHER!
YOU MIGHT BE MORE STOPPABLE IF POLICE CHIEF O'REILLY STOPS CALLING YOU WHEN THERE'S TROUBLE.
OR MAYBE NO ONE WOULD WANT TO BE RESCUED IF YOUR FARTS SMELL SO BAD.
HOW COULD THAT BE? I'M SO BRAVE AND HANDSOME – NOT TO MENTION HUMBLE.
SO WHICH WOULD BE WORSE – A VILLAIN THAT TAKES AWAY ALL MIRRORS, OR ONE WHO TRIES TO DESTROY THE SOURCE OF YOUR POWER?
DOES IT MATTER? BANANAMAN CAN TAKE ON ANY BADDIE, NO MATTER HOW BARBARIC.
ERIC? DID YOU JUST MENTION ERIC? FUNNILY ENOUGH, I WAS JUST TALKING TO ERIC WHO IS TOTALLY HERE, HE'S PROBABLY IN THE LOO . . .

WHICH OPTION WOULD YOU CHOOSE WITH ALL THOSE VARIATIONS ADDED INTO THE MIX?

SERGEANT SLIPPER

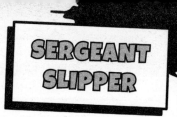

'Excuse me,' said Sergeant Slipper as he approached. 'I've heard a lot of commotion from around here, and I need to check that none of Beanotown's 4212 laws are being broken.'

'That's a lot of laws—' Rubi began.

'I've probably broken at least half,' Dennis muttered under his breath.

'—but our machine is completely legal,' Rubi continued. 'See for yourself!'

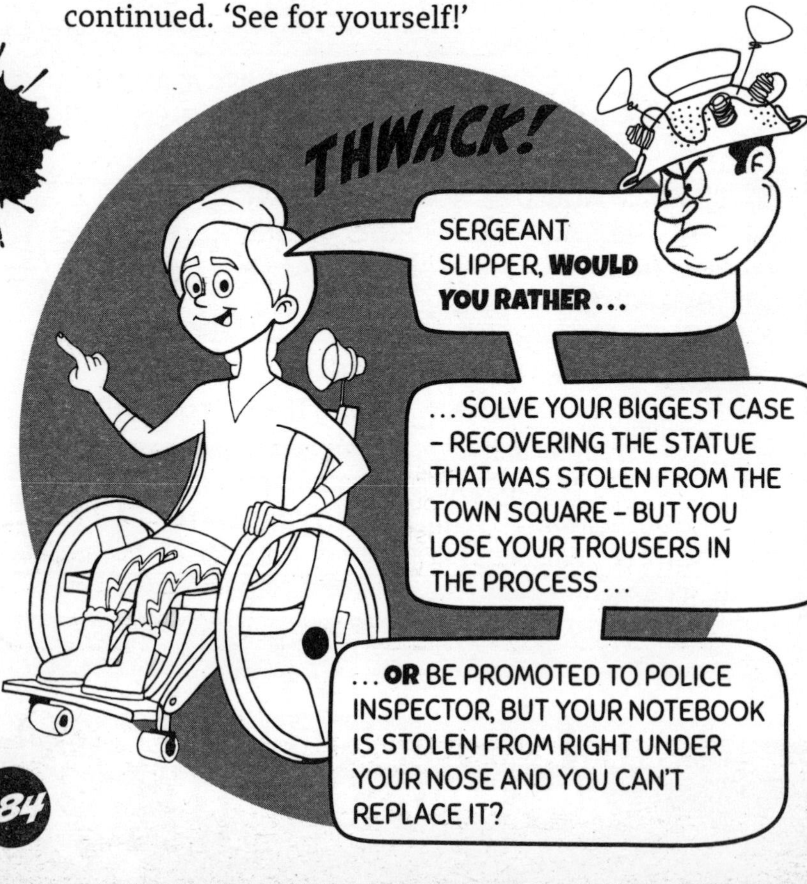
THWACK!
SERGEANT SLIPPER, **WOULD YOU RATHER . . .**
. . . SOLVE YOUR BIGGEST CASE – RECOVERING THE STATUE THAT WAS STOLEN FROM THE TOWN SQUARE – BUT YOU LOSE YOUR TROUSERS IN THE PROCESS . . .
. . . **OR** BE PROMOTED TO POLICE INSPECTOR, BUT YOUR NOTEBOOK IS STOLEN FROM RIGHT UNDER YOUR NOSE AND YOU CAN'T REPLACE IT?

WHAT DO SERGEANT SLIPPER'S NUMSKULLS THINK?

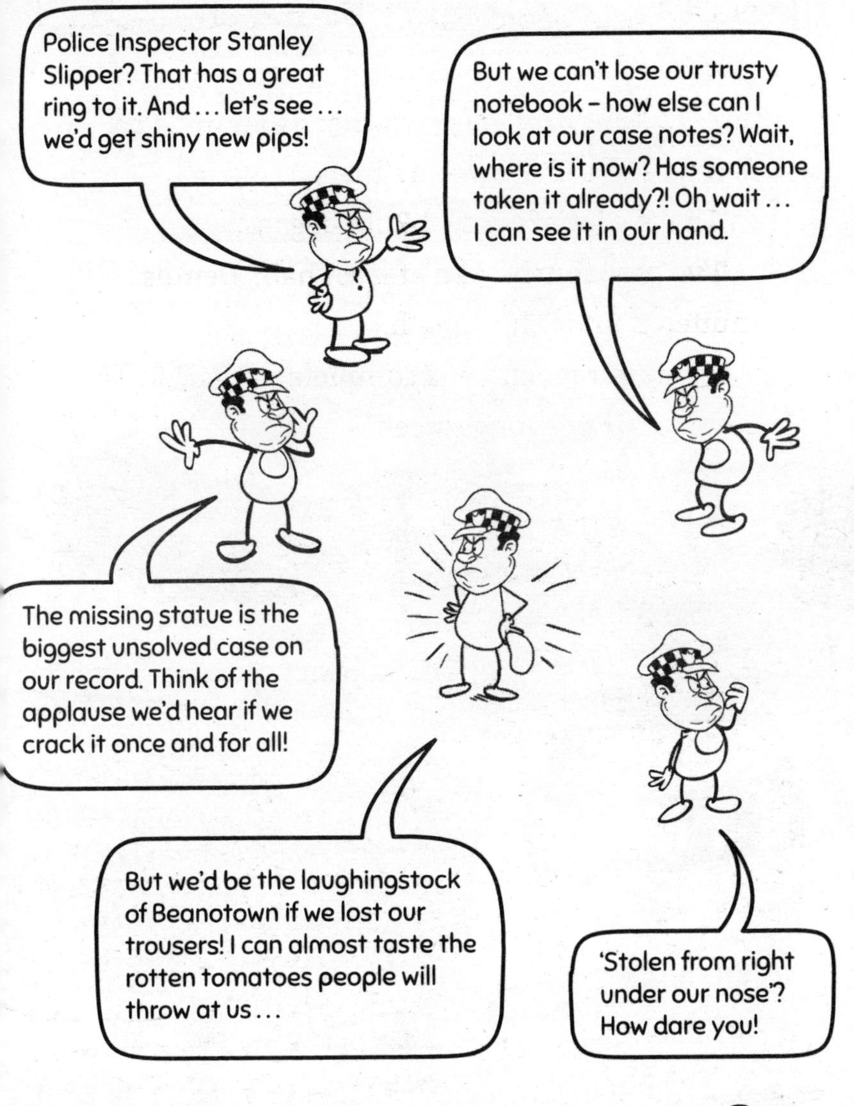

WHAT WOULD YOU DO?

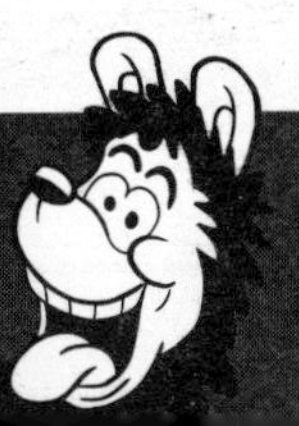

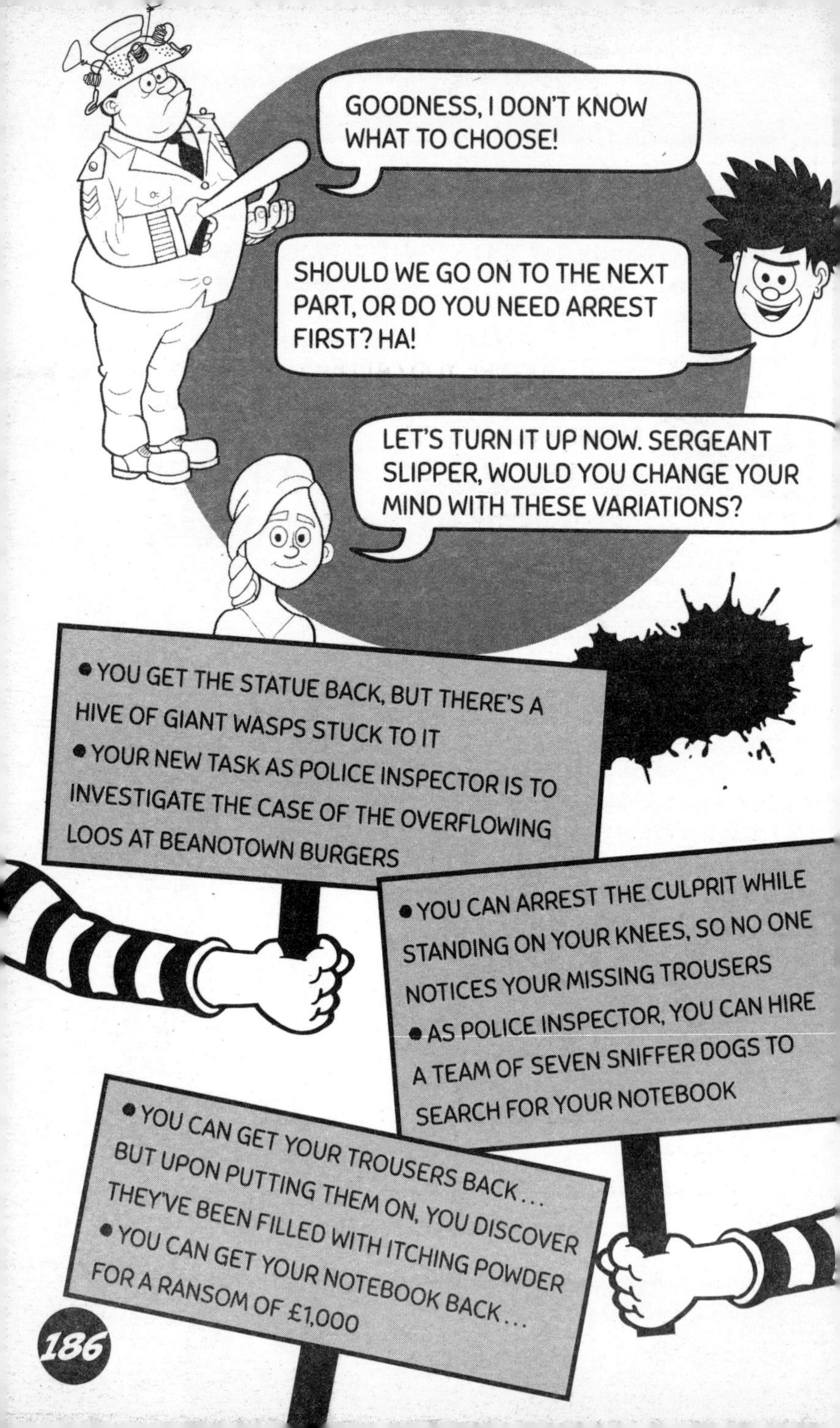

GOODNESS, I DON'T KNOW WHAT TO CHOOSE!
SHOULD WE GO ON TO THE NEXT PART, OR DO YOU NEED ARREST FIRST? HA!
LET'S TURN IT UP NOW. SERGEANT SLIPPER, WOULD YOU CHANGE YOUR MIND WITH THESE VARIATIONS?
• YOU GET THE STATUE BACK, BUT THERE'S A HIVE OF GIANT WASPS STUCK TO IT
• YOUR NEW TASK AS POLICE INSPECTOR IS TO INVESTIGATE THE CASE OF THE OVERFLOWING LOOS AT BEANOTOWN BURGERS
• YOU CAN ARREST THE CULPRIT WHILE STANDING ON YOUR KNEES, SO NO ONE NOTICES YOUR MISSING TROUSERS
• AS POLICE INSPECTOR, YOU CAN HIRE A TEAM OF SEVEN SNIFFER DOGS TO SEARCH FOR YOUR NOTEBOOK
• YOU CAN GET YOUR TROUSERS BACK... BUT UPON PUTTING THEM ON, YOU DISCOVER THEY'VE BEEN FILLED WITH ITCHING POWDER
• YOU CAN GET YOUR NOTEBOOK BACK... FOR A RANSOM OF £1,000

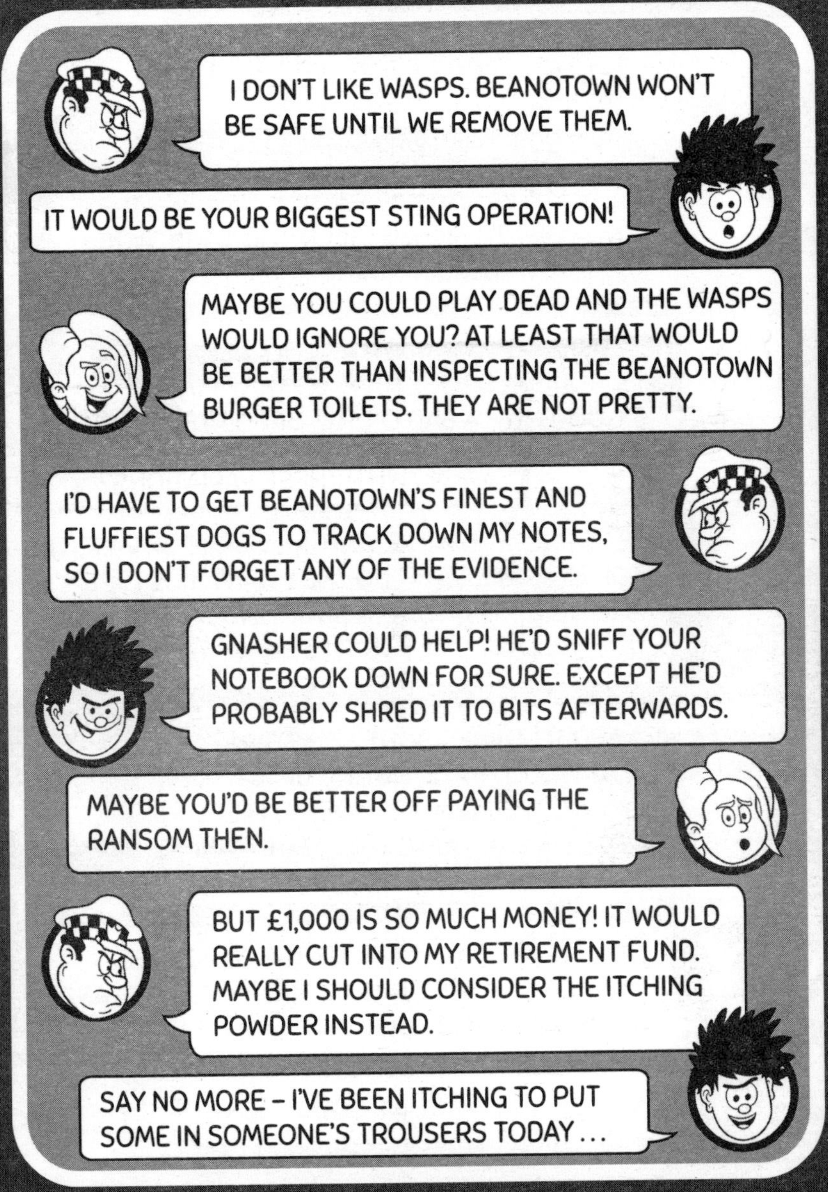
I DON'T LIKE WASPS. BEANOTOWN WON'T BE SAFE UNTIL WE REMOVE THEM.
IT WOULD BE YOUR BIGGEST STING OPERATION!
MAYBE YOU COULD PLAY DEAD AND THE WASPS WOULD IGNORE YOU? AT LEAST THAT WOULD BE BETTER THAN INSPECTING THE BEANOTOWN BURGER TOILETS. THEY ARE NOT PRETTY.
I'D HAVE TO GET BEANOTOWN'S FINEST AND FLUFFIEST DOGS TO TRACK DOWN MY NOTES, SO I DON'T FORGET ANY OF THE EVIDENCE.
GNASHER COULD HELP! HE'D SNIFF YOUR NOTEBOOK DOWN FOR SURE. EXCEPT HE'D PROBABLY SHRED IT TO BITS AFTERWARDS.
MAYBE YOU'D BE BETTER OFF PAYING THE RANSOM THEN.
BUT £1,000 IS SO MUCH MONEY! IT WOULD REALLY CUT INTO MY RETIREMENT FUND. MAYBE I SHOULD CONSIDER THE ITCHING POWDER INSTEAD.
SAY NO MORE – I'VE BEEN ITCHING TO PUT SOME IN SOMEONE'S TROUSERS TODAY ...

WHICH OPTION WOULD YOU CHOOSE WITH ALL THOSE VARIATIONS ADDED INTO THE MIX?

WRITE YOUR OWN

WRITING A **WOULD YOU RATHER** IS EASIER THAN YOU MIGHT THINK: THE TRICK IS KNOWING WHO YOU ARE WRITING IT FOR.

THINK OF A **WOULD YOU RATHER** AS TWO SIDES OF TWO COINS, SQUISHED TOGETHER, SO THAT YOU HAVE ONE GOOD WITH A BAD OR THE OPPOSITE BAD AND THE OPPOSITE GOOD.

LET'S PRETEND WE'RE WRITING FOR YOUR PARENT, FOR EXAMPLE. WHAT DO THEY WANT MOST? PEACE AND QUIET? A BREAK? A SHOPPING SPREE? LET'S USE THE LAST ONE FOR THIS EXAMPLE.

NEXT, WE NEED TO THINK ABOUT SOMETHING YOUR PARENT WOULD HATE. TIDYING UP ALL YOUR TOYS? CLEANING THE TOILET? SPIDERS? FOR THIS EXAMPLE, WE'LL ASSUME THEY HATE MAKING PACKED LUNCHES.

NOW, WE NEED TO THINK OF THE OPPOSITES OF EACH OF THESE THINGS AND MAKE THEM AS BONKERS AS POSSIBLE.

SO, FOR SHOPPING, WE COULD GO WITH:

- YOU WIN A THREE-HOUR, KIDS-FREE SHOPPING SPREE IN A STORE OF YOUR CHOOSING
- *OR* YOU ARE NOT ALLOWED TO BUY YOURSELF ANY CLOTHING FOR THREE YEARS

AND FOR PACKED LUNCHES, WE COULD GO WITH:

- YOU HAVE TO MAKE 30 PACKED LUNCHES EVERY MORNING BEFORE THE SCHOOL RUN
- *OR* YOU ARE GRANTED THE MAGICAL ABILITY OF FILLING LUNCHBOXES WITH THE SNAP OF YOUR FINGERS

NOW, WE HAVE TO PUT THE GOOD EXAMPLE FROM THE FIRST SCENARIO WITH THE BAD EXAMPLE OF THE 2ND AND VISA VERSA, WITH A BUT IN THE MIDDLE.

WOULD YOU RATHER...

...WIN A THREE-HOUR, KIDS-FREE SHOPPING SPREE IN A STORE OF YOUR CHOOSING, BUT YOU HAVE TO MAKE 30 PACKED LUNCHES EVERY MORNING BEFORE THE SCHOOL RUN...

...**OR** YOU'RE NOT ALLOWED TO BUY YOURSELF ANY CLOTHING FOR THREE YEARS, BUT YOU ARE GRANTED THE MAGICAL ABILITY OF FILLING LUNCHBOXES WITH THE SNAP OF YOUR FINGER?

NOW WATCH AS THEIR MIND NEARLY EXPLODES AS THEY TRY TO DEBATE THIS ONE OUT IN THEIR HEAD!

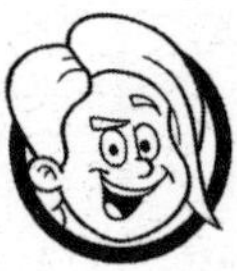

IF YOU REALLY WANT TO MAKE THINGS DIFFICULT FOR THEM, YOU CAN COME UP WITH VARIATIONS FOR YOUR **WOULD YOU RATHERS**. FOR THESE, WE SUGGEST TAKING BOTH OF YOUR **WOULD YOU RATHER** OPTIONS AND ADD ONE THING TO EACH THAT MAKES THEM WAY WORSE, ONE THING TO EACH THAT MAKES THEM TOTALLY BONKERS AND ONE THING TO EACH THAT MAKES THEM BETTER.

SO, FOR THIS EXAMPLE, WE COULD ADD THE FOLLOWING VARIATIONS:

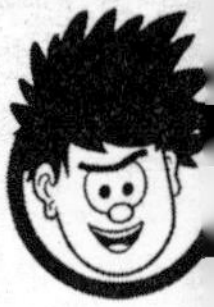

- ALL 30 PACKED LUNCHES ARE DIFFERENT
- ALL OF YOUR CLOTHES HAVE HOLES IN THEM

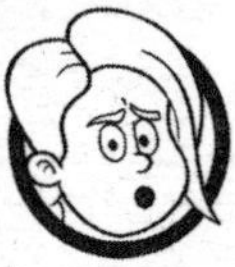

SEE HOW THESE MAKE BOTH SCENARIOS WORSE FOR YOUR PARENT?

- YOU HAVE TO SPREAD EVERY SANDWICH WITH YOUR NOSE
- ALL YOUR BELTS ARE MADE OF SAUSAGES

YOU CAN GO AS BONKERS AS YOU LIKE WITH THESE VARIATIONS – THE WILDER THEY ARE, THE MORE FUNNY THEY'LL BE.

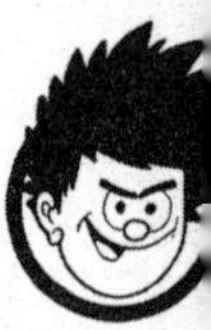

- YOU HAVE A LIVE-IN CHEF THAT COOKS YOU DINNER EVERY NIGHT
- YOU BECOME A TRENDSETTER AND NOW EVERYONE HAS HOLES IN THEIR CLOTHES

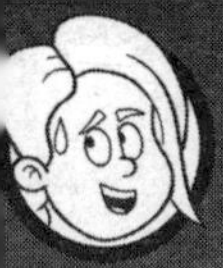

THESE LAST VARIATIONS ARE TO ADD A SMALL BIT OF RELIEF AFTER ALL THE HORRIBLE THINGS THEY HAVE TO CHOOSE BETWEEN. THEY SHOULD MAKE THE BAD OPTIONS IN EACH THAT LITTLE BIT BETTER – AT LEAST YOUR PARENT WON'T HAVE TO COOK IN THE EVENING AND PEOPLE LIKE THEIR CLOTHES.

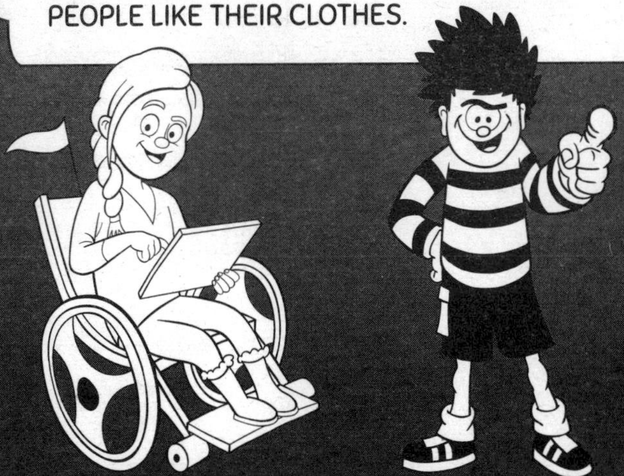

IT'S AS SIMPLE AS THAT! SEE WHAT **WOULD YOU RATHERS** YOU CAN COME UP WITH FOR YOUR FRIENDS AND FAMILY!

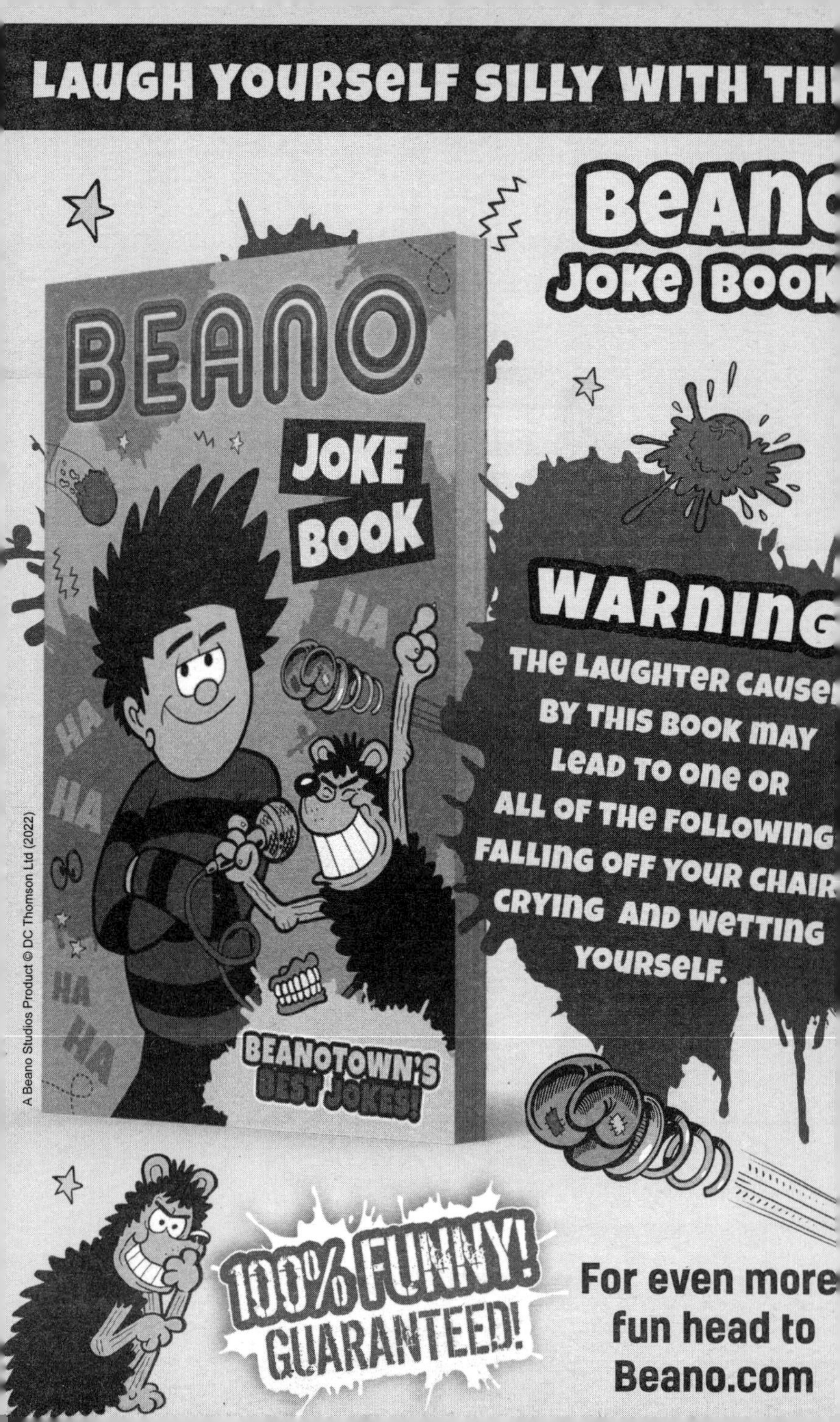

LAUGH YOURSELF SILLY WITH TH
Beano
Joke Book
BEANO
JOKE BOOK
HA
HA
HA
HA
HA
HA
BEANOTOWN'S BEST JOKES!
WARNING
THE LAUGHTER CAUSE
BY THIS BOOK MAY
LEAD TO ONE OR
ALL OF THE FOLLOWING
FALLING OFF YOUR CHAIR
CRYING AND WETTING
YOURSELF.
A Beano Studios Product © DC Thomson Ltd (2022)
100% FUNNY! GUARANTEED!
For even more
fun head to
Beano.com